The URANTIA DIARIES of Harold and Martha Sherman

VOLUME TWO: 1942

Compiled, Transcribed and Edited by
SASKIA PRAAMSMA and MATTHEW BLOCK

THE URANTIA DIARIES
of HAROLD and MARTHA SHERMAN
VOLUME TWO: 1942
Compiled, Transcribed and Edited by
Saskia Praamsma and Matthew Block

Cover photo: Archives and Special Collections at the University of Central Arkansas

Cover and interior: Syrp & Co.

ISBN: 978-1-7321796-1-5
eISBN: 978-1-7321796-2-2

Published by Square Circles Publishing
SquareCirclesPublishing.com

I am much fearful that you do not yet realize the great importance of your book, that its magnitude has not yet reached your consciousness. Do you not yet begin to know the tremendousness of the book of yours to posterity, into the dim and misty vastness of far, far future years? What if, under the same circumstances, there had been a similar "book" to accompany our present-day Bible? What a wonderful thing it would have been through all these years of Bible study. The Book of Urantia will be in existence just as long, or longer, and so will be your book as a component and explanatory adjunct to it for just the same period. How illuminating it will be to the readers a thousand earth years from now. You are the only historian of this present great event. Can you not see even a small part of the great importance of your task?

—Harry Loose to Harold Sherman, July 21, 1942

Appendices

Contents

Introduction

This volume, covering May to December 1942, records Harold and Martha Sherman's first flush of enthusiasm for the Urantia revelation as well as the events that culminated in the first major conflict among Urantia believers. It provides a far more accurate account of this period than the truncated and pseudonymized version Harold gave in the "Pipeline to God" chapter of his 1976 book, *How to Know What to Believe.*

The volume opens as the Shermans arrive in Chicago and find an apartment directly across the street from the Sadler residence at 533 Diversey Parkway. They renew their acquaintance with Dr. Sadler and his relatives, meet other Forumites, and begin reading the Urantia papers and attending the Sunday Forum meetings. Soon joined by Sir Hubert Wilkins, the renowned polar explorer whom Sadler had admitted to the Forum on Harold's recommendation, the new Forumites—Harold, Martha and Sir Hubert—are warmly welcomed by the people at 533.

Perhaps due to Sir Hubert's celebrity and Harold's recent success in Hollywood, combined with the men's ardent interest in the Urantia phenomenon, the Shermans and Sir Hubert soon became favored Forumites. They sat at the Sadlers' table at Forum events, and Sadler and his son Bill took them into special confidence, reading out to them accounts of interactions they had had with superhumans which weren't included in the Urantia papers. Sadler also gave the Shermans a detailed account of the early years of the Urantia phenomenon, which apparently few Forumites had heard.

At the very time that the Shermans and Sir Hubert (who was only able to come to Chicago for short visits) were engaged in their first reading of the Urantia papers, Sadler announced, at the annual Forum picnic, that the Forum's long-running role as a question-asking group was ending. Since about 1924, Forum members were invited to submit written questions which might influence the content of the developing Urantia manuscript. That role having been fulfilled as of May 31, 1942, the Forum was to continue studying the papers and to contribute funds for the eventual publication of the Urantia Book. The Sadlers had already formulated organizations—the Urantia Foundation and the Urantia Brotherhood—which would begin to function upon the publication of the book. The Foundation was to have absolute control over the production and translation of the Urantia Book, while the Brotherhood was to be the official membership organization of believers in the Urantia revelation.

But questions were just beginning for Harold and Martha as they read the manuscript and learned of the Sadlers' publication and organization plans. Indeed, as this volume describes, Harold was besieged with questions and concerns. Throughout the late spring and summer of 1942 he shared his concerns and suggestions with the people at 533 and with the Forumites he and Martha had befriended. Not satisfied with the Sadlers' responses, and encouraged when he learned that other Forumites shared his concerns to one degree or another, Harold helped write a petition, signed by almost fifty Forumites, asking Dr. Sadler to allow free and open discussion of the planned organizations.

Upon receiving the petition, Sadler, who had gotten wind of it beforehand thanks to two anxious Forumites, orchestrated a reaction which, in the course of a few days, succeeded in quashing virtually all sympathy for Harold and his proposals.

In the space of less than a month, the Shermans went from being favored Forum members to being largely shunned. They continued attending meetings for four-and-half more years as quiet observers. Harold shared his plight with a sympathetic Sir Hubert Wilkins, and the Shermans became close to a few Forumites who resisted Sadler's apparent attempt to ostracize Harold. These few shared their confoundment at Sadler's actions, which had revealed, to them, an unexpected, dark side to his character.

Throughout all these developments, the Shermans were in frequent correspondence with their mentor, Harry J. Loose, the eccentric retired policeman who had been a member of the Forum until 1934, when he and his wife Emily moved from Chicago to Monterey Park, California.

In addition to other advices, Loose encouraged the Shermans to keep a secret diary to use in a book Harold was to write about the history of the Urantia phenomenon. The Shermans began this diary on July 24, 1942 and maintained it for several years, even after leaving Chicago in 1947. They had also created a "Forum Calendar," in which they jotted down notes of events which occurred from July 26, 1941 (when Harold was introduced by phone to Sadler) to November 18, 1942. Every entry of the diaries and of the Forum Calendar is included in these volumes.

9/17/42.
Steinbeck phone

After the interview ē Dr. Sadler, H. phoned Mr Steinbeck & told him that the Dr had refused to tell him anything, asking if he & M. could come over & see the Steinbecks & Miss Carolyn Brown & secure more information ab them as to what he had said to F. members. Mr S. said he saw no reason why we couldn't get together but would discuss it ē Mrs Steinbeck & phone in tonight. This he did around ten o'clock saying that he & Mrs S. had been discussing the matter all evening & that he was phoning as he had promised tho he had been advised by a member not to do so. He said that Mrs S. had seen the Dr around 6 to this eve. & he had told her it was better that no one talk to us & that this matter be allowed to quiet down & that he would talk to us when feelings had become more normal. Mr Steinbeck said "I hope you appreciate our position Mr Sherman. Dr S. has been our leader & mentor for so long that to go against him now is almost like going against our faith & the truths that have come to us thru him." H said "I understand, but does it seem to you to be divine justice to isolate us from the fellowship of our F. members & to single us out as special objects of persecution when we all acted in good faith & in all sincerity in petitioning for a free discussion of Urantia subjects?" Mr Steinbeck said "No. Mr Sherman, this is what Mrs Steinbeck & I have been talking about most of the evening. It doesn't seem fair & right & for the time being you people may have to be the martyrs but out of this, we think great good may come." H. said "Our consciences are clear

A page from the Diaries

-2-

5/17/42 H & M. attend first F. meeting. Meet several members. Marcia & Mary guests of Bushlers for noon dinner.

5/20/42 Marcia leaves for Michigan for summer.

5/21/42 H. & M. guests of Doc. & Christy along c̄ Sir Hubert for dinner & evening.

5/23/42 Mary located at Hull House

5/22/42 - 25th Mother S. visits us in Chicago.

5/24/42. Second F. meeting. We attend every Sunday meeting of regular F. from this date except the two Sundays in New York. We find the papers hard to understand as read in F.

5/25/42 Began reading of papers in earnest every day from 9^30 to 12^30 & 1^30 to 5^30

5/30/42. Invited to Aunt Karles at Oak Park for evening with Bushlers & Sir Hubert who is back in Chicago for second reading of papers.

Mary interviewed & admitted to Forum membership.

6/3/42. Christy had dinner c̄ us in our apt. (We learned, afterward, that Christy seldom accepted invitations from F. members unless accompanied by the Dr. During the course of the evening H. asked her why the Bk. of U. contained no explanation of psychic phenomena, so common to millions of people, who, when they read the Bk. of U. which describes phenomena of a transcendent super nature, will wonder how to classify what they feel has happened @ times to them. Christy said she realized that this subject wasn't adequately covered & that the Doc. himself had had no personal experience to indicate to him that this phenomena really existed. She said, "Harold,

A page from the Forum Calendar

Biographical Notes on Anna and Wilfred Kellogg, Emma L. Christensen, and William S. Sadler, Jr.

In Volume One biographical profiles were provided for Harry J. Loose and Dr. William S. Sadler. These men played determinative roles in Harold and Martha Sherman's entire Urantia experience. This volume profiles the members of the Sadler family circle, a tight-knit group living in or near 533 Diversey Parkway, who were on hand when the Shermans arrived in Chicago. A few years before, the group had lost its central binding figure, Dr. Lena Kellogg Sadler, William's wife and professional associate of forty-two years, who died in 1939.

Each person in the group—William and Lena, their son Bill, Lena's sister Anna and her husband Wilfred Kellogg, and Emma Christensen—was a member of the so-called Contact Commission. This commission was supposedly charged by the superhuman directors of the Urantia revelation to be present at the sessions in which an unconscious man, whose identity was known only to the Contact Commissioners, transmitted communications from the revelators. Dr. Sadler also claimed to converse with invisible beings, such as midwayers, on his own.

In addition to their family connection, William, Lena, Anna and Wilfred had an important thing in common: they had all spent their formative years as Seventh-day Adventists. Seventh-day Adventism was a small but active Christian denomination which arose in mid-19th century America and had its headquarters at Battle Creek, Michigan. One of its dominant figures was Ellen G. White, who was recognized by Seventh-day Adventists as having the gift of prophecy. She wrote voluminously of her visions and of the messages she had received from higher beings such as the third angel of the Book of Revelation.

The two Kellogg sisters and their future husbands all moved, at various points in their lives, to Battle Creek to study or work at Seventh-day Adventist institutions. They all knew Ellen G. White and her immediate relatives and were imbued in the SDA culture of revelation. The Urantia phenomenon occurred shortly after the four had drifted away from Seventh-day Adventism. Being itself the communication of an ongoing revelation, this phenomenon was thus not wholly foreign to the four.

Anna B. Kellogg and Wilfred C. Kellogg

Anna Bell Kellogg, born in Waupun, Wisconsin in 1877, was Lena K. Sadler's younger sister by two years. She was the fifth and youngest child of Smith Moses and Maria Dickinson Kellogg, two Seventh-day Adventists with pioneer roots in Michigan. Smith's half-brothers, Dr. John Harvey Kellogg and Will Keith (better known as W.K.) Kellogg, were prominent citizens of Battle Creek; Dr. Kellogg was head of the world-famous Battle Creek Sanitarium, and W.K. went on to found the Kellogg Company, a multinational manufacturer of breakfast cereals and other foods.

Like Lena, Anna became a registered nurse, probably receiving her education, as Lena had, at the Seventh-day Adventists' Missionary Nurses Training School, in Battle Creek. In 1906, when Lena and William became physicians after graduating from the American Medical Missionary College, Anna accompanied the Sadlers to La Grange, Illinois. All three joined the staff of the nearby Hinsdale Sanitarium, an SDA-affiliated institution, two of whose original trustees were John Harvey Kellogg and William S. Sadler. Anna also traveled with the Sadlers on Chautauqua-Redpath tours as "The Sadler Company" from 1907 to about 1917. She lectured on nursing, cookery and domestic hygiene.

In 1912 she married her half-first cousin, Wilfred Custer Kellogg; they shared a grandfather, John Preston Kellogg.

Born in Vermont in 1876, Wilfred was a full nephew of John Harvey and W.K. Kellogg. In 1896, he moved to Battle Creek with his mother, Emma, and four siblings, after the death of his father, Charles, a circuit-riding Seventh-day Adventist minister. Wilfred had only a sixth-grade formal education.

He worked as a clerk for John Harvey Kellogg's Modern Medicine Publishing Co. and then at Kellogg's Sanitas Nut Food Co., where he was promoted to assistant general manager. From 1907 to 1909 he was manager of the sales department at W.K. Kellogg's Battle Creek Toasted Corn Flake Co., the forerunner of the Kellogg Company. At the time of his marriage, he was secretary of the Battle Creek Sanitarium, as well as secretary-treasurer of the Battle Creek Optical Co.

Wilfred and Anna were married on August 28, 1912 in Kenosha, Wisconsin, a state which permitted first-cousin marriages. Later in the day they participated in a double-wedding ceremony at the Sadler home in La Grange. From then on, Wilfred and Anna stayed close to the Sadlers. In 1914 their daughter Emma Ruth ("Ruth") was born, nearly fully deaf.

When the Shermans arrived in Chicago in 1942, Wilfred and Anna were living in an apartment around the corner from 533, at 2754 N. Hampden Ct., with Ruth, now 27 or 28. Anna worked as a nurse in Sadler's practice and Wilfred was Sadler's office manager. Ruth had been a psychologist at the Illinois School for the Deaf, in Jacksonville, Illinois.

Wilfred played a large part in handling matters related to the publishing of the Urantia Book and the securing of its copyrights. He was the first treasurer of the Urantia Foundation. Wilfred died in 1956 and Anna in 1960.

Emma L. Christensen

Emma Louise ("Christy") Christensen was born on January 29, 1890 in a rural county near Aberdeen, South Dakota. She was the sixth of eight children born to Danish-immigrant farmers Nels and Rosalia (Bald) Christensen. Her mother died when she was five.

She attended Carleton College in Northfield, Minnesota, majoring in English, and took a two-year extension course at the University of Minnesota in St. Paul.

On February 9, 1914 she married Christian J. Davidson in Clay County, South Dakota, but the marriage was short-lived; the 1920 census reports her as a single woman.

From 1915 to 1920 she worked in Minneapolis as assistant chief clerk in the Office of the Comptroller of the Currency, a bureau within the U.S. Department of the Treasury. In November 1921 she transferred to the OCC's office of National Bank Examiners for the

Seventh Federal Reserve District, in Chicago. The following February she was promoted to chief clerk, and held this position until her retirement in late 1946.

In July 1922, as reported in the Shermans' diary entry for August 14, 1942, "she was struck by a car and knocked unconscious; came to in [Columbus] hospital with Dr. S. working over her. Reported at his office at intervals till completely well. Dr. Lena became interested, and Christy divided her time between her own room and their home, eventually taking [their son] Bill's room (he being in the Marines) permanently."

Before moving in to 533 in 1935, she lived a short walk away from the Sadlers' and became a virtual member of the family. She traveled with them and Bill to Europe in 1928 and to Estes Park, Colorado in 1931.

Later in life she told multiple people that she had typed the successive drafts of the Urantia manuscript on a manual typewriter. She also was responsible for standardizing the spelling and capitalization of the text of the Urantia Book.

Regardless of any inner turmoil she may have experienced during the Sherman years, she became a stalwart of the Urantia Foundation and the Urantia Brotherhood. She was secretary of the Urantia Foundation and filled various positions on the Executive Committee of the Urantia Brotherhood, including president and vice-president. She was the last of the Contact Commissioners, dying on May 2, 1982, at the age of 92.

William S. Sadler, Jr.

William Samuel ("Bill") Sadler, Jr. was born in La Grange, Illinois on December 15, 1907, the only child of William and Lena Sadler. The Sadlers, along with Wilfred and Anna, moved to Chicago when Bill was a boy.

After graduating from high school at fifteen, he enrolled at Northwestern University. In 1924 he ran away from home to join the United States Marine Corps, applying under a false name ("Winston Stefan Stevens") and claiming to be 19 instead of 16. He served for four years, in Nicaragua and Haiti, visiting his parents on annual furloughs.

Returning home in 1928, he found a job as a clerk for the National Bank Examiners (which also employed Emma Christensen). He held that position for approximately three years.

On June 20, 1932 he again suddenly left home to join the Marines. A few days afterward he tried to commit suicide by overdosing on sleeping pills. He was in a coma for forty-eight hours and was revived at the U.S. Naval Hospital in Washington, D.C. Dr. Sadler was contacted and arrived at the hospital, where he learned that his son had been diagnosed as being in a "constitutional psychopathic state." Sadler confided to the attending physician that his son's behavior had been peculiar for years; that he was seclusive, prone to suicidality, and had recently remained in bed for three days, in an apparent catatonic stupor. Bill was discharged from the Marines under his father's custody.

On March 9, 1935 Bill married Leone Marie Gill. The couple had three children: William III (who died aged 19 in 1955), Patricia, and Charles. (Patricia became president of the Urantia Foundation in 1992.)

Soon after his marriage, he found work with the Standard Oil Company of Indiana, as investment custodian for its pension fund. In early 1944, he left Standard Oil to do personnel work for a company owned by a former Forumite. In their diary entry of February 10, 1944, the Shermans relate what their Forumite friends Lulu and Erle Steinbeck told them about Bill's career change:

> They said a family, they thought by the name of Berger, who formerly belonged to the Forum and who had gotten Bill his job at Standard Oil some years ago, had now hired him to do personnel work for their firm which services different industries through interviewing and checking on the qualifications of their employees.

In 1947 he started his own personnel and management consultancy business, Sadler and Associates, with offices at 333 N. Michigan Ave. in Chicago.

In 1956, a year after the Urantia Book was published, Sadler, then 48, left his wife and moved to an apartment on 900 N. Lake Shore Dr. He pursued a relationship with Florine Seres, a 23-year-old Master's graduate from Northwestern University who had joined his company in 1955. They married on August 5, 1958.

In November, 1962, he suffered a stroke while on a trip to New York. He died on November 22, 1963.

One of the few people to have unrestricted access to the Urantia manuscript, Bill became a leading interpreter of the teachings. With his father he taught the first groups organized for the systematic study of the Urantia Book. He was the first vice president of the Urantia Foundation and the first president of the Urantia Brotherhood.

Acknowledgment

Much of the information in these profiles was derived from *Dr. Sadler and the Urantia Book* (2014), by Sioux Oliva, Ph.D., as well as from Oliva's as-yet-unpublished timeline of the Sadler-Kellogg family. Other details were drawn from Martin Gardner's *Urantia: The Great Cult Mystery* (1995), and from the ubhistory.org and urantiabook.org websites.

Acknowledgments

We wish to thank the following people for the help or information they have given us:

Martin Gardner, who announced the existence of the diaries in his 1995 book, *Urantia: The Great Cult Mystery*, and said they'd be made available at the University of Central Arkansas in January 2000.

Our friends John Bunker and Karen Pressler, who traveled to UCA as soon as the diaries were released and copied them for us. More recently they helped us fill in gaps in the Sherman-Wilkins correspondence with letters they found in the Sir Hubert Wilkins papers at the Ohio State University Byrd Polar Research Center in Columbus, Ohio.

Mary Sherman Kobiella and Marcia Sherman Lynch, the daughters of Harold and Martha Sherman, who allowed us to include the Harry Loose letters as well as the Ara messages, both of which were still in their private possession when this project began. They also gave us permission to quote from Harold Sherman's published works. Both Mary and Marcia were gracious hostesses on the occasions when we visited them at their homes. They gave freely of their time, sharing memories and photographs, and have since become lasting friends.

The staff at the Archives and Special Collections at the University of Central Arkansas, especially Jimmy Bryant, David E. Bowie, Jr., Betty Osborn, Cynthia Frase, Artency Davis, Michelle Strouse, Sarah Langford and Aryn Denette, for helping us locate various materials.

The unnamed persons who provided documents from the Forum years, particularly the lists of names and addresses of Forumites and Seventy members, to the ubhistory.org and urantiabook.org websites.

Saskia Praamsma
Matthew Block
Pahrump, Nevada
May 2018

Part III

Cordially Received

1

Arrival in Chicago

May 6, 1942 found the Sherman family—Harold, Martha, 19-year-old Mary and 12-year-old Marcia—leaving Hollywood for Chicago. Harold was intent on getting his proposed Jane Addams play approved by the officials at Hull House, and both he and Martha were eager to begin reading the Urantia material at the Sadler residence at 533 Diversey Parkway.

HARRY LOOSE to HAROLD and MARTHA SHERMAN

Monterey Park, May 13, 1942

Dear Folks:-

This is Wednesday morning again—just one week ago today I waved you goodbye from in front of the house here—as you turned east on Garvey. You have all been on our minds very much this whole week. . . .

Get out of the expensive Rienzi as soon as you can and into less costly quarters. The Brewster should be able to accommodate you at much less expense. Mail to 533 is safe and convenient no matter where you locate. BOTH OF YOU READ JUST AS LONG AS AND STEADILY AS YOU CAN GET THE TIME TO. You will need all the information you can gain. Hope that Mother Sherman gets down from Marion for a short visit and then she and Marcia arrive safely up in Michigan. Will be glad to hear news of Wilkins—of his receipt of my last letter—his advancement—continued interest etc.—when he writes you—or makes contact.

Received yours from Gallup [New Mexico]—thanks a lot. Watch all operations on the car—greasing—oil changing, etc. . . . Be sure to give all at 533 our remembrances—and to tell Uncle Kellogg that I'll be writing him soon. All as well as could be expected here. Will be grateful to hear from you at any time—but don't let writing me infringe on time that could be better used doing something else more constructive. . . .

With best thought—and love from ALL,

Harry

FORUM CALENDAR *May 13, 1942*

Family arrived in Chicago from Hollywood. First stayed at Rienzi [Hotel] until a small apt. was located, following Mr. Kellogg's suggestion, at the Cambridge, on the 16th.

MARTHA SHERMAN to HARRY LOOSE

Chicago, May 14, 1942

Dear Harry,

Well, we are finally in Chicago and what an adventure we have had! You will never believe me when I tell you that we have actually BOUGHT 120 acres in the Ozark Hills. Yes—you were right—it is simply wonderful country and we are so thankful you suggested we drive through Arkansas on our trip East. I hardly know where to begin except that our first night in Arkansas we spent at a motel in Fort Smith and all night the rain poured, the thunder thundered and the lightning flashed. It was heavenly after our rainless year in Hollywood! And we loved every minute of it.

All the next day we drove through such greenness as we had forgotten existed—and incidentally over such roads as we never knew existed. Our old Buick was certainly put to the test and had to plough through mud up to the axles and even ford several streams which flowed right over the roadbed in places. Harold had to keep his eye pretty closely on the road but Mary and Marcia were delighted with all the wildflowers. We saw what appeared to be deep pink azaleas growing wild and the biggest blue violets I've ever seen and all sorts of other lovely flowers.

Anyway, to get to the story, we angled northeast through the state and how we got there I'll never know, until we stumbled onto a little town called Mountain View. It seemed a pleasant place so we took rooms at a rambling house called Dew Drop Inn for the night and the next day we found it was surrounded with low mountains.

Either the bright sunshine, or the green hills, or the blue sky or *something* got into our blood streams for, on impulse, Harold decided to see if there was a real estate man in town. There was! And he would drive us out to look at a piece of property that was for sale—120 acres! Really, Harry, I wish you could have seen that car! Mr. Webb, the real estate man, apologized for it by saying it wasn't very clean—he'd had to take some pigs to market in it that morning. Can you imagine putting *pigs* in the back seat of a sedan? But we all got in and he drove us over some very rocky roads about 10 miles out of town to a little unpainted house on the side of one of the highest hills.

I don't know what there was about that place—it certainly was untidy and the house was a shambles but the moment we stepped foot on the ground we felt a sort of inner peace. We found a man and his wife were living in the house—they were not the owners—but the wife was lying ill on an iron bedstead with three legs, and running over the floor and bed were 200 or more baby chicks. The man explained that since his wife was ill, it had been too much trouble to keep the chicks in the brooder so he had brought them all into the house where he could look after them more easily! That should have cured us but somehow it didn't—we still felt that inner sense of peace.

Then, when Mr. Webb suggested he'd drive us down the road (it was quicker, he said) to the lower part of the property where there was a stream, we were completely won over by the water tumbling over the rocks, and the woods on all sides. Harold said right then and there we'd buy it. Mr. Webb accepted a small down payment and said he'd get us the deed from the owners in Texas.

So, in a few days, we hope to hold the deed to our first property. After all our years of city apartment living it seems wonderful to say we actually own some land of our own! Of course, right now we haven't the faintest idea when we can get back there to do anything, but it is such a good feeling to know it's there. Probably most of our friends will think we're crazy—maybe we are—but there is just something so real and simple about it all, in contrast with the show and pomp of Hollywood, that we just know we're going to love it.

Hope you are keeping well and that we may be seeing you again before long.

Affectionately,
M & H

FORUM CALENDAR *May 16, 1942*

Harold and Martha begin reading papers from the beginning, Martha almost overcome and overwhelmed by depth of papers and wondering whether she could ever understand them.

Mildred Bucklin stopped in at 533, on an errand, and introduced herself. Finding Harold needed a typewriter she offered to loan him her portable and returned shortly with her husband and the typewriter. An immediate friendship sprang up.

HAROLD SHERMAN to HARRY and EMILY LOOSE

Chicago, May 17, 1942

Dear Harry and Mother Loose:

We are at last settled in your old home town of Chicago—in the Cambridge Hotel, 530 Diversey, directly across from Sadler's . . . in a one-room, light-housekeeping apartment with kitchenette on the fifth floor (507), with a little two-foot balcony looking out on the street from which we can look down and see Diversey and the Sadler house . . . so, you see, we have them under close surveillance. They can't do anything from now on that we won't know about . . . we can even see their sun decks on the roof where Bill Jr.'s wife goes to get her beach tan. Just now both children or all of them (I forgot how many) have the mumps . . . having just recovered from the measles.

The day after arrival it rained all day, so if we had not moved on schedule, we would have run into bad weather . . . as it is, going and coming, to and from California, we have never had bad traveling weather!

I have had the car fixed as you directed . . . greased and lubricated . . . also brakes checked, which took quite a beating over the bad Oklahoma and Arkansas roads. We drove through streams where there were no bridges. Exciting, primitive travel. We love that country out in the Ozarks and hope we may return to explore "our farm" before too long . . . but there is a big job to be done . . . and the project to be gotten under way before the Shermans can have much surcease from activity.

Martha and I started with our reading last night, and with Martha reading aloud we covered the first three chapters, largely dealing with definitions of terms and words used, and the attributes of God, the Father. Marvelous material, of course, but not as interesting as what is to come, and a bit heavy reading until the full meaning of all the terms begins to grow on one.

Wilkins is returning for study again on May 21st, so we will be seeing him. Here are excerpts from the letter I received which Kellogg asked permission to copy, since he said Wilkins' estimate of the Book was so concise and clearly put, he wanted it on record. All are extremely fond of Wilkins and so glad to have him a part of the Group.

Wilkins said: "Until the last minute before rushing to catch the train to New York, I was reading and just managed to get through the last chapter . . . The whole thing is so immense and astounding that one is lost for words to describe it. It is, however, likely to be subject to criticism by the established churches, both in respect to its origin and to its revelations which deprive some of the sects of the basis of their foundation. To me, however, it is the first connected, clear exposition of *the* 'faith.' The need for faith and the reward of faith—a combination of considerations which seem to confront Man no matter what race or color, and notwithstanding his stature of 'education.'

"*We* might be intrigued in the matter of faith because of religious training very early in our youth. But the wish to *know* something of the cosmic organization seems paramount in all humans, 'heathen' or otherwise.

"The papers will therefore fill a long-felt want.

"They will need—as have other writings—a good deal of *expounding* if they are to reach the multitudes, but that has been found necessary in respect to all 'teachings.' Yet the papers in themselves are more *absorbable*—if one has much capacity—as a whole, than any other theological 'tome.'

"I will arrive in Chicago on the 21st and spend two or three weeks in reading again the material. After that time I will probably get back to the farm (in Pennsylvania) until about August when I will probably go to Alaska—if the NIPS don't get there first . . . Hubert Wilkins."

He mentioned nothing about your letter, but I *know* he followed instructions . . . and I am overjoyed at his reactions to the papers, as I am sure you will be.

We have no set plan for going on to New York. I am to see Miss Carr and Schwartz at his office on Monday. I was furnished with written critical comments [*Ed. note:* about the draft of the Jane Addams play] from Mrs. Bowen, Carr, Allen, Humphries, and some others[1] . . . all are well-intentioned, some very constructive . . . others in igno-

[1] Officials connected with Hull House.

rance of necessary dramatic license. Your suggestions are in order . . . I WILL NOT do any more work on the play until I get the contract. They must have confidence in me from this point on, that I will make such changes as are in good taste and should be made . . . but I cannot be dictated to by people who do not know playwriting. I feel confident everything will work out fine.

No more word from the New York front [regarding the Mark Twain play] . . . from [producer Eugene] Bryden or [actress Marie] Cornell. I hope we can remain while Wilkins is here and study . . . then go on to New York, etc.

I received a remarkable letter from this former Catholic priest in which he said: "I am determined that, with the help of the Guide, in whose presence I live every moment, we shall never be poor again. Thanks to you, our present is flooded with sunshine. Now, as you know, my entire life is based upon the thought of the Guide, 'ever-present and ever-ready'. . ."

It seems evident that this man, [Charles] Ronayne, is being prepared to do a job. Dr. [Charles Francis] Potter, head of the Humanist Society, would be immensely interested in this material, as a Bible authority. [Dr. Seymour (Cy)] Wanderman, as a medical man.[2] A number of pieces now begin to fit together.

You are much in our thoughts and hearts . . . we had your 42nd wedding anniversary much in mind—its approach—and then, under the pressure of getting settled here, let it slip temporarily from consciousness on the day it really occurred, until too late to send you the intended wire of good wishes . . . but we KNOW YOU FOLKS know our love for you . . . and all that we wish constantly.

Sadler, Christy, and the Kelloggs send their best, appreciating your own regards . . . I have not seen young Bill yet . . . childhood diseases and war work are keeping him on the hump. We go to the Forum meeting this afternoon. I am typing on a machine loaned me by the Bucklins, new members (within last four years) who have a daughter, Winnifred, about Mary's age, they are bringing over for Mary to meet this Sunday morning.

Again our love to you and please keep us advised of doings and thoughts.

[2] Potter and Wanderman appear in Vol. 1. Ronayne and his wife were friends of the Shermans in New York. In 1941, while the Shermans were in California, Ronayne acted as Harold's agent, trying to interest publishers in Harold's various manuscripts.

FORUM CALENDAR *May 17, 1942*

Harold and Martha attend first Forum meeting. Meet several members. Marcia and Mary guests of Bucklins for noon dinner.

HAROLD SHERMAN to CHARLES F. POTTER

Chicago, May 17, 1942

Dear Charles:

Here we are, nicely situated in Chicago, where we intend to stay indefinitely as there is much research work to be done in this city. . . .

What I have been writing you is strictly private . . . I am overjoyed that YOU will have substantiated the work I was able to do with Wilkins.

Charles—IF I can get permission, I will have some things to tell you WHEN we come to New York which will blow your hat into the middle of the Atlantic Ocean. It will make the little extrasensory perception we have dabbled with . . . however successful . . . look as picayunish as a pimple on the moon.

I am not interested in doing any more telepathic experimentation at present . . . I have made my contribution in this field . . . but I *AM* interested in going beyond this field of manifestation into the realm of the UNIVERSAL where is contained the answer to all the riddles Man has tried to solve since he first became a human creature on this *dark* planet.

I know of few friends who are equipped to receive what has come to me, as result of my own search for truth . . . so much as yourself, with your profound knowledge of the Bible. I believe you have been uniquely prepared to render a great service to mankind in time to come. Keep that fine enthusiasm you have . . . your feeling that we might have something big and worthwhile to do together in the near future may have been most accurate.

Martha joins me in affectionate greetings!

HARRY LOOSE to HAROLD and MARTHA SHERMAN

Monterey Park, May 18, 1942

Dear Harold and Martha:-

May I thank you both for your fine letters of May 14th[3] which arrived today. I mailed you a letter in answer to the one from you written from Gallup—you should have rec'd it in the batch of mail

[3] Harold's letter has not survived.

Mr. Kellogg handed you. I hope that you will have rec'd it safely before now. Please acknowledge receipt of it.

I have rec'd some information to be forwarded to Wilkins through you. Get it to him at your earliest opportunity. Tell him the answer is "YES"—to make a confidante of his wife of much of what has occurred to him, and for him to impart to her gradually as much as she can comprehend of the information. Tell him she must be under a solemn pledge of secrecy—which must be kept *inviolate*. Tell him to keep my personality, name and address out of the details. Let me know of his safe receipt of the above. . . .

In re Mountain View—tell Arthur that much now depends on him—that there will be much for him to do and to overcome—that he must meet very seeming adverse conditions and carry on—when he and his family take possession of the farm.[4] . . .

For yourself and Martha—a "safe shelter in the time of storm that is to come." A "hide-out." A place to deeply meditate. A place to write. A place of meeting for the "select." A place of rest—recuperation—and safety. At least, "a home" for the tranquil years—when the battle is over—when the head is white and the step is slow and the shadows lengthen. A place to lay in your own soil when the mission is done and the day of release is at hand. A place of your "very own." Your "castle" and your acres. No "rent" but $4.50 a year as taxes. If you do not lose interest, if you keep the faith—even though you live there only a little time out of the year for some time—you should grow to love it—and to think often of it and its improvements and its future very very often. With so very little, it can be made into so very much. Read this paragraph over once in a while when doubts dismay you.

There is much added activity around the old house here. Much coming and going, much that portends. Some regarding "the book."

Handle your funds carefully. Do not take on any additional obligations. Be careful of commitments that would mean any drain on finances. Yes, you have been "cared for" greatly. More than you yet know. You should become increasingly aware of this. Look back. Yet you must have trials and adjustments to meet. Joshua ben Joseph had them. Yet he, too, was "greatly cared for."

---

[4] Harold had been making plans with his brother Arthur for Arthur and his family to move to the Shermans' Arkansas property.

Don't forget Wanderman and the Priest. Hope that you have dwelt some on "fire."[5] There is not much to tell of here. The day is beautiful and warm. Health conditions are the same as when you left. . . .

We miss you all—but it is "the way"—and "is to be."

Be brave—be certain—keep the faith—read "the book."

Love surrounds and supports you,

CHARLES F. POTTER to HAROLD SHERMAN

New York, May 19, 1942

Dear Harold:

Yours of the 17th at hand and fully relished.

Continent and half-continent apart as we have been geographically, we have kept close in spirit. We may be on Mars in our next incarnation, but even there we would find each other. Spirit transcends space, and even time.

You have been having something really important happening, and I, in my smaller way, have been progressing too. Next time we meet, we shall find a higher plane of meeting, I think. My wife, also, has made rapid progress, and has much to contribute.

Please keep in close touch with me, as best you can. Let me know your plans. Very interesting that last night a medium said, "Chicago vibrations here, very strong." He was very dumb and simple and interpreted it that I was going to Chicago, but I knew what it was.

I spoke Sunday to the Spiritual and Ethical Society in the Astor. I was very weak from my recent illness with acute bronchitis and influenza, and had already spoken at noon at the Ansonia to my own group. But I was somehow caught up and transported and made what my wife, my severest critic, called the best inspirational and inspiring talk she had ever heard me make. Very strange psychic phenomena, all beyond my very scientific and rational experience. Several women came to me afterward and, after consultation among themselves, said, "Excuse us for saying this, but we have to. You don't believe in the spirit world, but we never saw such a display of psychic lights as played around you all the time you were speaking. You were in a perfect blaze of light. What you said inspired us all: it was a very fine address in itself, but the thing we want to tell you is that you

---

[5] Loose sought to teach Harold and Martha about the special importance of fire. See Vol. 1, p. 223.

have a contact with the Universal Life Force; you have a spiritual connection, which you ought to develop for the good of the world. The whole world of spirits is with you. You may not believe in spirits but they believe in you. Your halo and aura was simply dazzlingly bright." Well, I discount that, of course—I have to, with my background—but I have to take it into account just the same.

The spiritualistic hypothesis implies so much that I cannot accept, yet one of these women saw a man beside me whom she so accurately described that I knew it was my father! I am much confused.

Cordially,

CFP

FORUM CALENDAR *May 20, 1942*

Marcia leaves for Michigan for summer.

HAROLD SHERMAN to CHARLES F. POTTER

Chicago, May 21, 1942

Dear Charles:

Something is happening to you and *I* know what it is but I cannot tell you in writing. I do not want to sound mysterious but there is a reason. You are opening up channels in your own consciousness and attracting new experiences which are preparing you for a great work to come.

I am glad you are giving me evidences of this development and awareness. Do you remember what I told you about yourself when we first met . . . that your greatest work was ahead of you? I told you this in the face of discouraging conditions . . . and struggle. I knew whereof I spoke—and I will prove it to you one of these days.

Spiritualism is NOT the answer to this phenomenon . . . nor the hypothesis. Do not become confused at this stage . . . observe but hold yourself apart from emotional acceptance because of what seems evidential results.

There are great forces around you . . . *have* been for some time . . . and some sensitively developed people can sense this condition . . . but they do not correctly interpret.

It means much to Martha and me that Mrs. Potter is developing along with you. This is for a reason also. And this Chicago impression has solid substance. YOU may feel impelled to join me in Chicago one of these days. Again for a *mighty* reason.

Contain yourself; keep this in confidence; know that incomprehensibly great things are getting ready to happen. We'll be seeing you before too long if present plans work out . . . as they have a habit of doing, at the right time.

Love to you and yours from us both!

FORUM CALENDAR *May 21, 1942*

Harold and Martha guests of Doctor and Christy along with Sir Hubert for dinner and evening.

May 22-25, 1942

Mother Sherman visits us in Chicago.

May 23, 1942

Mary located at Hull House.

CHARLES F. POTTER to HAROLD SHERMAN

New York, May 23, 1942

Dear Harold:

I have yours of the 21st. Thanks a lot. Very helpful.

Not so disturbed and confused, but still this psychic maelstrom.

Dreams by day and night. Images. Pictures. All soon truly substantiated amazingly. It would take a book to explain it all. I think it will soon clear up, but it is rather upsetting for a rationalist like myself.

Can a man live to be 56 and not have been aware of this *real* world in his subconscious? Always the sense of being on the verge of something truly and really great.

You are right—something is happening to me, and I don't know just what. Sometimes it scares me.

You know, Harold, there is a power or force in us somewhere, which, if we could harness and use it for the good of mankind, would outstrip the vaunted force of the splitting of the atom.

Force, power, tremendous vitality and strength—I get that feeling all the time now. The only words that express it adequately are "LIFE" and "LIGHT."

I hope you will get here soon: I am rather overwhelmed by this psychic climax, whatever it is. When I spoke to the Spiritual and Ethical Society last Sunday—although I was exhausted from two weeks' sickness, something happened, and they all knew it.

Forgive this rather maudlin and rambling letter, but you will read between the lines. I am planning my meetings for next fall and I am tempted to do something rather venturesome: I think I am going to do something big next year. Why do you and I both get this sense of impending greatness and power? Maybe only wishful thinking, but it certainly is strong.

I have signed up with Creative Age Press for my Pseudepigrapha book and am working on my autobiography,[6] but there is something much bigger right around the corner somewhere!

As ever,

HARRY LOOSE to HAROLD SHERMAN

Monterey Park, May 23, 1942

Harold:-

I am enclosing carbon copy of my letter to Mary mailed at the same time that this goes out to you. You are doing right in regards to the [Jane Addams] Contract.

I feel a little indefiniteness regarding Wilkins and wish that you would reassure me. I cannot isolate the feeling to any specific center. I hope that he arrived okay and that you have met. I do so want to keep his confidence and belief and respect. Has his contact with the "book" and its surroundings made any change in his prior view?? I have done so much for him that he does not know about. Suggest that he drop me a line—when the time and spirit move him. Anyway, let me know.

Love to you both,

FORUM CALENDAR *May 24, 1942*

Second Forum meeting. We attend every Sunday meeting of regular Forum from this date except the two Sundays [*Ed. note:* June 28th and July 5th] in New York. We find the papers hard to understand as read in Forum.

May 25, 1942

Began reading of papers in earnest every day from 9:30 to 12:30 and 1:30 to 5:30.

---

[6] Potter's autobiography, *The Preacher and I,* was published in 1951. Creative Age Press did not publish a book by Potter on the Pseudepigrapha.

HAROLD SHERMAN to CHARLES F. POTTER

Chicago, May 25, 1942

Dear Charles:

If you could only *see* what is happening from my point of vantage, you would then understand what is happening to you, through your inner consciousness—and WHY!

Now let me ask you something testily. Could you arrange for you and your wife to come here to Chicago to stay for perhaps six weeks, sometime this summer . . . if not six, necessarily *four* . . . and take a light-housekeeping apartment such as Martha and I now occupy, which you should be able to get for around $60-$70 per month.

I am not sure yet that I could gain permission for you to join us in this research and study—but if I can—and if you could quietly arrange your affairs to be absent from New York, before fall, for this period of time—I can promise you the greatest experience that can come to a human *soul* on this *dark* planet. I am choosing my words advisedly. And you would have to pledge, for your wife and yourself, absolute secrecy . . . for the knowledge which is being revealed . . . or would be revealed . . . is not to be given to the world, as yet.

This is worth every sacrifice you can humanly make; Martha and I have broken up our little family and despite the economic factors involved . . . have *made* ourselves available. What will eventuate will prove our life work; the forces motivating you are preparing you for your part in the same work. I am not permitted to hint too much . . . but there is a universe of incomprehensibly higher intelligences beyond the reach of our physical senses . . . and what we've experienced in telepathy, etc., is just the fringe of a great and infinite reality.

Is there some parishioner to whom you could go—who would underwrite, as a spiritual contribution, your trip to Chicago, to undertake some highly important research and study of a confidential nature, which is later to be revealed to the world . . . and which, you are assured by a friend in whom (I hope) you have every confidence . . . can mean MORE than life itself to every human creature—including *himself*? This knowledge (for *your* information only) concerns your eternal destiny as an evolving human creature; the complete history of the origin of this planet from the time it was formed, by a conscious thinking act of the Great Intelligence, to the day that the human creature first appeared upon it and began its long, upward, God-ward climb, to what we regard as the *present* day . . . and on beyond what we call death . . . to a specific knowledge of what awaits us beyond . . . and ALL the hitherto unknown truths which have baffled men throughout all ages.

What might be revealed to you is so colossal that no vocabulary of Man can even begin to give you any concept. There is a reason WHY you and Mrs. Potter have been so close in matters of this kind. You will NEED each other to discuss this knowledge, if and when permission can be obtained by me for your association.

Can I tell you confidentially this much . . . since apparently you need this much of an explanation of forces stirring in you . . . ? There dwells with every human consciousness or *evolving* soul (the human creature has not yet taken on immortality but is potentially heir to immortality of personality or identity) . . . there dwells in your consciousness, yet separate and apart from your entity—a fragmentized part of God or the Great Intelligence which can SPEAK TO YOU through what you would call your inner voice or consciousness. You can actually learn how to commune with Higher Intelligences and with the God of this Universe of Universes THROUGH this fragmentized part of HIMSELF, existent in and through you! NOW—does a LIGHT begin to dawn. You'll get beyond these little offshoot manifestations of psychic power pretty soon into another FIELD entirely . . .

Our love to you always—

HAROLD SHERMAN to HARRY LOOSE

Chicago, May 26, 1942

Dear Harry:

Your letter to Mary was perfectly timed as I think she needed encouragement from you. . . .

Mother was here to spend the weekend and returned to Marion, Indiana yesterday . . . not being ready to go on up to Traverse yet. Marcia is safely in our home town and happy . . . and Martha and I are now free to do continuous study on the book which we are finding easily up to all your advance notices.

All those in the Forum here who remember you wish to send greetings, especially Miss [Elsie] Baumgartner, who wrote you some months ago[7] and who says you predicted her affiliation with a "spiritual group" a long time before it actually happened.

[7] See Vol. 1, p. 351.

Wilkins is delighted beyond words and reiterates that he would always be eternally grateful to us for this association. We are reading in the front second-floor room, Martha and I at one end . . . and Wilkins at the other . . . we read out loud but it doesn't disturb him since he is deaf.

The Forum ends its primary function as a body this next Sunday, being at the end of its dispensation. It is to keep going, with a picnic June 6th at the home of Mr. [G. Willard] Hales, and regular Sunday discussion meetings, with the Forum eventually becoming the Urantia Society. I hope no Society is formed for a time after the book comes out as it seems to me that this would make it seem as though a new religion was being founded, and other churches and peoples would shy away. I sounded out the Sadlers today about plans; they say they have nothing yet on book publication and have received no instructions; I will make suggestions after I have digested the material as best I can in a first reading. It would take years to get a fair comprehension of it all.

Things that have been said in private conversation confirm again much you have told us. I was particularly interested in the Reserve Corps, entities in the flesh who have come here to do a job and are trained for it, often without their knowledge . . . it made me wonder IF . . . ? Particularly when it was said they looked into the future and were assigned to see that important developments went through on schedule . . . the older ones "tossing the torch" to the younger, etc. Being trained while they sleep . . . you know this all better than I.

Being here opens up so many avenues for discussion with you that I wish I were telepathically enough endowed to commune at length. Sadler doesn't know what to make of our experiments . . . he says, according to advices from Higher Intelligences—telepathy, while possible, is not now being practiced on Urantia. He has a different explanation in mind for the phenomena. I conjecture it has to do with thought adjusters.

I am having my temporary troubles with the Hull House people, as this copy of a letter I sent to Miss Carr shows . . . So far, I've had to deal largely through Miss Carr—with Mr. Schwartz playing shrewd and dumb in the background. His ignorance of theatrical affairs is appalling. I've had to make allowances for people in positions of authority all my life and suppose I'll have to continue being tolerant and patient.[8] Martha and I are well and happy and greatly enthused over the material. Glad you and Mother Loose are as usual. Tonight's paper says bombings are expected on the coast. Keep me advised of developments out there.

All send love and wish you could be here . . . I'll keep you advised the best I can at all times.

CHARLES F. POTTER to HAROLD SHERMAN

New York, May 26, 1942

Dear Harold:

I have yours of yesterday, airmail, and I wish Mrs. Potter and I could arrange to do what you suggest, but it is impossible. We are already committed to previously planned arrangements which cannot be changed. These arrangements concern other people.

Not that I am not very greatly interested in what you are doing (indeed I am, more than this letter may indicate), but it just cannot happen. I appreciate the fact that you and Martha have given up much to be in it, but, much as Clara and I would like to cooperate, it just is not possible this summer.

You wrote in a recent letter that you might be on to N.Y. for a trip soon. Can we not get together then and talk over this and other matters?

Your letter read unlike yourself—more like a Rosicrucian advertisement. Have you come to believe in a personal God? Surely you do not retrograde to that level! There is where the great mistake has been made. That inhibits real progress in this field.

As I see it, Harold, in all frankness, we have to avoid the Scylla of materialism on the one hand and the Charybdis of theism on the other. We must be neither materialistic nor gullible.

This fragmentized part of God who is a fragmentized part of me just doesn't click with my intelligence, nor with my feeling-consciousness. Maybe the words are wrong. I know, very well, that there is a power within me on which I can draw, not only in emergencies but for daily sustenance, a power which has nothing of "God" or supernaturalism in it, but rather a natural evolutionary force. It is a part of

[8] On May 22nd Schwartz notified Harold that the Board of Hull House had voted to reject his play. In his May 24th letter to Carr, Harold expressed his willingness to revise the play and his hope that Hull House would fashion a contract which would allow him to secure a Broadway producer before getting Hull House's approval of the play.

me. I am, as a man, the out-reaching bud-tip of the tree of life: I am the whole universe come to consciousness. But that does not mean that I have to believe in God, or in some nebulous Higher Intelligences or Master Powers of Tibet.

Maybe I have got you all wrong: if so, correct me. If you think I have a piece of God in me, very well, but I am fussy about this God-person. I'm not sure I like him. The word "God" has too many fringes and I shy from it. Maybe I have theophobia, or something like that. Anyway, know I like you and would admire working all this out with you.

Cordially,

P.S. Reading this over, it sounds cold. I'm working toward the same goal you are, but I'm very suspicious of this God—Great Intelligence—you mention. I think I really feel more in touch with the Life-Evolutionary Force than theists do, but I don't like the Jehovah-God idea. Let the theological idea go, and I'm with you. God is out, but this power, force, whatever you want to call it, is there. It is purely human and part of us. We can use it, contact it, but we cannot properly impute to it the old God qualities. It is infinitely more than that. This ESP power, or whatever you call it, is so much greater than God that we have not yet got a proper word for it.

HAROLD SHERMAN to CHARLES F. POTTER

Chicago, May 28, 1942

Dear Charles:

You should know me well enough by this time to know that I don't go overboard on religions or isms . . . nor do I fall for Rosicrucian advertisements, however alluring.

I think you have been so revolted by the old concepts of God that mention of the name (and we've got to have SOME NAME with which to describe or try to indicate INTELLIGENCE incomprehensibly superior to our own) prejudices you to any consideration of the possible origin and nature of UNIVERSAL FORCES which you now commence to sense flowing through you—perhaps for the first time in your 56 years.

Your reaction demonstrates to me again how PERSONAL and INTIMATE and INDIVIDUAL a thing is human experience. I do not like the word "God" as used by churchianity any more than you do

. . . but until better words are invented to convey the existence of INFINITE POWER, what are we going to do?

For the time being, since this knowledge will later be made available to everybody, let's just forget what I have indicated to you. It is too vast a subject at present, and since it is impossible for you to be here and be exposed to it and be confronted with the EVIDENCE . . . any hints I might be permitted to give you might cause you to COLOR them by your own preconceived convictions . . . and I would not be able to go far enough, unless you were in the same position I am, to present the case to you in acceptable form.

Suffice it to say, you have a great deal to learn about the nature of this universe and our relation to it—and so have I. Keep that fine mind of yours absolutely OPEN and FREE OF PREJUDICE and FIXED IDEAS . . . Great things are going to happen—man's knowledge is going to be terrifically extended in the not too distant future.

Meanwhile, we love you and send you our best wishes . . . can't say yet when we'll be on to New York.

HARRY LOOSE to HAROLD and MARTHA SHERMAN

Monterey Park, May 29, 1942

Dear Harold and Martha:-

I am returning herein the carbon copy of your letter to Miss Carr. There is nothing for you to get excited or worried about. . . .

The Reserve Corps is a little something different and not that to which you see a resemblance. It is too bad that that which you should have read [*Ed. note:* about the "hybrids"] has been deleted—both written and from the minds. I do not know the reason—but some good cause lays behind it—the operation much the same as the dematerialization of solids—it is quite often done when necessary.

That which you are reading is an old, old story to me—and there is much more—not understandable to most in the present state of development. I am much interested in Martha's reaction to the reading. Is faith more acceptable with renewed personal contact with the printed source and surroundings?? You can both now better realize how little I could impart orally. And this is but the first lesson—there is much more.

Sadler's reaction to telepathy, and the Astral, is not unexpected. He misinterprets some things. Accurate telepathy is not universal—nor is the ability to produce the Astral. And will not be during our present flesh experience. General development, to the present, is such that the availability to so operate at will would not be for the general good. You can visualize this. It would be the opposite. Like a man given a locomotive under full steam to run who had never operated one before. A terrific power not under control. All of this above does not include the fully favored—and has no bearing on their activities. . . .

I miss Martha's biscuits and the understanding atmosphere of association with you both—and grieve a bit that this phase of my flesh existence here has come to pass—with its gain and its loss—of you *all*. And now it has gone into the limbo of the past—and all that I have left is a memory to bide with—I have on those zipper tan shoes now.

Thank the well wishers—especially Miss Baumgartner—for their good thought. . . .

I look for your assurance regarding Wilkins as per my last letter. I am still a little unquiet. There are things forming for him.

Things here not so well but please do not remark in your letter when you write.

Love—as always—

FORUM CALENDAR *May 30, 1942*

Invited to Dent Karles' at Oak Park for evening with Bucklins and Sir Hubert who is back in Chicago for second reading of papers.

Mary interviewed and admitted to Forum membership.

HAROLD SHERMAN to CHARLES RONAYNE

Chicago, May 30, 1942

Dear Charles:

Wonderful things are happening to Martha and me, and we wish you were here to be sharing them. Much of what we are undergoing in the way of spiritual research and study we are not permitted to pass on, at present . . . but, if it ever might be possible for you to spend a month in Chicago, I would submit your name and make every effort to gain your acceptance.

You have been prepared, uniquely, to do a great work in the world—and your time is not quite yet. But you have been *chastened* and for transcendent reasons beyond your imagining or conceiving. Be of good cheer—the period of your punishing experiences is nearing an end . . . and the WAY in which you have pulled yourself out of this economic and spiritual morass in which you found yourself has been proof to Higher Intelligences beneficently interested in your welfare—that you could be trusted with one of the great spiritual assignments ahead.

We all have been TESTED . . . and are being tested. This life is a terrific training school for a future destiny of glorious possible achievement in "mansions and worlds" to come.

No, I don't have religion in the sense that the church people *think* they have religion . . . but there is being unfolded to my expanding consciousness the first full, true and scientifically provable story of the universe, the origin of our planet from the dark islands of space, the origin of the human creatures upon it, the relation of these evolving human creatures to the Great Intelligence or Universal Father, who Jesus really was and the great purpose of His sojourn on earth, what this life is being lived for, and what awaits us after physical death—on and on to the final indescribable possible attainment of the human creature, possessor at last of an immortal soul . . . the eternal retainer of individual personality and identity. . . .

All the perplexing problems of religiosity which have plagued you all your life—are going to be wiped away.

A new revelation is coming into the world from verifiable Higher Sources which will amplify all the truth that still exists in our present Bible and carry us on FAR BEYOND it.

I have been placed in touch with phenomena so far eclipsing the little mental work I have been able to do with Wilkins as to make it seem picayunish. BUT, we are led to great spiritual discoveries and unfoldments through our own meditation . . . and FAITH is not intangible . . . FAITH is SUBSTANCE.

Keep happily and confidently at your work; don't let any physical or economic thing disturb you any more. KNOW that fundamentally everything is all right. . . .

Great and good things are getting ready to happen. Free yourself of any possible lingering thoughts of inferiority or frustration. You may be a teacher of spiritual truths in the years to come on a scale never dreamed of. I am sorry that I can only hint at present . . . but I feel you have confidence enough in me to accept what I say on faith for the time.

It may be close to July 1st before we can come on to New York.

HARRY LOOSE to HAROLD and MARTHA SHERMAN

Monterey Park, June 3, 1942

Dear Harold and Martha:-

I am in receipt of small Martha's letter of May 30th and Harold's of June 1st.[9] I thank you much—both. Both of you write such good and descriptive letters. You do not acknowledge receipt of my letters. I address them correctly and when you do not remark their receipt, I wonder if they have arrived safely. Please acknowledge. You do not answer the personal question I have asked regarding Wilkins.

Bilocation has recurred on an occasion and at a location which has caused me much embarrassment because of inability to explain or refute the presence. And because of the inability to understand by the recipients.

I long unbelievably for you both. Something portends—I do not know what—yet. I am very tired and not so well. I will make my presence understandably known to you both afterwards if I am to go on.

The Sunday message at the Haleses' will be of importance. I do hope that neither of you will miss it. . . .

I have no knowledge at present of definite forwarding of the revelation. Except that you surely are connected positively with it in some way. Don't forget Wanderman and the Catholic priest—and that doctor from the Humanist group.

What you are reading, and more, I have known for so long—how difficult—and how slowly it has to be introduced—only little by little. It was to be, but I am so grateful that you are, both, in realization now—fully. ALL that has been given you is the TRUTH.

Martha, I am so glad to read full acceptance—with no mental reservations—in your letter. I know "doubting Thomas" has fled now. A year—and so very much has come to you. Could you return to the *old* thought now???? . . .

What did your Mother think of the little information that you could give her???? . . .

We are still here—at the old brown house—the days pass—noontime shades into night—and night passes—and we wait. I am very tired and I look away into the distance beyond that which the mortal eye rests upon. The shadows are surely lengthening. It would have been a wonderful thing if Ma and I could have been with you folks—

[9] Neither of these letters has been found.

if only for a little time—while you were there—and to have been there while Mother Sherman was there—to have met her—it would have been such a break in our routine. I have just finished the magazines that you folks brought over. There'll be no more coming now. Remember me—and Ma too—to little Marcia when you write. I miss the biscuits too—Martha. My life has been so much of "goodbyes" and this last one was the hardest of all.

Love from us both to you all,

2

QUESTIONS

FORUM CALENDAR *June 3, 1942*

Christy had dinner with us in our apartment. (We learned, afterward, that Christy seldom accepted invitations from Forum members unless accompanied by the Doctor.) During the course of the evening Harold asked her why the Book of Urantia contained no explanation of psychic phenomena, so common to millions of people, who, when they read the Book of Urantia which describes phenomena of a transcendent super nature, will wonder how to classify what they feel has happened at times to them. Christy said she realized that this subject wasn't adequately covered and that the Doctor himself had had no personal experience to indicate to him that this phenomena really existed. She said, "Harold, you know a lot about these things. Why don't you write up an explanation of the way you think it ought to be and let us submit it. Maybe the Angels of Progress will okay it for the book." Harold was astounded at this invitation and said he would prefer asking a series of questions which might be submitted so that the higher beings in charge of this revelation could answer them as they chose. This has continued to disturb Harold as we thought no human had the right to create any copy for the Book of Urantia.

June 4, 1942

Spent evening in discussion at Bill's.

HAROLD SHERMAN to the ANGELS OF PROGRESS et al., via WILLIAM SADLER

[undated, probably June 5, 1942]

QUESTIONS

There is considerable mention made in the story of the early human creatures on Urantia of the "ghost fears" which they persistently encountered, and which eventually gave birth to first religious concepts and even influenced moral developments. While many of these "ghost fears" may have been induced by natural phenomena, some still remain to be explained.

Countless people still have experiences in which they "see" the forms or "hear" the voices of those who have gone on. When the Book of Urantia states that no personality ever returns to the planet of its birth, these people will be very confused unless some explanation is given as to just what takes place at such times. What, for instance, do people about to die often actually see in their visions?

What does a so-called "medium" contact when he or she purports to bring "messages" from those who have recently passed into the next phase of existence, back to dear ones still on Urantia?

There have also been occasions when entities who have passed over under tragic circumstances seem to make even total strangers, as well as friends or relatives, brought into the environment of their tragedy, aware of their presence and the circumstances involved. Can an explanation be given for this? On occasion, people at great distances have had apparent "spirit visitations" and have been advised or given the impression of tragic happenings. How is this explained?

The statement is made in the Book of Urantia that telepathy, as we understand it, is not now in practice on this planet. Is this meant to be a *general* statement and are there exceptions under special conditions? If so, should not some explanation be offered to aid the understanding of scientists, as well as millions who have encountered a substantial amount of evidence which seems to point to the existence of genuine extrasensory perception?

No mention is apparently made of the occasional appearance on earth of so-called "astral" bodies or perhaps what might be called "Morontia bodies" by these papers. Yet the questioner and many others of sound mind and highly trained observational faculties have been witness to the appearance of definite, recognizable "astral or spirit" forms of human entities.

Such phenomena, as stated, have occurred without the aid of any so-called "spirit mediums," and the forms witnessed have been those of entities both living and dead. Not only that, but in some instances, these forms have *spoken* and have been heard by the physical ears of those present.

It would seem that the Book of Urantia, at the proper place pertaining to the development of man's mind and spirit, might well stand the insertion of an enlightening chapter relative to the entire field of what we understand to be "psychic phenomena."

Inasmuch as the Book of Urantia itself has apparently been made available through a "human subject" in a manner that investigators, from their viewpoint, would classify as a "psychic manifestation," it would appear absolutely imperative that these various phases of "psychic experiences" be adequately treated and explained.

The Book of Urantia is so all-inclusive in every other way that the conspicuous absence of satisfactory material relative to the cause and nature of these mysterious occurrences will leave many readers disturbed and bewildered.

Unless such a paper is presented, readers naturally interested in knowing the manner in which these revelations were made possible to humans, are going to be disposed to challenge their material authenticity no matter how remarkable the contents.

One of the recognized fundamental problems of this book's presentation to the public is admittedly going to be that of its *origin.* If any explanation at all is officially offered in written form, and if any group or representative of this group attempts to stand on such an explanation, and no chapter is contained in this volume pertaining to the field of psychic phenomena, then the human upholders of this volume are placed in a most vulnerable position.

The Book of Urantia answers literally *millions* of questions that humans have never had answered for them before. The most *pressing* question that is going to exist in the minds of all who read these revelations will be "how and in what manner did they come about?"

This question cannot be satisfied by any partial explanation if such explanation is unsupported by material in the book itself setting forth conditions and factors incident to similar phenomena. In fact, it now seems to this questioner as though such a chapter might be so presented as to answer *for all time* the fundamental question that is sure to rise in the minds of the readers as to the attitudes humans should assume in the face of all such phenomena as described.

Certainly *something* has been happening in countless substantiated cases which cannot be classified as hallucination, self-delusion, imagination, fear projection, emotional instability or a vagary of the subconscious.

If we can be indwelled by Thought Adjusters, and reached and influenced in consciousness by various orders of seraphim and by one or more of the Seven Adjutant Spirits, then is it not possible that, under certain moments of witting or unwitting sensitivity, we can also be influenced by the minds or spirits of those living or "dead"?

Whether or not communication with the so-called "dead" is possible or desirable, something evidential has taken place numberless times. This book is so authoritative as to what occurs from the time of death on, that it seems to me, in all humbleness, a great oversight not to have properly recognized and evaluated the various kinds of mental, psychic and spiritual manifestations so prevalent throughout all recorded ages, including the Bible times.

As transcendent and indescribably wonderful as are the contents of this book—would it not be even *more* transcendent and wonderful for it to be *known* that these Great Intelligences from higher planes of being *organized* for the purpose of visiting this planet Urantia and presenting the inspired and true revelation of the Creator, His Universe and His Creation?

To make a mystery of the origin of this revelation and a *partial* explanation of it, however well-intended, will be regarded by many as a practice of human deceit and insincerity actuated by definite motives. There is enough *profound mystery* contained in the book itself to satisfy any aspiring soul.

Its inspiration, it would appear, would be greatly enhanced by the knowledge that Intelligences from higher planes, interested in serving the evolving human family on Urantia, are *actually here with us*, though invisible to most, but reaching the consciousness of us all through their *developed and appointed* "human instruments."

This great fact, as demonstrated and supported by the contents of this *basically unassailable book*, is the greatest piece of NEWS that could ever be presented to humans at any time, anywhere, in the history of this world.

Jesus did not keep His origin a secret. He came into this world of humble parentage. His spiritual achievement as an actual son of man has been the one great light on this dark planet. The identity of the subject in this new revelation should rightfully *never* be revealed, but the nature of the book's origin should be so *authoritatively* explained by the Higher Intelligences themselves as to be *immediately accepted* by all skeptical readers, just as they will accept many of the profound and logical statements made about the Universe, the formation of the worlds, the creation of this planet, the work of the Life Carriers, and countless other remarkable revelations.

This book is beyond the human. It should be so constituted as to remain *forever* beyond the human. Pulling its origin down to a partially explanatory human level in an explanation offered *by* humans will serve to greatly impair its spiritual value.

I humbly petition the Angels of Progress and all those who have labored so long on this mission to consider the questions herein raised and the problem of so presenting the answers to these questions as to include an acceptable, understandable, authoritative explanation of the manner in which this revelation was made possible through and to humans, to the end that no Forum member or official will ever be placed in the vulnerable position of having to defend, explain, attempt to dignify or authenticate, the sublime contents of your revelations.

These questions and comments are submitted in all respect and in all humility.

FORUM CALENDAR *June 6, 1942*

Annual picnic at Haleses'.

HAROLD SHERMAN to HARRY LOOSE

Chicago, June 6, 1942

Dear Harry:

Just time for a note this morning as I want to get off a copy of these questions to you which I have sent in to Sadler.

I think Sadler intends to have a printed pamphlet telling the *partial* story of what happened—and, unless I am wrong, he is going to make himself vulnerable to all kinds of newspaper and scientific inquiry. IF the Higher Intelligences could only take care of this explanation in an authoritative manner in the book itself . . . then Sadler and all other humans wouldn't have to say a thing . . . they could stand on the book's explanation.

Martha and I are reading all day every day. Today is the day of the annual picnic and we wish you and Mother Loose could be here for it . . . we will be thinking of you. . . .

Our love and best thought for you always. More later. (Wilkins has been called to Washington and leaves after the picnic tonight. He is on fire. You never saw anyone so delighted with the material. He's an inspiration to everyone around here.)

CHARLES RONAYNE to HAROLD SHERMAN

New York, June 7, 1942

Dear Harold:

Your letter of May 30 was a welcome surprise, mainly because I was in debt to you for a letter. I had not answered your previous letter when this one arrived. You pardon me, I know, for you understand how dreadfully busy I am. (I should not have said "dreadfully busy," rather "delightfully busy.")

But in another sense your letter was a surprise . . . a surprise in the sense that there is much in it that I cannot seem to comprehend. I know that I have been chastened. I know that I have been through a testing. And I know that I have been through a veritable hell—economically, emotionally, and spiritually. All this I know and understand. I understand also that at the moment the pressure is easier, from all sides. I am grateful for the respite, more grateful than I can ever say.

What I fail to grasp is your assertion that there is yet a big job for me to do. I am not talking out of any false sense of humility when I say that I do not envisage myself in the doing of any big job. Not that I would shirk any such thing if it came along. Rather my feeling is that I am such a smallness (so to speak). My experiences have been punishing, it is true. I am glad for the growth they have engendered in me. But I am painfully conscious of the huge mass of human error and human superstition. I have been for so long a working part of that error. I know it from the inside. And I know that the inertia of human thought is so terrific that it will take a much bigger man than I ever hope to be to dislodge even the tiniest part of it. . . .

. . . By no stretch of imagination can I see myself in the role of a teacher of men. I was in the role for nearly a quarter of a century, and the experience has left with me a profound distrust of my own capacity to lead others. With the exception of this element of your letter, you give me nothing but encouragement and help. But I do wish with all my heart that I could have a long talk with you. Maybe I shall, when you come to New York. . . .

Blessings on you always,
Charles

FORUM CALENDAR *June 7, 1942*

Jo and Merrill Davis arrived in Chicago and we are invited to join them at the Doctor's for lunch before Forum. Doctor tells of the narrow escape from death near Denver while driving with Bill, Christy and Dr. [Lena] Sadler several years ago. [*Ed. note:* This occurred in Estes Park, Colorado, in 1931.] They go over a mountain 2000 feet and survive with only slight injuries. Car hauled up next day and driven away on own power.

Harold and Martha have fish dinner, South Chicago, with Davises (and Mr. Wilson, relative).

HAROLD SHERMAN to HARRY LOOSE

Chicago, June 8, 1942

Dear Harry:

The Annual Picnic was a wonderful affair; marvelous weather, interspersed in between a week of thunderstorms, the biggest gathering ever—130 people—a fine dinner served under trees on lawn . . . but Martha and Sir Hubert and I sat at the "guest table" on the porch, with Mr. Hales, Dr. Sadler, Christy, a Mr. Harre [*Ed. note:* Harrah][1] from Niles, Michigan, and Herschel Wilson, relative of Jo Davis and Sadler's, a new member.[2]

The entire membership is in love with Wilkins, who has made a tremendous impression . . . he had to leave after the picnic and we

[1] William F. Harrah (1871-1959) was a wealthy industrialist and banker who co-founded National Standard Company, a wire-products manufacturing firm based in Niles, Michigan. In a talk given to a Urantia study group in Oklahoma on February 18, 1962, Bill Sadler said that Mr. Harrah, while not the man who transmitted the superhuman messages to the contact commissioners, was similar to him in temperament and disposition, being a "kindly guy," a "tough businessman," and "an all-around, self-made man."

[2] Herschel Fleet Wilson, born in 1908 in Clinton County, Indiana; died in 1991 in Marion, Indiana.

drove him to the station to catch a midnight train for Washington, where he has been called on the Alaskan situation.[3] Wilkins told me he never could repay *us* in this lifetime for putting him in touch with the Forum and this great knowledge which he has no doubt comes from "higher intelligences," the most amazing document ever to come to earth. You should be hearing from him soon. How he has dug into this material—long hours every day for weeks! (By "us" above, I meant you and me.)

After dinner, everyone assembled in the Hales house, and young Bill read a special message directed to the Forum by the head of the Angels of Progress, in charge of this work. The Forum was officially released from its duties of asking questions and its direct responsibilities concerning the papers; it was stated emphatically that everyone was now on their own and that it would remain to be seen whether they would prove equal to this "test." It emphasized the need for unity and predicted there would be many human ideas as to how this Forum should be run from now on.

It was stated that the U.S. was facing its greatest crisis, all freedom-loving nations were—and we were not out of danger yet . . . no indication was given as to when the book might be released, although it was urged that the printing job be speeded (setting in type) . . . Appreciation was voiced by the Midwayers for the cooperation given by Forum members over this long period . . . it was a touching moment as people, long in harness, tried to realize that their long devotion to this cause was entering a new phase . . . Martha and I thought of you and Mother Loose at this moment . . . with tears of thanksgiving that we should be here, at least at the finish . . . (the Most Recents of Days). . . .

Oh, Harry—to have found such LIGHT on this DARK planet is such a soul-satisfying experience. . . .

Mother has been greatly helped by the little information we were able to give her. I shall approach Dr. Wanderman, Mr. Ronayne and Dr. Potter when we get to New York . . . I am sure they are all *ripe* for service . . . and will respond in the right manner.

Your letters have all come through fine and had not thought it necessary to specifically acknowledge them. It is a RED LETTER day when we get word from you . . .

[3] The Battle of the Aleutian Islands began in June 1942. U.S. troops fought to remove Japanese garrisons from two U.S.-owned islands off the coast of Alaska.

I am not trying to wonder where I may fit in here . . . just studying at present . . . and waiting for my part to be unfolded to me.

Jo and Merrill Davis were here yesterday and we drove them to Hammond, Indiana where we had a perch dinner at a place called "Lundgren's" . . . marvelous cooking. They were thrilled at our being in the Forum . . . and our connection with you . . . whom they remember well.

I received a wire from [veteran actor] Fred Stone that he can try the MARK TWAIN play out in summer stock at Dennis, Mass., in August. I will be glad to get this under way . . . it will help my reputation with the Hull House people . . . I am glad you feel the Jane Addams matter will work out okay despite all or any opposition in its right time . . . JENKINS of Occidental Life Insurance Company is coming here June 15th . . . I feel his interest is renewed in radio . . . wouldn't that be strange IF . . .?

LOVE TO MOTHER & YOU.

FORUM CALENDAR *June 9, 1942*

Bill and Leone have dinner and evening here with us.

HAROLD SHERMAN to CHARLES RONAYNE

Chicago, June 9, 1942

Dear Charles:

I do not want to seem mysterious and yet there is so much, just now, that I cannot say by letter.

First, let me ask you how many foreign languages you read and write—and how many of them you feel capable of translating an English manuscript into? Upon the nature of this answer might depend *years* of profitable, inspiring work in the not too distant future . . . leading into the big job I spoke of (this translation an immense job in itself!).

Yes, you are just emerging from a period of darkness . . . you are conscious, as am I, of the "huge mass of human error and human superstition," and this cannot be alleviated in a day or a year . . . but punishing human experience is doing things to the minds and hearts of millions. To plant seeds you first have to ruffle up the soil, do violence to it . . . and then Nature, with temperature and rainfall, does violence to the seed—and life manifests and something of beauty grows out of seeming ruthless operation of elements.

Don't try to understand it all now . . . but I am SO HAPPY to have seen you come this LONG WAY to stand where you now stand . . . better and stronger even now than you know. You *will* be put in touch with somebody at the right time who will lead you where you want to go. Everything is basically *all right* and you will find yourself walking more steadily every day. . . .

HARRY LOOSE to HAROLD and MARTHA SHERMAN

Monterey Park, June 9, 1942

Dear Harold and Martha:-

I am answering at once and in haste your airmail letter of yesterday enclosing the "Questions."

Sadler does not "own," he is but a temporary custodian of the revelation. He has no other official relationship to it. If he attempts his own personal aggrandizement for perpetuity in attaching his human name and personality to the finished printed document of the revelation, he is doing a tremendously wrong thing—a Judas thing—as a sop to his personal vanity. If he does this thing, he will nullify a great deal. He should have sufficient intelligence to see this himself without it having to be brought to his attention. If he cannot see it himself—over the selfish desire to attach himself personally to it forever—then someone should surely tell him. Any, and all, members of the Forum should have the same right exactly as Sadler to attach his or her name.

Your "Questions" was a brave and correct thing to do and should enlighten Sadler a lot if he will but read it with an open mind. If, however, his human love of self takes precedence over all else, he will be blinded and "will not see." Through this self-love, he can do a great deal of harm. Harm that it will take the mist of centuries to overcome and blind. Maybe your best avenue of adjustment, before anything really injurious happens, is through Bill.

What *should* happen now is this. Sadler should make contact and ask from the Intelligences an authoritative explanation of our truly evidenced psychic phenomena and an authoritative introduction giving the reasons for this revelation—and from whom the permission for such revelation comes. No human element is needed in this "explanation." All this as per your very valuable suggestions. This would obviate any attempted "explanations" in the future. The answer to inquiry would be, "Read the Book, that is all that there is to it." It would then stand or fall by its own merits—as it should—without any human explanations. The "Receiver" of this revelation should be forever shielded. He MUST be. If he is not, he will be "removed" in his own protection.

The "message" to be read at the Picnic will NOT be the last communication. There will be continuous maintained watchful contact kept on the reception and success of the revelation. There will be, at irregular times, further and added communications through the present Receiver—to Sadler. There will be an inner circle of the select in continuance of the Forum developing later. Watch the cliques develop—and the bickerings—and the differences in opinions—all the human entering in—just as in the time of Joshua ben Joseph.

There IS, and always has been existent, and will always continue to exist, what is, for lack of a better name, that which we call psychic phenomena. MUCH that humans call supernormal—or supernatural—is perfectly normal and natural and becomes so just as soon as the method of operation is understood. There is, however, much that is far and above this. For instance, is not the whole Forum evidence of the existence of psychic phenomena??

There ARE fleshed human instruments appointed to serve—that were definitely sent here for the purpose of serving—make no mistake about this. Joshua ben Joseph was so enfleshed for the mission he came here to perform. So were the Prophets. The list is too long to go into here. The very instrument through which the present revelation came is one. YOU ARE ONE. There are many, many others. "There were Seven."

There IS what we call telepathy. It is not general. At this period of our development it could not be with safety. Make no mistake—there IS the Astral. The ability of production of such is not general. At this period of our development it could not be so with safety. There is definitely bilocation and there are many other even more humanly mysterious manifestations than any of the above phenomena. What is called "Sight" and what is called "Hearing" are two examples that are definite—absolutely true—and most positive.[4] And all are possible to a degree by earned development—without the added gift of the easier ability so to do given at birth and not earned.

I have so often asked in my letters whether Wilkins retained his faith in me and I have not yet been able to get an answer to the ques-

[4] See Vol. 1, p. 333, for Loose's earlier remarks on sight and hearing.

tion. I would not ask you to remark on this without a reason. I make this request once more.

Returning to psychic phenomena for a minute. The change in the papers that "just appeared there," according to Bill, are evidences of existent psychic phenomena. Is not the very reception of these revelations also in this class. What happened to the hybrid papers also belongs here—even to the mental deletion of the many who knew. This same takes in the "witnessed writings" of which we have talked before. . . .

. . . We will look for your letter—and one from Martha maybe—after the doings at the Haleses—and that was three days ago.

Please acknowledge receipt of this when you write. Must close for now.

Much love from us both,

HAROLD SHERMAN to HARRY LOOSE

Chicago, June 12, 1942

Dear Harry:

I am glad you approve of my "Questions" and I know I have the inspired answer to the origin explanation of the book of Urantia—if the Higher Intelligences see fit to act upon it. For Dr. Sadler or any committee to publish a pamphlet in *partial* explanation of the phenomena, in order to provide a "story" that every member of the Forum will be compelled to "stick to," rather than the possibility of many telling "separate stories," strikes me as a great mistake. It simply gives skeptical newspapermen a "field day" opportunity to try to "get behind the scenes" and find the "real subject" . . . They will be looking for the "nigger in the woodpile" . . . they will think someone has an "ax to grind" and would brand this phenomenon as nothing more than "automatic writing," which many scientists have discredited as an operation of the "subconscious." This, no matter how remarkable and inspired the material.

Martha and I had Bill and his wife over for dinner Tuesday night and accomplished a great deal. I have never had opportunity to sit down and tell Dr. Sadler my own story in detail of HOW I was LED to this Forum . . . I could tell this would have been unwise and SO, I got opportunity to recite the amazing tale to Bill, under pledge of secrecy . . . and he was profoundly impressed . . . he said to me, "Harold, I have always felt, confidentially, that my Dad was holding out on me in some particulars . . . I don't believe he and Harry Loose directly correspond . . . I think there's a reason behind this . . . they may have agreed not to . . . and I have a hunch that Harry has played a bigger part in this development than is indicated on the surface." He went on to say that he was always deeply attracted to you . . . and in his memory now he entertains such a warm feeling of trust and affection that, if he were coming home with his paycheck for $51 and you said you needed $50, he would give it to you without question, nor be concerned if he ever got it back, knowing it would be for a good cause . . . and in line with the work . . .

Bill wonders what happened in those early days, and suggested himself that probably his Dad was "circumstanced" and that you may have had something to do with it.

Bill recognizes that his father requires some "handling" at times . . . and that he is quite set in his ways. He has advised me, if I have some ideas that I think worthwhile, not to make an issue of them or present them directly . . . but write them up and drop them in the office casually . . . and let his father go over them quietly . . . *by himself* . . . so he won't have the feeling that he has to go against his own judgment or beliefs by making a commitment one way or the other at the moment.

Dr. Sadler is as sweet a personality as we have ever met . . . and means the BEST, I am sure. Being new here, we are going slow and diplomatically. We know that we have been well received, by comments that come back to us . . . but I can feel that I am perhaps being *used* to see that certain things are done at this time which *should* be done.

I can foresee bickerings ahead from the "human element" and suppose these must be faced. Some of the members want to go out and preach these truths . . . not realizing that the truths will preach themselves . . . and that they must not make the mistake of forming another church or religion . . . or this revelation will suffer the same fate as the revelation of truth in Jesus' day.

I do not know that Dr. Sadler intends to identify his name with this book—BUT, if he issues a printed pamphlet attempting to explain it—and stands behind it—he might as well.

The corporation papers are drawn up for the Urantia Foundation . . . and the Urantia Brotherhood, ready to be executed . . . I realize that the book must be copyrighted and protected in every way . . . but

I would feel better, as I view it now, if a good, competent, established book publisher would *apparently* be the publisher of the volume. The name "Urantia Foundation" sounds like an organization set up to institutionalize the REVELATIONS . . . At present it would be heresy to ask Sadlers to consider such a material move as to let the book be printed under the banner of a recognized publishing house, with wide-open distribution channels . . .

Unquestionably, the Sadlers, with every good intention, consider the book of Urantia "their baby." It is Dr. Sadler's intention to put Bill and the two sons of Mr. Hales, the wealthy Forumite, in charge of the Urantia Brotherhood and Foundation . . . and let them run it, when the time comes, with other members on the board . . . and the doctor and Mr. Hales, etc., members of the board, too, supervising things from behind the scenes.

This whole matter is most DIFFICULT, as is everything of this nature when the human equation comes in . . . it is hard to say what *is* and what is *not* the right move, in some particulars . . . and I wish those Higher Up would give SPECIFIC INSTRUCTIONS . . . it would avoid a lot of human error and some wounded human egos a little later.

Apparently, however, everything is done for humans that they cannot do—but higher powers seldom intervene with real human problems.

BEFORE I FORGET . . . Wilkins INDEED has FAITH in you—so much so that he is going to the coast as soon as he can, not later than next fall, to try to see you again—when he hopes you can give him directions as to HOW to FURTHER his own PERSONAL development . . . and information beyond the book itself. He plans to come back here and study whenever he can get a few weeks available.

You should have received my letter about the Haleses' picnic by now. We are reading the papers about the Thought Adjustors [*sic*] today . . . and our feelings are beyond words.

Interesting about your new bilocation experience. Wish you would tell me more of details. Would like to know more of my hybrid connection for own personal good, since it is not now in papers. I am getting to the point where this more personal information would help, since the papers emphatically state, as written now, that no soul returns here. Midwayers always remain . . .

Love from us all.

FORUM CALENDAR *June 13, 1942*

Take Bucklins to dinner at Isbell's and evening here.

HARRY LOOSE to HAROLD and MARTHA SHERMAN

Monterey Park, June 14, 1942

Dear Harold and Martha:-

I am answering Harold's airmail letter I rec'd Saturday. . . .

I am glad that your today's letter mentions Wilkins. I may have to get in contact with him before this coming fall—for his benefit—a contact that he must make toward introduction to a future self-need in development. This, although I am not responsible for him in any further way. By the way, did you give him my message regarding his wife???

Do you now see how you are needed in Chicago????

Perhaps you have forgotten, but a long time ago, in Martha's presence, at the Canterbury, I tried so positively to get it to you both that there was no return to this earth for a released Soul—and so no repeated lives here as in Theosophy—and so, also, for the Soul no return here either. That still is very true. Except in certain dispensations, no old Soul returns to the planet of its earth life. And no recently released Soul ever does surely. The hybrid is distinctly a different matter. Though they nevermore will ever return here—except on missions of one kind or another—from other and advanced planets. This was adjusted some time ago when the hybrids made their case before the Ancients of Days and an adjustment was made. This has been in our present enfleshed life time period. At the prior period indicated, the hybrid was never fully in either of the dimensions.

However, there are observers, for many reasons, and students, and other enmissioned fleshed entities from other and more advanced planets, ALWAYS on this exactly the same as on all other planets. They have always been here. From the beginning, now, and forever will be as long as this planet exists. And they will be here to see to the destruction of it. All this, in addition to "a cloud of witnesses" that are not enfleshed and are unseen to the mortal eye—that has not received "sight."

The Midwayers, so-called, are something entirely different from the hybrid. They are not concerned and are not changed.

Mrs. [Carrie Merchant] Hales, married to the present Mr. Hales, had a great deal of money and property. She was the original one with the money. Hales married into it. Mrs. Hales is a long-standing "neuro" and a pre-Forumite, and not fond of Bill.

Just as a far possibility, I may, much later, come to N.Y. purposely to see Wanderman—Ronayne—Potter—etc. This is just a far possibility at present. You will be doing a great deal of travel before that time arrives. Though you will be there then.

The introduction to the Book should be as per my last letter to you. Nothing that is now done can halt its printing at the proper time. But O the mess that can be made of it—and the regrets that can follow—if it is not done as it should be. Bill has probably indicated the best way of handling it with his father, and in Bill you should have a very good friend. You are on the ground—you see things as they are—your correct logic should have much weight. I cannot advise. There is so much that I could say—but I cannot. It is very positive that there should be no human introduction. "THERE IS MUCH FOR YOU TO DO IN CHICAGO."

As far as your letter indicates, your talk with Bill was all right BUT I must advise no further revelations. No good would result and much harm surely would. I know that there would be repercussions that would have very unhappy endings. Please keep this forever in mind and be governed accordingly.

There is a book to be written eventually in which all these matters may be brought forth. Having this book in mind, I might suggest that you keep some sort of diary for future reference. Believe me, you will very surely need it.

Just think, between what I have been able to tell you and what you have learned from reading the Book, you and Martha, to my own personal knowledge, now know more of these things than any two humans have ever known before. Now that you have read the Book, how many more questions you could ask. And how little I can further tell you NOW.

Jenkins and Fred Stone sound interesting. I surely would like very much to be present in the flesh when you first talk to Wanderman, Ronayne, Potter etc.

"In the beginning, we were Seven."

Love to you both from Ma and I and remember what I have advised in re Bill and further revelations.

SIR HUBERT WILKINS to HAROLD SHERMAN

Hotel Annapolis,
Washington, D.C., June 14, 1942

Dear Harold:

For the time being I have been "commissioned" in the Production Development Branch of the U.S. Army's Quarter Master General Department, having to do with the resources available and the designing and provision of equipment for use in Arctic, Desert, Jungle, Mountain, and Tropical environments.

Since the Q.M.G.'s Department had not special equipment for these areas but "got along" with regular issue material, there is some job ahead. We have done a great deal this week at Washington and some of the other days of the week at some other point interviewing and inspecting, etc. It seems as though there will be a good deal of writing to do and it will probably be possible—since I can get to the farm from Washington by bus overnight, for me to spend at least a day a week on the farm.

I miss the daily readings and the informative and enjoyable conversations with you and your charming wife. Haven't seen Suzanne yet. She may go up to the farm if I can get there next week, or I may be passing through New York.

Had a letter from Mr. Robinson.[5] He sends regards and wanted to know your address, which I am sending him today.

Please give my regards to Dr. Sadler, Miss Christensen and Bill. I am writing the Doctor today thanking him for his kindness and hospitality.

The City Club is still the best address for my mail. They will forward it on from day to day.

Best regards. Let me know when you go to New York. Am told there is a whale of a story in the *Philadelphia Inquirer* of May 31st date but have not seen a *Full Page* story about *Thoughts Through Space.*

Hubert

HAROLD SHERMAN to SIR HUBERT WILKINS

Chicago, June 16, 1942

Dear Hubert:

You are much missed here—by everyone . . . and especially by Martha and me.

---

[5] Joseph Robinson, head engineer of the War Production Board in Washington, D.C. See Vol. 1, p. 346.

We have now reached the Jesus papers—and have had many "moving experiences." We are commencing to realize, more than ever before, that we are among the most *privileged* of humans . . . as you have so expressed . . . and this must imply a great spiritual responsibility in the time to come.

What a PERSPECTIVE is now added to our mental and spiritual horizons! Never again can we think or view things as before. It is all, as you have also said, absolutely indescribable. And to think that some day we may reach the development wherein *all experiences of all ascending creatures*, from the beginning of time to the completion of the seven superuniverses of light and life, may be added to our own consciousness!

I hope we can meet again soon in New York and discuss different aspects. I am sure that the S'es are going to need guidance from here on—unless received from other sources . . . on the human organization, etc. . . . or they will, with every good intention, fall into error. Can say no more here.

Sounds to me like the Gov't direly needs you. Hope you can work it out so you can spend part time on your farm, however . . .

I'll have to look up the *Inquirer* story . . . I got a wire from [Creative Age Press associate] Chadsey yesterday as follows: "Sales frozen by price . . . Mrs. Garrett of strong opinion that repricing necessary if book is to move . . . may we have your approval of new three-dollar price." I wired approval at once. Had just gone to Marshall Fields, Kroch's and Brentano's to try to buy a copy . . . found first two sold out . . . B's said this was their last copy—but they would sell many more if price lower . . . I found great awareness of book and contents . . . so perhaps new price, in these times, will help.

Martha joins in best to you . . . let's hear again soon . . .

FORUM CALENDAR *June 17, 1942*

Karles have 5:30 dinner here before Bill's lecture.[6]

June 18, 1942

Dr. Sadler and Christy our guests at Isbell's and here for evening.

On June 19, Harold wrote to Cy Wanderman, asking for medical advice regarding Martha's uncle. He also cryptically mentioned his involvement with the Urantia phenomenon:

[6] Bill Sadler held twice-monthly Wednesday night meetings at 533 to study Urantia Book topics.

Yes, we're getting nearer "dear old New York" . . . and I am getting more and more eager to see you . . . and to tell you MUCH. (Much that would have to be personal and confidential for the time being . . . but oh, Cy—simply "out of this world" it is so astounding, authentic and inspiring!). . . .

Martha and I hope to be able to get on to New York later and to see you folks . . . WE MISS you people a GREAT DEAL.

Our love always . . . and my gratitude for any suggestions you may be able to offer.

HARRY LOOSE to HAROLD and MARTHA SHERMAN

Monterey Park, June 20, 1942

Dear Folks:-

There is movement and activity about you. You see interesting people and go about a bit. In your reading of the Book, you are doing a pleasant and informative thing. There is much yet before you. Here we are much restricted in our field of activities and our vision is much limited. And our "future" is all behind us. So, I cannot write as interesting or newsy letters as either of you folks do. You know our situation here. So, it would seem that our letters are not a fair exchange and that we are getting the best of the deal. Martha, your letter was such a chatty and informative one.[7] You write so very descriptively. . . .

We remember Miss Douglas[8] well—and where she sat in the Forum regularly—but we do not remember the Carls [*Ed. note:* Karles]. Mrs. Hales will never tell you of her feeling toward Bill. It wouldn't be good policy for her so now to do—especially to you folks who are such recent comers. Mrs. Hales is a neuro of very long standing—a pre-Forumite—and gets pretty desperate with her neurotic troubles at periods. My suggestion in reference to her is to walk carefully in her presence—you will not find her very congenial—and she may at any time take the occasion to be downright impolite—in a way generally termed "snotty."

Hope that Ruthie's[9] young man comes home safely from the war—and that they live happy ever after.

Am so pleased with your progress with the reading. It is very correct that the TAs are gifts from God, the Supreme (as are ALL good

[7] This letter has not survived.

[8] Probably referring to Katharine ("Crinky") Douglas, an early Forumite.

[9] Ruth Kellogg, 28-year-old daughter of Wilfred and Anna Kellogg.

things) and are non-personal—only achieving personality through eventual uniting with the personality they come to uplift. They, however, ARE an entity distinct from the Soul to which they have become united (without such a distinctness, and separateness, they could never be helpful), and they can never be divorced from the Soul in this dimension after such complete union. They, during such union, remain such distinct entities that they are fully capable of individual response to the proper stimuli from such entity that has such authority at their command to be able to supply such stimuli. The Soul itself is forever guarded in its privacy from any authority whatsoever existing on this planet. And there are great authorities existent right here and now.

With full thought of what I have remarked a few sentences above, I want to remark something here that may explain some things further to you. I am still of the flesh, and "the power" is not always resident within me nor at my immediate command. It is not like turning on the water at the faucet. There is much, so very much, you have yet to comprehend in the Book—and there is more that is really not at all comprehensible in the present status. So much yet to learn and so much restriction. I never will be able to tell you.

The long and very interesting story of the hybrids has evidently been deleted from the minds and from the papers. Why I know not. But be assured, it was for a good purpose.

I do not know what responsibilities will be Harold's in the forwarding of the Book. I only know that the long process of care and growth which culminated in what you are both now doing—your acquaintance with the revelation—was not for idle purpose. You may be assured of that. However, my responsibilities are long over. Harold is fully awakened—but what the future holds for him in the further development of the revelation—I do not know. My own period of usefulness in regard to this particular matter is finished. I have no knowledge of any further activities there are for me, if any.

A minor matter exists—that of a contact with Wilkins for the delivery of a certain thing—by late summer. And that is not of sufficient weight but that it could be delivered by any other entity beside myself. It would be better so. I have had no further communication from him—since the letter I read you folks while you were still here.

Martha, we love to get letters from you and from Harold but, just because of this, do not let us selfishly intrude on the time at your disposal when you might be occupied in some more interesting or profitable activity.

Love from us both to you all,

Harry

FORUM CALENDAR *June 21, 1942*

Mary decides to start reading by herself on Sunday afternoons instead of attending Forum readings which she cannot grasp.

3

Dissension in the Ranks

HAROLD SHERMAN to HARRY LOOSE

Chicago, June 21, 1942

Dear Harry:

Thank you for your fine letter of June 14th.

Yes, there is apparently *much* for me to do in Chicago. And what diplomacy it is going to take!

Harry, I wish you were seated in this room right now and I could talk a lot of things over with you. This week we have had Dr. Sadler and Christy out to dinner and up to our little apartment for a talk; we are going to take the Kelloggs out next week; we have talked with the Bucklins, members of about five years' standing. And from what we sense, there is dissension in the ranks which is being suppressed only because of affection for the Sadlers.

Now that the dispensation of the Forum has come to an end, after these long years of devoted study and work . . . Forum members thought they were going to be permitted some "say" as to the form their organization would take in the future . . . or as to whether it should be continued at all. The "message" read at the Haleses' picnic seemed to indicate that the Forum was to be kept on, as a means of having Dr. Sadler present an outline of all other religions so that members would be more tolerant and understanding . . . and also as a means of reading the papers AGAIN and trying to understand them. Dr. Sadler has now let down the bars so that new members can be proposed and can come in to the Forum meetings on Sunday and read the papers.

But, Harry—the Sunday meetings are *deadly* beyond belief. Bill Jr. is reading the first chapter now about the Universal Father and First Source and Center, etc., which is subject matter designed for the Einsteins of the world, to begin with, and not for public consumption and understanding through mass presentation; then the second hour is devoted to Dr. Sadler's recounting the history of other religions and reading their church charters and articles of faith, etc. The attendance is fair but everyone heaves a sigh of relief when the time is up . . . and a woman behind me whispered, "Thank God, that's over," this afternoon.

If any new members are brought in "cold" on these Forum meetings without having been exposed to the papers, they won't be able to make "head nor tail" out of what is going on . . . there is no human appeal; it is such heavy going that veteran members are nodding or drop to sleep; everyone fidgets, and a superhuman effort is required to concentrate this length of time . . . but the Sadlers plow sublimely on, unconscious of what is stirring in the minds of the listeners . . . the unrest . . . etc.

At the Haleses' picnic, Dr. Sadler referred to three anonymous letters of criticism of Forum procedure he had received . . . and kidded them . . . and then, in the same breath, he invited everyone to submit letters—if they had any suggestions—but to SIGN THEIR NAMES . . . and he could promise, if there were any PARANOIACS in the group, he was capable of taking care of them. Such a comment, even humorously intended, was sufficient to discourage most honest and sincere members (which I believe them ALL to be) from expressing their own opinions.

The latest development is for Dr. Sadler to announce a music committee—saying that he believes the evolving Urantia Society will want a list of hymns which express the true spirit of the Urantia religion. This committee is to select hymns from different church hymn books which they think okay, and these are to be used when the Forum reconvenes in the fall. Today Dr. Sadler said: "My—what a profoundly interesting and exciting place the Urantia office is going to be—with the world's attention fixed upon it—telegrams, long-distance telephone calls and volumes of mail coming in from all over the world." In his comparison of religions he says, "We can't go along with this or that . . . this is not in accord with the Urantia religion," etc.

Harry, can it be possible that the Sadlers have missed the GREAT NEW MESSAGE OF JESUS . . . and that they are really preparing to perpetuate themselves through an organization? Dr. Sadler has already said that he intends for Bill and the Hales sons to take charge of the Foundation and the Brotherhood . . . and he and Mr. Hales will run it from behind the scenes or help them.

The doctor is so dear and sweet—and Bill, himself, means so well—it is hard to conceive how blind they are . . .

The Bucklins are horrified at thoughts of a Foundation and Brotherhood being announced at about the time of the Book's publication . . . feeling that this revealed truth is for all the world . . . and not to be TIED to another material organization which would represent just another SECT. We have had to be careful in the expression of our own opinions and are good listeners . . .

We know that we are well thought of and that we enjoy the confidence of the Sadlers . . . The fact that no Forumites are permitted to express any opinion or take part in the human planning . . . and the fact that all committees announced are appointed by the doctor . . . and that this appears to be crystallizing into a two-man organization—father and son—with the JOB COMPLETED . . . is disturbing to many. They had been told through the years that the Sadlers were simply custodians of this knowledge . . . now they are commencing to wonder.

Of course there are many who are *evangelically* inclined. Dr. Sadler introduced Father or Reverend Rosson [*Ed. note:* Charles Rawson] to the Forum today, who told the members he had been asked to take out a religious half-hour on the local NBC radio station, beginning two weeks from Sunday . . . 7:30 to 8 a.m. . . . and that he was going to turn it down until he consulted the doctor, who told him he thought it must be a "circumstanced event" and that he should take it because later he might be in the position to present the Urantia message over the air. The more "religiously or emotionally inclined" are now looking for "circumstanced events" . . . and many consider Sir Hubert and myself in that category . . . but whether this is true or not, it is dangerous when the rank and file commence making this interpretation . . . and thinking in terms of organizational activity.

Harry, if I am wrong in my reactions or my feelings of what should be done from this point on—then I instantly stand corrected before any message of instructions that might be received from higher sources, and like the Apostle Thomas, I then say, "Let's go!" and heartily get in the harness and pull my load, whatever the assignment.

But so long as this situation is left to remain a "human problem," then I think I have a right to think this thing through, in the light of my experience, and to determine, from an unprejudiced viewpoint, what I think should be done.

Martha and I are in the midst of the Jesus papers now—and are inspired and moved beyond words. We are beginning to learn much about Abner . . . and his close relationship with Andrew . . . and strange feelings stir occasionally within me. There is so much I would like to ask but I want to keep this letter on the problems at hand.

It is my thought now—when we have to go on to New York—that I will write Sadler a long letter, setting forth my reactions and suggestions . . . and leave it with him to MULL OVER through the summer . . . I have been invited to write my suggestions, so he cannot get peeved at me . . . or *should* not . . . and perhaps I should not be too concerned about his immediate feelings in the light of a possible great mistake which could be made. But, while I am willing to assume the responsibility of making my own decision—if that is expected of me now . . . I would appreciate your own further counsel, if this can be granted.

I was thrilled at your suggestion that you might join me at some later time in New York—to meet with these unusual men—Wanderman, Ronayne and Dr. Potter . . . Martha and I want nothing so much as to devote the rest of our lives to this work . . . and, Harry, I am not interested in any personal glory . . . I would work as a complete unknown if I could accomplish whatever task is to be required of me in that manner—and if best results could be obtained in that way. I am waiting for guidance and asking the TA for it . . . This is the bird's eye view up to date . . . if I am to be the one to wake the Sadlers up . . . or give them a new perspective . . . despite the tough assignment, I'll do it.

FORUM CALENDAR *June 22, 1942*

Bill here all evening discussing psychic questions.

June 23, 1942

Kelloggs our guests at Isbell's and here for evening.

HARRY LOOSE to HAROLD SHERMAN

Monterey Park, June 24, 1942

Dear Harold:-

I have rec'd your letter telling so much of how things are progressing with the forwarding of the revelation. So much that is so sad and disheartening. Of course Sadler is wrong. I am writing in haste what will probably turn out to be a somewhat incoherent letter. You must put it together in thought. No, you do not worry me in telling me the difficulties that you can see the advancing of the Book of Urantia and the Forum have been evidencing. They will continue to do so. Such is the human. This has been anticipated.

In the light of the present developments, do you begin to see why it was desired Wanderman, Ronayne, Potter and the other four to be gathered about you??[1] When you talk with them, begin at the very beginning—hold nothing back—except where the present papers now rest—and in whose custody. They will have to be satisfied to wait until the Book is in print and available before such names and addresses can be given. Remember this, or immediate difficulties will present themselves. I am also included in this "no name or address" procedure. I would believe also that the matter of the hybrid be withheld until a later date until there is better and fuller understanding. You must assure Wanderman, Ronayne, Potter, etc. that this is a true revelation to this age and that, depending on certain circumstances developing, or some not developing, they may play a part of consequence in its unveiling.

The Kelloggs know some things, and have suspected other things, for long, but they will not tell of them. The same for Christy. The same for Bill. Sometime Bill may open up and tell you *some* of them that they all know—and some that they suspect.

Do not be too upset or disturbed yourself at the turn of events. Just as soon as the Book is published and available to the public and you have a copy in your hands, you have all that is needed. Coupled with your greater and longer knowledge that is not concerned with the Book.

No member of the Forum should have preference indicating a line of procedure over another member. All these things should be subject to a vote of the entire Forum assembled, and the majority

[1] See Appendix A for an undated letter apparently written about this time in which Loose instructs Harold to form a group of seven.

carries. Discussion on the floor of such method of procedure, or line of action, should be free to any Forumite before such deciding vote. This goes for Sadler, Kellogg, Hales, Christy and any others of the inner circle.

You will eventually find yourself that Mr. and Mrs. Kellogg are more approachable, have better reasoning and are more open of mind than any of the others of the inner circle. That goes for Sadler, Hales, Christy, etc. Some present things are not approved by the Kelloggs.

I have not, and will not, write to Wilkins. It is not my place so to do. It is possible that he has received some bad advice somewhere. I will not indicate. I have now yet to be assured in re Wilkins. Was there a mistake made??? I am wondering. I do not know.

Future events will only tell if I am to go to New York.

I mailed a letter to Martha [*Ed. note:* dated June 20th]—a part of which had to do with a very condensed bit which I hope is understandable regarding the TA. You have read it by now. In a prior letter [*Ed. note:* dated May 29th], I expressed interest in the result of Martha's direct contact and personal reading of the Book. But I suppose that I expressed myself badly and this became confused in understanding and became something in reference to a continuance of faith personally in myself. I am very sorry that I wrote so badly as to cause this confusion.

I am very glad that you are keeping a diary. You will need it much when the time comes for its use. I am glad that you finally found that old letter[2] and also have kept my other correspondence.

I am also much pleased that you seek nearness to and the counsel of your TA. You will not go wrong, or do wrong, if you follow his counseling.

I have no further jurisdiction over your continued activities and no direct knowledge of what they are to be. You must think things out and make your own decisions. I will always be glad to help, if I can, with any of your individual decisions or activities.

The book you will eventually write will tell so very much to clarify obscured matters to a then much interested world in the book of Urantia, and it will be an authoritative verification of it. It will have a sale and interest equal to the Book of Urantia itself.

---

[2] Loose is apparently responding to a letter from Martha, in which she mentioned keeping a diary and having recovered Loose's first letter to Harold. See Vol. 1, p. 93, where the loss of this letter was reported.

I grow very tired and long much for you and small Martha. My work is really done. A few odds and ends only to catch up.

It is so sad that Sadler is so blind. He was so well chosen for the part he has had. And he has performed so wonderfully up to the present. "There is much for you to do in Chicago."

I cannot advise you as to your further immediate procedure. Whether it be by a long talk with Sadler to show him the error of his ways—or a letter in detailed fullness for him to mull over after you have gone to New York. Or whether a long talk with Bill, who would carry at least the gist of it to his father, would be the best means of attack, I do not know. You are on the ground and know best how to decide this. Who should call Sadler's attention to his oft-repeated assertion that he is merely the Custodian of this revelation and NOT the owner—and what rights the Forum has in all matters of interest and progress. He will have to have these things brought to his attention by someone—sometime—for his own benefit alone—if not for anything else. Also for the benefit of the Book and for all concerned—which does not mean just the Forumites—which body is but a tiny percentage of the number concerned.

Harold, with all your good intent, with all your better knowledge, with all your good thought—you TOO will find the further way not smooth—not without its knocks and bumps and sad surprises—BUT be not downhearted—be not afraid—know that others, TOO, were "prophets without honor in their own country," and yet they kept the faith and carried on. The torch has been tossed to you, my dear friend, and yours be the task to seize and carry it onward. Just reading the papers will not suffice, NOR HIDING YOUR PERSONALITY UNDER A BARREL either. You have a large job on your hands. What you do with it—and how you do it—is your problem. Assisted by that extremely dear little wife of yours—that comfort in the night of storm—small Martha. And will you need the "hideaway" to recuperate at????

I am glad that you are now advanced to Abner and Andrew. And note their love for one another. There is a great deal there. You would not believe if I told you the whole story. I have been on the point, often—and then fear of question and disbelief has overtaken me. There is lots of time, however, maybe not in this dimension but I look forward to it in the time to come when things will be so very much clearer to you—and I can see so many laughs and much humor in the recounting of things that happened and were so serious and complex here.

And now I find that I have written you such a long letter—and so in haste too. I hope this long letter will not bore you. When I mailed my letter to Martha, I was just coming to the conclusion that it might be best that I did not write anymore. That I might influence some of your decisions or that I might take from you some part of responsibilities that are yours—that I might thus in some way impede your own development.

And, too, that you might have much more pleasurable or exciting or interesting things to do than the writing of letters to me.

By now you have a better understanding of your growth in knowledge and spirituality in "three years" than you had before. It will come.

Anyway, Ma is just the same—and so am I—a bit more tired perhaps—and I get so lonely for you and for small Martha—at times.

But now your way is pretty clearly indicated—AHEAD.

So with much love to you both from Ma and I,

HAROLD SHERMAN to WALTER M. GERMAIN[3]

Chicago, June 24, 1942

Dear Walter:

When you do you have to be in Iowa City?

In the event we are not called to New York we would like you to be our guest for a day in Chicago—as there are many things which need to be covered.

Could you come a day early? Is there any train which would get you in here early in the morning . . . and a train you could take on to Iowa City late in evening to get you there following day . . . so you could have a good stretch of hours in Chicago?

This is STRICTLY CONFIDENTIAL . . . but the *real* reason for Mrs. Sherman's and my being in Chicago at the present time is for the purpose of research and study. Walter—in a metaphysical manner surpassing anything known by our scientists, there has been made available to a spiritually selected group, from Higher Unfleshed Intelligences, for the *first* time in the history of this planet, the entire,

[3] Police inspector in Saginaw, Michigan. See Vol. 1, p. 66 for last mention of him.

true and authentic story of its creation, the origin of human creatures upon it, their evolution, the relation of these human creatures to God, the Great Intelligence; their intended destiny, what really happens when death occurs, the indescribable path of progress open to surviving souls, and ALL other higher truths which Man has, for centuries, sought to gain, are HEREIN unfolded. No words can describe the WONDER of this revelation; and the true, complete day-by-day story of JESUS is told . . . WHO he WAS . . . and WHY he came to earth. We have evidence now that there are BILLIONS of INHABITED WORLDS in this UNSPEAKABLY GREAT UNIVERSE. For the present, this vast knowledge can be known only to a few . . . but later, at the right time, it is to be published in book form . . . and it will amplify the CHRISTIAN RELIGION beyond all bounds . . . and win also the support of SCIENCE, completing the marriage of Science and Religion . . .

Your own spiritual hunger can here be satisfied and appeased for all time . . . and your own individual destiny revealed. I believe you are to play a great part in the work for all HUMANITY ahead . . . with the ending of this period of approaching chaos. I only wish it were possible, should I get permission for you to be taken into this little group here which numbers people from every sect, for you to come here for a week or two and do some reading. This knowledge cannot be imparted except at its source and then only to those who take the pledge of secrecy until the time for public presentation arrives.

It is my personal feeling that you have been *prepared* for your part in this greatest of all services—the dissemination of true and authenticated knowledge of the actual spirit and origin of Man and his glorious destiny in the worlds beyond . . .

You will have to accept some of these statements I have made here on *faith* for the time being . . . but I feel you know me well enough to be certain that I know whereof I speak.

My wife and I are gladly making every sacrifice to avail ourselves of this ASTOUNDING spiritual wisdom. We have been reading from 9:30 to 5:30 every day for a month and have not yet completed the material. The history of this planet for millions of years back—is SOME history . . . and the full and complete description of the UNIVERSAL FATHER, a PERSONALITY, a SUPREME BEING, with whom we are inwardly attuned the instant we learn how to contact the spirit circuit of this universe, is thrilling beyond any power of expression.

Nothing is taken away from the progress already made by man, socially, economically, scientifically or spiritually—but INFINITELY MUCH is ADDED . . . and all the missing links are fitted in.

You BELONG. There is a reason WHY we have been brought together . . . we will soon have to "be about our Father's business" . . . I will try to remain here until you come through—but even if this can't happen, we'll arrange a time. Best to you!

FORUM CALENDAR *June 24, 1942*

(Dr. Sadler's birthday)

Harold leaves suddenly for New York re Twain material.

June 25, 1942

Martha is guest of Christy and Dr. Sadler for pick-up supper followed by movie.

MARTHA SHERMAN to HAROLD SHERMAN

Chicago, June 25, 1942

Dearest,

It was good to hear your voice for even a few minutes and I can just pretend you're really down town and not far away at all. Anyway, I can't actually feel you are ever far away from me anymore—your presence seems always to be with me. . . .

An hour after you left yesterday Christy phoned to see if I wouldn't have a pick-up supper with her and the doctor tonight and of course I accepted figuring I'd return early to get your call. I spent some time both morning and afternoon rereading the TA papers and was just about to leave at 5:30 to change for dinner when in walked the doctor to take me right upstairs then. So we were having a very early dinner when you called, and afterwards the doctor took us to a double movie—Sabu (Kipling)[4] and *The Lady Has Plans*. Neither extraordinary but the coloring was exquisite in the first and the second exciting so I enjoyed both for a change. After which I said goodnight and came home. I don't know what's the matter with me but my heart was pounding with excitement during the picture and I was positively shaking afterwards! It's so ridiculous for I certainly wasn't scared! . . .

Mrs. Bucklin phoned to ask us for Saturday night but, of course, that is postponed. She said she was eager to tell you about the first meeting of the song committee!

---

[4] The movie was *Jungle Book*, starring Sabu.

Nothing more to report momentarily—I canceled your other appointments. Expect you will have plenty to tell me about NYC. Give my love to all interested parties. I never can put my love for *you* into words—only I'm sure you know it is there—always.

Referring to that day, Martha wrote the following on a separate sheet of paper:

ADDENDUM—PERSONAL

On Wednesday, June 24, 1942, Harold left on business for New York. Learning that Martha was alone, Christy phoned and asked her to come to 6 p.m. dinner, Thursday night, and then go to a movie and, of course, Martha accepted. During the day Martha did some review reading of the papers and was just finishing up on one of the TA papers, a little after 5, when Dr. Sadler came into the Forum room and said, "I've come to get you. We're waiting for you upstairs."

Martha said, "Oh—I expected to have time to run across and change my dress first," to which the Doctor replied, "Oh, you're all right." So Martha followed the Doctor up to the 3rd floor living room. As she looked about the room expecting to see Christy, the Doctor suddenly put both arms about her and kissed her squarely on the mouth, saying, "You can't help it if I love you, can you?"

Martha drew away and sat in a chair, too stunned to make any coherent answer, but finally said, "Where's Christy? I thought she was here."

"Oh, she'll be here in a few minutes," Doctor said.

And just then Christy did come in, her arms filled with packages and looking a little surprised to find Martha ahead of her.

It was the maid's night off and all three helped prepare the cold picnic supper—the Doctor saying hardly a word but hurrying about like any bad little boy anxious to be of assistance to cover up his guilty deeds. There was a sort of self-consciousness about the whole supper.

Immediately afterwards we all went to a neighborhood movie which we did not see all the way through having missed the beginning, so were out before 9 p.m. when Martha excused herself and went directly to her own apartment.

It might be noted that Christy acted *forced* also—as though she suspected something was amiss. She took the Doctor by the hand and led him like a child to his seat in the movie—because of his bad eyesight.

The following day Harold phoned for Martha to meet him in New York, so Saturday Martha left for the East where she reported to him what had happened. In the interim she did not see the Doctor again, and upon her return July 12th to the Forum kept him at arm's length with a short handshake.

FORUM CALENDAR *June 26, 1942*

Mrs. Bucklin has lunch with Martha.

June 27, 1942

Martha leaves for New York.

SIR HUBERT WILKINS to HAROLD SHERMAN

Hotel Annapolis,
Washington, D.C., June 30, 1942

Dear Harold,

Thanks for your note. Sorry will not be in the city until the week after next as am pretty busy at Washington and elsewhere. Just returned from a trip to Dayton. Have now for the first time in my life a swivel chair, my name on a desk and just got a 2000% rise in salary (which however doesn't make the total very great) but for that I do most of the swivelling, not the chair.

Best regards to you and Martha.
Sincerely,
Hubert

P.S. Still trying to recall to memory daily what I can of the 'material' but as you indicate it is a colossal job.

FORUM CALENDAR *July 8, 1942*

Harold and Martha return to Chicago. Germain.

July 9, 1942

Continue reading. Bucklins spend evening here.

July 11, 1942

Completed first reading of papers.

July 12, 1942

Tea at 1:30 with Christy and Doctor followed by Forum. Bucklins here in evening.

SIR HUBERT WILKINS to HAROLD SHERMAN

New York, July 15, 1942

Dear Harold,

Congratulations on your 44th. Since reading the papers and reflecting on my 54th this coming Oct. I have an entirely different attitude toward Earth time and human life and birthdays. Had hoped to see you in New York when I came in today but was glad anyway to get your note and to know that you are back in Chicago where you have access to the book. I would like to be back there again and will try to arrange to spend as much time there as possible. However, it is too far to commute from Chicago to Washington—almost too far to commute from the farm but I have been getting up to the farm for week ends. Came to New York this time for a change.

You were right about pain, but in right shoulder and under right ribs. I fell twice on the slippery wet grass at the farm last week end. Once might have broken my shoulder but for the fact that I was carrying a big watermelon and landing on that broke the fall. Didn't do any good to either the melon or my shoulder. The next day fell on a bucket of water and almost pushed the hook of the handle into my spleen. Have been pretty stiff and sore since but today is first day I am not conscious of pain each time I move.

Lectured at West Virginia University last Wednesday. Haven't been to any factories but our office in Washington has a resemblance to such—it is full of gadgets and supplies. Most of them articles found unsatisfactory in service and which have been sent in to "Development Service" for redesign. In the last two weeks I have redesigned flea powder, dog harness, a sledge, show shoes, tropical helmet and am now working on a motor snow sled. Let me know your movements. The [City] Club still forwards my mail and is my best address. Regards to you both and our mutual friends at Chicago, especially the Sadlers.

Hubert

HARRY LOOSE to HAROLD SHERMAN

Monterey Park, July 15, 1942

Dear Harold:-

I have rec'd your letter from Chicago.[5] I am glad that you have finished reading the Book. Remember that in reading the Book, even

[5] Letter not found.

as explanatory as it is, and it is very full, that this Book is not alone for the great masses with their present limited abilities of comprehension; there is much in it beyond their abilities to comprehend. There is very much there present that is understandable only to those who have an ability to comprehend beyond the usual met intelligence, or, better expressed, mass intelligence. Please also be aware that there is much more that is greatly beyond the Book and which is not understandable to even these greater minds. There are, also, certain rare individual capacities, very few, to whom a greater degree of this knowledge is comprehensible.

When you express yourself, "Strange feelings stir occasionally with me,"[6] and where you express yourself, "I sense," in relation to something not fully realized or understood, you additionally evidence that which I am trying to express. I say this because I know "you." The same expressions voiced by other individuals would in no way necessarily mean anything deeper, or of more value, than just the words so spoken. Neither of these phrases are surface with you. However, there is much that you are not yet in readiness for. Much that I would be so glad to give you in continuing addition to that which you have already gained. And yet, I must again repeat, "I know so little." You and small Martha have grown so greatly in understanding though. I believe that you both must have pretty full realization of your growth.

My friend, the Priest,[7] cannot come to see me anymore, but he has sent me some very comforting messages lately.

I told you and Martha long ago that ALL is an individual proposition.

In other days, Cleodotus was a Roman soldier—a bold, brave man—with a wondrous power of expression in the spoken word. He was converted to Christianity by a man by the name of Abner, who established a Church in Philadelphia in Perea. Cleodotus went boldly about the Father's business in places far from there—converted many—and died a tragic death in the service of the Father.

I am enclosing two letters which should join the other material that you are saving to be used in a Book that you are to write. They are self-explanatory. They are the only letters of yours that I retained

[6] See Harold's June 21st letter to Loose.

[7] See Vol. 1 for numerous mentions of "the Catholic priest" from South America with whom Loose claimed to be in astral contact.

in my possession. *ALL else is burned.* No use for them to be possibly found by non-understanding minds at any time later on.

Some years ago, because of certain possibilities that might have presented themselves, some old school friends of yours were induced to reside in this section. All from the little town of Marion. All well-known to you—or, I should possibly have said, known by you. I was kind of lonely for you recently, and so one of these old schoolmates was called, by subterfuge, to come to the house here last Sunday. I had never met him before, and he surely was most interested and surprised when I brought up your name. I showed him *Your Key to Happiness* and *Thoughts Through Space* and your picture therein. He entertained us on the front porch all afternoon with long stories about your school doings, and his. He sure was interesting. He was quite reluctant to go home. He was in your very class in High School. His name is Glen B. Fields, of old Marion, Indiana. He is in a small Government job here. There is nothing particular to gain by writing him except a renewal of old memories—you now have nothing in common with him. However, if you do have a desire to correspond with him, I will send you his address if you so request.

Hope that Arthur thinks well of the farm in Arkansas. Is Fred Stone and the show Mark Twain running as a summer tryout??

You must find your own way to be "about the Father's business," beset as always by all manner of material, and mental, interference, and fearsome things. I will not advise you. Seek counsel with your TA. He will not advise you wrong—although he will neither advise you the "easiest way." Did Joshua ben Joseph have an easy way???? The whole world is filled with those who wish to be "about the Father's business"—provided it is an easy way—a way that does not entail either sacrifice or suffering or much endeavor. The "seed" flourishes mostly but a little time and then perishes. "Take no thought of what ye should eat nor what ye should put on"—find that verse and read it.

Sadler does not "own" the Book. Forum members, any Forum member, has as much right of "ownership" as has Sadler. Sadler is now, and has been for all this time, the "custodian." Sadler cannot dispossess you of Forum membership—now or ever—it is written in a far higher place. If you have the best interests of the Book at heart——————(??????????).

An honest digression of opinion with Sadler could only bring his respect. And might help him much. And would probably be in accord with other members. "Be not as a sheep that is led." There are many such—far too many.

I am relieved finally and positively of need for any further contact with Wilkins. I am very glad for this.

O what a book you will eventually write. "This is the apartment in which he once lived."

There is no denying that I love to hear from you—BOTH. But I must not selfishly take up your time—nor influence your decisions in any way.

Remember that the demand for your book will last as long as the Book of Urantia and will be a verifying component part of it. They will go together. Descendents of yours for generations in the misty future will be receiving royally on the continuing sales of your book. I hope they do much good with the money returns in the years to come. I have often wondered if you fully were aware of these things.

My physical condition is not of the best and Ma has her usual troubles. However, for the present, we are going along pretty good. Much love to you both, and don't allow us to impose too much on your time in writing. "You have much to do in Chicago." We are merely a phase in your development that is now of the past. May I ask you to please acknowledge receipt of the enclosed.

Again, our love to you both,

HAROLD SHERMAN to HARRY LOOSE

Chicago, July 20, 1942

Dear Harry:

Thank you for your fine letter with enclosures of my two letters which I am adding to my file.

I am writing at once for I am greatly disturbed by your reference to this person *Glen B. Fields* and your saying that you attracted him to your house by *subterfuge.*

To the best of my recollection, I have never known a boy or man by the name of Glen B. Fields. I DID NOT go to school in Marion, Indiana. My schooling took place in Traverse City, Michigan, and I did not go to Marion to live until after I was married . . . and then, as you know, for only three years. During that time I became extremely well known in Marion through my newspaper work and civic activities.

When I went to New York later, I wrote a sport book, *Get 'Em, Mayfield!*, based on the Marion, Indiana, High School basketball team.

If this Glen B. Fields "entertained you on the front porch all afternoon" with *long* stories of my high school doings"—he is not only one of the biggest LIARS in America but possesses one of the most fantastic imaginations.

I would certainly KNOW and REMEMBER any fellow who could tell such stories about me . . . and if you received the "*impression*" that this man was a schoolmate of mine and *attracted* him to you, then *you* must have been *misdirected* this time and become CONFUSED.

This concerns me a great deal, Harry, and I hope you can get to the bottom of this and give me an explanation. I cannot conceive, in the first place, of a man having the GALL to so misrepresent—claiming he was in my class in High School which would have *had* to be in Traverse City, NOT Marion, Indiana—to begin with . . . and there was *no* Glen B. Fields *there!*

I'd like to FACE this party who *could not* have made any mistake of *identity* since you showed [illegible] my *picture* in *Thoughts Through Space.*

For *you, yourself* to be TAKEN IN, if this is a partial explanation, is in itself disturbing.

I will do my utmost here in every *good* way, you may be sure - - - and our love and gratitude goes out to you in a constant stream.

When my typewriter arrives I will write you a longer letter—about developments. Mark Twain play again postponed due to "conditions."

Please inform me as soon as you reasonably can about this Glen B. Fields mix-up.

Our love and best to Mother Loose and yourself. Glad you're both in usual health.

HARRY LOOSE to HAROLD and MARTHA SHERMAN

Monterey Park, July 21, 1942

Dear Harold and Martha:-

Your airmail letter of July 18th rec'd Monday.[8] I mailed a letter to you by regular mail Wednesday, July 15th. It had enclosures necessary to be included in the Book you are to write. You should have received it Saturday—but the mail is sometimes subject to odd delays in this

[8] Letter not found.

war time—and you should surely receive it today—Monday. I hope that you will acknowledge its receipt in your next letter for the enclosures are really important to you.

I am much fearful that you do not yet realize the great importance of your Book. That its magnitude has not yet reached your consciousness. Do you not yet begin to know the tremendousness of the Book of yours to posterity—into the dim and misty vastness of far, far future years. What if, under the same circumstances, there had been a similar "Book" to accompany our present-day Bible. What a wonderful thing it would have been through all these years of Bible study. The Book of Urantia will be in existence just as long, or longer, and so will be your Book as a component and explanatory adjunct to it for just the same period. How illuminating it will be to the readers a thousand earth years from now. You are the only Historian of this present great event. Can you not see even a small part of the great importance of your task?? You have been given so very much—from the beginning. You know so very much. You have been helped so much. Only that which you have not yet acquired growth to grasp has been withheld from you.

You have been in contact with one of the Seven.

I fear for you, that you do not yet grasp fully, nor accept fully, the most tremendously great responsibility that is yours to carry. Try to visualize a thousand years from now, a grouping, much the same as today, studying the Book of Urantia and turning to the Book of the historian of that then far-off time, the Book of the man, Harold M. Sherman, written in corroboration and authentication of the Book of Urantia. Of the trials and tribulations—of the squabbles and petty differences arising. I sorrow and I fear you are not realizing what a great weight of responsibility is upon you. A responsibility not just to you and yours, and those of this generation, but a responsibility to the untold millions of truth seekers in the aeons of time yet to come. I am sad and sick of heart that I, mayhap, have somewhere failed to impress this great responsibility upon you. Can you not see the impress on history alone that this epoch period will make?? "This is the apartment in which he once lived" will only come true through the great endeavor befronting you.

Accumulate every memo possible—a copy of the list of the original Forumites would be interesting—your name is there—and Martha's and Mary's—Bill or Kellogg would co-operate in this. Please be aware and well know that the fact of the Book you are to write must be kept inviolate between you and Martha. Knowledge of others of this intent would much shut off supplies of information and meet with instant disapprobation—and other difficulties. Please be guarded. This has been one of the greatest efforts since the beginning of things. I lean so heavily on small Martha to keep you steadfast to your task. There is a reason for small Martha in all this—and a very good one. Please remember too, that the Book of Urantia has been long of earth time in recording. So do not become impatient in the wait for the time of production of your authentic Book. Work at your Book even now—build your story piece by piece and bit by bit—and as perfect as possible—of course it will have to be gone over and corrected when the time comes, but you will have "much done" anyway. . . .

Your typewriter should have been left with me all packed and ready to send on when you wanted it. I could have expressed it at once. . . .

Harold, I will always be glad to hear how matters are progressing. But don't let us selfishly impose upon your time. I must not bore nor tire you with my long letters. Maybe they are really too frequent. Don't ever feel it necessary to write me any "duty letters."

You are "on your own." I cannot accept any further responsibility for your activities—or thought. You have a grand mind. You surely have the information. You have been blessed beyond your present realization. You have a most terrific asset in small Martha—don't ever for a minute forget this fact. If ever the road was "made straight" for anyone, surely yours has been. Yours has not been made easy "in the flesh," nor has mine, NOR WAS THAT OF JOSHUA BEN JOSEPH.

Yes, I long for you—both—unbelievably—selfishly—but, what is to be will be. However, do not ever forget that you will be helped—as you help yourself—and you always have your TA for comfort and for counsel. Helped mentally—and spiritually—even more so than in the material things of this world. "Take no thought of what ye shall eat nor of what ye shall put on." The torch is in your hands—beyond that of Sadler or Hales or any other human. Yours is the torch and you are running with it for all the world to see—and those beyond—who also watch.

Forgive my long letter. Mother is the same. I am not well. Our best thought and love to you both.

HARRY LOOSE to HAROLD SHERMAN

Monterey Park, July 22, 1942

Dear Harold:-

Your letter of July 20th received. Am glad for your acknowledgment of the receipt of the two letters for your file. I mailed a letter to you yesterday morning in answer to your last. Ma and I and Jo and Auntie were sitting on the front porch when the mailman arrived with your letter. I read it aloud and I got the biggest legitimate laugh that I have enjoyed in a long while. Maybe I do not write as understandably as I should or you entirely miss the point. Maybe this letter will brighten things up a bit.

I know very well that you were a Traverse City resident and were schooled there. We have spoken of this so often that there is hardly any point in repeating it here. You have told us of the house where you lived—the location of the trees in front from which Edward fell while Mother and Dad were not at home—and of their final arrival—the continuing illness of Edward and his passing. How you left Traverse to go out on your own—and the last goodbye to your Dad on leaving—and how it affected you. There is a great deal more. It is all very plain. No one here was "taken in."

The man, Fields, is from Marion, Indiana, where he was born, raised and schooled, and where his mother and father still reside. And yet he sat on our front porch, with Ma and Auntie and I and Mrs. Fields and a woman from our neighborhood here, all as an audience. He had told us about his old home town of Marion, and when I asked him if he knew a Harold M. Sherman, a one-time resident there, he immediately answered in the affirmative and evidenced surprise and pleasure at hearing the name. He talked of you so intimately that, to make myself sure of the identification, I went in and brought out *Thoughts Through Space* and showed him your picture therein which he at once recognized. He described the High School which you attended and where you were in his very class. He described class studies and school activities. He said that you never went in for athletics and that you were a slender young fellow and not of the robust type. That you were distinctly different from most young fellows of your age and not understood very well. That you had a newspaper route, cut lawns, and kept generally busy. He knew Edward and of the fall from the tree and of Edward's death. He did not know Arthur but knew of him, that Arthur was so much younger. He knew that you went to New York City. The only recognizable miss he made in the story was that he wasn't sure that, at the time he left Marion, you had gone to Northwestern University up in Chicago or to New York. He said that he was 44 years old and that you must now be either 43 or 44 yourself. He sure had his information—even though the location was wrong.

He telephoned me night before last and said that he was coming to call on us again, on a Sunday, and that he would phone before coming so as to be sure that we were at home. When he comes again, I fully expect that we will hear more of your school life and early activities. Remember that while all this was going on, we knew very well of Traverse City as I have before remarked. However, the whole matter was very interesting. We were in the presence of either a very remarkable evidence of strange and unusual psychic phenomena—— or a very remarkable case of honest mistaken identity. I am inclined to believe the former explanation because so much of this sort of data has occurred, or similar data hard of explanation, in my life period—it kind of follows me around. It may, however, be the mistaken identity thing. The recognizing of your picture does seem somewhat evidential, however. Whichever or whatever it is, Fields has no wrong motive or intent. I would remember this if you write to him.

My judgment would be to wait a time before writing him and see if he really does visit us again with his wife and see what more he has to say of you, if anything. Though I have no surety of his coming again, or when, if ever. I have only his call on the phone to go by. However, do as your own judgment dictates what is best. If you do decide to write him, write a friendly, diplomatic, letter. There are one of two things happening—and he is very honest and sincere—and an unfriendly or undiplomatic letter would antagonize the man very needlessly. The man is Glen B. Fields, Deputy Collector, U.S. Treasury Department, Internal Revenue Service, 11th floor, U.S. Post Office and Court House, Los Angeles, California. His home is in Bella Vista, a suburb not far from us here, but I do not know the street address. I am now finished writing of, or about, Glen B. Fields unless he visits here in the near future and continues his memoirs—in which your name figures.

Now that the above story is indited in its fullness, I want to add the following. I want to be sure to make it very positive that I am very far from infallible. I make plenty of errors and I look forward to probably making mistakes and errors as long as I live in the flesh—exactly the same as yourself. If you will look closely over my early correspondence, you will undoubtedly discover some. But, wherever found, they are honest errors and mistakes with no wrong intent. Perhaps truths hard to explain or badly expressed—all with honesty of purpose. If you will look backward, you will possibly observe some errors of your own—exactly the same as the rest of us—and all happening with honesty of purpose as a background. So, I make no excuses—nor should you—and remember that I again most positively state that I am very far from infallible.

If your belief, or confidence, in me is shaken, or destroyed altogether, I will grieve of course. I have had sad things happen to me before. My work is done anyway—and that which was meant for you has happened—the "seed" is well planted—and you have gained much—and you cannot lose that which you have gained—you cannot do it—experiment and see for yourself. And so you have profited—and will continue to profit.

With the best of thought and with much love to both you and small Martha,

Harry

4

Two Letters to Dr. Sadler

DIARY[1] [*undated*]

Special

Harold's thought—You cannot create the body before the spirit is born. The spirit in which humanity receives the Book of Urantia must create its own body. Any attempt to create the body now—before the truth is presented to the world in the form of this book—is to create a stillborn child, since the real spirit of mankind's reaction to the book cannot be in it.

FORUM CALENDAR *July 22, 1942*

Guests of Betty and Jim Hicks evening.

July 24, 1942

Guests of Mr. and Mrs. Luther [and Harriet] Evans with Karles.

DIARY *July 24, 1942*

Harold checked his ideas concerning book publication and Forum future with Dent Karle and found him to be in general agree-

[1] This is the first entry not to be included in the Forum Calendar. From here on in the Shermans' notebooks, the diary entries are recorded separately from the Forum Calendar.

ment. Karle felt the Forum has been repressed and members must be permitted to express their views. He further stated the Sadlers seem reluctant to relinquish their hold on group or give anyone else any say.

FORUM CALENDAR *July 26, 1942*

Last Forum meeting for summer.

Potluck supper at Bucklins' with Mrs. [Elizabeth] Githens.

July 27, 1942

Dinner guests of Kelloggs and Ruth.

July 28, 1942

Bucklins here evening.

HAROLD SHERMAN to WILLIAM SADLER

Chicago, July 29, 1942

Dear Dr. Sadler:

Since you asked me some weeks ago, during one of our discussions about the future of the Forum and the publication of the Book of Urantia, to put such thoughts and ideas as I had in writing for consideration, I am now doing so following my completed reading of the book itself and my greater acquaintance with the Forum as a body.

I have given great deliberation to all possible angles of the approaching problems which I foresee arising as you near the time when you feel the Foundation and Brotherhood should be established and when you are finally instructed that the book itself should be published.

In what I am now to present so frankly, please know that all is said with the greatest of affection and with no intent of personal criticism. But, in the absence of any further specific instruction from Higher Sources with respect to Foundation, Brotherhood, Forum, Book or general procedure—I feel that these points I am about to submit should be given the most sober and considered reflection by you and your associates before any further steps are taken, that no unwitting great mistake may be made in the presentation of this Revelation to the world.

First, let me say, that I accept wholeheartedly and without any reservation whatsoever the Book of Urantia and the Revelation it contains. And, if what I set down here should ever be "countermanded" by instructions from Higher Sources, then would I be the first to withdraw any objections or suggestions and "go along" with these instructions, so received, in full spirit.

If, however, we are to be left, as humans, with the problems of organization and publication to solve—then perhaps my own personal experience and background—coming into this group with a new and different perspective—may have a definite value. Please know also that I have no personal ambitions with respect to the Book of Urantia or its contents. I suggested some months ago, by letter, without having had opportunity to read the book, that channels of radio, stage and screen should and could probably be utilized at the proper time for dissemination of the truths it contained, under the "guise of entertainment." I see even greater possibilities in this now—but all of these developments will eventually come whether I, or any of us, have anything personally to do with these channels or not. The TRUTH and its RIGHT presentation to the world is ALL that matters—and if it is better for NONE of us to have any public identification with this book at any time, then this [illegible].

I cannot conceive how any finer human selection could have been made by Higher Intelligences for the faithful fulfillment of a long and arduous task than that conferred upon you and your wife, whom I shall always regret not having known in this life. What you and the small group of devoted "contact commissioners" have accomplished through these long years will live throughout the whole universe of Nebadon. Not to have faltered or swerved from your high purposes during this long time is to have gained a spiritual reward beyond price—for the human is so subject to err and to "grow faint." It is not necessary for your name or the names of any of us associated with this Forum to go "ringing down the corridors of earth time." Your name, and the name of your dear wife, is established in the realms beyond, wherein is true glory. And SERVICE is our glory here, which is an inner experience that does not require the plaudits of the multitude.

I say the above because I see, so clearly, the most serious of complications ahead which, from your own position and viewpoint, may not yet have become apparent to you.

You have told me that you intend to get out a pamphlet, describing in part the phenomena attendant upon the origin of the Book of Urantia. Obviously, either the Urantia Foundation or yourself, as an identity, or both, must stand behind this statement. You have explained that such a statement is absolutely necessary to avert all manner of perhaps well-intentioned but distorted versions of the book's origin which might be told by different Forum members. It is your intention that this pamphlet give the "official version" and that the explanation begin and end there.

From a totally outside viewpoint, knowing the opposition this book is bound to arouse in certain quarters and the pressure that will be brought to bear through newspapers and even special investigators to "get to the bottom of this" and "discredit it and those associated with it," if possible . . . I foresee GREAT, HUMILIATING and DEVASTATING results from the issuance of such a pamphlet.

First, the very nature of your work and practice, which has been such an asset to you in developing and protecting this Revelation through all these years—now becomes your *greatest liability!* You were able to quietly assemble, through the years, men and women who you knew, through personal contact, could render a vital service. Some of these people were your patients. You have even referred to the possible presence of some "paranoiacs" in the group, as you have mentioned certain anonymous letters that have been written in. I'd like to say that, in my association with your Forum members, I have found them to be an exceedingly devoted and well-balanced group. BUT—consider how this Group, with your own name and background associated, will be regarded by the *outside world!*

Newspaper reporters and investigators are certainly going to follow up on this pamphlet—they are going to request a fuller explanation, an introduction to the subject himself, a demonstration. The people of Christ's day wanted "proof," the performance of "miracles." You will experience such a demand in intensified force today.

You may think now that you can "stand pat" and end it all by saying, "Gentlemen, this is all that can be said or will ever be said. You have the whole story, all that will be told. You must test the truth of the Book of Urantia by its contents."

But your interrogators are not going to be satisfied. Not securing further information from you—with your Urantia Brotherhood then existent and open to the public, they will invade it. They will contact original Forum members and question them; perhaps purposely insult them and their belief in the book, an old reportorial trick to get people to talk. Then "unofficial explanations" will be offered which will not jibe with statements made in the pamphlet; then new clues will be developed . . . perhaps in ways you do not now anticipate, the identity of the "human instrument" will be disclosed and his life turned into a hell on earth.

And then—cruelest of all, will appear a newspaper headline something like this:

SPIRITUAL REVELATION
PRODUCED BY DERANGED MINDS:
PATIENTS OF FAMOUS PSYCHIATRIST
USED TO CONTACT SPIRIT REALMS.
New Life of Christ Reported,
Written by "Angels"; Scientists
Studying Unusual Document
Dr. William S. Sadler Declares
Revelations to be Genuine

And now picture the unfortunate and harassed position you and all original Forum members find themselves in. You are thrown entirely on the defensive, your protestations against such an interpretation being placed upon your Group, and the origin of the paper will only then be destined to make matters worse—since you can offer no further explanations. The whole Book of Urantia has now been dragged down to a human basis, associated in the public consciousness with people of neurotic and mentally unstable tendencies. It is quite possible that one or more of these Forumites may crack under this emotional strain and "commit suicide" or "do something" which will add to the unfavorable publicity. And those interested in discrediting the Book of Urantia will leap upon such happenings and make the most of them in an attempt to damn by scorn and ridicule and depreciation this GREAT and TRUE REVELATION.

I see the POTENTIALITY of all this happening and MORE—as though it were revealed to me . . . as it *has been!* This whole picture, as I am unreeling it, has passed before my inner vision. Not once—but many times—with ever increased clarity.

There is no human way—*absolutely none*—that you can employ to overcome this *liability*. The instant you and your institution are linked with the Book of Urantia, directly or indirectly, the "HEAT IS ON." A TERRIFIC WEAPON is given all enemies of the Book at the very start which will discourage literally millions of truth-seeking humans from ever reading it. To permit yourself to be placed in this VULNERABLE POSITION is to assume a responsibility beyond your human capacity to withstand. Knowing you to be so completely sincere and devoted to this mission as you are—I am sure it would actually kill you to feel that you had, in any way, wittingly or unwittingly, taken any action which had impaired the reception of this TRUTH by the world at large.

The same holds true for Bill, who has a magnificent mind and a great capacity for service. But, unless great care is taken, his own ability to serve will be completely jeopardized and discounted by wrong public reaction.

This TRUTH is obviously for ALL the world . . . not one little group or a number of groups. Anything that is done—in the presenting of this book to the public which in any way tends to alienate, directly or indirectly, the interest of any person of any faith or no faith at all, is therefore WRONG.

The fact that NO religion, in past history, has PERSISTED *without* an organization, is no indication whatsoever that THIS REVELATION will not so persist.

A study of this very Book of Urantia, clearly and unequivocally states that Christ did not found a religion. He exhorted his followers to "preach the gospel to *all* the people," but the instant they organized for this purpose they confined and segregated the TRUTH and created great groups of people OUTSIDE THE FOLD . . . as against little groups of people INSIDE THE FOLD . . . and the TRUE SPIRIT OF CHRIST was stifled in the BODY of a CHURCH. From the time of that great mistake, the great value of the LIFE of CHRIST has largely been lost upon humanity.

Such a mistake MUST NOT be made AGAIN. This Book of Urantia must not have barriers placed between it and its reception by peoples of all faiths. Unless we are to be self-appointed missionaries of the Book of Urantia and the TRUTHS it contains—we do not have to concern ourselves with its adaptation to the various orders of religious faith in the world. This adaptation is the problem of EACH TRUTH SEEKER. The adjustment must voluntarily be made by different church leaders and members of their congregation who are impressed by the SPIRIT OF TRUTH within them . . . and their own SPIRIT MONITORS that they are in the PRESENCE of a new and greater REVELATION. Anything we can say, as members of the

Urantia Brotherhood, setting ourselves up as "authorities," can only constitute a barrier—in the nature of "priests" who would attempt to interpret for the multitude OUTSIDE the church. In other words, without so intending we will have made the same mistake as the followers of Christ in His time—our Urantia Brotherhood, no matter how brilliantly conceived or managed, will be regarded by those of different church orders as a *new kind of church*—and unnecessary prejudices and complications will instantly arise.

We do not need to PROTECT the TRUTH. It has a LIVING QUALITY if we do not kill it by wrong human presentation.

In making the TRUTH *available* to *all*—we must anticipate and remove all possible hazards before we start. The TRUTH is transcendently greater than any of us. As the last communication from Higher Intelligences stated: "We are in a testing period." And we each must question our own personal feelings and aspirations with relation to this PROJECT.

The Forum has completed its dispensation. It is natural and human that all would wish to continue this inspired association. It is natural and human that a bigger and finer organization would have been visualized in the form of a Urantia Brotherhood, perhaps later a Urantia Society. It is understandable how Higher Intelligences, those in charge of this Revelation, would have kindly commented upon the plans of organization at present, although the Angels of Progress demurred. It would have been most unkind, at the end of this long dispensation, for any severe criticism or suggestions to have been offered. From my little knowledge of Higher Intelligences, their leadership is always kindly; they are conscious of our human frailties and proneness to err, even with every good intention.

BUT—we are rapidly approaching a crossroads at which point the direction we take can influence the entire world reception of the Book of Urantia.

Should this approach not be examined with great and *impersonal* consideration from every possible human angle?

IF it is unwise for the public EVER to have your name associated with this BOOK OF URANTIA because of the vulnerable background your profession now represents—*is it also wise for this book to be published by the Urantia Foundation and to be supported by a Urantia Brotherhood?*

This query may come as a shock to you. But let's proceed further along the line of human probability.

If you had this Book of Urantia placed in your hands, an entire stranger to this revelation, would you be more disposed to evaluate its contents if you saw it bore the imprint of an established publishing house than you would if you saw on the title page: "Published by the Urantia Foundation"?

Would you not think, at once, there was some new cult or ism or religion behind this? The moment you saw "Urantia Foundation"?

You have stated that it took *you* a long time to be convinced of the truth and source of these revelations, even so. How much more difficult then will the position of the thinking person be who comes in contact with this Book of Urantia for the first time, with no background appreciation whatsoever, and particularly if he has *anything prejudicial* presented to him at such a time!

"Urantia Foundation" implies a group behind it. "Urantia Brotherhood" definitely implies a body of people who had a "priority claim" on the knowledge contained in the book, which sets them up as authorities. If such a group, in its meetings, is singing "church hymns passed upon by them" as being Urantian in spirit, this authority is thus demonstrated——and those on the outside, members of other organizations and church bodies, are made to feel that they cannot get as CLOSE to this TRUTH as those SO ESPECIALLY FAVORED.

At the very start, then, a SCHISM is created; a BARRIER is erected; and PREJUDICIAL CONSIDERATION of the BOOK OF URANTIA begins!

I have not read the incorporation papers of either the Urantia Foundation or Brotherhood but have been told about them by Bill and yourself and several members of the Forum who recall certain features from a previous reading. I understand, with respect to the Brotherhood, that provision has been made for the issuance of charters to other groups of people who may wish to form themselves into such a body. Also, that these charters may be cancelled or withdrawn if the conduct or interpretation of the members of any chapter is such as to be judged foreign to the spirit and purposes of the Urantia movement by the parent organization.

Such a procedure is highly dangerous since it sets up "human authorities" and "human interpreters" of the truth and develops organized divisions of opinion when the TRUTH should be FREE to ALL. This it can *never* be—*when* it is ORGANIZED!

It is clear to me that no *one* human or *group* of humans *has* been appointed by Higher Intelligences or *will* be appointed to interpret the Book of Urantia and the REVELATION it contains. This interpretation was definitely intended to be left to the INDIVIDUAL, and for us to so intercede ourselves, with every good intention, is in *direct violation* of the mandate that we are *only custodians* and *not* possessors or owners of this TRUTH.

The TRUTH of the Book of Urantia cannot be distorted so long as it is contained within the confines of the book itself. But the instant human organizations are set up to promote and interpret this truth, rather than permitting humans to seek out the truth from the one unimpeachable and unchanging source—the book—all manner of human prejudice, distrust and disunity will result.

The TRUTH CONTENT of the Book of Urantia is so *mighty* and *unassailable* in itself that it needs no supporting statement pertaining to its metaphysical origin. Any attempt to explain it, undignifies it, and pulls it down to an already generally discredited "psychic phenomena level." And the fact that the origin can never be fully explained or tested or verified makes the dilemma even worse.

If the pamphlet reveals your own identity to the world as an endorser of the phenomena and this subjects you to embarrassment and humiliation, and the Urantia Book to possible wide discrediting because of the psychiatric and neurotic angle—then the Urantia Foundation and Urantia Brotherhood opens up similar sources of *great vulnerability*. The moment these incorporation papers are filed, the names of the officers of both organizations are public knowledge to all who wish to so ascertain them. Once the Foundation and Brotherhood become operative, anyone may contact the persons in charge. And the same unhappy result will occur. This is a human inevitability by the very nature of your past activity and present setup, highly honorable in itself, but highly damaging in the light of the world's concept of psychiatric practice as associated with consideration of the Urantia papers.

You may feel that other organizations may spring up for study of the Book of Urantia if you do not enter the field with the Urantia Brotherhood and that, since this is apt to happen, it is a lesser evil or hazard for your organization to be established.

Actually, however, the Urantia Brotherhood, however well designed, if set up before or at the time of the book's publication, is like *creating a body before the spirit is born*. The SPIRIT OF TRUTH, awakened in the consciousness of humanity, must create its OWN BODY. And it *cannot* do this—IF a *body* has *already* been formed before this SPIRIT has come alive in the evolving souls of all who may read this book. What you DO have, under such circumstances, is a STILL BIRTH. The TRUE SPIRIT can NEVER enter the BODY of the Urantia Brotherhood because the minds of those affiliated with other organizations and churches feel themselves APART from the Urantia Brotherhood—*never* able to *equally* share with those who have been original charter members, associated directly with the REVELATION itself, and thus self-constituted authorities and "personal possessors," through the Urantia Brotherhood, of this TRUTH!

The TRUTH must not and cannot be contained in an organization. The minute this happens it becomes *exclusive*, *segregated* and *perverted*. The TRUTH must come alive and exist in the minds and hearts of all peoples regardless of their present religious connections or non-religious tendencies. They must not feel that any "official interpreters" or organizations stand between them and the TRUTH.

If such a development is permitted, it will *deny* the TRUTH to untold millions in this present world crisis and postpone its otherwise wide acceptance for centuries yet to come!

If no organization exists—and no identities are established in association with the Book of Urantia, then the Forum members cannot be contacted or easily known and a complication of difficulties arise.

With the BOOK being published by a *recognized* publisher, instead of with the imprint of the Urantia Foundation, everyone can have access to the book at the same time, including past Forum members. All persons are thus privileged to organize little study groups for themselves, unofficially, whether they are contacting the book for the first time in their communities, or have had a previous knowledge of it. And the TRUTH is thus enabled to find its way naturally and spontaneously into the hearts and minds of people everywhere.

Think of what personal and human hazards are eliminated IF NO pamphlet, with its necessary identifying sponsorship, is issued; IF NO Foundation bearing the name of Urantia is associated with the printing of the book, and IF NO Urantia Brotherhood is permitted to exist!

On the surface, it appears as though the Book of Urantia, in this modern world, has no chance for proper introduction or survival, unless the above steps are taken. But consider that the present day and age affords entirely different means of conveying TRUTH to the minds and hearts of humanity than was possible in Jesus' time.

We have the printed page, the newspapers, magazines, radio, stage, screen—all mediums for reaching human consciousness quickly, independently and *individually!* These mediums have no "motives" or "axes to grind" such as all organizations must have. Every organization's excuse for being is to be "for" or "against" something.

But these *mediums of communication* exist to be USED by Man to transmit knowledge, in various humanized and dramatic forms, to his fellow man. And these mediums can readily and mightily serve as the APOSTLES of the BOOK OF URANTIA . . . In *this* manner the TRUTH can be called to the attention of every human who, unprejudiced by any organization setups which might cause him to reject the Book of Urantia, sight unseen—now makes direct, undiluted and undistorted contact with the TRUTH in book form. Once impressed by the TRUTH, he is FREE to do what he wishes about it at once—in "spreading the gospel, according to his own light and in his own way, among his own friends and acquaintances."

Such an individual, receiving the TRUTH in this way, has nothing to question *but* the TRUTH as presented in the book. He does not have to question the character and possible motives of any human individuals or organizations behind the book. He is in *direct* touch with the SPIRIT of CHRIST. He does not have to go anywhere or join anything to have this SPIRIT revealed. It is IN him and OF him and no earthly person or organization can add anything that he does not now possess. The LIFE of CHRIST is having an unrestricted opportunity to influence him without the interjection of any well-intentioned Brotherhood with its different, equally well-intentioned "human ministers or interpreters."

THE BOOK OF URANTIA, in addition to its being a TRUE REVELATION, will be the SPIRITUAL SOURCE BOOK for truth seekers for ages to come. But, while we feel assured of this, we must not lose sight of the problems confronting its proper publication and presentation to the peoples of this present era.

I, as you know, have had over fifty books published which have sold into the millions of copies. You also have had a wide publishing experience. You can appreciate it, then, when I tell you that I made the mistake of trying to publish one book—an adult novel—on my own. I thought my own name and the market I had builded would be sufficient to enable me to have the book printed at my expense and distributed through the Union News Company to booksellers everywhere, and that I could make a large profit by so doing.

I should have known better. I did not actually learn until then that book publishing and selling is a tremendously intricate business. Without a recognized and established publishing house behind you, without a well-trained and aggressive sales force, without a thoroughly tested and operating means of distribution, and without competent publicity experts who know how to exploit your special type of book in a manner to impress both public and reviewers—the chances of any book, however good, becoming a best seller today (production and selling costs being what they are) are negligible.

This difficulty is almost *infinitely* increased when your product is that of a book which appears destined eventually to replace our present BIBLE!

It is wise and absolutely necessary and right procedure for this book to be under your complete editorial control during preparation—and to be set up in type in such a manner as is now being done. With a manuscript of this unusual origin and nature, this could not successfully and with proper protective measures have been accomplished otherwise.

But, as I look into the future, I see great hazards attendant upon the attempted publishing, exploiting and distributing of the Book of Urantia under sponsorship of a Urantia Foundation and a Urantia Brotherhood.

In the first place, you need the co-operative aid and publishing experience of a *going* publishing concern to avoid the many pitfalls which any new publishing house would be bound to encounter. The Book of Urantia cannot and must not get off to a *false* start. Your new publishing firm would have NO RATING with publishers, booksellers, reviewers or public—and, in addition, would have to combat the instantly created prejudice of being considered the possible front of a new religious order. Not to mention the other complications as herein before outlined.

You are in a particularly advantageous position when the right time comes, should you and your associates decide to follow this procedure, to call in an established publisher and conclude a most favorable arrangement.

The Book of Urantia will then have been plated, ready for printing. You have paid the typesetting and plating costs which gives you a major interest in the publishing venture.

The publisher, if interested, agrees to publish, placing his imprint on the title page in place of the "Urantia Foundation," which is deleted. To all intents and purposes, this Book of Urantia then goes on the publisher's list as one of his releases for spring or fall. It, of course, is the FEATURED BOOK on the list and is so represented by the sales force. The book is distributed by the publisher through the usual channels and everything is handled in a most regular and businesslike manner. The fact that this established publisher has had this unusual manuscript brought to him and has recognized its extraordinary merit by publishing it, gives to the Book of Urantia an immediate prestige value in the trade it never could have acquired had it been introduced by an unheard-of Urantia Foundation and Brotherhood.

Then, too, did you attempt to publish on what must inevitably start out as a comparatively small-scale venture, with the Urantia Foundation and Brotherhood sponsoring the book, you run the great risk, not only of widespread discrediting, but of organized efforts to force the book off the market. Certain religious organizations are immensely strong, as you know, and if your publishing house is not able to weather a mighty storm, the Book of Urantia—priced as it would have to be priced—unless you had great capital—could not stay long in print.

Therefore, UNLESS the plan of publication anticipates the hazards and is so organized as to rise above them—you are apt to meet with a crushing and devastating defeat from the forces of evil still active on this earth.

As I see it—the risk is too great to consider bringing this REVELATION out in a limited, high-priced edition *alone,* depending largely on word-of-mouth selling and organization support. It can be too easily stopped by opposing forces before it really gets started, under such circumstances.

The only way to make sure that the Book of Urantia is extensively and firmly launched in human consciousness is to undertake a publicity and advertising campaign such as no book hitherto has ever received!

Such a campaign requires the donation of large sums of money by individuals spiritually interested—but such individuals *can* be found—and will gladly give of their substances to bring spiritual advancement to this planet.

Given an established publisher, and the power and right to have your representatives sit quietly in with him on all developments, yet remaining always behind the scenes, you can then arrange for the opening announcement of this book.

This announcement should come in the form of beautifully written, *full-page newspaper advertisements,* appearing in every daily paper in the country on the *same* day!

These ads would be seen by uncounted millions, and copies of the book would be available, on assignment if not on order, in every book store or place where books are sold!

Since the TRUTH must be within the reach of all peoples, the book must be published in several priced editions at the same time—with a paperbacked edition selling for $1.00!!

It should remain to be determined whether the Book of Urantia ad should contain the endorsement of men and women scientists, educators and others of prominence in all lines of endeavor who have read and reviewed the book prior to its publication date. Endorsements, if any, should be in the scientific field but *under no circumstances* from the religious field, for any endorsement by the clergy of any sect or sects, at the start, would make it seem as though the Book of Urantia specially favored these particular religious orders.

But this advertisement should be as attractive and inviting as some of the ads prepared for *Compton's Encyclopedia* which show background scenes of heavenly space, the formation of the earth, lower forms of life, and evolving man. It is possible, too, that announcements of this new revelation—the Book of Urantia—could be made over the radio networks—at the same time.

That I might check the feasibility of my own vision with respect to the way it seemed this book should be handled, I talked confidentially with a book publisher friend when I was in New York. Without revealing the exact nature of the book, except to say that I knew of the existence of a manuscript of such spiritual power that, when properly published in book form, it should revolutionize world thinking—I asked this publisher's opinion of my ideas.

The publisher said: "Not only do I think your ideas are feasible—but some such spectacular and distinctive method of simultaneously calling public attention to such a book *must* be utilized—as any quiet publication of it will be squelched by different religious groups who feel it opposed to their interpretation and the commercial existence of their order. But once the book is so announced, and its importance so established, it *cannot* be squelched. It has developed too many centers of support and interest throughout the country. It may still be opposed in certain quarters but it is bound to make a place for itself!"

Knowing that such an advertising campaign would require a large sum of money which the book itself could not hope to earn back in a long time, if ever, I asked the publisher if he thought such money could be raised.

To my astonishment, this publisher said: "Sherman, I have confidence in your judgment. If this book is what you say it is and I could be permitted to read the manuscript and decide for myself, I feel reasonably sure I can get a close personal friend, worth fifty millions, who is interested in helping humanity, to donate a million dollars toward the exploitation of such a volume!"

This publisher will be free in September to visit me here and, if you have by that time decided to consider this entirely different method of procedure, you could then confer along the lines indicated.

As you can see—something is developing here of tremendous possible magnitude!

This would mean that your proposed Urantia Foundation should never be incorporated under the easily recognizable "Urantia" title, and your name should not be identified with it. "Progress Foundation" might be better and this organization, actually a holding company for receiving and dispensing funds in relation to the Urantia Book, would be kept quiet anyway.

The Book of Urantia, if an established publisher handled it, should be copyrighted in the name of the publisher so this imprint may appear on the title page and wherever else it has to be used.

Then, the publishing house assigns the copyright and all rights vested therein to your Foundation. Any individuals or organizations desiring to gain access to any of these rights are then compelled to approach the publishing house as the apparent copyright holder, with their propositions. They cannot get at you personally and your identity never needs to be disclosed unless some Forum member *talks*—and, even so, you are so far removed from any personal connection that you can, under such circumstances, easily defend yourself and avoid being drawn into any controversies, which would happen constantly were you "out front" and on the "firing line."

Representatives, of your choosing, could meet as required to pass upon proposals made through the publishing house for different adaptations or uses of the contents of the Urantia Book. The Book of Urantia is thus strictly "on its own," unencumbered by any human influence or interpretation—a TRUE REVELATION—*direct* from GOD, THE UNIVERSAL FATHER—to *each* and *all* of HIS earth children, regardless of race, color or creed.

Your "Urantia Brotherhood" incorporation would not be filed. Your Forum Group would be disbanded months before the book is published so that no connection with it could be established. Members could meet about, as friends do, in their individual homes, if they so desired—but with the understanding that they were to hold as secret and inviolate their years of devotion to this work. Their interest in the book, when published, must be expressed as though it were on a par with those who have never belonged to the Forum and are seeing the book for the first time.

Later—it may be pointed out to the Forumites—the public reaction to the Book of Urantia may become so pronounced and vitalized that a Urantia Brotherhood may be formed without prejudicing any religion . . . and with chapters possibly affiliated with all churches—so that greater unity rather than disharmony is created.

But, until and if that time arrives, it is thought best not to attempt to promote the Book of Urantia and its REVEALED TRUTH through another organization which is bound to be regarded and opposed by all other denominations and groups of people as a new religious sect.

Perhaps, if you would care to submit this letter to the Angels of Progress, they might be disposed to pass upon it, and we all might be granted that guidance we so direly need for the important work ahead.

This has been written in the most loving consideration and with the deepest of respect and regard.

Sincerely,

FORUM CALENDAR *July 29, 1942*

Bucklins here evening. Harold read letter re organization prepared for Dr. Sadler.

HAROLD SHERMAN to HARRY LOOSE

Chicago, July 30, 1942

Dear Harry:

I see nothing to gain through writing Mr. Fields. I never knew him and he couldn't have known me. So I prefer to forget the whole thing.

Nothing that could ever happen would shake my confidence in you, so be not disturbed.

I am herewith enclosing, with stamped envelope for return, a copy of the letter I am today leaving with Dr. Sadler. His ego and that of Bill Jr. are running away with them, at present. It remains to be seen what this letter can accomplish. So far as I know, I am the first Forumite who has dared "cross" the doctor or be other than a "yes man." I hope to preserve cordial relations regardless, and this letter was written as delicately as it could be done in consideration of the vital matters which had to be presented. Please let me know what you think of it.

You are right that "there is plenty to be done here in Chicago." If he should accept the outline given him in my letter—I am sure the BOOK will get off to a tremendous world start! This is the part of the job that I *could* handle with every confidence of success.

As to the book I am later to write, there are so many inconsistencies in the story of early beginnings that I am, at present, much confused. Until I can sift out the true from the false and exaggerated, I would not know how to proceed or to whom to give credit.

I hope you can one day give me more definite enlightenment to clarify many points. I agree with you, such a book at the proper time might be of great value and interest.

Martha joins me in love to Mother Loose and yourself.

FORUM CALENDAR *July 30, 1942*

Leaves letter for Dr. Sadler @ 533.

Bill reads us apocrypha[2] in eve in his apt.

[2] Various superhuman communications claimed to have been received by a member or members of the contact commission. See Chapter 6 for the Shermans' notes of the apocryphal data they had heard from Bill Sadler and Dr. Sadler.

DIARY *July 30, 1942*

On July 26 the last Forum meeting before recess was held and it consequently took a little more social atmosphere. As we were saying our adieux to the Doctor on the stairway, Harold suggested casually that it would be fun for the Doctor and "Christy" and ourselves to take a jaunt down to Marion for a few days—they to visit the Merrill Davises and us the Baldwins. To our astonishment a couple of days later the Doctor called and said he could get away the weekend of 14 of August, and would Harold write the Davises and make all arrangements. We had not dreamed of such a quick and complete acceptance. So Harold *did* make arrangements and all was set before he submitted his letter of frank discussion on the Forum and Book activities. We wondered, of course, very much whether this would alter the Doctor's attitude but felt it must be done regardless.

[*Harold wrote:*]

July 28, 1942

Dear Jo:

I have this morning been delegated by your Cousin Will, as secretary-manager of the proposed Sadler-Christy-Shermans' tour to Marion, Indiana.

Dr. Sadler, in going over his dates for August, suggests Friday, August 14th, as the starting time—with his arrival in Marion scheduled, minus blow-outs and plus enough gas to get us there—late in the afternoon. STAY—to be until Sunday afternoon, August 16th.

This appears to be the only weekend or time the doctor can get away. If convenient for you and Merrill, you are to so signify. I told the doctor he should write you, and he said, "No—tell Jo I'm *preaching* to five hundred Presbyterian ministers this week, all week, and I'm busy. You folks arrange it."

Despite the fact that you originally suggested this jaunt, I still am unaccustomed at inviting relatives to another relatives' home to visit!

The Shermans will stay at the Spencer House—rather than barge in on Aunt Flora in the heat of the summer . . . we'll want to see Lillian and Aunt Flora, of course, and have some visits with them while you are enjoying the doctor and Christy—but perhaps we can have one good get-together while there . . . So—if this time is convenient and if you can suggest THE time we all might have a good visit . . . then we'll try to arrange to see some other Marion people in the brief remaining time.

Don't hesitate to state—if your own "brain concussion" or other factors interfere on [*Ed note:* The rest of the letter is lost.]

FORUM CALENDAR *July 31, 1942*

Hear Dr. Sadler talk (with Mrs. & Ruth Kellogg) at Presbyterian Seminary.[3]

Bill and Leone our guests at Isbell's followed by apocrypha reading at their apartment.

DIARY *July 31, 1942*

This a.m. Harold and Martha went with Ruth and Mrs. Kellogg to hear the Doctor lecture to a group of ministers at the Theological Seminary. The Doctor kept everyone highly entertained with stories of the difficulties ministers have with their women parishioners.

One statement he made created great hilarity among his listeners but considerable embarrassment to himself as he made a mental "slip." He mentioned that women always fell for doctors and ministers and that men liked "sinners." He meant to say "singers"! In retrospect we have decided that he was truly speaking his own mind!

HAROLD SHERMAN to SIR HUBERT WILKINS

Chicago, July 31, 1942

Dear Hubert:

Just a quick note to tell you that you have a most cordial invitation to join the Doctor, Christy, Martha and I at the home of Doctor and Mrs. Merrill Davis in their home at 723 Euclid Avenue, Marion, Indiana, on the weekend beginning August 14th to 16th inclusive. These are the unusual people I wanted you to meet but they arrived in Chicago the day after you left. Remember?

I am driving the Doctor and Christy to Marion on Friday, August 14th, for this weekend. Jo Davis says in her letter to me: "Can't you get Sir Hubert to join us? We'll feed him on a Hoosier fried chicken dinner he would never forget—and no doubt he needs the outing. I'll be glad to issue the invitation with an o.k. from you. We feel he would enjoy coming."

Bill has been reading us the APOCRYPHA and, as wonderful as the book material is, this is *more* wonderful. I neglected to ask if he

[3] McCormick Theological Seminary. Dr. Sadler lectured on pastoral psychiatry at this Presbyterian institution from about 1930 to 1956.

had read you any from it. If not, you MUST return and spend a week going into this! Martha and I have never been so thrilled. It seems a shame it must be destroyed when the book is released, but one can understand why.

If you might be free to join us in Marion, we could drive you back to Chicago with us . . . and would hope that you could stay a few days. We expect to stay, Martha and I, at the Spencer House there . . . Dr. S. and Christy will stay at the Davises', no doubt. I suppose they would want to put you up at their fine home, too.

The *Times* review [of *Thoughts Through Space*][4] was splendid—thanks for sending it. We're crazy to see you!

HARRY LOOSE to HAROLD SHERMAN

Monterey Park, August 4, 1942

Dear Harold:-

As per request, please find herein returned the carbon copy of your letter to Dr. Sadler contained in your letter of yesterday.

We are glad to have been given the privilege of reading it. There is no other comment except to heartily agree with its expressions and to hope that it accomplishes its mission.

Love from Ma and I to both you and Martha.

FORUM CALENDAR

August 5, 1942

Luther and Harriet Evans here for 8 p.m. dessert and evening.

August 6, 1942

Betty and Jim Hicks here for 8 p.m. dessert and evening.

August 7, 1942

Dr. Sadler comes over in a.m. for talk with Harold re organization letter. Stays for lunch.

DIARY

August 7, 1942

Dr. Sadler dropped over for a visit with respect to letter from Harold, which he stated he had read for the first time in the middle of the night last night. He was obviously impressed by its contents, he stated, one quarter of which the Forum group would oppose, one quarter of which was against directions, and one half to be consid-

[4] This review has not yet been found.

ered. He said further he had turned the letter over to Christy, who in turn would give it to Bill, and they would later enter upon a full discussion of it.

He revealed he had been instructed by those Celestial Beings in charge that he was not to participate directly or indirectly with any activities following publication of book, as to the foundation or as to the Brotherhood. He was to act however behind the scenes as counsellor. An attempt by Mr. Hales, one of the Forum members, to contribute $50,000 towards the book's publication was prevented by direct message from higher sources, indicating that support was desired from people of all classes rather than any one individual who might seek consciously or unconsciously to glorify his own identity in connection therewith. Dr. S. stated he did not see how the Forum group could be disbanded, since they felt they had a mission, and used this as one of the reasons for the necessity of eventually having a brotherhood.

Referring to the early days when he was investigating this phenomenon, Dr. S. said he called in several fellow physicians as observers and also the well-known magician Thurston,[5] in an attempt to get some plausible explanation of what was occurring. These men were as confounded as Dr. S. It was during this time that Harry J. Loose came to him as a patient and was introduced to this phenomenon by Dr. S. When asked a point-blank question as to whether Harry Loose had actually witnessed the human instrument through whom the phenomenon was being performed, Dr. S. declared he could not answer, he had taken an oath not to do so. When reminded that he had told us Mr. Thurston had seen the phenomena, he said, "Yes, but Thurston is now dead, and so long as any of the individuals who have been associated now live I can tell you nothing." He did say however that Harry Loose often reassured Dr. Lena by saying, "Don't worry about the chief. He'll come around. He'll believe in this," indicating that Harry was "sold" on what was happening long before Dr. S. himself became convinced.

Dr. S. went on to say that Harry, 20-25 years ago, had come to him as a patient, being nervously upset over attempts of his buddies in the police department to frame him. He was a man of great physical powers but had been shot through the abdomen and had had a

[5] Howard Thurston (1869-1936) was a popular American stage magician.

serious operation some time before which had no doubt contributed to his nervous condition. Dr. S. stated that it required several years for Harry Loose to be straightened out and that he did not feel he could travel alone anywhere during that time.

[*Marginal note:*] The Doctor felt that newspapermen would respect men of medical profession and would not give them unpleasant notoriety.

[*Marginal note:*] The Doctor admitted, this day, he was unfamiliar with most of the Forumites' personal vocations and activities and knew them only as Forumites. Had not had time to meet them socially and so really knew little of what each might contribute of value to the development and presentation of book.

11 p.m. Christy phoned to say she had just finished reading Harold's letter. She was crying as she spoke and said God had surely spoken through Harold; she had been so worried over this whole problem and that this was the complete answer. She had told the Doctor so and she knew Bill would be of the same opinion when *he* read the letter. She said Doctor felt Harold might alter opinions slightly when he had actually read the incorporation setup paper and the Brotherhood plans but that she, Christy, knew it wouldn't make any difference, but please read them as quickly as possible anyway so as to be on an even footing with the Doctor.

In conversation with the Bucklins, Hickses, Evanses, Mrs. Githens and Karles—all had previously expressed concern over the future handling of Book publication and Forum activities.

FORUM CALENDAR *August 8, 1942*

Harold and Martha read charters.

DIARY *August 8, 1942*

Read Urantia Foundation and organization plans in a.m. and in p.m. Harold composed a letter to Dr. Sadler stating his reasons for feeling they were basically wrong, advising against the foundation and stating that he felt the Doctor's identification with the book would subject him to ridicule. On concluding the letter he was led to open the Bible at random and his eyes first fell upon Luke 14:29: "Lest haply, after he has laid the foundation and is not able to finish it, all that behold it begin to mock him."

HAROLD SHERMAN to WILLIAM SADLER

August 8, 1942

Dear Dr. Sadler:

Thanks to your kindness and fine cooperative spirit, Martha and I, this morning, had opportunity of reading the papers concerned with setting up the Urantia Foundation, Corporation, Brotherhood and subsequent Societies.

A careful study of the documents demonstrates to me more conclusively than anything heretofore that the points raised in my previous letter to you are sound and valid . . . and that there is IMPERATIVE NEED of basic reconsideration to avoid possibility of a great and irreparable, though obviously well-intentioned, mistake.

The TRUTH *cannot* and *must not* be OWNED . . . and it *IS* OWNED, by the very nature of these planned bodies, despite every human effort and protestation to the contrary.

I have no doubt that the attorneys who drew up these organization plans are fine men, and that they have patterned the proposed Foundation, Brotherhood, Corporation and Societies after the best of all existing orders in any way similar to the high purposes of the Urantia development. But they are *not inspired,* neither do they have sufficient background of spiritual comprehension to foresee what this type of setup will most certainly and inevitably precipitate in the way of discord, misunderstanding and conflict.

You have been so close to this whole evolving enterprise for so long, and you and your little group know what is *in your hearts* and what *you* would do in management of the Foundation and Brotherhood . . . but you are launching such organizations amidst a sea of other humans who will become identified and whose inner spiritual or base motives you cannot divine. You think you have made provision against all possible human contingencies but this *cannot* be done.

Instead—what you have in these proposed organization setups can easily tend, under wrong management, toward developing COMMERCIALISM and FANATICISM.

Obviously, your organization setup is conceived with the thought and belief that all officers, trustees and directors are going to be of the highest spiritual type . . . and yet strict allowance has been made for the removal of those who should not prove to be so qualified.

Your attorneys realize, and so do you, that there may be many embarrassing situations arising, once the organizations are operating, requiring stringent action to protect the very principles upon which your enterprise has been founded.

The VERY FACT that this is EVEN POSSIBLE should cause you to PAUSE and CONSIDER whether the formation of an organization, under such existing circumstances on this planet at this time, would not be the greatest of mistakes and involve you, the Urantia Book and all concerned in a heartless complication of disrupting experiences, defeating, FOR THE TIME BEING, much of the long years of devoted work you have all put in.

I see clearly the INTENT but one cannot guard against the HUMAN WEAKNESSES of ENVY, JEALOUSY, GREED, EGOTISM, LUST FOR POWER, and other such traits—all of which, by the very *structure* of your organization setup, are given *full* opportunity for expression here.

Under such conditions it, unfortunately, possesses all the potentialities of a HIDEBOUND RELIGIOUS ORGANIZATION—with members of such Foundation, Brotherhood and Society *forced* to HEW TO THE LINE of interpretation and conduct under fear and threat of EXPULSION contained in the very by-laws!

Any member, through difference of opinion or interpretation or some act considered hostile or damaging to the Urantia purposes, may be subjected to the stigma and disgrace of removal from office or membership by action of a board or a majority vote . . . and then, if desirous of petitioning for reinstatement, must be subjected to the further personal humiliation (deserved or undeserved, as the case may be) of being tried by a committee of his self-constituted and duly elected "human peers," either Judicial or Executive in function.

By what God-given right can ANY group of humans presume to pass upon any fellow human's degree or character of spiritual illumination and interpretation? It is the INALIENABLE RIGHT of *every* human, of whatever faith or no faith at all, to SEEK TRUTH in his own way . . . and find and recognize the TRUTH, *without compulsion,* once it is placed within his reach!

The URANTIA BOOK, properly introduced and widely publicized, will place this TRUTH within the *reach* of *all!*

As long as the URANTIA BOOK remains ALONE and BY ITSELF as the ONLY SOURCE OF TRUTH . . . *free of any human organization* . . . it will *forever* remain IMPREGNABLE as a TRUE and DIRECT REVELATION of GOD to man.

The TRUTH becomes vulnerable and subject to distortion the INSTANT any "authoritative or official interpretation" is set up concerning it.

Only a member of a Urantia Brotherhood or Society can really *impair* the TRUTH contained in the URANTIA BOOK, and this is because of the "vested authority" *implied* in such an organization and its announced purpose of promoting said book.

Urantia Teachers, so certified, to instruct those interested and non-believers, are as vulnerable in the world at large as followers and leaders of a movement like the Ballards' "I AM,"[6] and will probably be so classified by unsympathetic, scoffing and opposing observers.

But the sublime and *real* truths of the URANTIA BOOK can *never* be twisted or perverted so long as they are permitted to remain in the book itself, accessible to all earnest seekers of truth—but never garbled through well-meant but varying interpretations of Urantia Brotherhood members or teachers who will be drawn into endless arguments, controversies and strife by those both within and without their own organizations.

Any attack made on the URANTIA BOOK by members of churches or organizations represents only their personal opinions and does not hurt the book nor alter its truth. BUT—if their attack can be made on HUMAN UPHOLDERS of this truth in the form of URANTIA BROTHERHOOD members, then the URANTIA BOOK can lose dignity and caste through the *ridicule* and *belittling* of its *own supporters!*

In any organization setup, however well conceived, I see the following insurmountable human hazards:

I. Any human identification with the URANTIA BOOK, whether through an individual or an organization of individuals, lays the book open to:

1. Highly vulnerable human sources of contact for attack by non-believers and those strongly opposed, who will try to disprove "authenticity" of the Revelation by DISCREDITING of its upholders.

2. Possibility of varying errors of interpretation on part of Urantia Brotherhood and "certified teachers." This will cause ever-widening and disturbing controversies and cost the URANTIA BOOK great spiritual prestige it would otherwise acquire *on its own.*

---

[6] See Vol. 1, p. 237 for more about the IAMers.

3. Development of spiritual intolerance and religious feuds on a scale never before seen on earth through the resistance of all other churches to what they regard as a new religion in the form of the Urantia Brotherhood. Despite the fact that the charter invites membership of all faiths without renouncement of present affiliations, it is obvious that many will have to change their beliefs or they will not be interested in joining, and this alone is going to cause many religious leaders to feel that the Urantia Brotherhood has been organized to take members from their churches regardless of protestations to the contrary.

4. Unwise and prejudicial methods of promoting the Urantia Book are bound to occur under the spiritual zeal of Urantia Brotherhood members, and needless opposition will thus be aroused.

5. Existence of an organization implies possession of "special inside knowledge of interpretation" not possessed by the URANTIA BOOK itself and detracts from the book's own importance and authentic revelatory value. Also discourages many members of other churches who do not care to join the Urantia Brotherhood, from ever seriously considering and accepting the TRUTHS contained in the book itself.

If the above points are well taken, as well as the comments made heretofore which have a bearing upon the entire situation—then the plans calling for the publication, distribution, translation and publicizing of the URANTIA BOOK, in addition to all plans of organization, should be *drastically revised.*

Briefly, it seems that the steps taken should be these:

The Urantia Foundation should be exceedingly simplified and have to do only with the affairs of the URANTIA BOOK'S publication, distribution, and translation . . . and such monies as may be forthcoming from all rights vested in such enterprise.

Provision should be made for the receiving of endowments, donations, and contributions of whatever sort but there should be no necessity for the maintenance of an office and staff. It is clear to me now that affiliation with some reputable publishing company, equipped to handle the publicizing, selling and distribution, is not only advisable but a primary essential.

No Urantia Foundation or corporation possesses or can possess the publishing knowledge or facilities to present a book of this tremendous character to the world. The Foundation's chief function, once a publishing affiliation has been made, should be, through its board of trustees, to cooperate in every way with this publishing house. All propositions for utilization of any rights inherent in the book will come through the publishing house and will be passed upon by the trustees who have, at all times, the high destiny of this book in mind. These trustees will render their services without compensation. This is for them a true labor of love, which will forever keep them from being placed in the position of accepting or rejecting a monetary proposal, which might otherwise hold a basis of profit for them and thus prejudice their own judgment.

All monies earned by the URANTIA BOOK are to be spent in further publicizing it or to make free copies available to many who could not otherwise afford possession of it. No money should be expended and no human efforts made by any organization or group with any recognizable or identifiable headquarters, and this publicizing should be done through and with the publisher.

In this manner the BOOK OF URANTIA is enabled to expand its influence *in* and *of itself* with no possibility of this influence being detracted by organizational effort and the opposition such methods of promotion would be bound to arouse.

The URANTIA BOOK, *unorganized,* is thus FREE for acceptance by every member of *every church organization* and *every human everywhere.*

It is true that every religion which has persisted in the past has had an organization, but though the organizations themselves kept alive the *religions,* they LOST THE TRUTH—making this PRESENT REVELATION *necessary!*

It is not for us in this generation, looking toward the future of all evolving souls on Urantia, to pattern the presentation of this REVEALED TRUTH on the precedents of the past. If we do, we commit the *same spiritual folly* as transpired following the sojourn of Christ Michael on earth—and VIOLATE His *very admonitions* in the BOOK OF URANTIA *itself.*

Devotedly and sincerely,

5

Idealists and Ideaists

FORUM CALENDAR *August 9, 1942*

Potluck at Karles. Present—Mr. & Mrs. Evans, [Al and Charlotte] Dyon, [Lee Miller and Katharine] Jones, Bucklins, Winnifred, Mary, Jones daughter [Katharine aka "Ticky"] and Harold & Martha.

DIARY *August 9, 1942, p.m.*

Dr. Sadler came over to personally answer points raised in the second letter and to "bring Harold up to date" on Forum discussions and messages received from higher sources relative to the formation of both the foundation and brotherhood.

Dr. S. stated that others had felt as Harold now felt, notably Clyde Bedell and Bill Jr., who were ringleaders among those opposing existence of an organization. After many arguments, pro and con, over a period of the last 8-10 years, a vote was taken and what has evolved to be the present Foundation and Brotherhood form of setup was elected 4-1 (vote). Later, this, on a motion, was made unanimous with the exception of one individual who still held to the conviction that no organization should ever be established.

Harold stated there were many Forum members at the present time who felt strongly about book and organization plans, but the Doctor said these were distinctly in the minority; that he knew who these people were; that their minds couldn't be changed and that he wasn't going to argue with them.

Dr. S. referred to some communications he said the contact commissioners had received from time to time but which had not been passed on to the Forum members—which communications had been in support of such an organization. He stated Sonsovocton (33rd lieutenant) had said that were it not for an organization, more than 50 would spring up in the first 10-15 years following book publication, and great confusion and distortion would result. This "lieutenant" in charge of the Angels of Progress further declared that Dr. S., as a psychiatrist, should know he could not influence the mind of an idealist and therefore he should not argue with him. Dr. S. emphatically declared that the organization setup, having been passed upon by the Forum, was water over the dam and could not, and would not, be changed.

When Harold reminded him that the Angels of Progress had not been able to endorse this organization in their last communication even though it had been favored by the Angels of the Churches and that therefore much opportunity existed for perfecting improvements before such organization might be born, Dr. S. said, "Oh, no. That's all settled. The Angels of Progress have indicated that while they weren't pleased with the present setup they would go ahead with us anyway and would iron out the mistakes as we went along." Dr. S. advised Harold to do no more thinking about the organization but to put his mind on the problems of publication which yet remained to be solved. He did state, however, that he would not act upon the Brotherhood organization until he received direct orders so to do from the Angels of Progress.

Harold expressed relief that Dr. S. was to be guided by further instructions and said he felt, if the book were published without an organization, that no need for an organization would be found to exist and that the Angels of Progress at such a time might so advise. Dr. S. waved this possibility aside by saying that they had received a mandate, which the Forum members knew nothing of, to have an organization, and the only question remaining was that of the time for its origin. Dr. S. brushed aside all attempts Harold made to present objections, and left with the repeated admonition that he confine his thoughts to making suggestions on the book's publication.

Potluck at Karles', Elmhurst. Present—Bucklins, Joneses, Dyons, Karles, Shermans, Evanses (and children).

The men entered into a frank discussion with Harold of the Forum, organization and book problems, and he found them all to have been privately concerned but unable heretofore to express their opinions either to one another or to Dr. S. In direct opposition to Dr. S.'s statement that these problems had been thoroughly aired and thrashed out before the Forum, these men were unanimous in stating that, while some questions had been raised and some comments made, the Forum members for the most part had been *told* of plans originated and consummated by Dr. S.'s little group and asked to vote upon them. Increasingly through the years, and particularly since the death of Dr. Lena, they had all observed a more dictatorial attitude on the part of both Dr. S. and Bill and the tendency for them to discourage any real expressions of opinion from the floor. All committees had been appointed by the Doctor rather than being selected by the Forum body and all plans instigated by him.

Asked by Harold if they were all familiar with the Foundation and Brotherhood charters, they said the charters had been read to the Forum, but so rapidly they could not be properly evaluated, and that the Forum had then been asked to pass upon them, the assumption being that the membership would give Dr. S. and his contact commissioners a vote of confidence. Karle told Harold he had seen vicious possibilities of commercial and fanatical uses being made of the Foundation and Brotherhood, and had sought to go on record to no avail. He and Bucklin on one occasion had dropped in upon the Doctor to present their case and had been unable to get in a word edgewise.

Reference was made by Harold to the power vested in the parent Brotherhood body to disenfranchise any offending chapter or individual, and all men agreed this opened the way for rabid abuse of spiritual power and authority. They all stated they did not see how the establishment of an organization could be interpreted in any other way than that of a religious order and, in their opinion, would tend to alienate millions from giving consideration to the Book of Urantia.

These men brought up the possible harmful influence that connection of Dr. S.'s name as psychiatrist would have upon not only the book but any proposed organization. It was their opinion that any such association would be highly dangerous. All agreed that their identification as Forum members with this new organization would subject them personally and their families not only to ridicule but to possible physical harm by representatives of those institutions and/or individuals who might be strongly opposed. Therefore—it was also agreed that these members had every right to have "their say" in whatever was to be done in a public way since they were bound to be individually involved and to have to assume responsibility whether they so wished or not.

Karle stated that this was the time for Forum members to get together and discuss these vital points, and that he felt other members should be quietly sounded out as to their convictions. He further stated that he thought no such unity would exist in the future as had prevailed in the past because all had been devoted to the task assigned, and, now that their dispensation was finished, felt that the time had now arrived for expression of their long-restrained views and opinions.

Harold said he was surprised that restrictive control of the Forum body still was maintained by Dr. S. when he had expected that this group would now be free to decide its own destiny in the absence of any specific instructions from Higher Sources. It was the consensus that some plan of action be considered to bring these matters up on the floor of the Forum and to the direct attention of Dr. S. and his contact commissioners. The unanimity of thought held by these men, several of whom have been members for many years, was illuminating and indicated the existence of substantial discontent with respect to current developments.

FORUM CALENDAR *August 10, 1942*

Dr. Sadler comes over at 9 a.m. for further discussion.

Bucklins here evening.

DIARY *August 10, 1942, Mon. a.m.*

Harold had an early visitor in the person of Dr. S., who brought with him the two letters Harold had written. He stated that he, Bill, and Christy had conferred on them last night and were agreed that for purposes of presentation to other contact commissioners, and subsequently to Forum members, Harold's comments upon the Foundation (book publication) and organization and Brotherhood (organization) should be separated and two new letters written dealing with these problems individually. Dr. S. explained that he did not wish to prejudice the consideration of Harold's valuable suggestions regarding book publication by association of any organization criticisms or comments, since all organization matters were a "closed book." He said, "We have gone all through this organization business with the Forum and it's been okayed. I expect if we act upon your publication suggestions we will have another fight on our hands and I don't want to mix it up with organization questions."

Harold said he did not want the division of these two subjects—organization and publication—in the form of letters dealing with each separately to in any way detract from the force and conviction of his views dealing with the proposed Brotherhood. Harold specifically asked Dr. S. if he intended later to submit his letter on the organization setup to the Forum body for consideration, and Dr. S. said, "No, I do not! I told you this was a closed book. We already have our authority both from the Forum and from higher sources to proceed as we see fit."

Asked again by Harold if he was right in understanding that Dr. S. intended to wait (as he had previously stated) for instructions from higher sources before setting the Brotherhood organization in motion, Dr. S. replied (completely reversing his statement of the day before), that this was not necessary; that they would probably not set up the Brotherhood at the time the Foundation was established, but that they had authority now to proceed with the organization whenever they thought best.

In support of this declaration, Dr. S. revealed that there had been other confidential communications received by them which they had not passed on to the Forum and which he now wished us to see, since these messages further stressed the need for an organization. Asked why he did not present these communications, he said he did not want to influence the minds of the members, and that Sonsovocton had stated that these members were already overawed by previous messages read them. It was Dr. S.'s contention that the members should be free to make up their own minds, uninfluenced by such authoritative communications as the contact commissioners (he and Bill in particular) had received. (That these members had not felt themselves free to express their opinions had been made evident to Harold at last night's meeting at the Karles'.)

Dr. S. likened certain objecting Forum members to "idealists" as contrasted to "ideaists," a distinction which had been made at one time in a "conversation" held with Sonsovocton. She had advised, according to Dr. Sadler, that he should know better as a psychiatrist than to argue with an idealist because the idealist is right and knows he is right, but unfortunately things will not work out his way. As an illustration, Dr. S. referred to Abner as an "idealist" and Paul as an "ideaist." He said that Abner was not much appreciated on Jerusem but would be when he arrived on Edentia. In contrast he spoke of Paul the ideaist who had compromised with all manner of organizations and religious orders and had thus kept the message of Christ alive in the world. Dr. S. said it was regrettable that Abner and Paul couldn't have gotten together . . . but that if it hadn't been for Paul, they had been told, they wouldn't have had any springboard in the world from which to launch the Urantia Book.

Dr. S. referred to Gandhi as an Abner type of idealist who was employing Christ's attitude of pacifism and said this was all very well, but you had to meet force with force in the world today and must not fear the consequences. Harold took exception to this statement which could only be interpreted as classifying him with Abner, and said he, Harold, was no pacifist nor was he afraid to face any consequences, but that until further light was shown him he would have to stand upon his already expressed views with respect to the organization.

(It has since occurred to us that Paul was really the pacifist, since he was the compromiser willing to trade values and spiritual interpretations for dissemination of Christ's message to all peoples, while Abner courageously held out for the true and unadulterated presentation of Christ's life and works on earth.)

Asked by Harold what his attitude would be if some of the Forum members should wish to make their further views known with respect to the organization, Dr. S. said, "I would pay no attention to them. I know certain idealists still exist and have been so told by Sonsovocton that they had not changed their minds. But I have also been told we are to go ahead with our organization and, since this has been passed on by the Forum, the subject will not be reopened." (To reinforce his statements he said we would be permitted to hear the shorthand notes made (by Christy) on several occasions when special instructions were given the contact commissioners, which had never been revealed to the Forum.) It was evident that Dr. S.'s mind was absolutely set, that any changes which might now be proposed by any Forum members with respect to the organization setup would be staunchly opposed to the point of being given no consideration whatsoever.

Dr. S. stated that he knew of the attitude of every Forum member when Harold asked him if he was aware that certain Forumites had differences of opinion, but that he was not concerned; the Forum had already voted on a 4-1 basis in support of this organization setup and there could and would *not* be any alteration made in the present organization plan. He further went on to say that Harold had naturally only attracted to himself Forum members who thought his way; that these were all known and were in the minority. (The Doctor apparently had no comprehension that he himself had probably been in touch only with those who subscribed to his own views, and that his dictatorial attitude had silenced the others.) Dr. S. gave as his explanation for the need of an organization the necessity of an authoritative body of interpretation to prevent any other organization being formed which might pervert this truth.

Harold pointed out that the organizing of a religious body following Christ's time on earth did not prevent the origination of multitudinous other organizations, each endeavoring to preserve and convey their own interpretations of Jesus' life on earth, until today we have this present state of utter confusion and conflict. The Doctor admitted this was so but said this was a chance we would have to take, and that we would not be expected to be held responsible for what happened to this organization after we were gone—this was a problem for future generations. He said the important thing was to preserve and protect the true interpretation for a long enough time after publication of the book would definitely establish it, and that this was why an organization was needed. He refused to see or to view this organization as a religious body or to realize that it was bound to be so regarded by practically all peoples outside it—and that, as a consequence, the Book of Urantia would likely be opposed by all religious organizations and attract to itself only for the most part those individuals not having any definite spiritual affiliations.

Dr. S. did not seem to see the inconsistency of his declaration that all people were free to interpret the Book of Urantia as they chose, against the fact that an official organization existed to *tell* them how to interpret it. He seemed to feel that the authoritative existence of such an organization would serve to bolster all religious bodies in their understanding and acceptance of the Book of Urantia. He stated at one point that Sonsovocton told him that we needed a government to guarantee freedom, it being his implication that the Brotherhood would be an organization to end organizations.

When asked what difference it would make if there were different interpretations arrived at by different individuals and organizations, Dr. S. said, "They'd be welcomed—they might throw a new light on the truth." When queried then why a Brotherhood needed to exist, Dr. S. again returned to an old contention: "It was needed to prevent unauthoritative bodies from originating who might pervert the truth." It became obvious that not only was this subject a "closed book" as far as Dr. S. was concerned, but that he had an absolutely "closed mind" concerning it.

HAROLD SHERMAN to HARRY LOOSE

Chicago, August 11, 1942

Dear Harry:

Things have been happening so fast around here this past week that I would need a Burroughs adding machine to add them up. It's hard to know where to begin, there are so many developments that should be reported.

I am glad you approved of the letter I wrote Dr. S. . . . and here is the second one, which please read and return for my file.

After the first one had *reposed* over there for a week, I got sudden word from Dr. S. who said he had just gotten around to reading it and wanted to talk to me about it. He came over and spent two hours, during which he said he liked the "publication plans" but that the Forum had already passed on the organization . . . voted for it, 4 to 1 . . . and that this was settled, and that he thought I would change my mind about the organization setup once I had read the charters and by-laws. I LISTENED, but said nothing in rebuttal . . . however, Dr. S. *did* say that, inasmuch as they expected to be instructed WHEN to release the book . . . he thought they would ALSO be instructed WHEN to start the organization and that he intended to WAIT until he got the order to go ahead before starting such organization. I said, "Doctor—if this is your plan—then I am satisfied. IF you get orders to go ahead on this organization, I'll abide by these orders . . . but IF YOU DON'T, then I will stand on my own judgment."

That evening, late, Christy phoned me. She was CRYING, Harry . . . and said she had just finished reading my letter which the Doctor had given her . . . and she said, "Oh, Harold—you must have been inspired by God to write this . . . you don't know what a great load you have taken off my heart and mind . . . I am SO RELIEVED . . . I can't tell you how worried I have been for years . . . THIS IS THE WAY IT SHOULD BE DONE . . . POPSY wants you to read the charters and by-laws of the Foundation and organization . . . HE THINKS YOU WILL CHANGE YOUR MIND WHEN YOU'VE READ THEM . . . BUT *I* KNOW YOU WON'T . . ." This was all Christy could say over the phone . . . but she is in an AWFUL SPOT and for her to give me this tip-off that she agreed with me was grand of her. She said she was turning the letter over to Bill and said that Bill was originally against an organization UNTIL Dr. S. sold him ON it.

Last Saturday morning, Martha and I ran over and spent several hours studying the charters and by-laws . . . and this second letter tells you what we think of the whole business.

I took this letter over Sunday noon and passed it in to Christy at the door, who seemed afraid to stay down in the hall and talk to me . . . and I got the feeling that she thought Dr. S. might be suspicious. I doubt if she'll be able, for some time, to see us alone. But we are to take the Doctor and Christy on a motor trip to Marion, Indiana this coming weekend for them to visit the Davises, while we visit Mrs. Baldwin, Mother's sister . . . Mother being in Michigan.

Sunday afternoon we got quick action from the Doctor. This second letter "got under his hide." I was so outspoken in my feeling about his organization setup . . . and he now knew that the reading of the charters and by-laws hadn't changed me . . . so he came running across the street to spend two hours in trying to win me over.

Dr. S. said, "Harold, you've reacted as other Forum members have in the past . . . this organization thing has all been discussed and thrashed out and DECIDED UPON . . . the Forum VOTED to go ahead . . . so this is a *CLOSED BOOK*. Nothing can be done about it or will be done . . . And YOU would have felt differently and been able to JUDGE this thing differently had you been here . . . but since you weren't, I want to BRING YOU UP TO DATE . . . GIVE YOU A LITTLE PAST HISTORY."

Then Dr. S. told of several "off the record" messages from Sonsovocton (if I am spelling it correctly), 33rd lieutenant of the Angels of P. . . . in which "she" favored the organization . . . I asked, "Why did you not make these communications known to the Forum?" and he said, "Because I wanted the Forum members to make up their own minds without being influenced by higher sources." Then he went on to say that they were going ahead despite anything the Forum members might say or do. I reminded him of what he had said the previous conference . . . that he intended to wait until he got "orders from on high," and he said, "Oh, no—you might as well know that we've had enough approval so we consider we've got the green light . . . and we'll set up this organization whenever we feel the time has arrived, without any further instructions . . . or any word from the Forum!"

This was a startling statement to me and indicated how dictatorial he had become.

Sunday night we were invited to a potluck at the home of the Karles in Elmhurst . . . attending this meeting were the Bucklins, Evanses (relatives of Clyde Bedell, an old member), the Joneses, the Dyons (old members—1925), the Karles and the Shermans . . . ALL OF THE MEN, in a frank talk which developed, expressed GREAT CONCERN at the way things were going . . . and felt that something would soon have to be done about it.

Yesterday morning, bright and early (Monday), Dr. S. came over, bringing *both* the letters I had written him.

"Harold," he said, "I want you to do something for me. I want you to rewrite these two letters and SEPARATE the PUBLISHING SUGGESTIONS and put them in ONE LETTER . . . and then put all your comments about the ORGANIZATION in ANOTHER letter. I think your publishing ideas are very good and that these should be presented to the Forum to be passed on when we reconvene September 13th . . . BUT, I can't present your ideas MIXED UP with your organization comments because this would only PREJUDICE members of the FORUM *against* you . . . since the organization has been *passed* on and (repeating once more) is a CLOSED BOOK."

Dr. S. said he could not even show these present letters to the *other* members of the CONTACT COMMISSIONERS because of certain comments I had made, which he was sure I WOULDN'T have made . . . had I been more advised and had a better background here . . . One point he particularly did not like was my reference to his "psychiatric reputation" and its possible effect upon the public mind. He said, "These other contact commissioners know I have no intention of being active in this setup, and this would only serve to reopen something we have already discussed . . . so when you rewrite these letters, don't refer to that at all." (This leads me to believe that Doctor does not want this VULNERABLE POINT brought up . . .

and, HARRY—AREN'T ALL THE CONTACT COMMISSIONERS ENTITLED TO CONSIDER EVERYTHING OF VITAL INTEREST TO THE PAPERS? WHAT RIGHT HAD DR. S. TO WITHHOLD SHOWING MY LETTERS TO THE "KELLOGGS" WHOM HE MUST HAVE BEEN REFERRING TO?)

We had dinner with the Kelloggs several weeks ago, in their home . . . and they are so tremendously loyal to the Doctor, which is fine . . . but I feel they are disturbed . . . and don't dare say anything. Their bread and butter depends upon him. NOW, I am sure that Dr. S. only intends to show the Kelloggs and others my PUBLISHING LETTER and to file the ORGANIZATION letter away.

I asked him if he intended later to read the "organization letter" to the Forum, if anyone raised a discussion again about organization plans, and he said, "No—you don't seem to comprehend, Harold, that this organization matter is finished."

I said, "But, Doctor, I happen to know that different Forum members are concerned over the future status of the Forum, and what if they bring up questions on the floor?"

"We'll pay no attention to them," he said. "I won't even argue with them. Oh, yes, I know there are a few 'Idealists' in the Forum, and Sonsovocton told us one time that '*they are right*' . . . but that they 'wouldn't have their way.'" (Could this have been a prediction that the Doctor would have HIS WAY . . . only he didn't interpret it correctly?)

The doctor went on to say: "ABNER was an *idealist* . . . he believed in PRESERVING the true life message of Jesus . . . but PAUL, he was an *ideaist* . . . he believed in compromising with different existing organizations, trading spiritual truths and interpretations here and there . . . in order to carry on the message of Jesus . . . and, but for Paul, we wouldn't have any springboard today to launch this Book! . . . But, ABNER was really right . . . however his plan didn't work . . . he and Paul should have gotten together . . . but on Edentia, the world where ideals are realized, they look upon him as a great soul. . . . Now, Harold, you are an ABNER type . . . and I'm telling you it won't work . . . we've got to have an organization!"

I said, "Doctor, Paul's organizing didn't prevent *other* organizations from springing up. You say you feel if you organize that you'll keep other organizations of different interpretations from developing . . . but look at all the churches and sects which exist in the world today and the confusion and strife they have caused. I feel a U. Brotherhood will immediately ANTAGONIZE ALL CHURCHES and PEOPLES who will feel it is another religion . . . and will therefore shun the message in the book." Dr. S. said, "That's not for us to worry about . . . if we can protect this book with an organization for ten or fifteen years, it's up to the next generation to carry on the fight . . . that's not our responsibility . . ."

I am quite sure that arrangements have already been concluded with the Haleses on the business end of the Foundation . . . it's to be largely a two-family proposition . . . and the trustees have POWER, "as if they owned the papers," a statement in the by-laws[1] . . . to do what they wish, to sell any rights, to spend money as they wish, to vote themselves salaries or fees for SPECIAL services rendered . . . although they are to serve without compensation as trustees.

HARRY—if I only could get some DIRECT word from the Angels of P. to know that my views are RIGHT. Bill Jr. said to me once, "If anyone ever walked in and gave me MY NUMBER . . . I would say, 'Brother, TAKE OVER . . . YOU ARE IN CHARGE.'" If only I could be given some authority to IMPRESS these people across the street, when the right time comes . . . or IF ONLY some message would come through from the HIGHER-UPS, CONFIRMING the points I have made . . . and setting the stage for a CORRECTION of present EXISTING EVILS! . . . I am hopeful and I am praying.

I know that Forum members are checking with each other during this vacation period and there is to be a *mighty stirring* this fall. I will do all I can to preserve peace and unity. Everyone says, "Dr. S. will not listen to suggestions from anybody . . . he has even discouraged questions almost completely in the Forum since Dr. Lena died . . . there has been a great change in Bill and his father since then." Much feeling which has been restrained for the past few years is due to break out shortly . . . now that the work is done . . . and now that they see Dr. S. does not consider that the Forum members have any vote or power to think or act in themselves. They never had a chance to discuss the organization plans . . . they were simply presented to them and they were asked to vote on them "as was."

[1] Article 6.15 of the Declaration of Trust Creating Urantia Foundation (first published in 1950) stipulates: "The Trustees shall have the power . . . to sue in any court of law or equity to protect or enforce any rights or interests of the Trustees in or related to or in any way connected with any of the Trust Estate or any part thereof or interest therein, the same as if they were the private and individual owners thereof . . ."

I will be interested in such comments as you care to make concerning all this. You were more than RIGHT when you said there was "plenty of work to do in Chicago." It's almost a full-time job now and I have had little time for creative work or thought . . . but am going forward in the belief we will be taken care of financially. ALSO—your suggestion of keeping a DIARY has been INVALUABLE . . . we would have been LOST without it . . . and IF BIG MISTAKES ARE MADE . . . the book you say I am to write is the ONLY THING that can straighten things out.

My—how I pray Dr. S. is saved from making a colossal personal and egoistic mistake. He WANTS it known he has been connected with this development . . . and says he will simply stand on his professional ethics, when asked about it . . . saying he knows of the work but can say nothing for "professional reasons." How little he knows what a BLAST will be awaiting him from a skeptical press motivated by opposing forces.

Mary is coming along fine; Marcia, too, in Michigan . . . we are well and happy here . . . and DOING OUR UTMOST . . . with constant love and appreciation going out to you. Our love also to Ma Loose and Josie and Auntie.

FORUM CALENDAR *August 11, 1942*

Discussion with Bill Jr. eve.

DIARY *August 11, 1942*

Invited to Bill Sadler's to have further readings of earlier material during the development years of this [sleeping] subject, who was inducted into the Reserve Corps of Destiny, a discussion was first entered into between Bill and Harold with respect to Harold's views on the organization plans. Bill declared he had bitterly opposed all organization ideas some years before but became convinced he was wrong when he considered that no religion had survived without organization. He took the same attitude as his father in stating that Harold, as an Abner-the-idealist type, was right and therefore he would not argue with him—but that Paul, who established an organization when Abner did not, and compromised with other existing orders and beliefs, preserved the message of Christ down to the present day.

Bill emphatically declared that, regardless of whatever any Forum members thought or did, if no one else set up a Urantia organization, he would do it himself. He further stated: "Harold, I've been teaching these Urantia papers for years and I am saying to you that no one abominates organizations more than I; I think most of them are rotten and I can foresee there is going to be considerable opposition, but I feel we must have an organization to prevent organizations just the same—and while I don't want it myself, I'm nevertheless going to occupy a position that many others would love to be in. I don't covet to sit in this high place but I've got to do it at whatever cost to my family or myself or my personal desires."

Asked suddenly by Harold *on whose authority* he would set up such an organization and place himself at the head, Bill impulsively replied, "On my own." He seemed to realize this statement was a bit too precipitate, and added, "Or rather, I would exercise the best wisdom of which I was capable in the light of these papers in so doing." Then asked pointedly by Harold what would be his attitude if the message from Higher Sources should be received strictly advising against an organization of any kind, Bill declared, "I would challenge it! I would have to be sure in my own mind if it would be true or false. Such a message would be contradictory to existing information, and I would have to be sure of its source because I don't anticipate any such message and would be very slow about acting upon it."

(Bill here indicated that he was at variance with his father's last statement when he said he intended to wait for specific instructions from higher authority as to the time of setting up the organization. Dr. S. had said that they were ready to proceed upon their own authority when they judged the time was right, as he interpreted the last message to have given them "the green light.")

Bill expressed a liking for the publication ideas submitted by Harold and said he felt they were well worth considering. Harold stood firm on his present convictions against any organization setup, and Bill specifically stated that most of the organization plans were conceived through joint action of his uncle (Mr. Kellogg), his father and himself. He argued that the entire universe was highly organized, and wasn't it sensible to have organization here.

Harold brought up the matter of punishment for Urantia Brotherhood offenders (either chapters or individual members) and asked what would give any humans the authority to judge others. Bill referred to the action taken against Caligastia and his rebellious supporters, and said that some system of protection against those who would try to pervert the truth must be established on earth as it has been in the higher realms. He admitted to having conceived this phase of the Brotherhood charter himself.

Bill, looking into the future, pictured himself, as the head of the organization, being questioned during office hours by fellow Standard Oil employees who might refer to his society as a "screwball" setup and would ask him if he believed that there were different orders of beings flying around "invisible in space." In answer to such queries, Bill said he would make some such reply as, "No, I don't think they are flying around in space. But I think it's quite possible these beings are operating *outside of space*." By such a reply Bill intimated that he would make these skeptical employees "think" and thus arouse their interest in reading the Book of Urantia to find out what it was all about. Bill stated also that he would say, "Listen, fellows. My time belongs to Standard Oil, but if you'd like to discuss this with me after hours, okay, I'll be glad to tell you all about it. But you've got to read the book first."

Expatiating further, Bill said, "Of course we're going to have many knotty problems, for instance—what are we going to say to an Arabian prince who has three wives and who wants to preach Urantia? Are we going to turn down a good prospect like this just because he happens to believe in polygamy? No! The way we'll get around such a situation is this—We'll set up an Arabian chapter and then it won't be necessary for us to pass judgment on them at all since they'll run this chapter in accordance with the laws of their country." (It became obvious that Bill and his father have autocratic control of the Urantia Book and its message in mind.)

Bill declared, in answer to Harold's question, whether they didn't desire acceptance of the Urantia Book by all existing churches, "No, I think that would be the worst thing that could happen. I think the first great support we're going to get with the Urantia Book will be from that great number who are not now identified with any churches or who are dissatisfied with present affiliations." Harold suggested that what Bill was organizing, then, was a new religion which would be in competition with all existing religions. Bill shrugged his shoulders and said, "Mebbe so."

Harold then said that the first group who always jumped on the bandwagon was the so-called "neurotic or lunatic fringe," and that the organization would be immediately embarrassed by such membership of well-meaning but for the most part self-deluded individuals. Bill said, "Yes—like Mildred Bucklin. She joined up with about every screwball organization she could find until she came upon Urantia. Her husband Russell said to her, 'Well, Mildred, at last you've found something really worthwhile.'" (This revealed an attitude of smugness and intolerance on Bill's part, boding ill for his future relations with members of any subsequent organization if they did not agree with his point of view.)

Told by Harold that there were many differences of opinion among present Forum members, Bill said yes, he knew that "there wasn't much spirit of truth in quite a few of them." Harold stated his conviction that all of them were sincere even though possessing different viewpoints, and Bill expressed doubt as to this. Harold further suggested that it might be wise to hold an open discussion and let these people give expression to their views, and Bill said, "Yes—it might be a good idea." Harold, feeling that Bill did not have much sympathy for those who did not agree with him, said that he thought every tolerance should be extended to the differences of opinion on the part of Forum members, and Bill said, "Yes, but it's pretty hard to be tolerant with some of them. I just can't get along with a few of them. They don't like me and I'm having a hard time trying to like them. But even Christ had his troubles with members of his organization."

Bill, illustrating his idea of the need for compromising the truths contained in Urantia, referred to Christ's conversion of the prostitutes. He seemed to think that Christ's attitude was the condescension of a superior Being in recognizing these fallen humans, and by so much indicated Bill's own superior subconscious attitude with relation to his purported possession of the truth and his intended dissemination.

August 12, 1942

In a frank talk with Clyde Bedell, Harold learned that Clyde had been concerned through the years with the proposed nature of the organization and with the obviously growing dictatorial tendencies of both Dr. S. and Bill Jr. When Harold outlined his publication ideas and conviction that no organization was needed to disseminate the truth contained in the Urantia Book, Mr. Bedell said instantly that this whole plan was sound and automatically reduced all previously existing vulnerable points to a minimum. He said that he could be counted on to support any action which might be taken by Forum members to bring about needed changes, and that he felt if any petition to the Sadlers should be rejected that said Forum members should resign in a body from any organization participation. He said he felt their private endorsement of the book, unallied with, and unprejudiced by, affiliation with an organization, could accomplish much more good and reach a far greater number of people.

Bedell said it was apparent that the Sadlers were preparing to take every step to insure ownership, which would forever keep the truth from being free. He stated that he felt the publication of any pamphlet purporting to authoritatively explain the phenomena behind this spiritual revelation would be utterly wrong and rob the book of its true revelatory spirit. Moreover, existence of this pamphlet and partial, unsatisfactory human explanation would prevent the book, even in future generations, from being regarded as a true revelation, uncontaminated by man, of the nature and origin of the Bible itself. For the same reason, Bedell said he could now see the validity of Harold's contention that no organization should exist, since the organization would attempt to repeat the mistake made by the pamphlet in explaining the source of the Book of Urantia, which would be subject to the attacks of ridicule and disbelief.

He was in favor of the book's being published at a much more popular price, and said he had always opposed the fixing of what must amount to a prohibitive price to the majority of humans on the Book of Urantia. One's ability to receive the truth should never be limited to his economic standing. Bedell said he had tried to offer many carefully thought-out suggestions through the years, which had not been heeded, and that he was convinced that no real consideration was going to be shown to the Forum membership regardless of the fact that these same members had contributed through their monies and their services to the very creation of this book itself. He said this very fact might enable the Forum to take a stand later which would legally be supported if necessary and enforce consideration as to their deserved status.

Harold said, "I am not so sure but what we have established some rights here which we have not realized and which we can act upon to help clarify this situation."

CLYDE BEDELL to HAROLD SHERMAN

The FAIR Store, Executive Offices
State, Adams and Dearborn Streets
Chicago, August 13, 1942

Dear Harold:

I am enclosing a carbon of the memorandum dated October 30, 1933.[2] It will cover only a small fraction of the area you have since covered so thoroughly.

I found with this paper, penciled memoranda of a little talk made perhaps the same year or a year later, reading, "If I can do so without raising your blood pressure unduly, I would like to repeat my annual warning that the present proposals are for something which will appear to clear-reasoning people to be selfish and bigoted—something which is afraid to trust itself to propagation by reason."

Also, a query as to what dispositions of assets at the end of the copyright period. Still another, "We must take care lest the doctrine suffer by the apparent intolerances of those dedicated to its dissemination." Also "Provision for trials and expulsions repugnant."

Please preserve the enclosure for me.

Yours,
Clyde Bedell

FORUM CALENDAR *August 13, 1942*

Dinner at Hull House—Winnie, Mary, Bucklins, Harold & Martha.

HARRY LOOSE to HAROLD SHERMAN

Monterey Park, August 14, 1942

Dear Harold:-

I am again writing in haste and so this letter will be "spotty" and not very smooth in composition or expression.

Enclosed herein please find returned the carbon copy of your Sadler letter for your file. It is a very excellent continuation of your first letter. It needs no more comment than did your first letter. It is truthful and accurate in its charges and recommendations. Fight for what you know to be right with every weapon at your command. It is your present task. Do not FEAR. Sadler is highly vulnerable. His whole position is pitiful. You are much stronger in your position—and very

[2] See Appendix B.

much stronger entrenched than what you are now aware. Sadler is so open to attack and from so many directions. Openly or otherwise, remind him at every opportunity of his repeated statement, "I am only the Custodian of the papers. I do not own them." This statement is the real truth—and has been so often impressed upon him. He knows this so very well—but he has a convenient memory—with ability to forget that which is personally distasteful. Please know that 76% of the Forum are very tired of the dictatorial and possessive attitude and "ownership" complex that has been evidencing stronger and stronger in the past few years' period. And 70% of the Forum think with you.

The Forum reconvenes on my birthday—Sept. 13th. Demand the floor at the Forum at the first, or at some of the very earliest meetings. It cannot be refused you. If in any way dictatorially interfered with BY ANYBODY you have civil law to fall back upon—even the threat of it would suffice in any situation. Vigorously and ceaselessly attack every wrong. If necessary, send copies of your two letters to the entire Forum membership. Attack, attack and attack. You will profit MUCH by this—Forumites long wishing to escape the domination will see their pathway clear. Witness Christy. What better proof.

NONE of the Haleses should have anything to do with the continuance of the Book matter beyond the activity of any other Forum member. This is definite and positive—and beyond further consideration. I strongly advise you to avoid them socially as far as decently possible. Any HALES association in furtherance of the BOOK beyond that of any other Forum member should be attacked and attacked and attacked. 90% of the Forum membership dislike and distrust the Haleses—though you might not at once get such honest expression—but I KNOW.

Get on the Seven—while you can—it has not yet opened to you but quite some of the future lies in the usefulness of the Seven.

I am glad that the value of your Diary is at last being arrived at. It will be the eventual only true record of these early times. Can you not realize?? Do not let it be known that you are keeping such a Diary—or that you anticipate writing a book eventually.

Seek counsel with your TA. Lean heavily upon and draw strength from Martha. Do not wander from her mentally. I cannot make it strong enough or positive enough. DO NOT BE AFRAID. Do not become close to—nor in any way under the influence of, the Haleses. I warn you. Avoid them whenever possible. At last resort, in the possible eventual, the Court may have to adjust some of these matters. Such a Contract as you describe could be halted, and voided, by any Forum member in Court—alleging his non-understanding of what was being done in Forum voting. The Forum was not of Sadler's choice but WAS A DICTATED THING. The Forum as a collective body—and individually—has rights in Law that Sadler's dictum cannot dispossess.

I want you to know now that you, personally, are not liked by the Haleses. You may rest assured that Sadler has long ago fled there for comfort, solace, and advice—and support—during this period. Hales has read both your letters. The Haleses fear you.

So much has been done for you. You have been shown so much evidence. And yet you have periods of being the "doubting Thomas." I should not censure you for this, for Joshua ben Joseph had his periods of non-full-understanding—and doubts—and fears—in his early period—and he much sought guidance and strength and reassurance from his Father in prayer—and he listened to and advised with his TA. He was sorely tempted by the flesh and the (D)evil also.

I, too, the same as you, falter and fear at times also—and the way grows long and hard and stormy and I fail to understand. Yes, there are things that, to my mind, you should additionally know. Maybe these things will come to you. I hope and pray so. I do not know. And because I do not know, I cannot definitely promise you. I really have no right to continue to try to even advise you in any way. You know far better than I what your *duty* now is. You have a fine mind and abilities far beyond mine. You have Martha with her understanding—and her spiritual strength. I stumbled the long pathway alone. Yes, you will make mistakes. Every prophet and "see'r," every "holy man"—without exception—from the beginning down to now has made them—you are not any exception—and I certainly have not been an exception. Time will teach you so much more than I could possibly impart. You are in a present position where you have to make decisions on your own responsibility. There is no one else. The great weight of light for future generations rests upon your shoulders right now. You know it, too. Are you afraid??

I very probably write you "too long" letters. Letters that you may not even read in full—or that leave no impression upon you. Please read this slowly and understandingly the second or third time so that it gets to you fully. Martha, please cooperate in making this happen.

There is a limit to these letters—I tell you that I am not going to be here very long to write them.

I get confused too—and there are many times when I do not see my pathway clearly. I have nowhere to go but to my prayers and my TA. My way has been very hard and bitter too. I am not complaining, please remember, but only trying to evidence to you that you should not look forward to a soft and easy pathway in this matter. Was the pathway for Joshua ben Joseph easy? John was beheaded. And he was not the only one. Some suffered death by fire. Cleodotus died a martyr's death. I write too long—I try to help you too much—I wonder if I am making a mistake. . . .

Last Sunday's magazine section of the *Examiner* here was very interesting with its story about *Thoughts Through Space.*

Love to both you and Martha from Ma and I.

6

"Forum Data" and Apocrypha

The following passages have been drawn from the first of the Shermans' fifteen notebooks. The first entries are undated; the dated entries range from July 27, 1942 to August 14, 1942.

* * *

Forum data (Bill, Dr. S. and other Forumites)

Original seven — H.J.L. —

Next seven? Dr. William Sadler, Dr. Lena Sadler, Mr. & Mrs. Kellogg (Dr. Lena's sister)

Thurston (Wilfred? Kellogg)

First message — "And, as I slept, I dreamed."[1] (Bill)

First contact with subject — 1911

Formation of Forum Group — 1926?-1942 about 200 members

Passed by Midwayers for purpose of developing questions

Names of Forumites *complete* list. How chosen/sponsored — Faith

[1] From John Bunyan's *The Pilgrim's Progress (From This World to That Which Is to Come, Delivered Under the Simultude of a Dream)*, a Christian allegory from 1678: "As I walk'd through the wilderness of this world, I lighted on a certain place, where was a den; and I laid me down in that place to sleep: And as I slept I dreamed a Dream."

Little *social* contact among group until 1942
Formation of 70[2] — 1940. Monday alternate
Formation of Bill's study group. (Interest lacking last 2-3 years.) Alternate Wed.

Forum services officially dispensed with June 7, 1942. (Paper read June 6th at picnic at Haleses'. Angels of Churches approve; Angels of Progress not satisfied. Prediction made concerning possible disunity among members since the overall protection of harmony of purpose was being removed and they were out on their own.)

Forum picnics
"Apocrypha" papers
Committees appointed by Dr. S. (under some pressure by certain members)

Music — "Christy," Mrs. Bucklin, Mr. Rawson
Flowers —

Date for "plating" permission
Study of church creeds begun
Years covered in actual book preparation
Rewritten 3 times. How done

Statement made which aroused inappropriate laugh re Jews. Reaction of Forum watched and statement withdrawn.[3] Questions could be asked verbally or mentally or written. Every question clearly formulated answered.

Selection of Sadler building—its adaptability and location

Description of subject—businessman uninterested in philosophy. Wife came to Sadler for help with husband who did unusual things in sleep—number of witnesses—write with both hands and speak at

[2] The Seventy was a group of Forumites selected and led by Dr. Sadler that met regularly. According to Sadler's unpublished essay, "History of the Urantia Movement" (1960), it was formed in April 1939 and initially contained seventy members.

[3] Mark Kulieke, son of Forumite Warren Kulieke, wrote on p. 17 of his 1994 booklet, *Birth of a Revelation*: "Other papers were edited after being read to the Forum. For instance, one of the papers stated that the apostle Nathaniel had a good sense of humor for a Jew. At this comment the members of the Forum chuckled. The next time they got this paper from the safe, they discovered the phrase 'for a Jew' was deleted."

same time. Subject entirely unaware of phenomena. On occasion all asked to withdraw for a moment while certain papers were destroyed.

1942. Up until 3 years ago (until demise of Dr. Lena?) discussions were informal and enjoyed by all. At that time they were told papers were complete and Bill discouraged further outside reading and research. Since that time papers were revised again but discussions have never been free and open as before, and Bill (who had said he would never become a teacher) became more and more pedantic.

Dr. Lena — died of cancer 1939 (Aug.). Found sitting in her chair at 4 a.m. by Doctor, who had no idea she would go so quickly—expected her to live until after Xmas. A few days later came communication that she had passed straight through to Mansion Worlds (as Reserve Corps of Destiny member) and did not have to wait till general roll call.

Lincoln — Possible Reserve Corps of Destiny member. Had unusual dreams which he wrote down (and which made his wife Mary Todd think him crazy) which were sealed and filed in Springfield, Ill., to be opened in _ years after his death. (1947)

Young people come to Forum a few times and then drop out. No appeal to them as presented.

Other groups possibly made aware of same material (Omaha)

Mrs. Hales sufferer from depressions - longtime patient of Doctor.

Bill — ran away from home at 15. Father afraid to cross him ever since. Stubborn traits still persist, notably inability to get out of bed in a.m. and down to work. Has developed Benzedrine habit for stimulating mind. Nervously picks finger- and toenails below "quick."

Dr. William Sadler:

Book in hands of Revelatory Commission until, about two years ago, control was given over to Angels of Progress for next 100 years. Angels of Churches had hoped for that assignment. Thirty-third lieutenant (no name given) of Angels of Progress in immediate charge. Nov. 1941. "Sonsovocton" head of Angels of Progress. "33rd" a Seraphington graduate previously in charge of similar revelations on other planets. Introduced by D.E.F., secondary midwayer, working with Revelatory Commissioners. Two-way conversations carried on and advice given from time to time.

Kelloggs: History. Dinner at their home with Ruth (7/27/42)

Subject discovered 1911

Forum founded 1926

Question period closed May 31, 1942

Dr. Lena died Aug. 9, 1939

Mrs. K. stated H. J. L. never was present when subject produced information. Both Mr. and Mrs. K. stated they were (always) present.

Bucklin: History.

Contact Commissioners subject, Dr. Lena and William Sadler, Mr. and Mrs. Kellogg, Christy and Bill. If any one of these dies, orders are given for book to be published *18 months* later. This was given ( ) years ago. When Dr. Lena passed on, a Midwayer was commissioned to take her place and order was postponed for future emergency.

Bill Sadler (7/30/42):

(Story of Tabamantia visit, part of apocrypha papers which are not to be included in U. Book:)

Tabamantia (apocrypha) Sept. 13, 1924 makes visit to this planet via receiving station at Big Tree (Grizzly Bear) [*Ed. note:* Grizzly Giant] for first time in 40,000 years. Chicago group one of 978 (sleeping contacts) waiting in preparedness for this visit. Sixty-eight "projectile contacts unannounced" arrived, and as each came the "contact" was shocked as though a high-voltage current fairly lifted him from the bed. Tabamantia himself arrived. He is the sovereign supervisor of all experimental worlds, having once been a mortal on the very first planet on which there was a rebellion in all the super universes. He delivered a withering indictment against the methods of the Angels of the Churches which permitted the existing situation on Urantia and the almost total loss of the Adamic strain. He especially praised the TAs.

In commenting on the work of the (contact commissioner) group, he stated they were no better than other similar groups but were selected by the first assistant to the governor for good reasons (possibly the fact that one of the contact commissioners (Christy) could take shorthand).

Tabamantia's visit was such a physical and nervous strain for subject that only first half of his one-night visit was held in Chicago. Second half was given to Omaha group.

Five days before Tabamantia reached Urantia, an outpost stationed somewhere in the universe perceived the presence of the Tabamantia vehicle, recognized by its insignia its enormous importance, and computed by its direction that it was headed for Urantia. So the outpost, who had been on guard at this station for 700 years, flashed the news to Urantia. There all the preparations were made to have the various contact groups ready for the use of the visitor, who arrived on a Sat. (9/13/24), at about 6 p.m. (Grizzly Bear). There he was greeted by a great host of seraphim and heavenly creatures standing in the shape of a cross (Urantia the World of the Cross) and singing somewhat the equivalent of "All Hail the Power of Jesus' Name." There registrations and speeches took place, and it was not until 10 p.m. that he announced himself in Chicago, and not until then was the Chicago group aware that they were to be chosen. During all this momentous happening a mortal man slept quietly at the base of this very tree.

Tabamantia also criticized the Angels of Progress for permitting mankind to so far advance in material inventions that mechanically he was far outstripping his mental and spiritual development, and *absolutely ordered* no further inventions to be given. Mankind *must* labor to survive. The finest stocks had been permitted by these mechanical means to destroy each other while the inferior races were allowed to multiply. Had not intended white race to exterminate fine red man. Regretted black man had been brought to this country though they were race least apt to intermarry. The order intended on this earth was a caste system of violet at top to black race at bottom. And in government a *republic*, as first founded in America, not a monarchy nor a democracy (domination of mediocrity).

Tabamantia paid great tribute to *TAs*. This included in Book of Urantia. [*Ed. note:* See 108:3.5-6.]

Surprise visit from entity—*"student visitor"*—from a distant planet on which beings have no bodies, hence no size nor features such as eyesight. Thus they do not see color! They do not die as we do and have no recollection of birth. Their only concept is *knowing*. Many of their order die permanently in trespassing beyond the limits of their own energy sources. They have no TAs. They do not breathe.

Cardif—[of] an order of dual-personality beings able to use two-brained subject for registration on this planet.

Broadcast from capital of Nebadon to all sleeping "contacts" and all orders of beings in charge of all inhabited planets: "Word has just been received of the arrival on one of the outermost planets of the super universe, of an ambassador from the capital of a hitherto unknown and undiscovered universe." He had been in transit 500,000 years, and a like number of years more would transpire before he arrived in Nebadon. This fact being established, a Melchizedek Son was immediately dispatched as an ambassador from Nebadon to this universe. It will require a million years for him to reach this universe and he will arrive at *their* capital 500,000 years after their ambassador reaches Nebadon. Great joy was expressed that another link had been established with fellow creatures so far, far away, akin to those residing in Nebadon.

Everything which passes through the brain is recorded there whether conscious or unconscious. Hence Higher Intelligences can read the records of past events in a contact's brain. *Dual intelligences* (both male and female) use *both* sides of brain of subject. Various "circles" of brain activity are used by various entities.

No knowledge was of value to this planet unless it first passed through the mind of a mortal.

John the Potter (one of the four-and-twenty elders) and ABC and DEF in charge of subject. Twenty-four elders in charge of this planet (Machiventa Melchisedek, Moses, Enoch, etc.), 16 of which are full-fledged members and active, the other 8 in reserve.

Subject's TA had served six times previously. Subject has no knowledge of events except as related to him later by others. In beginning subject wrote with alternate hands. (Produced sealed notebooks fully written.) Later was used as a speaking voice by Intelligences.

Bill (7/31/42):

Bright and Morning Star of Avalon from a neighboring universe—visits Urantia (Chicago) in February 1925. Had the same relationship to Avalon as Gabriel to Nebadon—representing the Second Great Source and Center. He found and had so recorded by the various orders that Tabamantia's indictments were *just*, but, considering the unusual destiny of mortals here and the numerous mistakes which had been made, a universal viewpoint rather than a planetary viewpoint should be taken, and hence he was adding universal mercy and tempering the previous indictment. He was a most gracious and benign influence, maintaining he was ordered for this service because, coming from *another* universe, he was able to take an impersonal and hence impartial viewpoint.

Preparations for his arrival were not as extensive as for Tabamantia—even so there were 72 sleeping contacts ready, one of which, however, was not usable as he was asleep in a car. His communication was divided between Chicago and Omaha, as with Tabamantia. He stated the midwayers had been of irreplaceable service and were most necessary as the connecting link with man. Only one of them was permitted to leave with Jesus to become one of the four-and-twenty elders of this planet. The others remained to serve mankind and had not slept for 37,000 years, since their creation. They are to continue here in service till Urantia is settled in Light and Life.

Bill (8/4/42):

Student visitors not permitted after actual book revelation work was begun, but previous to that time they were in constant attendance. Their remarks very enlightening as to how observers look at our planet. One spoke of being on a planet where the storms (thunder) were so terrific that they took great toll of life, particularly during a 30-day season when everything without protection perished. They erected homes or shelters consisting of seven layers of asbestos. Between each layer were gas chambers. Our thunder was the mere whisper of an echo of theirs. These intelligences were non-breathers.

Another student came from a world of small, 11-inch entities and he was amazed at our size. Remarked that he wished *their* planet had "*animals*" indwelt by T.A.'s. He had been experimenting in the development of a form of life called Spornagia, very faithful animals and intelligent, even able to talk.

One visitor remarked that this was most interesting planet ever visited, containing as it did animals indwelt by mystery beings, most of whom are not aware of this presence and who live in such (sublime) uncertainty! Not doubting for the past million years these mystery beings existed, he nevertheless had never seen evidence of any until his being brought in contact with the indwelt mind of this mortal subject on Urantia. After listening to the detached TA of this sleeping contact he declared he would rather hear this mystery being talk than God himself.

The *TA* in question, having been granted permission to address the little mortal group in attendance, made a stirring plea to those assembled to communicate a message to the subject of his indwelling upon the return of this subject to mortal consciousness. TA explained that he probably would be unable to speak direct to the soul of his "betrothment" until after he had completed his life in the flesh, and his entreaty was that the mortal of his indwelling not fail him; that he accept greater and greater guidance, and assuring him that he, the TA, would be attending him, through whatever was to come, to the very end with the most sympathetic, understanding and loving devotion.[4] When the TA had finished speaking, ABC the midwayer, who had set up the lines of communication, remarked ecstatically, "Wasn't he wonderful! You know, I really saw him that time as he bridged over from the fourth to the third circle in this mortal's consciousness. I had to watch awfully close. It was just a flash. I've never doubted the existence of these wonderful beings but it's seldom you can ever catch any sight of them."

A *Trinitized Son* (about 1922) awakens to his first consciousness on this, 606 of Satania, World of Cross, the world of his identification. John the Potter this night instructed ABC (midwayer in charge of communication) to stand by for an unusual contact on the 10 o'clock draught, a time apparently when many sleeping contacts are held in readiness for whatever service may be necessary. On this occasion, a new type of being presented himself to this mortal group introducing himself by saying, "Who am I? Who are you?" And when told where he was, he seemed to get his bearings and said, "There are really three of us—my father, mother and myself—but you see only two. One of my parents is invisible but whether it is my father or my mother, I do not know. My parents, of a high spiritual development, elected to participate in an act of creation and so petitioned. Their oneness of purpose in the desire to create a new trinitized idea for service on the worlds of time and space having been passed upon, they were set aside by themselves and protected by a band of seraphic hosts

[4] A similar account appears in the Urantia Book, in 110:7.0.

while they undertook the majestic task of bringing forth a new sublime creature. Many couples, no matter how spiritual, often fail in this attempted reproduction, but my parents remained in creative meditation for the period of a million years, endeavoring to so synchronize their singleness of purpose and spiritual devotion to this idea as to bring forth this new being. When it seemed as though their heroic and concentrated effort was to meet with failure, there was suddenly a great flash of light, and I stepped forth, but one of my parents, in this indescribable moment of creation, became invisible and we are now co-existent with each other yet still possessed of our individual identities. I am here now, having been brought to the World of the Cross for purposes of identification and for taking the oath of loyalty and service required of all Trinitized Sons."

ABC here interrupted to state that lines were being laid straight from Salvington (central universe) [*sic*] so that the oath might be administered by a seven-times-incarnated Son. There was then heard the voice of such a Son (unnamed but might have been Michael of Nebadon). The swearing-in ceremony was transcendently awesome. The last pledge had to do with the acceptance by the Trinitized Son of a possible mandate to surrender his own life on behalf of lower creatures whose uplifting would be placed in his charge. In the making of such a sacrifice, it was understood that it would mean complete severance from this 3-in-1 attachment with his parents and his entering into a state of complete isolation. It was emphasized, before this Trinitized Son was given opportunity to take this pledge, that no other oaths of allegiance meant anything unless he should be ready and willing to subscribe to this final condition. The new Trinitized Son gave a soul-stirring and unfaltering answer and then was welcomed as a full-fledged member of his order of beings. ABC: "The last time I saw this happen was 3000 years ago."

It was remarked here that Bestowal Sons serve from 6 to 604 years, but on the latter planet everyone accepted the Son and it was approaching Light and Life. Each Son worked with his hands in some *builder* work on the planet of his bestowal, such as carpenter, potter, tiller of soil and "transparency." (604—This Son left a glass replica of the mansion world to which they were going, to each of his apostles.)

Contact group—Special delivery of special instructions—During the controversy over the Jesus papers, the need for special instructions to one of the contact commissioners arose and this communication was delivered direct to her (commissioner in question) by unseen hands and dropped from mid-air on her desk. It was a startling experience which was humorously commented on by the midwayer at the next "session."

(*Bill's attitude.* Stated his intentions of reading to us apocrypha from 1924—back to early beginnings, parts of which had never been read outside the original group before. This over several nights of reading.)

Celestial Being of high development stopped off here en route to Uversa to pay a visit to the World of the Cross. He was highly developed in Chemistry and was going to teach on Uversa to repay in small measure a great favor bestowed by Lanaforge many years ago. Asked why he had come by way of this little planet, he said, "Why, Urantia is known throughout all Nebadon as the world where the Creator Son lived his 7th bestowal life and was crucified by his own creatures." Asked if some of the mortal group then present would see him on Uversa, he replied that they might and if so would be walking through his laboratories, and that with his back turned he would turn about and in one glance the memory of this earth visit would return to him, as it would to them, and they would recognize each other without a word being spoken.

Anniversaries are real events in the higher realms. At such times special favors are granted to the ascending intelligences.

One celestial being recorded he was here on the anniversary of his mortal birth which occurred millions of years ago. He referred to a mortal associate of that far-distant past and said that should he desire it, as a special birthday bestowal, he could have the lines of communication laid to any place in the universe and reach and talk to this friend of so long ago.

Student visitors have usually served hundreds of thousands of years before they visit other planets, systems, etc., except under specially conducted observation tours.

Dr. Sadler (8/7/42):

Student visitors were frequent welcome guests at meetings with subject, and on occasion they would carry on a *private* interview with a *single* mortal commissioner while remaining members were sent from room. These were held in *strictest confidence* until apparently two of these individuals talked or confided in each other following such a personal talk about 15 years ago. Since that time there have been *no* private talks, indicating the student visitors had meant exactly what they said when they used the word "confidential." The orders had been disobeyed and the privilege thereafter withdrawn.

Bill (8/11/42):

Thought Adjusters, having previous experience, use that experience on their present wards. John's TA had previously guided a painter so John received inspiration in form of pictures.

(*Re sleeping subject*) Subject at first dreamed dreams and wrote them down on awakening—"And as I slept I dreamed." 1911. "I *seemed* to be taken by a guide in full regalia before a tremendous structure near an ocean," etc. As these dreams continued they took the form of automatic writing and spoken word. He would write with both hands and speak at the same time. He would find fully written pages on awakening. Finally he was taken to Dr. Sadler for examination, and original contact commissioners would then be called in to witness actual phenomena.

(*Types of Contacts*)

Midwayers - ABC. DEF.

John the Potter   Nathaniel

Thought Adjusters - attached and detached - (*I have come with the Battle Plan of Verdun!*)

All authorities for Book of Urantia

Visiting students

Tabamantia - Bright and Morning Star (?)

Sonsovocton   Angels of Progress - Churches - Seraphim

Clearinghouse for old "rehearsal rolls" never consummated in fact and "talked out"

Soul (evolving) of subject. "Ten o'clock draught"

Trinitized Son

Christy (8/14/42):

Emma Christensen [Christy] came to Chicago Nov. 1921. Got position in present office (Bankers –). In 1922 she was struck by a car and knocked unconscious; came to in hospital with Dr. S. working over her. Reported at his office at intervals till completely well. Dr. Lena became interested, and Christy divided her time between her own room and their home, eventually taking Bill's room (he being in the Marines) permanently.

In 1923 the first general forum group met for free Sunday afternoon discussion of religion and philosophy, with Dr. Lena as hostess. This became so popular, as each brought his friends, that they moved to second floor and group pooled funds to buy chairs. For a year they carried membership cards and were then told not to repeat any of the "messages." Meanwhile, the first paper (on the Universal Father) had been received (1924) and read and discussed, arousing many oral questions, and were then told to carefully formulate and write them. Out of these questions came the first (56) papers, which they thought then was the whole story. Later came all the Jesus papers and an expansion of the first group.

7

"BATTLE PLANS"

FORUM CALENDAR *August 14, 1942*

Drive to Marion, Ind., with Christy and Dr. Sadler. Leave 12:30 arrive 5:15.

DIARY *August 14-16, 1942*

Christy, Doctor Sadler, Harold and Martha left for Indiana at 12:30, Aug. 14th, reaching Marion at a little after 5 via our car. On the drive to Marion, Harold again stated to the Doctor that a large number of Forum members were expressing different views and that there was a confusion of ideas as to the Forum's relationship to the coming Urantia organization, and that he thought the Doc would be surprised at the number which held such views. Christy spoke up and said, "Poppy, I think Harold's right," but Doc S. said, "Oh, no. I know what they think. They don't misunderstand this relationship at all."

The Doctor then decided to have a shave before he went out to the Davises, so we dropped him at a barber shop and waited in the car till he was through. This gave us a short time to talk with Christy alone.[1] During this time she told us that she was in *full accord* with Harold's letters. She stated the Doctor was going to be terribly crushed by the Forum group attitude which she knew existed. Her advice was, Harold having once gone on record, to sit back and let the Doctor come around in his own way. She said, "I'm confident he will get specific

[1] This may have been the occasion in which Christy shared her personal history as detailed on pp. 126-127.

instructions and that he will follow them even though opposite to his views. He went along with the revelatory commission and was surprised when the Angels of Progress took over, but has gone along with them."

Christy felt that Harold and Martha were supposed to come along to open up the way, and suggested presentation of ideas in three separate letters: first, publication plans; second, elimination of pamphlet explaining source; third, organization views, so that each issue could be taken up and considered on an individual basis, unprejudiced by involvement with the others. She said the Higher Intelligences pass on issues when definitely stated, but waited for humans to develop the issues and ideas first. They never suggest the way.

On this night, while in Marion, Indiana, Harold had a vivid dream of a documentary scroll being held before him. He got up, using a pencil and pad from Martha's pocketbook, and wrote at high speed and terrific energy the record of his dream, "Battle Plans for Book of Urantia." Martha spoke of it to Christy the following day and showed Christy a copy of it privately on the return trip to Chicago on 8/16/42.

* * *

On the night of August 14th, 1942, while on a visit to Marion, Indiana, Harold M. Sherman was shown the following document in his sleep. He was then awakened and instructed to record it, word for word, while the image of it still remained in consciousness.

This is an exact transcript:

BATTLE PLANS for the BOOK of URANTIA

Preamble

The Book of Urantia presents the general trend picture of the Universe, leaving it to evolving man to work out his specific destiny here.

*

Man is not to be coerced into believing, neither is he to be drawn from any other fold.

When even a candle light burns in darkness it may be seen from afar and attract all who are lost and wandering to it.

How much more so, then, when a Great Light shines out in the black wilderness of man's own spiritual groping!

Man-made organization cannot, in itself, enable man to find God.

If this had been so, all men would have found God long ere this.

But the Spirit of Truth, the Guardian Angel and his Thought Adjuster, the organization working with man's evolving soul, can and will enable man to find God once the true Light exists in the Book of Urantia to show him the way.

Even the prostitute inherently knows the *right*, but no earthly organization can cause her to *do* the right, nor will it knowingly accept her for the Kingdom, since human creatures prefer to be saved in company of beings of their own choosing.

To God, the Father, the prostitute is as close to Him as the most righteous of His human children.

God has already set up an organization not built by human hands for her to join, and when she has united her temporarily lost soul with the Spirit of Truth which is being constantly and lovingly poured out upon her, she is *then* led gently by her Guardian Angel to the place of indwelling of her Thought Adjuster, and spiritual communion takes place.

Heretofore man has sought, on earth, by the setting up of organizations, to do the work which belongs to God.

Man is an organization *in* and *of* himself.

When he organizes *outside* himself, he debases that which he seeks and deprives himself, more often than not, of the spiritual joining together of his inner organization of body, mind and spirit, since he has been led and ensnared to believe that the Truth and its interpretation exist in a worldly organization outside himself.

But Christ Michael has repeatedly said to his erring creature, man: "My Truths are not of this world, nor is my Kingdom."

Yet man, as did the Jews, still tries to organize the Truth and place it between walls of human organization, thinking that it may the better be preserved.

Can a light shine as brightly and as distantly in the darkness when walls enclose it?

Do not wall out the Light from your brother of whatever race, or color, or creed may be his evolvement.

Place the Light, instead, within his reach and let him be drawn *to* it as beasts of the wilderness seek out a warming fire on a cold and desolate night.

Such beasts feel the glow within themselves.

Would they feel it if the fire were walled away from them?

How can anything stand beside the Truth and why should it be surrounded and enshackled?

For what divine purpose?

To appease and delight man's vanity?

So that man may say to all the world: "Look at *me!* I discern the Truth better than my fellows! Come to *me* and *I* will give you Light!"

But mortal man is *not* the Truth; nor can he discern it for others.

A Great Light has now come to earth through man; let this Light then shine *through* man *in* and *of itself.*

For man to interpose himself between the Light and his fellow creatures, who would receive it, is to weaken, diffuse and cut off the truth-shining rays of this Light as they otherwise might reach, unadulterated, the human soul and find lodgment there.

God is in His heaven and all will be well with the world if God's work of reclaiming man, is left to God.

Man's acceptance of the Truth does not rest upon organization. If this were so, the world would not now be in such crucial need of more Light.

More organization simply means greater diffusion and confusion of Light.

Let the Book of Urantia shine out upon all the world as the Spirit of Truth now shines out, for all to see and perceive.

Let the evolving soul of each human reach out and unite with this Light, and not an organization *shielding* this Light.

The Light will not be received by any two humans alike. Then how can a body of humans equally, and without adulteration, dispense the Light to others?

God is the Great Dispenser and the Light is to exist *in* man, not entrapped by organizations *outside* of man.

Man's soul cannot be activated from without.

This delicate adjustment must be made by the Spirit of Truth and the Thought Adjuster working together in answer to man's free will desire.

Man-made organization can never accomplish this.

Ponder well the admonitions herein spoken, for the Truth that can make man free is now at hand if man will KEEP FREE THE TRUTH.

* * *

FORUM CALENDAR *August 15, 1942*

Jo Davis dinner party and evening.

August 16, 1942

Jo Davis lunch and return to Chicago by 6 p.m.

HAROLD SHERMAN to HARRY LOOSE

Chicago, August 17, 1942

Dear Harry:

As you will see by the enclosed, your letter, arriving this Monday morning, upon our return from Marion with Sadler and Christy, was a CONFIRMATION THEREOF . . . "Battle Plans for the Book of Urantia" and you say FIGHT . . . ATTACK and ATTACK and ATTACK!

Things are beginning to happen. I am receiving my instructions. This document seems to me UNANSWERABLE. How can Sadler or *any* human stand before it? I am getting offers of support from prominent members of the Forum highly regarded by the Sadlers . . . which will shock them when they are confronted by these "old faithfuls."

Christy told us privately, on the trip, that she knew Doctor was going to be hurt and almost crushed by realization of how Forum members felt one of these days. Dr. S. stated to us: "I know how every Forum member feels; you can't tell me . . . and the majority are in favor of the present organization." To my statement that I felt most members have been in awe of him, consecrated to the task at hand, and have withheld expressing their real views . . . he brushed it aside, unwilling to believe it or consider it.

It is significant to me that this message I received was headed, "Battle Plans" . . . I am not afraid of the fight . . . and would much prefer fighting it out in the privacy of this group than before the whole world when it would be too late to prevent great impairment of the Truth.

You may be sure, Harry, that I have caught the torch you have flung to me and I will seek constant illumination in order that I may carry it as it should be carried.

I am forever amazed at your *knowing* back in Marion of the part I was destined to play, so many years hence.

It gave me strange feelings to be back again in Marion, the scene of our first earthly meeting . . . and to be there, this time, with the doctor and Christy!! The Davises remember you pleasantly . . . and we are not involving your name in this situation, of course. We are very close-mouthed about inner developments but are now talking quite frankly to different Forum members we feel we can approach, awakening their own convictions.

A group of Forum members want to canvass all those they feel might be receptive, and petition the doctor to open the whole organization subject for discussion at the first reconvened meeting, on your birthday.

I am seeing Russell Bucklin for lunch and "Dent" Karle for dinner this evening about this matter. While I probably will have to bear the brunt eventually . . . it strengthens my position to have strong support from the field.

I am putting in some airmail stamps for your use . . . since, when you feel prompted to write me, during this time just ahead, I would like to get the inspiration of your letters a little quicker than ordinary mail which I find is often delayed appreciably due to defense shipments, etc. Love from us both to you both . . . I'll keep you advised.

FORUM CALENDAR *August 17, 1942*

Dent Karle dinner here. (Elsie unable to come last minute.)

DIARY *August 17, 1942*

Lunch with Russell Bucklin, La Salle Hotel. Harold was advised by Bucklin that Mrs. Githens, who has been greatly concerned lest the Sadlers plan organization of another church, feels the Karles, particularly Mrs. Karle, are too staunch friends of the Doctor's to be approached too quickly with respect to new publication and Urantia society plans. She seemed to think Mrs. Karle to be so emotionally attached to the Doctor as to even go to him privately against her husband's counsel and advise the Doctor of the growing differences of opinion. Bucklin thus suggested, having respect for Mrs. Githens's evaluation, that Harold use caution in discussing the subject with the Karles, and expressed relief that Mrs. Karle could not keep her dinner engagement this evening with us. Bucklin stated that Karle had voiced great concern over the fact that the Sadlers had not taken Forum members more into confidence in regard to organization plans, and that he also felt Bill's immature leadership might later prove a great public liability.

Referring to a visit he had last night with the Rawsons and another Forum member by the name of Harry Beatty [*Ed. note:* Beattie] whom he characterized as a "true Alpheus twin," Bucklin said, "I found Charlie Rawson just busting to talk Urantia, and during the course of an automobile drive he told me of several recent talks he had had with Dr. S. in which the main subject of discussion was Harold Sherman." Rawson said the Doctor described Sherman as a promoter and said that while he had many good ideas, he had a lot to learn and that he'd learn in time.

[Bucklin continued:] "Rawson then turned to me and asked me point blank, 'What do you think of this fellow Sherman?' And I replied, 'I think he's got many splendid ideas that Dr. S. would do well to seriously consider.' Then I made a few follow-up comments in explanation of this statement, which led Rawson to ask, 'You don't mean that you think the Sadlers intend to set up a new church?' And I said, 'I meant just that.'" This thought appeared to shock Rawson and his wife as well as Harry Beattie. Rawson now began to see clearly for the first time that if this happened he would one day be placed in the public position of having to choose between his church and the Urantia society, and that church members of all other denominations as well as ministers would have to do likewise.

Rawson's wife is a clearer thinker than he and his greatest asset. She expressed immediate concern, and Rawson was not slow in following up her comment by saying he had had no such concept of the Urantia Brotherhood and that he thought it would be most unwise for the Sadlers, especially Bill, to be at the head of such an organization. "When I saw how these three were reacting I then decided to really give them something to think about and said, 'I had it on unimpeachable authority that Bill had stated he intended to occupy a high place and that he would even challenge Higher Sources if any advice ever came through that seemed to contradict the present plans of organization.'" Confronted with this information, the Rawsons were considerably sobered as was Mr. Beattie, and the opposition to one Harold Sherman seemed to have somewhat lessened.

Shown by Harold a copy of the "message" he had received in Marion, Ind., Bucklin said he felt its use unidentified as a "message," as additional ammunition against the organization, would have more effect. This opinion was independently endorsed by Clyde Bedell at a later afternoon meeting which Harold had with him at the Fair Store.

Bedell said that he thought the message remarkable but that Sadler, when hard pressed, would not hesitate to ridicule or discredit such comments as coming from any other source but the subconscious, whereas he would have to consider their logic if presented on the basis of human argument alone.

Bedell gave Harold permission to read *his* letter to any of the members he chose, stating that he had never made a secret of his views and saw no reason why these subjects should not be fully discussed. He expressed the desire to confer with Harold and Martha and any other members we would care to bring with us at his own home a week from Tuesday (Aug. 25).

The Karles were invited for dinner, but due to registration duties Elsie could not come and Dent accepted alone. Harold read him his two letters to Dr. S., also his "Battle Plans" dream, but did not tell its source. Dent said he was in general accord and felt they were well written, although he was not sure the Brotherhood idea should be given up completely: Thought it might possibly be a matter of "timing." He has great confidence in Dr. S.'s good sense. Feels he will await instruction. Thinks Bill is immature and would not survive with the Forum group 5 min. without his father's association. He believes Bill Hales (Jr.) is a swell fellow but has never had to face a problem in his life. He believes the Hales family 100% sincere and thinks they would withdraw if they thought they were interfering.

Russell Bucklin joined the general discussion about 10:30 p.m. Dent said, "There has been no *new* religion since Christianity. All 'new' religions are a variation of it."

The possibility of drawing up a paper at Clyde Bedell's (a week from Tuesday) was brought up—this paper being a petition for a re-opening of these issues for open discussion at the Forum early in September and signed by as many members as possible.

Made a list of "sure" first group, to be expanded. (See attached list.)[2]

(Note—Had talk with Elsie Karle after evening spent at Luther Evans's on Fri. July 24th while walking home. She said, in an outburst of emotional praise of Dr., that she believed she'd go along with him even if he *were* wrong.)

[2] See next page for list.

List drawn up -
8/17/42
Frank Karle
Russell Bucklin
H. M. S.

Mr. and Mrs. James Hicks,
4947 Wolcott Ave.,
Chicago, Ill.
Ardmore 1139.

Mr. and Mrs. Clyde Bedell,

Mr. and Mrs. Russell Bucklin,
2758 Hampton Court,
Chicago.
Lincoln 1037.

Mr. and Mrs. A.H. Dyon,
619 N. Central,
Chicago.,
Columbus 8387

Mr. and Mrs. L.J. Evans,
468 Deming Place,
Chicago.
Lincoln 1287.

Mrs. Elisabeth Githens,
5245 S. Cornell Ave.,
Chicago.

Mr. and Mrs. Lee Miller Jones,
7023 Chappel Ave.,
Chicago.
Fairfax 6940.

Mr. and Mrs. R.D. Karle,
181 Kenmore Ave.,
Elmhurst.
Elmhurst 3092.

Mr. and Mrs. E.W. Steinbeck,
2828 Pine Grove Ave.,
Chicago.
Buckingham 1700.

Mr. and Mrs. Harold M. Sherman,
530 Diversey Parkway,
Chicago.
Lakeview 6401.

HAROLD SHERMAN to JO and MERRILL DAVIS

Chicago, August 18, 1942

Dear Jo and Merrill:

After checking up our "box office returns" and the waistline dimensions of star performer Dr. William "Risqué Story" Sadler, I am glad to report that our three-day stand in Marion, Indiana broke all records for something or other, despite the attempt to rain us out, instigated by rival manager Billy Connors, who came running in with his own "risqué stories" in a mean and underhanded effort to steal the limelight.

Halfway home we decided to wire you: "DYING OF HUNGER... SEND SQUIRREL FOOD IMMEDIATELY" . . . but the four NUTS concerned couldn't find a Western Union Office open and my brain wasn't working well enough after that big noon lunch comprised of all the leftovers in the Davis household for the past month, to send you the message by telepathy.

I'm still trying to figure out all the things you had in that HASH, but if you want a button off of one of Merrill's hospital gowns and your missing shoe horn, please advise.

The star performer slept intermittently on the trip home with his hands gently caressing his stomach which, in turn, rested lightly (because of the gas on it) against the front windshield, and made my steering difficult. Every once in a while he would burp and a watermelon seed would fly out—but aside from this I could perceive no other outward effects of the wrestling match his digestive tract was having with the strange and wonderful assortment of inedibles he had managed to down in one of the greatest displays of gastronomic prestidigitation ever witnessed by mortal man.

During slight intervals of consciousness, Pot Belly Sadler would murmur: "What a time! What a time!" and he was not referring to Bulova watch time—but a HELLUVA time!

And even when a big truck swung into our lane and ran us off the road to avoid a head-on crash, he murmured: "That's all right—I've LIVED now—let me die happy!"

Seriously, Jo, we never had a better time . . . and we all thank you and Merrill for putting on such a show of genuine hospitality. We are devoted to you both, Martha and I . . . and we hope we may see more of you in the years to come than we have been permitted in the past.

I have written Dr. Seymour S. Wanderman, 88 Central Park West, New York City—phone: Trafalgar 7-3976 . . . telling him about you people, your various talents[3] . . . [sons] Joseph and Dick . . . and that you were leaving for the east around August 22nd, and would probably be phoning him to ask when you might see him. If you go to Philly first, I suggest you phone him from there and see if you can't call on Dorothy and Cy some evening. There are trains every hour from Philly. Dorothy is one of the country's greatest pianists . . . Cy owns many wonderful oil paintings . . . both know many wonderful musical artists as well as painters (non-musical except the harmonies they create in color) . . . and you should have an all-around evening of enjoyment. I leave it to Jo to get Dorothy to play for you . . . and Merrill, to get Cy Wanderman to tell of some of his research work. I wish both your boys could make the visit with you as they will be meeting one of the truly great physicians in Dr. Wanderman. He is so modest about the great work he is doing with respect to cancer, arthritis, rheumatic fever, strep viridants (may be misspelled but you know what I mean), leukemia, etc.

I can think of no two couples I would rather bring together . . . as I told Cy in my letter, I have recommended you both to each other with the TOP HUMAN RATING . . .

Please give our best to your fine sister, whom we enjoyed getting better acquainted with . . . and to her lovely daughter, Jackie . . . and accept our love and our thanks for an unforgettable weekend!

If and when you see Cy and Dorothy, please give us a report on the visit or come back through Chicago and stop off for a day.

Best to you!

Sincerely,

DIARY *August 18, 1942*

We decided, on short notice, to ask the Kelloggs and Ruth over this evening. They accepted immediately. Harold developed the conversation along Urantia Book and Forum lines and then told Mr. Kellogg of the unusual dream he had had concerning him. Mr. Kellogg expressed interest and Harold read the dream which seemed to impress Mr. Kellogg, but he could throw no light upon it. Harold then

[3] Mary Josephine ("Jo") DeMarcus Davis (1892-1983) was a musician and an artist, as well as a patron of the arts in Marion. See the article about her at http://wikimarion.org/Josephine_Davis.

read the further dream having to do with the turtles and the discord between them,[4] and when the Kelloggs asked how Harold interpreted it, Harold said, "I feel it has to do with coming differences of opinion in the Forum and that there won't be much we can do about it."

Harold then stated that we had heard varying comments from Forum members regarding the nature of the intended new organization, and when he found the Kelloggs' interest to have been sufficiently aroused, he related the unusual spiritual experience which came to him the first night on the visit to Marion, Ind. He then read them the "Battle Plans for Book of Urantia" document, and they were so moved by it that Ruth requested it be read again, which Harold did. Mr. Kellogg's comment was, "That's very interesting." Mrs. Kellogg said, "Yes, indeed it is." And Ruth said, "You know, when you read about these humans standing in front of the light and shielding it from others, I could just see the picture of millions of people being kept from the direct rays of this Light by the body of a human so interposed that the rays were diffused and shooting off sidewise in such a manner that no one could get the real truth at all. It was horrifying!"

Mr. Kellogg then got up to go, it being 11:30, and said, "You've given us a great deal to think about." Harold explained that he was going to submit this document and other matter pertaining to book publication, which he also outlined to the Kelloggs, to the Sadlers for consideration. Mr. Kellogg said, "Do that. It might prove very helpful."

As they were leaving, Ruth asked to remain a moment to speak to Harold, and said, "I don't know as you know that I am not a contact commissioner. I'm only a member of the Forum, but I shall never forget this evening and feel privileged to have been here. I am not in agreement with Bill, and I'm afraid our disagreement will become complete one of these days. I am not in accord with his ideas concerning a church. I feel as you do that anyone can gain the Truth direct from the Book of Urantia itself. I know that there is trouble coming and I don't see how it can be helped, but I feel more relieved tonight over the destiny of the Book of Urantia than at any previous time, and I want you to know that I am with you."

Reference was then made by Ruth to Bill's ego and the fact that such a tendency had not seemed observable by the father, nor the dangers inherent therein. She left with the assurance that what was

[4] The record of neither dream has been found.

said here tonight would remain inviolate with her. The Kelloggs liked the publication presentation plans, and Mrs. Kellogg said, as they were leaving, "This should burst on the public all at once."

FORUM CALENDAR *August 19, 1942*

Matterns arrive at Lincoln Park Arms. Mrs. Githens and Bucklins our dessert guests and evening.

DIARY *August 19, 1942*

The Matterns arrived in town today, and Harold phoned Dr. S. late this p.m. for permission to come over and see him. He was told to come at once, and Harold presented the Matterns as candidates for membership in the Forum, remarking that H.C. had once been tempted to take his life at about the time he came across a copy of *Your Key to Happiness*. Harold characterized H.C. as the "crusader type," and Dr. S. said he was afraid of such a man since this thought of suicide indicated an unstable tendency, and the fact that he was a crusader would probably make him so impatient to spread abroad the knowledge contained in the Urantia papers as to cause him to talk about them ahead of time. Dr. S. said, "We want crusaders when the book comes out but not before, as they might be dangerous."

Harold said he could vouchsafe for H.C. and wife as being dependable and trustworthy, and Dr. S. agreed to interview them tomorrow night. He took occasion to remark that he had talked with a professor in Chicago University who had commented disparagingly on *Thoughts Through Space* and particularly Wilkins for getting mixed up in this E.S. nonsense. Dr. S. remarked that it might not be so good for Harold to be associated with the Book of Urantia, as most scientists were apt to pooh-pooh his telepathy book. He gave Harold no chance to explain that some outstanding scientists in this field had already reviewed and favorably commented upon it.

The Doctor then referred to Mrs. Hales as a manic depressive and told how through the years she had run through cycles of high pressure activity wherein she had to be permitted to indulge her own notions. During such periods, Doctor said, she was apt to turn against anyone and, in her last outburst a year or so ago, had taken a violent dislike to the Doctor and had burned all the autographed books he had given her. She had also spent $18,000 of her husband's money relandscaping the premises, having big trees dug up and planted elsewhere. Mr. Hales, much concerned, in protesting to the Doctor, said, "My God! Can't you stop this woman?" And Doctor advised, "You can afford it. If you oppose her she will take out her manic depressive on you in some worse way." When Mrs. Hales emerged from this mental condition, according to the doctor, she was most remorseful, particularly over her destroying of his books, but Doctor said no one could predict when something might send her off on a "mental binge" again. Dr. S. did not seem to realize that he was making out an excellent case against the advisability of having any of the present Forum members publicly identified with the organization.

He spoke of receiving a 200-word telegram from some woman in Detroit who referred him to her rating in *Who's Who*, and to ask permission to fly here and see him with respect to what she had read about his "metaphysical adventure" in the last chapter of his book, *The Mind at Mischief*. Doctor said this woman was probably "a nut" but that he intended to see her next Monday; that these people who had the sudden urge to do things, who bombarded others with special deliveries and telegrams, are usually psychopathic.

Harold was left with the impression that Dr. S. did not have too high an opinion of the mentalities of many in the Forum, although he said their membership had never been dependent upon their degree of education, ability, or economic status—only upon their freewill desire to learn of this spiritual knowledge.

The Bucklins brought Mrs. Elizabeth Githens, Christian Science practitioner, in for the evening for an exchange in views on Forum problems. Mrs. Githens said she could now reveal the authors of three of the four anonymous letters written to the Doctor about a year and a half ago in criticism of Forum proceedings. She said that Mrs. [Lulu] Steinbeck, now head of the Seventy, was one, Mrs. [Della] Ward (Alma, Michigan) another, and herself the third. Mrs. Githens promised to report the name of the fourth when she had gained permission so to do. She was indignant that the Doctor should have referred to these letters as coming from "paranoiacs," and said that his and Bill's more dictatorial attitudes dated from that time.

She said she had lost all respect for the Doctor's integrity, and that he had stated to the Forum that he intended to present a talk on "The Evolution of the Soul" based on information contained in the Urantia papers whether he received permission from on high or not.

Subsequently he *did* receive such permission, so he reported, and the talk was given before a selected group in Lansing, Michigan.[5] Some Forum members felt strongly at that time that, inasmuch as he demanded secrecy from all of them, he was committing a breach by himself discussing any phase of the Urantia papers outside the Forum.

Harold read to Mrs. Githens copies of the letters he had written the doctor criticizing methods of book publication and organization, which letters Mrs. Githens highly approved. She then revealed, in confidence, a shameful squabble which occurred between Trustees and Board of Directors of the Christian Science Church in Boston, and which reached public attention and did the church great damage about a dozen years ago. Mrs. Githens stated that, in her opinion, all church organizations were highly vulnerable and that the Christian Science Church itself would not survive another generation since the young people were not taking it up. Mrs. Githens felt strongly that any organization set up to promote the Urantia Book would meet with a like or worse fate. She said that about seven years ago she had given Dr. S., at his request, a copy of the Christian Science manual and by-laws [*Ed. note: Manual of the Mother Church,* 89th ed., 1910] and that some of the methods of control in the proposed Urantia Brotherhood and Society had been patterned thereafter. Mrs. Githens was not surprised at learning that Bill had said he would challenge any higher authorities if the message ever came through advising against organization. She expressed the conviction that the Sadlers were so bent on having their own way that they would attempt to ride rough-shod over all opposition.

In a talk with Russell Bucklin on trying to determine a plan of action to bring this whole matter before Dr. S., Harold stated that he felt, since he was such a new member, that someone else should represent, personally, the views of any protesting group. Clyde Bedell, who had long been a leading dissenter, was thought to be the best choice for this task. Asked how the subject matter of his letters to Dr. S. could be made known to the Forum members, Harold suggested that he turn the letters over to Bedell and have him do a rewrite of them, putting them in the form of a presentation to be read by him at the first reconvened Forum session as a basis for discussion. Harold further suggested that mimeographed copies of this presentation be

[5] See Vol. 1, Chap. 16, for more information about this lecture and the Shermans' and Loose's reaction to it.

made available for distribution to every Forum member at the close of this meeting, and that they be instructed to take their copy home and study it, and come back the following Sunday prepared to act upon it and to express their own ideas.

Since Bedell had invited Harold to his home this coming Tuesday night with permission to bring the Bucklins and the Karles for a conference, it was decided that a petition would be drawn up to be revised by Bedell and put in form for signing by all Forum members interested on the occasion of their meeting at the Karle home (a week from this Saturday) on August 29th. The purpose of this petition, addressed to Dr. S., would be to get him to grant permission for an open discussion of Forum problems at this first reconvened meeting. In the event of Dr. S.'s refusal, this petitioning group would then call an entire meeting of the Forum elsewhere.

In emphasizing the responsibility each Forum member really carried, whether he realized it or not, the following thought occurred to Harold: If these Forum members permitted themselves to become a part of an organization plan which prejudiced millions of human souls, now living or yet to be born, from receiving the truth, then these very Forum members would have been directly responsible for denying the development of survival value to many of these millions and would then be instrumental in depriving them of their chance for attainment of individual immortality. If we are to believe that the Book of Urantia is a true spiritual revelation, then this fact is inescapable. Harold suggested that this awesome point should be scored at the conclusion of Bedell's presentation, and the Forum members left to ponder whether or not they wished to assume such unspeakable responsibility as to subscribe to any fallible human enterprise which might keep this spiritual revelation from reaching the souls of untold evolving human creatures.

Harold emphasized that every Forum member must appreciate that his identification with the Forum had not been accidental; that there was a definite reason why each had been selected or drawn to the Forum body; and that now they were in it, they could not dodge their responsibility either by walking out on it or going along with an ill-advised plan. It was Bucklin's conviction that this point alone would cause the most sober reflection; and that this denial of the truth, through wrong methods of presentation, would be a far worse crime in the light of our present understanding than the murder of a fellow human. Bucklin felt that this idea would so impress the Forum members and so influence Dr. S. as to leave him next to nothing to say; that for him to act in defiance of this consideration would indicate an egoistic, dictatorial attitude beyond all bounds.

Mrs. Githens stated that she felt the Sadlers would not back down but bitterly oppose the suggestions as a whole, but that we all must stand firm and self-controlled in the face of their outbursts.

ELIZABETH B. GITHENS, C.S. to HAROLD SHERMAN

1707 Stevens Bldg.,
Chicago, August 20, 1942

Dear Mr. Sherman—

A word of appreciation of your courage in accepting the commission plainly given to you at this point in the history of the Great Revelation.

Please be free to call on me if and as I can help, and do not hesitate to use my name as one in full accord with the masterly outline you have drawn.

Some day I should like, if I may, to hear again the "Battle Plans." To me, this bears its own stamp of authority as a communication.

Sincerely,
Elizabeth B. Githens

8

How the Papers Came Through

FORUM CALENDAR *August 20, 1942*

Harold introduces Matterns to Dr. Sadler for Forum membership.

DIARY *August 20, 1942*

This a.m. Harold prepared a clipped petition as a basis for the Tuesday Bedell meeting.

At 8 p.m. Harold took the Matterns over to be interviewed by Dr. S. and heard the most detailed account yet given of the manner in which these papers came through. Dr. S. said:

"About 35 years ago, when Dr. Lena and I were young physicians together, we decided to move, but the place we suggested was not yet available and we were directed to a furnished apartment in the neighborhood which we took for several months until our place was ready. We had been there about two weeks and some of the tenants had apparently learned we were physicians, and one of them—a woman living directly below us—rapped on our door about 11 p.m. as we were in the act of retiring. She said, 'Will you please come downstairs with me. Something has happened to my husband. He's gone to sleep. He's breathing very strangely and I can't wake him up.'

"We slipped on some bathrobes and went down to her apartment where I saw a medium-sized man, approaching middle age, asleep in bed, breathing very fitfully. He would take a couple of short quick breaths and then hold his breath for a time long enough for any normal human to have gotten black in the face, but nothing happened. I took his pulse and was surprised to find it was normal. I then tried to arouse him with every known method, even to sticking pins in him, but failed. His wife seemed to be a somewhat nervous and superstitious type. She was frankly frightened, even though I assured her that he seemed to be in good physical shape despite his peculiar actions.

"We sat about and waited for him to return to consciousness, during which time his body gave several violent jumps and starts. Finally, after about an hour, he awoke and looked around and saw us. We had propped him up on pillows and he now turned to his wife and asked, pointing at us, 'Who are these people?'

"She explained that we were doctors she had called in when she found she couldn't awaken him, and he said, 'What's wrong? What's happened?' I asked him, 'How do you feel?' He said, 'I feel fine!' I said, 'What have you been dreaming about?' He said, 'I haven't been dreaming at all!' I said, 'You've been jumping about on the bed.' He said, 'I don't know anything about that. I can't understand it.'

"I made him promise that he would come to my office the following morning for a complete physical exam. This he did, and I gave him every test but found him to be in excellent physical shape. I got his family history and there were no cases of insanity or epilepsy among any of his antecedents or present relatives. In my investigation of psychic phenomena I had witnessed many so-called trance states, but this phenomenon he experienced seemed to be something different. Most of the trance cases I had contacted were that of emotionally unstable or hysterical women. But here was a hard-boiled businessman, member of the Board of Trade and Stock Exchange who didn't believe in any of this nonsense and who had no recollection of what happened during these strange, unwakeable sleep states. I told him I would like to keep him under observation, to which he readily agreed.

"Nothing happened for several weeks and then, one night, about the same time, his wife called us and said he was having one of those spells again. We went down and I gave him some more tests and tried new ways to rouse him, all without effect. His labored breathing, its sudden breaking off, and then no breathing at all, would have been alarming had not his pulse remained strong and even throughout. The whole thing was baffling. When he awakened he was as before, unconscious of anything having transpired. This sort of experience was repeated at irregular intervals and at different times of night until the fall of the year, when we were able to move to the residence of our choice. This man's lease expired that same fall and he moved into an apartment house *in the same block in order to be near us.*

"One night, when we were called to his new address, and as we sat by the bedside, Dr. Lena noticed that he kept moistening his lips as though he were preparing to speak. She said, 'Perhaps he wants to talk to us. Maybe if we asked him a question we'd get an answer.' She did so, and to our great astonishment he did reply but it was not his voice. It was that of what we afterward learned to be a student visitor, on an observation trip here from a far-distant planet. This being apparently conversed with us through this sleeping subject, and expressed ideas and philosophies which struck us as entirely new.

"I had been led to believe, through previous study and research, that all such manifestations, however phenomenal, were the work of the subconscious. I, therefore, got this man in my office several days later, since other entities were apparently coming through him, and secured his permission to submit to hypnotism that I might explore his subconscious. It was difficult to get him under, but when I finally did so, I was amazed to find no consciousness whatsoever of the subjects discussed by these purported beings which we had, by this time, started to record (*in longhand by all and later combined*—Bill).

"I now felt that I needed help in solving the causes behind this mysterious phenomenon and I called in other doctors and scientists, friends of mine as well as Houdini and Thurston. They were equally unable to furnish any explanation.

"We now, finding that we could communicate by direct voice with different student visitors and other beings, began to look forward to each 'contact,' as we came to call it, and enjoyed the opportunity of asking questions which always brought the most stimulating and unexpected answers. We took to writing out questions in advance about the universe and to asking them, whenever given the chance. Finally, as a test, I worked out fifty-two questions privately and memorized them in my own mind, deciding to wait to see whether these so-called student visitors might be able to divine what was in my own consciousness.

"One night a particularly electrifying personality seemed to be present from a distant planet and had greatly excited us by his comments. As he was about to go, I addressed him, saying, 'How can you prove that you are who you say you are?' He said, 'I cannot prove it, but you cannot prove that I am not!' He then stunned me by continuing, 'However, I have just secured permission to answer forty-six of the fifty-two questions you have been holding in your mind.'

"Dr. Lena spoke up and said, 'Why, Will, you haven't any such questions, have you?' And I had to admit, 'Yes, Lena, the exact number.'

"This personality then proceeded to give me the answer to the forty-six as promised. When he had finished, he said, 'If you people really knew what you had here, you wouldn't take up our time asking silly, trivial questions like this. You would ask us something really significant and important.'

"We got home around 1:30 that night but there was no sleep in the Sadler household. We stayed up the rest of the night discussing and formulating questions that we might be prepared for the next contact.

"At this point I must go back and tell you that a few months previously I had made a lecture trip to the University of Kansas, and while there I wrote a letter to my son Bill suggesting that, since we seldom went to church, though I often talked *in* churches, I thought it would be a good idea if he and his mother would consider inviting in, regularly for Sunday afternoon tea, about twenty or thirty friends with whom we might discuss religion or any other subjects of mutual interest, and perhaps I could give them a little talk to stimulate these discussions.

"When I returned home the following Sunday noon, I found Dr. Lena and Bill had already acted upon my suggestion and were having about thirty people in that afternoon. This was about the 1st of October, 1923, as I recall.[1]

---

[1] We have been unable to find any newspaper reports of Sadler lecturing at the University of Kansas. However, we have found notices of him lecturing in small towns in Kansas in January of 1923. On January 16 he spoke at a senior high school in Fort Scott on "Faith and Fear, or How the Mind Influences the Body" and on "Americanitis, or the High Pressure Life." On January 22, he lectured in Junction City, probably on the same topics. (See Appendix C for clippings announcing these events.) In later years, Sadler told some Urantia Book readers that the first meeting of the Forum occurred on February 11, 1923, shortly after he had returned from giving a lecture on Gestalt Psychology in January 1923 in Junction City. (See Carolyn Kendall's "A History of the Contact Commission and Forum" and Barbara Newsom's "The Urantia Book—The Early Years.)

"The event just described, wherein we were challenged to ask worthwhile questions, had taken place about a month later, in November. I was asked by some members of this little social group, which we soon came to call the Forum, if I wouldn't tell of some of my experiences in abnormal psychology; and since we had not been prohibited from talking about the phenomena we had been witnessing, I related to them my encounter with this sleeping subject and the strange communications we were receiving through him and told of our being challenged to ask real questions.

"It suddenly occurred to me, as I got to the point—why not enlist the services of this group in the asking of such questions, and I called upon them to help me. I said, "Come back next Sunday with all the profound questions you can think of having to do with God and the Universe and I will see if these Intelligences can answer them.

"The following Sunday this group arrived with over 4000 questions. Dr. Lena and I spent several days sorting and classifying them. Then we held them in readiness hoping for the opportunity of 'calling the bluff' of these higher Intelligences. We were, as we thought, 'loaded for bear.'

"Some weeks went by and nothing happened. We thought we had them stumped and then one morning at 6 a.m. the phone rang. It was this man's wife calling. 'Come over quick.' she said. 'What's happened?' I asked, 'Is he still asleep?' 'Yes, but that's not it,' she replied. 'Please get over here. Hurry!'

"We dressed like volunteer firemen and arrived out of breath. She led us to the desk in his study and picked up a voluminous manuscript of 472 pages written in his own hand. I said, "Where did this come from?" She said, 'I don't know. He made some strange noises in his sleep and woke me up, and I saw it here on the desk.' I said, 'Has he been out of bed?' She said, 'Not to my knowledge. I don't see how he could have gotten out without waking me, and he's not awake yet.' I said, 'Is this his handwriting?' She said, 'It's his handwriting, alright. But I don't see how he could have done it.'

"I took a look at the manuscript and saw to my great astonishment that it was the answer to all the questions that had been formulated by ourselves and our Forum group. I couldn't wait any longer. I took this bulky manuscript into the bedroom and wakened the subject. I said, 'Do you know what you've been doing in your sleep?' He said, 'I haven't been doing anything.' I said, 'Oh, yes, you have. Look at this. Isn't this your handwriting?' He stared at the manuscript. 'Yes, it's my handwriting,' he identified, 'but I didn't do it.'

"I estimated that it would have taken a normal individual seven to eight hours writing at top speed to even copy what had been written, and the subject matter was so profound and yet so intelligently set down that I knew it was beyond human capacity to achieve. I phoned my daughter (C) and told her to bring over at once a grip device for testing muscular fatigue. I reasoned if he had physically written all this, his right arm would give evidence of it, but the device registered no fatigue whatsoever.

"We took the papers home and had them typed. They concerned the Universal Father, the Supreme Being, the Central and [*Inserted:* SUPER-] Perfect Universe and the Isle of Paradise. It was an unforgettable occasion when I appeared before this Forum group and said, "Well, we got the answers to our questions alright." And they sat awestruck and speechless as we read the papers to them. This was all we needed. Reading of these papers led to hundreds and thousands more questions, and more papers commenced coming through, and we found there seemed to be an organized group of high Intelligences on the other side prepared to present to us the whole 'astounding story of the Universe, leading from God, the Universal Father, down to the origin of the human creature man and his ultimate glorious destiny beyond the reaches of time and space.'

"This continued for perhaps seven to eight years, when what we considered the first edition of the papers was finished. At that time the Forum received its first direct message and its members were advised that, now, since their knowledge had been expanded, they should be able to ask more intelligent questions and that if they would do so, as they commenced a rereading of each paper, these intelligences would completely revise the entire tremendous manuscript.

"From two to two-and-a-half years ago this job was finished, and again we all thought that the manuscript was finally complete; but we were told, at this time, that the world events for which this revelation was designed were rapidly culminating (this was in 1939, several months before Hitler started his assault on the countries of Europe), and we could begin to see that those who had this revelation in charge did not intend to make it public until after the Second World War.

"More than a year was taken up, at a previous time, in celestial litigation between the Angels of the Churches and a midwayer ABC (?) and his staff who wished to tell the full true story of the life of Jesus. Permission was finally granted, and 75 papers came through giving the first detailed and comprehensive account of Christ's life on earth from his birth to his death, half again as large as the Old and New Testaments combined.

"This book is eventually to be published without any human personalities being identified in any way and no authorship ascribed to it. These higher beings have refused to use their own names and have only specified their *type* of being in the universe. There are only a few of us humans still living who were in touch with this phenomenon in the beginning, and when we die the knowledge of it will die with us. Then this book will exist as a great spiritual mystery, and no human will know the manner in which it came about."

(The Matterns were apparently favorably passed upon, and permitted to sign an application for Forum membership.) Dr. Sadler was greatly impressed by the fact that the Matterns had been led to locate in a small apartment hotel [the Lincoln Park Arms] within two blocks of Dr. S.'s address without their realizing that they were anywhere near the location of Harold and Martha. They had merely looked for apartment hotels in the newspaper and saw Wellington Arms, Sheridan Road, and decided to try that. It was full, and they were referred then to the Lincoln Park Arms or the Cambridge and suddenly discovered they were on Diversey near Harold and Martha.

9

Planning the Petition

HAROLD SHERMAN to SIR HUBERT WILKINS

Chicago, August 20, 1942

Dear Hubert:

We had a wonderful time this past weekend with Dr. Sadler and Christy... visiting at the Davises... and we kept hoping up to the last minute that you might walk in or wire that you were coming.

Things have been happening here . . . as will be evidenced by the enclosures. Please read them in the order clipped. There is great difference of opinion on the part of Forum members with respect to the proposed organization. Many of them feel as I now do—that NO organization should be formed . . . the Doctor and Bill and the other "contact commissioners" like very much my publication idea, as outlined in this first letter, but Bill's ego has been running away with him of late years, as he has visualized himself the head of the U. Brotherhood... and a man of world importance.

The doctor is blind to the Forum feeling rising up against him and what many feel his dictatorial attitude. All feel he and the contact commissioners have accomplished a tremendous task through the years of bringing through the papers . . . but that their work, when this is done, is THROUGH . . . and that there are too many human hazards and fallacies connected with their public identification with the BOOK.

As a result of this feeling, a petition is to be sent to the doctor, asking for a free and open discussion of all Forum problems at the first reconvened meeting, Sunday, Sept. 13th . . . this promises to be a HOT session. Clyde Bedell, whose letter (copy) I enclose, has seen this coming for years . . . he is a brilliant person, brother-in-law of the Hicks whom you met, advertising manager of the Fair department store here, and downtown civic leader.

I feel that you should be advised of what is going on, insofar as is possible by letter.

I think you will agree with that large number of Forum members who see things as I have outlined them in these two letters to the doctor. My signed letters are the first ones he has received which have not been anonymous . . . apparently other members felt he would lambaste them so severely if they revealed their names that they did not dare identify themselves . . . but they are ready to do so now when this matter comes to public attention.

The very stubborn and determined qualities which have aided Bill and the doctor in their long devotion to the papers—now become damaging if not properly controlled and directed.

The doctor's present attitude seems to be that the Forum has already voted upon the organization setup and has no more to say about it. Actually he simply presented the charter to them one day and asked for what amounted to a vote of confidence on it.

Hubert, the human equation is weak . . . and man's ego is the most vulnerable of all. It is distressing to find this condition existing even here and Bill and the doctor oblivious of what they would do to this great book by wrong presentation to the world.

I would appreciate your own private comments to me. At a later time you may have to throw the weight of your own experience and judgment into this situation along with ours . . . Please return these letters to me for my FILES . . . Best to you—

THE CLIPPED PETITION

August 20, 1942

Dear Doctor Sadler,

We, the undersigned members of the Forum, having met informally during this vacation period, have given thought to the approaching vital problems of book publication, organization of the Foundation, Brotherhood and Societies, and our expected individual and collective responsibilities in the participation therewith.

Because the work for which the Forum was originally organized or designated to serve has now been concluded, and we are arrived at a new phase of service wherein possible public identification with book and organization may occur as the order is received to publish and it is decided that the time is at hand for setting up Foundation, Brotherhood and Society, we feel that great care, consideration and planning should be given to this whole enterprise and that the following questions should be debated, analyzed and answered to the satisfaction and acceptance of all.

1. Is it wise for the Foundation to attempt to publish this book itself, or might it be more practical and profitable to affiliate with a publisher of established reputation and experience?

2. Is an organization designed to disseminate the truth advisable, or needful, if a new publishing plan is introduced capable of launching the book in a manner to bring it to the attention of all the people?

3. Would a new organization be interpreted by the public at large as a new religious sect? If so, would such an organization create more prejudicial harm than good in the attempted furtherance of this revelation?

The purpose of this letter is to ask that you grant us, the undersigned, an opportunity of presenting to all members of the Forum, at the first reconvened meeting, Sun., Sept. 13th, a statement of the points we feel should be freely discussed to the end that we may all participate, through the expression of our views and ideas, in the establishing of plans which, to the best of our combined human knowledge and experience, will serve the highest purposes in enabling the successful and most widespread and unprejudiced launching of the spiritual revelation contained in this book.

Since every Forum member should bear an equal sense of responsibility with respect to all future developments, we feel that each should be granted the chance to express himself fully on the imperative matters confronting us and that the time has now come when such consideration should be given.

If this suggestion is agreeable to you and your fellow contact commissioners, that the first reconvened meeting of the Forum, on Sept. 13th, be opened to free discussion of all phases of the book and organization project, will you please so advise us, addressing your letter to Clyde Bedell, not later than Friday, Sept. 4th.

Respectfully,

HARRY LOOSE to HAROLD SHERMAN

Monterey Park, August 20, 1942

Dear Harold:-

I am acknowledging receipt of yours of August 17th with enclosure ["Battle Plans"].

I have read the enclosure. It is very interesting and confirmatory. I will make no further comment until I have had opportunity to observe continuing developments. The way that I read the enclosure, *IT IS MEANT FOR YOU ALONE.* For this reason, I would keep the matter of the receipt of such advisory or illuminating data very much between yourself, Martha, and I. If you violate this procedure at this time or before some unknown time in the future, you will deliberately lay yourself wide open to very severe and unkind criticism. There are very few within or without the Forum that are far enough advanced to appreciate, or even recognize, the true from the false. If you do not keep the reception of these messages strictly between us three, Martha, I and yourself, you will find that other members of the Forum, ex-patients of Sadlers, will be receiving advisory messages regarding the Book also—and, of course, very much at variance with your own communications. You must surely see the points involved and why I counsel keeping these, and continuing advice, strictly between yourself, Martha, and I. Now is not the time, nor the period, for the reception of messages for the understanding of either the Forum members or the general public. I do not believe that such will ever come. It is not your mission. It is my belief that any and all continuing messages and advice, no matter how received, will be for your own personal guidance.

You will have plenty of help, and very little antagonism, in the reconstruction of many things.

Call attention to those Forum members that you interview of the oft-repeated statement personally by Sadler, "I am only the Custodian of the papers. Not the owner."

Remember, very few of the Forum members have any idea of their rights as a Member.

There is a tremendously valid reason to oust the Haleses from any other standing than that of a Forum member like all the rest. This applies to ALL the Haleses. I am now giving you foreknowledge and a warning. I would strongly advise you to keep your distance from them socially.

I will, of course, very much appreciate hearing how matters are progressing—and will be glad to help in any way that I can with my best thought in any developing situation.

You will enjoy every minute of the battle and its developing intricacies—and, I feel sure, of its eventual ending. Though the end of the "battle" will never come in your lifetime on this earth nor in the lifetime of the great-grandchildren of our time. I mean the real controversy that its publishing will institute.

I can only add—"Attack—attack—attack" all that is not the truth and that is unlike good.

Much love from both Ma and I,

HAROLD SHERMAN to HARRY LOOSE

Chicago, August 21, 1942

Dear Harry:

Thanks for your ever-valuable counsel which is always 100%. We shall follow instructions as usual.

This message was so powerful but I have not spread it broadcast, awaiting word from you. Would it be all right to use it, just as straight argument, without any indication of its source? (at the proper time?)

I recognize the dangers amidst Forumites of neurotic tendencies.

A group of Forumites, some of whom would astound the doctor, who feels sure of them, are planning to organize and petition him to let the first meeting of the Forum in the fall be thrown open to a free discussion of all plans—publication and organization. I am getting much material recorded in my diary.

The Matterns arrived yesterday, saw the doctor last night, and have been taken in . . . they are prepared to stay here for six weeks and to read the book through. . . . They have developed MUCH since your talk with them on the coast and are conscientious, dependable people who will render a service one of these days . . . Mattern is a fighter . . . a power in his way . . . and will be fine support later. Everything is under control and we are moving into the front-line trenches. Wish I could commune with you . . . what I'd have to tell you NOW . . . but you know and have foreseen it all. . . .

LOVE from us all to you both!

FORUM CALENDAR

August 21, 1942

Jesus' birthday at Forum. Sadler roof party.

DIARY *August 21, 1942*

An excellent attendance gathered on a hot night for the 13th annual celebration of Jesus' birthday, it now being computed as 1,948 years since he came to earth in the image of man. The usual simple ceremony has been the reading of particularly inspirational excerpts from the Jesus papers, but on this occasion Bill surprised by presenting an obviously and designedly selective series of papers dealing with organization problems as they confronted the apostles of John and Jesus working together. The Bucklins, Mrs. Githens and Ruth Kellogg, among others, recognized that Bill had a purpose in reading these papers—and intended subtle propagandizing of Forum members toward his point of view on organization matters as if in attempted answer to Harold's recently written letter criticizing the proposed organization setup. The effect on the assembled audience was one of slight bewilderment and apparent disappointment.

There was nothing of inspiration in the meeting and Bill dismissed them after about an hour, saying it was a hot night and that he guessed he'd read about enough. The Sadlers and Christy then began a recruiting of the select few members whom they wished to join them upstairs in a little social get-together. This display of favoritism did not go unnoticed among many Forum members who were completely disregarded and were left to depart without so much as a warm hand clasp or friendly word of greeting insofar as the Sadlers or Christy were concerned. Harold was invited upstairs and turned to speak to Bedell, who said he had not been asked, but Christy overheard and quickly included the Bedells in the invitation. The group who gathered on the roof comprised the Hales families (Junior and Senior), Ark Pettie,[1] the Bedells [Clyde and Florence], Bill and Leone, Dr. Sadler, Christy and ourselves.

Conversation was kept religiously off all Forum subjects. The two Bill Juniors sat off by themselves and conversed clubbily all evening. Harold had a little visit with Mrs. Bedell whom he had not really met before, and Martha was entertained at length by Mr. Hales Sr., who related how he reached his present financial position and told of his various philanthropical activities such as donating a women's gym to Oberlin (former home of his mother), and his acting as trustee on three different other institutions such as Presbyterian Seminary, etc.[2]

---

[1] J. Hawthorne ("Ark") Pettie (1904-1989) is buried in Arkansas.

[2] This seminary is where Sadler gave his July 31st lecture and where he was employed as a lecturer on pastoral psychiatry. See p. 86 of this volume.

He stated that he kept a careful check on all people who purchased grain supplies from his company by offering them a free auditing each month, and when he found they were not conducting their business wisely he refused them credit. He seemed particularly trying to impress Martha with his business acumen.

In connection with this evening occasion, Christy had phoned the previous day to be sure we were going to attend, something neither she nor the Sadlers had ever done with respect to any prior meeting. In the light of what was read as intended rebuttal material to Harold's organization criticisms, it seemed apparent that they wished to be sure we were present. At one point (without being able directly to quote the line), Bill said, "Jesus trusted all his disciples *save one,*" and looked steadily at Harold. He also sought to justify the penalizing provisions in the charter by reading excerpts of Jesus' advice to his disciples in the settling of disputes and the correcting of a fellow apostle. Bill, trying to make out a case for organization, did not seem to realize that times and conditions had radically changed since Jesus' day and that the only way of spreading the truth then was by word of mouth. Even so, Jesus' most oft-repeated admonition was, "Take up your cross and follow *me.*" The "follow me" referred to Jesus and not an organization.

The Bucklins came over following our return (11 p.m.) from the little roof party and were incensed that Bill should have made such use of the Jesus birthday occasion. They were also disturbed that such favoritism should be shown a few Forum members, and Mr. Bucklin stated it was plain to be seen there was going to be a "knock-down-and-drag-out fight ahead." The Bucklins recommended that Mrs. Steinbeck, new president of the "70," be included in the coming meeting at the Bedells', saying that she was greatly concerned over present developments. The Bucklins reported that the Dyons had asked the Rawsons to their home for the Sunday evening gathering, which indicated that the Dyons were not wholly sympathetic and that little should therefore be said at this meeting.

August 22, 1942

Harold thought it advisable to have Ruth Kellogg over for a private talk. Martha phoned her and she responded, saying she would be over in a half hour, which she was at 11 a.m., and stayed till a quarter of two.

Harold expressed his views testily to her, finding Ruth very reserved at first but at the finish having her say, "I have changed my ideas radically in the last few days, and this meeting has opened my eyes to many things I never saw before." She was given to understand that what was said here was strictly confidential and that she would never be quoted, Harold saying he thoroughly understood the difficult spot she was in.

Ruth frankly intimated that things had changed a great deal since the death of Dr. Lena, who had been the link between the two families. She said she would like to be able to spare the blows which she could see were coming to Bill Jr. Harold told her that many Forum members were getting ready to protest certain developments and explained that we wanted Ruth to thoroughly appreciate our position so that she, in turn, could act as a catalyst in helping stabilize the reaction of her own parents and the contact commissioners when these unpleasant matters might come to a head.

Ruth, now feeling free to express herself, intimated a sympathy for our point of view, it being understood that nothing could probably ever be said in public, and she would have to do whatever she could to be helpful undercover. While Ruth was not a contact commissioner, her close association with them all places her in a unique and strong position. She indicated that she is diametrically opposed to many of Bill's ideas, and realizes how positive by nature and headstrong both Dr. S. and Bill are. We have now, by expressions of opinion direct to Dr. S. and Bill and through them to Christy and through careful voicings of our opinions to the Kelloggs and Ruth, served notice on them all of the pending difficulties ahead and given evidence of what our stand will be.

FORUM CALENDAR

August 23, 1942

Evening at Al Dyon's. (Rawsons, Lee M. Jones, Karles, Bucklins, Evanses, Harold & Martha)

DIARY

August 23, 1942

Harold phoned the Sadlers this a.m. intending to report Booke Carter's article in Sunday's *Herald American* entitled "Why I Embraced Biblical Hebrewism," but got Bill Jr. on the phone instead who appeared to be in a talkative mood.

Bill's first statement was his high approval of the Matterns, who he said were a most unique couple, and that Mr. Mattern himself was definitely a "second-miler." It seems that Leone and Mary, both being Catholics, had taken immediately to each other, as Bill had taken to H.C. Bill read them the chapter on the twelve apostles, and they had a stimulating discussion on the subject of faith. Bill's experience with the Matterns led him to say that he had never seen so clearly the necessity of permitting each individual in the Forum to express his particular talents and views while maintaining the unity of the whole.

Harold commended Bill for this observation and predicted again that there was going to be a wide division of opinion among the Forum members with respect to future book and organization plans. He counseled Bill to be most tolerant and considerate and to be mindful that, while opinions might differ, all were sincerely devoted to the goal ahead. In that connection Harold said that he hoped Bill would remember his and my devotion to the Sadlers and the papers, regardless of what stand we eventually might feel we had to take. Bill said he remembered his own stand of some years ago and did not see how he could be less tolerant than others had been to him. Harold said that he felt Bill needed to develop the social side of his nature and fraternize more with all members so that they felt they understood him, and he in turn might understand them. Bill thanked Harold for his suggestion and said he was becoming more conscious of this need in himself. Bill, in the course of his conversation, said, "Harold, in advancing truths in the Book of Urantia I have decided to be all things to all men." This appeared to be his concept of what Harold meant by his suggestion that Bill develop a social consciousness.

Harold emphasized that many Forum members possessed abilities which would be most serviceable in time to come, which Bill and his father were not at present aware of. Bill said he had no doubt this was true. He said, "You know, familiarity breeds contempt, but in our case familiarity has bred acceptance. We've just taken the people on their expressed desire to know this Truth, and we've been so busy at our tasks we haven't had a chance to get much acquainted with many of their backgrounds."

Harold urged Bill not to be disturbed at whatever might happen and to keep an open mind, since he felt that many Forum members had some excellent ideas which should be considered on the basis of their logic without emotion. Bill promised that he would remember these admonitions and said he realized he didn't know it all, and that when people stop learning they stop growing.

Bill, referring to his meeting with the Matterns last night, said H.C. had occupied the chair Harold had usually occupied and that, after they had debated the subject of faith for some while, Bill told Mattern, "I will not dispute your views, my friend. Harold Sherman sat in the same chair some nights ago and we exchanged comments about organization matters, and when he got up to go at the end of the evening I'm sure he was no more convinced of my views than he was at the beginning, but he still remained my friend." Bill used this illustration to indicate it was his present intention to maintain a friendly attitude in the face of criticism. It remains to be seen whether he will be able to live up to his resolution under fire.

Harold felt the entire unexpected conversation to have been profitable in that he had again been enabled to plant the seed of approaching controversy and to state our position in relation to it. It is our hope, of course, that these difficulties may be met with a preservation of good feeling on all sides.

Present at the Dyons' were Mr. and Mrs. Dyon, Mr. and Mrs. Bucklin, Mr. and Mrs. Dent Karle, Mr. and Mrs. Rawson, Mr. and Mrs. Evans, Lee Miller Jones, and Mr. and Mrs. Sherman. It was thought, when the Dyons extended the invitation to the Rawsons, that frank discussion of Urantia problems would have to be curtailed. It did not seem possible that the Rawsons, with their church background, would or could be receptive to the ideas being entertained by other members of this group. The Dyons themselves, nice as they were, were placed on the doubtful list. However, once sociabilities had been exchanged, it was Mr. Dyon himself who opened up the subject by asking Harold to continue along the line of his comments made at the Karle gathering a couple of weeks before. Harold cautiously refrained from letting himself be drawn out at first, and explained that his comments had been made more or less in the nature of asking questions of older Forum members in order that he might get a clearer perspective of publishing and organization plans.

Harold said that there was one thing not yet clear and could those present enlighten him: "Did they understand that the Urantia Brotherhood and subsequent societies were to be what amounted to a new religion?" The Forum members thought not. Harold then asked how such an organization could keep itself from being so interpreted by the outside public. This query seemed to be a new and disturbing thought to some of those present.

Rev. Rawson was drawn into the discussion by Harold asking him whether he would consider and accept the Book of Urantia, if he were a stranger to it, and if he knew an official interpreting body such as the Urantia society existed in the form of what he would regard as the new religion. Rev. Rawson was hesitant about answering such a question, but his wife spoke up and said, "You know, Charles, you would be very suspicious. You always are of any development like that."

Harold then pressed home the point: Was it advisable, if the contemplated Urantia organization would arouse such a prejudicial reaction in many who otherwise would secure and read and accept the book, for such an organization to be created at all?

Asked how the Book of Urantia might be presented to the public and its truths disseminated, Harold stated, "Through the medium of publicity and all modern means of communication." Rev. Rawson was not so sure that such a spectacular ballyhoo should be indulged in and called it "casting pearls before swine." He was challenged in this statement by Karle, Bucklin and Evans, all of whom argued that the best plan of presentation was that one which brought the truth within the widest reach of humans. Karle put it: "The more swine you cast the truth before the more pearls you are apt to find."

Harold referred to possible scandalizing and ridiculing of any organization and the leaders connected therewith. Rev. Rawson seemed to feel that we must be able to face such ridicule as Christian martyrs, but Bucklin and Karle both took issue by saying, "Why invite such ridicule if it can be avoided?" Dyon expressed what was considered to be a consensus of opinion when he said that Forum members had been brought along to think only in terms of an organization and had been given no opportunity to consider or originate any possible better method of launching the Book of Urantia. He declared it a good thing that Harold had arrived and had raised these questions as well as instituted new possible ways of proceeding so that the whole subject might be reopened for free discussion. All intimated that the Sadlers were so positive in their attitudes that a mere request from Forum members that they be heard would likely be brushed aside, and that a substantial front must be organized to compel attention.

Rev. Rawson then spoke up and said that since he appeared to be the only minority representation, and since all members apparently felt as they did, why wouldn't it be a good idea for this group and any others sharing like views to petition Dr. Sadler for a hearing. Since this was just the plan contemplated by Bucklin, Karle, Harold and others, Rev. Rawson was commended for the suggestion. More was therefore accomplished this evening than had been anticipated, with the Rawsons developing at least a receptive attitude toward the whole situation and the Dyons expressing vital interest. Rev. Rawson had said that we should go on record as to how we felt with the Doctor, and that if he did nothing about it our consciences would at least all be clear; we would have done all we could. He was immediately challenged by other Forum members, notably Elsie Karle, who said, "*My* conscience would not be clear and it won't be until I know we have done everything we can to work out the best and right way to present this truth to the world!"

It is now possible that the Rawsons themselves, who might have been considered as strongly in the Sadler camp, may be signers of this petition. Asked point blank by Harold whether he, Rawson, had ever been able to get very far or stand up against the Doctor in an argument, he laughed sheepishly and made honest confession, "I wilt." Dent Karle, Bucklin and all concurred that the Doctor was unapproachable on an individual protest basis.

A common meeting ground was tentatively arrived at when the declaration was made by Karle and Bucklin that the setting up of an organization might be a matter of timing—that some time later, after the book was published, a spontaneous public demand for an organization might then make its establishment possible without prejudice or misinterpretation. Rawson said if this would be the attitude of the Forum members, then he could go all the way with them, but Harold emphasized that no arbitrary starting date should be set, since it could not be determined when an organization might be feasible or desirable until the book was out and the public reaction carefully and impersonally evaluated. This point seemed to meet with general acceptance.

Harold opened Bible upon inspiration at bedtime: Deut. 18:17-22.

FORUM CALENDAR *August 24, 1942*

Dinner with Matterns.

DIARY *August 24, 1942*

Harold phoned Dent to give him Bedell's address in Park Ridge and found him on the verge of phoning Harold to discuss certain points of procedure. Harold stated that he thought it essential that the meeting of the Forum be taken out of Sadler's hands, and that a chairman be appointed who could command the respect of all and whose knowledge of parliamentary law would enable him to insure the freest of discussions and prevent possible intimidation of Forum members.

It was Karle's feeling that unless the whole plan of procedure was thoroughly organized, the Forum could be tricked into accepting a proposal from the Sadlers which would enable them to accomplish their purposes substantially as they wished at a little later date and, once having committed the Forum, compel this body to stand behind their activities. In Karle's opinion, too precipitate action on the problems involved would be dangerous if the Sadlers were permitted to call for a vote of confidence and to make a sentimental appeal in that direction. Karle also felt that any acceptance of a compromise arrangement would be fatal since it could be interpreted as authority for the Sadlers to proceed unless specific restrictions were placed thereon. Karle subscribed to the conviction that each Forum member should be supplied with a statement of the problems under consideration and given sufficient time to prayerfully deliberate on them before being called upon to give any definite opinion or suggestions.

Karle agreed with Harold that Bedell would be an excellent choice as the man to present the matter to Forum members. He said such a man should be prepared to defend his position and to absorb all repercussions. Karle declared that we must be so organized as to be prepared to meet all eventualities. He said it was entirely possible that the reaction of the Sadlers in public would prove so illuminating to Forum members as to militate against their own contentions. He said it was possible they might imply that this stand of the Forum members was ungrateful and an unwarranted trespass upon the hospitality extended under their roof, but that if such an attitude were manifested it would reveal such a desire for possession and ownership of the Book of Urantia as to strengthen the cause of the protesters. Harold suggested that a secretary be employed to make shorthand notes of all proceedings, that the Sadlers might be held to account for their statements and an analysis made of all ideas, suggestions and criticisms. Karle felt this should by all means be done. He said that the meeting tomorrow night at Bedell's should be a strategy meeting and the one at his house on Saturday night a general meeting in which specific plans are not revealed but only the petition requesting a free discussion presented for signature. In this manner, Karle pointed out, we thus preserved our punches and kept individual members from being too concerned over possible measures which might subsequently have to be taken.

He felt that the Rawsons were as impressed as they ever could be, and that Rawson, with every good intention, would always be willy-nilly because of his background. When Karle was told by Harold of the propaganda in favor of an organization which Bill had marshalled from the Jesus papers for presentation upon the occasion of the Jesus' birthday meeting, he said this was a sample of what might be expected. Harold told also of the specially selected gathering on the Sadler roof afterward and his feeling that this anti-social attitude toward the group as a whole was highly inconsiderate. Karle stated this had been the practice for many years and he agreed that such procedure was not wise or productive of harmony and understanding and mutual confidence which should exist. He concurred with Harold in the belief that a taking over of the Forum management by Forum members themselves would give to that body new life, unity, and human feeling.

Evening with Matterns. Harold felt it best to frankly acquaint the Matterns with the existing situation here and found them to be already aware of conditions based upon their own observations. This in itself was indication of how flagrant these conditions have become. Dr. S. stated in Harold's presence when H.C. and Mary were interviewed that no human personalities were ever to be associated with the Book of Urantia. H.C. remembered this and said he would remind Dr. S. of his declaration at the proper time. H.C. stated that he sensed something rotten and a feeling of absolute ownership concerning this book material during the Saturday evening spent with Bill when he discoursed upon organization plans.

H.C. confessed that he had even worried about Harold forming an organization based on truths contained in *Your Key to Happiness*, and he declared emphatically that no truth could be organized and that it *must* be kept free. Both Mary and H.C. observed what they termed Bill's "dramatics" as he read the paper on the twelve apostles and his obvious desire to project himself and his views instead of the truth so contained. Had Harold not spoken to the Matterns when he did, they might readily have thought us to be blinded to the attitudes of the Sadlers and to actually be in support of their plans. Our talk considerably cleared the atmosphere, and H.C. said he did not wish to meet any Forum members until these subjects came up for discussion, when he would present his free and uninfluenced viewpoint. H.C. said it was evident the Sadlers meant to hold onto this truth and that it would take a fight to pry them loose from it.

FORUM CALENDAR *August 25, 1942*

Evening at Bedells'—Mrs. Steinbeck, Miss Carolyn [*Ed. note:* Caroline] Brown, Evanses, Karles, Bucklins and us.

DIARY *August 25, 1942*

Bedells'. Present were Bucklins, Karles, Evanses, Mrs. Steinbeck, Shermans and Bedells. Harold was asked to read his two letters written to Dr. Sadler as a background for discussion of publication and organization problems. Bedell, when Harold had finished, said, "Harold, you are 1000% right on your conclusions. We have all been asleep for the last eight to ten years. Some of us protested from time to time on various occasions, as I did in 1933, but we really permitted ourselves to be talked down and took no *concerted* action against developments of which we did not wholly approve. It has remained for you to awaken us, and I agree that we must do something about these matters at once."

In the discussion that followed, Clyde Bedell agreed to write the final draft of the petition, which all sympathetic Forum members are to sign, asking Dr. S. for permission to hold a free discussion on all subjects relating to the Urantia project. Bedell further agreed to write the presentation based upon the points raised in the two letters Harold had written to Dr. Sadler, and to make this presentation himself when the free discussion meeting should be held. Karle consented to be chairman of this proposed meeting, and a Friday noon luncheon appointment was set up between Bucklin, Karle, Bedell and Harold, at which Bedell's letter of petition was to be checked over and approved so that it could be prepared for signing by all interested Forum members on the Saturday night meeting at the Karles' home. These four men for the time being are to constitute the strategy board and will later plan all details for conduct of the free discussion sessions.

It was the consensus that a number of meetings would be required for Forum members to adequately consider and act upon the problems involved. Harold suggested that since the Forum members had rendered such a service in the asking of questions, quite possibly they could render an equal service in questioning all phases of the Urantia project to the end that the right solution might be gained. Mrs. Steinbeck, as head of the Seventy, confessed her long dissatisfaction with the inconsiderate treatment of Forum members and the general way things were going. All seemed to believe that a surprising number of Forum members could be secured who would sign the petition calling for a free discussion.

Inspirational Bible opening after meditation—Jeremiah 36:6-7.

HARRY LOOSE to HAROLD SHERMAN

Monterey Park, August 25, 1942

Dear Harold and Martha:-

Harold, your letter of Aug. 21st received. I am glad for the arrival of the Matterns and that they are to remain for 6 weeks reading the Book. I hope that the Matterns have not mentioned my name. Be sure to caution them at no time so to do—except to Martha and yourself.

When the proper time comes, you will know without question. When this period definitely comes, and the "message information" can be used for *good*, it surely is mentionable. But I would strongly suggest that you so do without pinning yourself to a definite source. Now is surely not the time. Events do not yet substantiate. Such present announcement would be very premature and certainly very harmful, and leave you wide open for criticism. For the present, do not impart the source to anyone except Martha and myself. As I have before written you, I do not think your mission has anything to do with the reception of higher information for the Forum members. It is my belief that any and all continuing messages of advice and information, no matter how received, will be for your own personal guidance. . . .

You are embarked on a very serious mission, one on which you will need much guidance and support. I am sure that such guidance and support will be given you. Consult always and ever with Martha. Have no secret thoughts or mental reservations from her. Keep continual contact with your TA and have a period of meditation—preferably just before going to sleep—and PRAY. Do not "forget" nor lapse in any way in your prayer period. If ever you needed prayer in your life, you surely need it now. And don't make prayer just a continual asking for "more" without giving "thanks" for all that has already been given you. Pray for guidance—direction—strength—more love and more capacity to love.

I suggest the lady publisher of your last book as one of your Seven. Ask her to come on to Chicago and read the Book. After she has read the Book, have her bring on the woman of great wealth whom she knows and of whom she has spoken to you. Have this lady read the book. She, too, might be another of the Seven. Please remember that these are suggestions only.[3]

I will continue to remark the undesirability of the Haleses, one and all, in any other part of this movement than that of Forum member, until you write back to me of your reception of this information and its impression upon you.

I will be very much interested in all developments as they mature. I am now but a spectator interestedly watching. "Yours is the torch—yours is the race."

Thanks a lot for your nice letter received today, MARTHA.[4] I haste to get the following to you. There is absolutely *no* restriction to prevent Dr. Sadler from writing whatever memoirs he so cares to write regarding his connection with the Book of Urantia. He can do this right now or at any time in the future. To help you over any small qualms of conscience in reference to his name not being directly connected with the Book of Urantia, I will tell you now that he *will* write such a book of memoirs. He has right now every intention so to do. And so do a half a dozen more Forumites—who are especially ill-fitted for the performance. You, personally, will read the book that Sadler will write. You will read other printed matter regarding the Book written by Forumites who will also name themselves. Harold has the same right of written expression as Sadler or any other Forumites. NONE of them have the right to include themselves in the Book of Urantia itself. Harold's connection with the Book of Urantia began 20 years before he even knew that there was such a book. His entire "build-up" since that time has been for a purpose. This should all begin to be-

[3] Eileen Garrett, the well-known medium whose Creative Age Press had published *Thoughts Through Space*. In Harold's July 29th letter to Dr. Sadler, he referred to a publisher friend of his who had a wealthy friend who might help finance the promotion of the Urantia Book. Harold refers to the unnamed publisher as a "he", but he likely meant Eileen Garrett. See pp. 81-82 of this volume.

[4] This letter has not survived.

come more apparent to you both. Harold's "Book" will be the authoritative accompaniment to the Book of Urantia in which the history of the movement—so much authentic data—so many substantiating truths—so very much—too much to even think about now—will explain so much to the truth seekers a thousand years from now. . . .

I wish that I could tell you more of the Haleses but I cannot. I can only warn you to be very careful.

There is now a "shot," or vaccination, that is given for hay fever. I have read that it works in quite a percentage of cases. Have Harold ask Sadler about it. Harold is sure needed on the job too urgently to have hay fever run him off now. "There is much for you to do in Chicago."

I will be much interested in continued developments as they appear. Don't be parted from Harold for a moment, Martha, and give him all strength and courage.

Much love to you both from Ma and I,

HAROLD SHERMAN to WILLIAM SADLER

Chicago, August 25, 1942

Dear Dr. Sadler:

At your request, I am herewith putting in writing my views and ideas concerning publication of the Book of Urantia. This plan of publication is the result of careful study of the Urantia papers, the purposes to be served by this Spiritual Revelation, and your present program for presenting this Truth to the world.

What I am to suggest is based upon my own publishing experience. As you know, I have had over fifty books published which have sold into the millions of copies. You have also had a wide publishing experience. You can appreciate it, then, when I tell you that I made the mistake of trying to publish one book—an adult novel—on my own. I thought my own name and the market I had builded would be sufficient to enable me to have the book printed at my expense and distributed through the Union News Company to booksellers everywhere, and that I could make a large profit by so doing.

I should have known better. I did not actually learn until then that book publishing and selling is a tremendously intricate business. Without a recognized and established publishing house behind you, without a well-trained and aggressive sales force, without a thoroughly tested and operating means of distribution, and without competent publicity experts who know how to exploit your special type of book in a manner to impress both public and reviewers—the chances of any book, however good, becoming a best seller today (production and selling costs being what they are) are negligible.

This difficulty is almost infinitely increased when your product is that of a book which appears destined eventually to replace our present BIBLE!

It is wise and absolutely necessary and right procedure for this book to be under your complete editorial control during preparation—and to be set up in type in such a manner as is now being done. With a manuscript of this unusual origin and nature, this could not successfully and with proper protective measures have been accomplished otherwise.

But, as I look into the future, I see great hazards attendant upon the attempted publishing, exploiting and distributing of the Book of Urantia under sponsorship of a Urantia Foundation and a publishing office of your own.

In the first place, you need the co-operative aid and publishing experience of a going publishing concern to avoid the many pitfalls which any new publishing house would be bound to encounter. The Book of Urantia cannot and must not get off to a false start. Your new publishing firm would have no RATING with publishers, booksellers, reviewers or public—and, in addition, would have to combat the instantly created prejudice of being considered the possible front of a new religious order.

You are, however, in a particularly advantageous position, when the right time comes, should you and your associates decide to follow this procedure, to call in an established publisher and conclude a most favorable arrangement.

The Book of Urantia will then have been plated, ready for printing. You have paid the typesetting and plating costs, which gives you a major interest in the publishing venture.

The publisher, if interested, agrees to publish, placing his imprint on the title page in place of the "Urantia Foundation," which is deleted. To all intents and purposes, this Book of Urantia then goes on the publisher's list as one of his releases for spring or fall. It, of course, is the FEATURED BOOK on the list and is so represented by the sales force. The book is distributed by the publishers through the usual channels and everything is handled in a most regular and businesslike manner. The fact that this established publisher has had this unusual manuscript brought to him and has recognized its extraordinary merit by publishing it, gives to the Book of Urantia an immediate prestige value in the trade it never could have acquired had it been introduced by an unheard-of Urantia Foundation.

Then, too, did you attempt to publish on what must inevitably start out as a comparatively small-scale venture, with the Urantia Foundation sponsoring the book, you run the great risk, not only of widespread discrediting, but of organized efforts to force the book off the market. Certain religious organizations are immensely strong, as you know, and if your publishing house is not able to weather a mighty storm, the Book of Urantia—priced as it would have to be priced—unless you had great capital—could not stay long in print.

Therefore, UNLESS the plan of publication anticipates the hazards and is so organized as to rise above them—you are apt to meet a crushing and devastating defeat from the forces of evil still active on this earth.

As I see it—the risk is too great to consider bringing this REVELATION out in a limited, high-priced edition alone, depending largely on word-of-mouth selling and organization support. It can be too easily stopped by opposing forces before it really gets started, under such circumstances.

The only way to make sure that the Book of Urantia is extensively and firmly launched in human consciousness is to undertake a publicity and advertising campaign such as no book hitherto has ever received!

Such a campaign requires the donation of large sums of money by individuals spiritually interested—but such individuals can be found—and will gladly give of their substances to bring spiritual advancement to this planet.

Given an established publisher, and the power and right to have your representatives sit quietly in with this publisher on all developments, yet remaining always behind the scenes, you can then arrange for the opening announcement of this book.

This announcement should come in the form of beautifully written full-page newspaper advertisements, appearing in every daily paper in the country on the same day! Simultaneously, announcements of this new spiritual revelation would be made over national radio networks.

These ads and radio announcements would be brought to the attention of uncounted millions of people in this manner, and copies of the book would be available, on assignment if not on order, in every bookstore or place where books are sold!

Since the TRUTH must be within the reach of all peoples, the book must be published in several priced editions at the same time—with a paperbacked edition selling for $1.00!

It should remain to be determined whether the Book of Urantia advertisements should contain the endorsement of men and women scientists, educators and others of prominence in all lines of endeavor who have read and reviewed the book prior to its publication date. Endorsements, if any, should be in the scientific field but under no circumstances from the religious field, for any endorsement by the clergy of any sect or sects, at the start, would make it seem as though the Book of Urantia specially favored these particular religious orders.

But this advertisement should be as attractive and inviting as some of the ads prepared for *Compton's Encyclopedia* which show background scenes of heavenly space, the formation of the earth, lower forms of life, and evolving man. It is possible, through the use of illustration as well as inspired wording and authoritative endorsement, to thus capture the INSTANT ATTENTION of the entire country!

That I might check the feasibility of my own vision with respect to the way it seemed this book should be handled, I talked confidentially with a book publisher friend when I was in New York. Without revealing the exact nature of the book, except to say that I knew of the existence of a manuscript of such spiritual power that, when properly published in book form, it should revolutionize world thinking, I asked this publisher's opinion of my ideas.

The publisher said: "Not only do I think your ideas are feasible—but some such spectacular and distinctive method of simultaneously calling public attention to such a book *must* be utilized—as any quiet publication of it will be squelched by different religious groups who feel it opposed to their interpretation and the commercial existence of their order. But once the book is so announced, and its importance so established, it *cannot* be squelched. It has developed too many centers of support and interest throughout the country. It may still be opposed in certain quarters but it is bound to make a place for itself!"

Knowing that such an advertising campaign would require a large sum of money which the book itself could not hope to earn back in a long time, if ever, I asked the publisher if he thought such money could be raised.

To my surprise, this publisher said: "Sherman, I have confidence in your judgment. If this book is what you say it is, and I could be permitted to read the manuscript, and decide for myself, I feel reasonably sure I can get a close personal friend, who is interested in helping humanity, to donate a million dollars toward the exploitation of such a volume!"

This publisher will be free in September to visit me here and, if you have by that time decided to consider this entirely different method of procedure, you could then confer along the lines indicated.

As you can see—something is developing here of tremendous possible magnitude!

This would mean that your proposed Urantia Foundation should not be incorporated under the easily recognized "Urantia" title, and your name should not be identified with it. The Foundation would be simply a holding company for receiving and dispensing funds in relation to the Urantia book and would be given no publicity.

The Book of Urantia, if an established publisher handled it, should be copyrighted in the name of the publisher so this imprint may appear on the title page and wherever else it has to be used.

Then, the publishing house assigns the copyright and all rights vested therein to your Foundation. Any individuals or organizations desiring to gain access to any of these rights are then compelled to approach the publishing house as the apparent copyright holder, with their propositions. They cannot get at you personally and your identity never needs to be disclosed unless some Forum member reveals it—and, even so, you are so far removed from any personal connection that you can, under such circumstances, easily defend yourself and avoid being drawn into any controversies, which would happen constantly were you "out front" and on the "firing line."

Representatives of your choosing, or the Forum's could meet as required to pass upon proposals made through the publishing house for different adaptations or translations or uses of the contents of the Urantia book. The book of Urantia is thus strictly "on its own," unencumbered by any human influence or interpretation—a TRUE REVELATION—direct from GOD, the UNIVERSAL FATHER—to *each* and all of HIS earth children, regardless of race, color or creed.

With the BOOK being published by a recognized publisher, instead of with the imprint of the Urantia Foundation, everyone can have access to the book at the same time, including past Forum members. All persons are thus privileged to organize little study groups for themselves, unofficially, whether they are contacting the book for the first time in their communities, or have had a previous knowledge of it. And the TRUTH is thus enabled to find its way naturally and spontaneously into the hearts and minds of people everywhere.

On the surface, it might appear as though the book of Urantia would need more support to further its purpose in this modern world. But consider that the present day and age affords entirely different means of conveying TRUTH to the minds and hearts of humanity than was possible in Jesus' time. In His day, the truth had to be carried by word of mouth.

Today we have the printed page, the newspapers, magazines, radio, stage, screen—all mediums for reaching human consciousness quickly, independently and individually! These mediums have no "motives" or "axes to grind" such as all organizations must have. Every organization's excuse for being is to be "for" or "against" something, and for this book to have its own publishing house would alienate many people against it.

But these mediums of communication exist to be USED by Man to transmit knowledge, in various humanized and dramatic forms, to his fellow man. And these mediums can readily and mightily serve as the APOSTLES of the BOOK OF URANTIA . . . In this manner the TRUTH can be called to the attention of every human, with nothing prejudicial associated with the book which might cause many to reject it, sight unseen.

The BOOK OF URANTIA, in addition to its being a TRUE REVELATION, will be the SPIRITUAL SOURCE BOOK for ALL truth seekers, for ages to come. Its TRUTH CONTENT is so mighty and unassailable in itself that it needs no supporting statement, such as the pamphlet you propose publishing, explaining partially the "metaphysical phenomena" behind it. Any attempt to explain this SPIRITUAL REVELATION undignifies it and pulls it down to an already generally discredited "psychic phenomena" level. And the fact that its origin can never be fully explained or tested or verified, makes the dilemma even worse. The Book SHOULD and CAN stand on its own AUTHORITY and the authority of the recognized publisher who publishes it. Beyond this you need nothing. It will find its own way in the world.

Devotedly and sincerely,

DIARY

August 26, 1942

Bedell phoned from downtown saying he had finished the first draft of the petition and asked permission to bring it out and check over with Harold, which he did. Harold found it to be a masterly job, and Dr. S. and his associates given due credit for their accomplishment during their long years of devotion to the evolving Urantia papers. It was agreed that every effort would be made to maintain harmony of the group as well as the good will of the doctor and other contact commissioners. Request was made in the petition for the Forum's right to a chairman of its own choosing and for permission to examine all charters and by-law provisions, as well as to consider the entire publishing and organization venture at the opening meeting Sept. 13. It is expected, if all goes well, that many weeks will be spent in careful deliberation and development of plans, but the reaction of Dr. S. and Bill to this petition is as yet unpredictable.

HAROLD SHERMAN to HARRY LOOSE

Chicago, August 27, 1942

Dear Harry:

Things are happening so fast here that it is difficult to keep you up to date. Martha and I have become the focal point of a substantial group of Forum members who are much concerned that they are not being taken into confidence by the Sadlers, and that the Sadlers apparently are preparing to go ahead without consulting the Forum body at all.

Meetings have been held around at different homes, such as the Bucklins, Karles and Dyons (these latter you might remember) . . . and a "strategy board" meeting was held at the home of Clyde Bedell (now advertising mgr. of the Fair Store, who is a WHIZ . . .). As early as 1933 he wrote Sadler a letter warning him that the type of organization he had in mind was rotten and that only ill could come of it.

At this meeting, attended by the Bucklins, the Evanses (relatives of Bedell), the Karles, Mrs. Steinbeck (now head of the Seventy Group) and ourselves—it was decided to draw up a petition and have it signed by as many Forum members as possible, asking the Sadlers to permit a free discussion meeting, covering all phases of book publication and organization plans. (On the first reconvening date of the Forum, Sept.13th.) . . . A BIG MEETING of all Forum members interested is being called at the Karles' in Elmhurst for this Saturday night, when the petition (drawn up by Bedell, at my suggestion) is to be signed. If Sadler won't permit such a meeting, action will be taken at some other place and Forum members assembled.

I am trying to preserve harmony and am moving forward prayerfully, asking for guidance . . . and it is my intention to work with Bill and his father and try to help them control their own personal feelings, and keep them in line, if this is at all possible. But Bill told me personally, some nights ago, when I asked him if he should receive word from Higher Sources NOT TO ORGANIZE, what would be his attitude, and he said, to my amazement: "I WOULD CHALLENGE IT!" (This indicates his state of mind, how determined he is to put his plans through, even to the point of intimating that such a message might be FALSE or the work of Caligastia, if it came through. Amazing what the HUMAN EGO and HUMAN AMBITION can do to a man. (Everyone wanting to sit on the right hand of God, etc.)

We have tactfully approached the Kelloggs, and I had such a strange dream concerning you and the Kelloggs, which I am sending . . . and which I read to them . . . they were strangely and strongly impressed by it . . . and they interpreted the turtle impression as "coming trouble" . . . the "violin" as having something to do with necessary harmony. In a private talk with their daughter, Ruth, she intimated that she is not in agreement with Bill's plans at all . . . and while we said we would not quote her, there is evidence that all is not harmony among the "contact commissioners." I foresee a possible 3 to 2 split when the test comes . . . Christy and the Kelloggs against Bill and his father.

Dr. S. asked me to rewrite the two letters I sent you, putting the publication plans in one letter and the organization criticisms in the other. This is because he wants to act on the publication plans and DODGE THE ISSUE of the organization setup if he can. I have turned in the publication letter but not the one on the organization yet . . . which he intends to pigeonhole anyway. He told me he did not show my letters to the Kelloggs as he didn't want to disturb them . . . since the organization plans were all decided upon, and no use bringing up any other arguments against them. (In other words, he decides what the other "contact commissioners" should see and pass upon, without their knowledge—a rather autocratic attitude, it would seem to me.)

Harry, on the anniversary of Christ's birthday, August 21st, Bill took this occasion to select passages from the Jesus papers, ALL OF WHICH *seemed* to support an organization so that he could propagandize Forum members, in anticipation of coming objections in the fall. It was the CHEAPEST EXPLOITATION of what should have been a spiritual occasion, I have ever witnessed. After the reading, Bill dismissed the Forum members like so many cattle, herding them out of the place, while Christy and the doctor grabbed hold of a few "favorites" and invited them upstairs for a "social gathering." They had intended to bring us together with members of the Hales family . . . but I turned to Bedell to ask if he had been invited, and he said "no" and Christy overheard . . . and became embarrassed and invited the Bedells upstairs also. So the Sadlers, Bedells, Haleses and Shermans were on the roof for an hour or two. Bill Hales and Bill Sadler went off by themselves and were palsy-walsy for the whole time, talking confidentially and fraternally to each other.

Dr. S. has told me that the two Bills were to run the show—the Foundation and Brotherhood, when it gets going, with Papas Hales and Sadler directing behind the scenes. But this PLAN will NEVER go through. The Forum members are now up in arms against this. How INCONSIDERATE the Sadlers are of the Forum members as a whole . . . the obvious playing of a few favorites . . . when, were I in charge, I would recognize all on an EQUAL BASIS . . . And this will be done when the Forum reconvenes . . . at last, Forum members will have something to say . . . the doctor's authority is to be removed, whether he fumes and rages or not. Bill is the one who is going to crack up . . . many think he is losing his mental balance the way he is acting, anyway.

I now take recognition of your comments about the HALESES and tell you we have already been on our guard . . . and, more so, since your instructions . . . there is something decidedly UNHEALTHY about their clubby attitude with the Sadlers . . . and I agree with you, they MUST NOT have any connection any more than any other Forum member. The doctor himself told me that Mrs. Hales had cracked up within the past year again . . . and had burned up all of Sadler's autographed books he had given her . . . turning against him . . . now she is temporarily on good behavior again and regretful of her past acts. But what she will think of us when she knows we are SO OPPOSED, you can imagine. I wouldn't put it past her to try almost anything to get rid of us . . . there is no insanity worse than religious insanity . . . people even feel justified in killing others as an imagined mandate from God.

Harry, how involved the human animal has become on this earth . . . and what a battle to straighten his muddles out. To think that a great spiritual revelation like this is temporarily in jeopardy because of existing conditions. I cannot believe that the Angels of Progress will permit things to go astray . . . and I hope and pray they are with us every step of this fight.

The Matterns have shown up on the scene at a most critical time, and Mattern is a TERRIFIC POWER. I have never seen a man with such will and resolution. And to show you how observing he is, he spent one evening with Bill, who read him the paper on the Apostles, and then Mattern said to me: "Say, Harold, if it wasn't for my faith in you and Martha, Mary Mattern and I would have walked out on this setup. Tell me honestly, what kind of a racket are the Sadlers running over there. They think they own this revelation and they don't intend to let go of it. I didn't know they were going to have an organization to put this book out. Why, you can't present the truth this way . . . that's what's wrong with the world now . . . the truth isn't free!"

I then explained the situation to the Matterns and they are continuing their reading and acting dumb . . . but observing. Mattern remembers Dr. S. telling him, on first interview, "No human personality is to be connected with this" . . . and he is going to remind the doctor of this statement when the meeting takes place, and say that he would never have joined the Forum group if he had understood they were to develop into a new religion . . . that this was not his understanding.

Incidentally, Harry, Mattern is curious and eager to know more about himself and his own place in this scheme of things and seems to recall that you promised him further word about himself.[5] He is such a go-getter and he has been so impressed by you—of all the people he has met—I think it would do him great good, if you cared to do so, for him to get word direct from you, which I am sure he would keep confidential. He is staying at the Lincoln Park Arms Hotel, 2738 N. Pine Grove. (H.C. Mattern . . . everyone calls him H.C.)

Martha and I have been busy into the wee small hours night after night on this development and it looks like much more work ahead. Accordingly, while it is a "personal wrench" of no small proportions to consider being without Marcia, we are planning to act upon your suggestion [to send her to Traverse City] . . . as we cannot see how it

[5] See Vol. 1, pp. 369-370.

would be any life for her here . . . with her father and mother engaged almost every evening . . . and having to sleep part of the days in order to get new energy . . . I have not been able to touch the rewrite of the Jane Addams play as yet . . . this has been a full-time job . . . and I am proceeding in the faith that we will be taken care of on the monetary side. I think we will get this petition on record and slip up to Traverse for a few days and make arrangements for Marcia's schooling . . . and then come back to resume the battle here. We know she will be happy in Traverse . . . and there is not now any assurance of a larger apartment here to include her, or even an extra room.

Back to the Sadlers, I think it has been an economic pull for the doctor with Bill and the Kelloggs needing financial help or compensation . . . and he has increasingly sold himself a bill of goods that the Urantia papers were to provide him an income for the rest of his life and Bill's family also. Actually, if he did what should be done . . . and kept the truth free, the BY-PRODUCTS of this book would open up legitimate opportunities for financial return which would take care of him. But trying to OWN IT and SEW IT UP the way he is . . . will kill the truth.

In meditation the other night, I was caused to open the Bible to Jeremiah, chapter 36, 6th and 7th verses:

"Therefore, go thou, and read in the roll, which thou hast written from my mouth, the words of the Lord in the ears of the people in the Lord's house upon the fasting day: and also thou shalt read them in the ears of all Judah that come out of their cities. . . .

"It may be they will present their supplication before the Lord, and will return everyone from his evil way; for great is the anger and the fury that the Lord hath pronounced against this people."

Perhaps, at the proper time, without any reference to this message as from a higher source, the communication I sent you should be read. Perhaps other bits of information which come to me should be used by me as my own . . . for I do not seek to be any message bearer . . . and I know how dangerous this is . . . so many unstable people imagine they get messages and suffer hallucinations, etc.

Well—it's a terrific thing I've moved in on . . . and it just about requires all the past experience I've had to hold up my end. It's amazing how the Forum members have rallied about me . . . but I'm not trying to do it all . . . I'm apportioning the work to as many as I can . . . so it can be a united effort.

Martha is standing by me wonderfully as she always has. I couldn't "take it" without her. Hay fever is bad but I've had it before . . . and it takes more than that to run me out of my assignment. In fact, I've never been trained to run from anything. We have filled two notebooks practically already . . . of our diary . . . and what a story this already contains.

Our love to you and Ma . . . and please let me keep you in stamps since it is heartening to hear from you.

FORUM CALENDAR *August 27, 1942*

Sir Hubert our guest at Isbell's. Christy reads Tabamantia indictment to Sir Hubert and us in evening.

DIARY *August 27, 1942*

Late this p.m. Harold received a surprise phone call from Sir Hubert, who had just arrived in city from Mishawaka, Ind., where he had been on war work. Harold immediately invited him for dinner, finding Sir Hubert had not yet received his recent letter explaining the current situation here, that he might bring Sir Hubert up to date. We had dinner with him at Isbell's, and Harold dated him for the "strategy board meeting" with Bedell, Bucklin and Karle at the University Club tomorrow noon as well as for the big meeting of Forum members assembled for purposes of signing the petition at the Karles' on Saturday night. Harold declared that Sir Hubert's arrival could not have been better timed since he could be a great influence through his presence here and the weight of his own counsel at this moment. Sir Hubert expressed pleasure at being here and stated he would have come had he been compelled to commute back and forth to Mishawaka. It seemed to us that Sir Hubert's coming might be attributed, as Dr. S. has so often said, to his being "circumstanced." Certainly his signature on the petition can mean much.

After dinner, Harold arranged with Christy and Dr. S. for Wilkins to be read the Tabamantia indictment and the Bright and Morning Star of Avalon papers. We spent two thrilling hours with Christy and the Doctor, these papers retaining their power and inspiration for us on second reading and greatly impressing Sir Hubert. We were impressed anew by the farewell statement of the Bright and Morning Star who, addressing the little mortal assemblage beside the sleeping contact, said he "had no censure to offer them but that one day they would stand in the presence of the record they had made during their short life here as spiritually endowed human animals" and he hoped, then, "that they would not have been found to be wanting in the trust placed in them and the mission they had been destined to perform." Dr. S. pointed out that these great beings like the Bright and Morning Star of Avalon had a regard and consideration for us even in our lowly state since they can perceive our glorious possible future as a Finaliter.

FORUM CALENDAR *August 28, 1942*

Lunch at University Club. Bedell, Wilkins, Bucklin, Karle and Harold. Discuss petition. Sir Hubert signs.

DIARY *August 28, 1942*

Early this a.m. (about 7), Harold was awakened with the feeling that he had been in conference with F. L. Reed, head of his former publisher, Grosset & Dunlap. Harold was surprised to find himself discussing with Mr. Reed the popular-priced publication of the Book of Urantia. It seemed that he had already completed arrangements with another publisher for the higher-priced edition, and Mr. Reed was startled at his proposition that Grosset & Dunlap bring out a popular-priced edition at the same time. Harold saw that he had in his hand what seemed to be part of an opening advertisement announcing the Book of Urantia. He showed it to Mr. Reed, who studied it thoughtfully but uncertainly, and Harold suddenly remembered that Mr. Reed was a staunch Catholic. While he was wondering how to overcome this possible barrier, Mrs. Reed, who had died some ten years before, suddenly appeared and earnestly entreated her husband to publish this book. Harold felt he had gone as far as he could in presenting the matter himself and that he should leave Mr. Reed alone with his wife.

There then seemed to be a lapse of time and, as Harold awakened with a photographic memory of the advertising copy, Mr. Reed appeared to be trying to get him on the telephone with regard to the Book of Urantia. Harold arose as quickly as possible and reported his memory of the advertising copy. Consciously he had never conceived of the idea of two different publishing concerns bringing out two differently priced editions of the Book of Urantia at the same time. Such a procedure would be a most radical departure from any previously known publishing venture and an absolute sensation in the trade.

FOR A THOUSAND YEARS TO COME!

Never before, in all countless ages of the past, has anything happened like this on earth!

Never before has the evolving soul of Man been placed face to face with the revealed Truths of the Universe!

Never before has God spoken direct to His creature, Man, through the printed word.

Jesus left no written word when He departed, after His crucifixion, this World of the Cross.

Your present Bible is therefore the word of God and the story of His Creator Son, as revealed by the prophets and scribes of old.

But now, for this new age just dawning, there comes to Man, through a Revelatory Commission of Celestial Beings - a new and further revelation!

Now, this planet, and all human creatures upon it, are to have a new spiritual awakening.

NOT through a new religion! But, through a BOOK which is destined to amplify and clarify and make firm the Truth in all religions - and for all humans of all faiths and no faith at all.

URANTIA, the true name of this earth planet on which you reside, is but one of BILLIONS of inhabited worlds!

It was designed and created several billion years ago, as earth time is counted, by the Architects of this Universe, acting upon a mandate from God, the Universal Father.

When all was in readiness, a special order of Beings known as Universe Life Carriers, brought the first early forms of life to this planet and planted them here.

And your ancestor - primitive man - was permitted to evolve and start his own self-willed, God-seeking climb, from the lowliest of beginnings to the highest possible universe attainment, in realms beyond the state we call Death.

The whole wondrous, compelling, authentic story is contained in this modern revelation -

THE BOOK OF URANTIA!

Text of the advertising copy in Harold's dream

What may come of this as pertains to so many other things which are unfolding, remains of course to be seen.

"Strategy luncheon," University Club. Present were Bucklin, Jones, Karle, Bedell, Wilkins and Sherman. This meeting was called for the purpose of considering and putting in final form the petition drawn up by Bedell. Wilkins' presence proved an added stimulus, and several of his suggestions for changes were very much in order. It was decided that a committee of three old-time Forum members would call upon the Doctor and present this petition personally, telling him they would return for his answer at a later convenient time. Everyone stressed the importance of maintaining the good will of all if humanly possible.

Wilkins seemed doubtful Doctor could be so adamant and was in favor of tempering the petition wherever possible. He confessed he had seen the Doctor only when on good behavior, and did say that he would have hesitated in joining the Forum had he known it might develop into a religious order. (Karle reported he had just heard another committee had been appointed to prepare a ritual for a form of worship for the society.) All assured Wilkins that the steps they were taking were imperatively necessary if any constructive results were to be obtained. Wilkins left his signature on the petition and said that he would like to be notified when it had been submitted, as he wished to write his views to the Doctor. Wilkins seemed to feel that an organization might spring up or be necessary, and it was not until later, in a further talk with Harold, that he suddenly apparently saw all the hazards involved.

Bedell stated in the meeting that he had found Miss [Marian] Rowley an idolatrous worshiper of Bill; and Karle reported that a talk with Mr. [Edward F.] Hill disclosed him to be in support of the present Sadler plans. Neither Bedell nor Karle opened up on their contacts as a consequence.

Bucklin was given the revised petition so that his wife might type off the final copy and have it ready for signing upon occasion of the Saturday night gathering of Forum members at the Karles'.

Phone conversation eve. with H.C. Mattern. Mary and H.C. reported to Harold that they had been wading through the first fifteen chapters and asked him, "Harold, can you tell us when this reading is going to get easier? It's awfully tough going, and we confess it's mostly words to us so far, but we've got faith that we'll come out into the clearing as you and Martha have told us, and that what we read will come to mean a great deal to us."

H.C. then said to Harold that he was wondering how a book of this kind could ever appeal to humanity at large, and Harold said that he felt that a little booklet should be issued with each book sold, entitled "How to Read the Book of Urantia." In this way, scientists, astronomers, chemists—all different types and professions of people down to the ordinary man on the street—would be given the key as to where to start reading and how to approach the material contained in this amazing book. H.C. declared that something like this was absolutely necessary, for average humans would never get past the first page.

This reaction of the Matterns was indicative since they do represent an average couple, but they possess excessive determination; and where they might persist, the majority of others of similar background would have long since refused to continue. Developing methods to enhance the readability of the Book of Urantia then becomes a major problem and is apt to remain so, requiring a tremendous publicity and promotional campaign under supervision of an advisory board and an established book publisher.

FORUM CALENDAR *August 29, 1942*

Evening at Karles' for signing of petition. Mrs. Steinbeck, (3) Evanses [Luther, Harriet and Avice], Miss Cook,[6] Bucklins, Dyons, Mrs. Bedell, Miss Brown, Mr. & Mrs. [Robert and Ruth] Burton, Mrs. Githens and us.

DIARY *August 29, 1942*

Since deciding to run up to Traverse City the first of the week to check affairs there (re Marcia), Harold went across to see Mr. Kellogg and asked him to arrange through the Chicago Motor Club a routing for the trip. He was greeted with unusual warmth by Mr. Kellogg and also by his wife, who came in later to give him a hearty handshake and to say what a joy it always was to see either one of us.

On learning that Ruth was in bed with an asthmatic attack, Harold asked them to convey his sympathy, and Mr. Kellogg said, "I'll do that. Ruth is tremendously fond of you and your wife and very

[6] This could be either Agatha or her sister Edith.

How to Read
THE BOOK OF URANTIA

Not as you have ever read any book before, because nothing like this book has ever existed before.

A mere glance at the mighty Foreword will tell you this.

An attempt to read and fully comprehend the first page of the first chapter on, "The Universal Father", will tell you more.

You will know, even in so short an acquaintance with the BOOK OF URANTIA that you are in the PRESENCE of revealed TRUTH - that what your eyes and mind behold is beyond the power of human expression.

Your first feeling may be: "How can I ever expect to understand this, though it be the Truth?"

But there are KEYS to your understanding - ways for you to read this BOOK and get from it the MESSAGE it contains for your own mind and soul.

The BOOK OF URANTIA was purposely conceived and transmitted by a specially assigned Revelatory Commission of Celestial Beings - to speak authoritatively and convincingly for the next thousand years of earth time, to all grades and types of human consciousness on this planet.

Through this BOOK, the scientist, astronomer, geologist, physicist, chemist, geneticist, historian, teacher, philosopher, sociologist, economist, public official, religionist, father, mother, youth, child and layman of any and all races, color and creeds, may find the TRUTH and apply it to their individual and collective backgrounds and needs.

How do YOU classify yourself in the world of humans? This will be your KEY to the reading of the BOOK OF URANTIA - the KEY which will open its TRUTHS to you simply, clearly and with a spiritual power never before experienced!

IF you are a SCIENTIST, your <u>first</u> interest will be....

IF you are an astronomer, your first interest will be...

ETC.

Outline of Harold's suggested booklet (see p. 184)

much interested in the things you are interested in." This told Harold a great deal. Apparently the Kelloggs had thought us to be partial to the Sadlers, and having revealed our stand to them had served to intensify their own demonstration of friendship.

Eve. Karles'. The Bucklins and Mrs. Githens rode out with us to the Karles', and en route Mildred [Bucklin] exclaimed, "This is the first real job I've done for Urantia. I consider it a privilege." She had reference to the fact that she had stayed up late the night before to make the fine copies of the petition.

Present were Karles, Dyons, Mr. and Mrs. Luther Evans, Mrs. Githens, Miss Cook, Mrs. Evans (2), Mrs. Steinbeck, Miss Brown, Mrs. Bedell, Bucklins, Shermans and Burtons.

Dent Karle opened this meeting with a few preliminary remarks having to do with discussions which had taken place among Forum members with regard to the approaching Urantia Book publication and organization problems. He indicated how these discussions had led to the decision that a petition should be drawn up and presented to the Doctor, requesting a wide-open airing of all questions now confronting the Forum. Karle then read the petition and called for comments upon it. Practically everyone seemed in accord but the Dyons, who asked for further information on different points and expressed themselves as feeling that some of the terms in the petition were too strong. They were reminded that the Doctor and Bill were two such strong personalities that unless a positive, well-substantiated request was made for a fair and unprejudiced hearing, they would not be apt to pay much attention.

Al Dyon asked Harold to outline some of the points he had raised at a previous gathering in the Dyon home, and Harold decided to read his letters to Sadler to the group since all points were covered more emphatically in these letters than he could express offhand. The letters seemed to make a profound impression on those who had not heard them heretofore, and Miss Cook, one of the oldest Forum members, seemed particularly concerned despite her high regard for Bill.

An invitation was then extended to those present by Dent Karle for them to sign the petition. As they were in the process of doing this, Al Dyon got a hold of Harold and asked if changes could not be made in the petition to "soften the blow" for the Doctor. Harold declared that, knowing the Doctor's reactions, as all in the Forum did, they could expect him to explode temporarily no matter how the petition might be worded.

Mrs. Dyon came up and said she objected to the clause referring to the contributions which had been made, and said that they did not wish their money back under any circumstances. Harold explained this was not the purpose of the reference to contributions but simply to remind the Doctor that the Forum members considered that they had not only a spiritual interest in the Book of Urantia but a material interest as well. He reminded her that this was basically simply a request for a free discussion which she said she thought was advisable. Harold then stepped aside to let the Dyons decide between themselves whether they wished to sign the petition. By this time everyone else had signed.

After a moment's hesitation, Mrs. Dyon said, "Well, Al, we've got to be going home. Are you going to sign this or aren't you?"

Dyon picked up the pen and said, "Yes, dear, I'm going to sign it."

When she saw her husband's action, she took the pen from him and said, "Then I'll sign it with you."

Mr. Burton, who had been hearing of these matters for the first time, had expressed himself earlier as having voluntarily offered his services to the Doctor in drawing up the charters for the Foundation and organization. He revealed he had been a lawyer specializing in corporation affairs but that the Doctor had disregarded his suggestions and proffers of help. Mr. Burton criticized the charters as finally drawn up as being "too prolix," prepared in this manner to impress the client, as it evidently had the Doctor—and with this grandiose wordage to seem to justify a high fee. Mr. Burton had attempted to influence Al Dyon at the last, as well, by saying he felt free discussion an excellent way of protecting the interests of all. The Dyons when they left were still jittery, although Al Dyon was soberly impressed at the possibility that a publicly discredited organization might reflect not only on him personally but upon the life of his daughter.

Harold pointed out that it was better to face a little unpleasantness in privacy now than to permit something to be done publicly which might humiliate the Doctor and cause him to turn to Forum members and say, "If you felt some things were wrong, why didn't you say so? Why did you wait until too late to do anything?"

As Harold shook hands with Dyon and told him goodnight, he said, "Well Al, now we'll all die together."

HARRY LOOSE to HAROLD SHERMAN

Monterey Park, August 30, 1942

Dear Harold:-

Your extremely interesting letter with the dream enclosed received. Your activities certainly indicate that you have been "going some." From what is written, and what I also read between the lines, I surely do not see anything to criticize. You seem to have things pretty well in hand. In any movement concerning a number of people however, you must always be prepared for a stab in the back. So be expecting something of that nature to arrive from some point that you least expect—and be very thankful if such does not materialize.

Without naming the source at any time, any information that comes to you can honestly be used as your very own—for such it is. It would be fatal however, at this period, to name a source for any information. Such action would give the opposition the very ammunition that they would appreciate. Can you imagine a full Forum meeting with Bill Sadler, and others, cross-questioning you as to the authenticity of the source of your communications???? Remember how they questioned Jesus as to the authenticity of his source of information??? How could you escape it—if Jesus did not—you must prepare yourself for question and disbelief in the future as you continue in this work. Remember that Bill Sadler, or any other Forumite present, would be entitled to ask questions at any open meeting. Do you visualize the irreparable damage that could happen?? Remember, though, that you can firmly and honestly state that you are definitely NOT ACTING ALONE nor entirely on your own initiative. That your way has been, and is continuing to be, indicated to you—which it most truly is. This is really the truth of the matter. After making a positive declaration of the above, then UNDER NO CIRCUMSTANCES DIVULGE THE SOURCE. The procedure indicated will be received with respect and confidence, and will be helpful. . . .

I am very glad to read your recognition of the Hales situation. ALL of them are dangerous. More so than you now can visualize. You will recognize more as time goes on. Avoid them all—whenever possible.

In your activities, be sure to arrogate as many duties as possible to others that they, too, may feel their importance in the problems at hand.

"Eternity and I" still hangs in its accustomed place upon the wall. Its swinging rhythm is perfect. It is much admired, but—you now see where the philosophy contained therein is much different than that to which you have now advanced.

So glad that "H.C." and Mary are with you. He gives you strength and courage besides the comfort of his physical association.

Remark in your next on my suggestion for the reading of the Book by your lady publisher—and her friend—the lady of wealth.

The first part of your night vision was distinctly and positively a thought projection from a troubled mind in search of the harmony of truth. Your para-sensitive mind seized upon it immediately for registry and dissection. You definitely and unmistakably identify the seeker as Kellogg. He comes to you proffering the instrument by which harmony is best expressed. He is still troubled and unsure—much because of his loyalty to Sadler—and he asks to reassure himself by your answer if you have heard from "the one." In this question, he directly refers to Sadler with whom there have been many conversations dealing with your present and probable future activities. Not alone conversations between them, but in the presence of other auditors. You may be very sure that you, and Martha, have been much under discussion. This should be no surprise to either of you. You surely expected such. However, these conversations have not been happy ones which refer to you.

Sadler is definitely afraid of you—and is at a loss to know in what plane to place you. He knows that you have greater knowledge of this whole matter than what you have outwardly expressed; and with this greater knowledge of an understanding of the entire picture, far beyond the casual Forumite, he recognizes an authority that is quite strange to him. He is fearful and a bit bewildered as to procedure. And he is filled with regrets that you were admitted to the Forum as a member and wishes that it could be all undone. Kellogg is fully aware of all this—including Sadler's mental state. Christy could tell you some things if she wanted to talk. Kellogg—both Mr. and Mrs.—have a great liking for and belief in you—and there is no fear of you. I must impress you now with the fact, which I am ready to believe that you have already arrived at without any help from me—that BOTH of the Kelloggs are the superiors of the both Sadlers. You define it for yourself—I have for myself. Your acceptance of the Kellogg projection was an action of your subconscious which put some of its own dress upon the impress by the symbol's use, though fortunately, it made no attempt to disguise Kellogg to your consciousness. The Kelloggs are much troubled in mind. They know the Sadler-Bill-Haleses present setup is all wrong.

The turtle represents many things in dream or vision life. It is usually a symbol of good. However, it also does picture other states. The turtle is always used in the projection of the very "earth-earthy." It is not the only symbol used for such projection but it is one of such. The matter of your vision of the turtles is a very distinct thing in itself with no relation to the first part of the message. I can tell you that it was not complete and that you will probably have a continuance of it in some form or another. In very plain English, the three who have assumed a high place where they did not belong, through their own activities, which incur assistance, are cast down after difficulties between themselves in which, for a time, one will devour the other. In this instance of symbolism, the turtle represents a something that pertains to the very earth and belonging to the earth—something of low origin—a lack of spirituality—a lack of the ability or the capacity to absorb spirituality or to grow in things spiritual—a parasite growth upon the spiritual—a non-acceptance of the spiritual because of lack of understanding. The incomplete vision represents the desire of the subconscious to express a definite something to the conscious mind. Something in the nature of a warning—an attempt to deliver a message—an attempt that is incomplete. There is more that can be read—more possibilities—but that is sufficient for now—and the message has not concluded. This I will add: the three who are actors in the symbol drama are sufficiently near to you to be practically under constant observation. At any rate, be continuingly careful. There should be no lapse or letdown that you are caught off-guard.

Well, I find that I have written quite a long letter again. I sure am much interested in matters as they progress. Much love to you both and much good thought always,

FORUM CALENDAR *August 30, 1942*

Evening at Bucklins with Karles and Evanses.

DIARY *August 30, 1942*

The Karles informed us last night they had been invited to the Bill Hales' that evening at the last moment. H.C. Mattern reported that he had seen the Sadlers leaving in two cars, having been told by Bill when inviting him out to dinner that they were going out to see one of their strongest supporters. It is our feeling that the Sadlers and the Haleses got together for purposes of discussing Harold's publication plans since he turned in his new letter to the Doctor several days ago.

On phoning the Bucklins this a.m., Harold found them to be upset over the reactions of the Dyons. They came over to see us about it and said they felt the Dyons should be given a chance to withdraw, as Mrs. Dyon particularly might go to the Doctor or talk among other Forum members, expressing her disagreement with certain clauses in the petition. Harold did not share their feelings, stating that he thought our group should stand firm, that any offer to let the Dyons out of signing, after they had done so, would weaken our position and imply that perhaps our stand *was* a bit too strong. He said that certain emotional reactions must be expected on the part of some Forum members whether they signed or not, and he did not see any major hazards even if such attitudes should arise.

The Karles were phoned and their opinions asked, and they substantiated in general Harold's point of view. Dent Karle said, "I have known the Dyons for years. They've always been a willy-nilly couple. They mull over things pro and con and then finally decide to go along. I think any reopening of the subject with them at this time would serve to get them all up in the air again, and the chances are they have talked it out and become more settled in mind. In any event, before they would do anything, I'm sure Al Dyon would phone me and discuss the matter as he has done on other occasions before."

Elsie added her comment by saying that the last thing Mrs. Dyon had said to her before leaving was, "I'm not in agreement with some of the clauses in the petition but I do *definitely* believe that a free discussion should be held."

The Karles then decided to come in tonight to consult with the Bucklins and ourselves with respect to future plans and developments.

FORUM CALENDAR *August 31, 1942*

To Traverse for Marcia.

10

The Petition

Dear Dr. Sadler:

I

We, the undersigned, about to address you formally on a matter of vital importance to us all, cannot refrain from taking this opportunity to pay you the homage and respect which—despite our affection for you—we have expressed all too ineffectually and too infrequently through the years.

We wish to say to you that—with the Forum group approaching its first season as an independent informal group with no specifically designed task to sustain through the year—we are suddenly acutely aware of the preciousness to us of the years we have been associated with you, our friend and mentor.

We wish to apprise you of our sincere appreciation of what you have meant to us personally through the years in which we have enjoyed companionship with you. We have delighted in your humor, your revealing anecdotes and illustrations, your kindliness and your supreme devotion to the great experience which drew us all together.

We wish to register how impressed it is in our hearts that you have been singularly honored in connection with the Urantia papers. Our emotions crowd within us when we face the fact that it was through you as an integrating focal point that the magnificent experience of the Forum touched our lives.

We are proudly aware that in future worlds, our beloved Doctor of these long and fascinating years, will be pointed out for the part he played in the Urantia Revelation.

Dear friend, this tribute to you has been earned to a degree we cannot express in words. Not one of us whose life you have touched but is better for it. We will be forever grateful for everything you have meant to us in the days which have brought us to this vital, moving, momentous fall of 1942.

II

We, the undersigned, facing for the first time a season of independent association with each other, you, and the Urantia papers, have been impelled to newly appraise the situation in which we find ourselves, and in which we may ultimately find ourselves, in relation to the Urantia Revelation.

Owing a responsibility to the Revelatory Corps, we view the future gravely and with yearning for an auspicious introduction of the Urantia Book to the world.

In a very few years, it may be possible to look upon the printed Book we have so long followed in manuscript form with mingled awe, reverence and thanksgiving.

We know the Urantia Papers plan has been in the making for many years. We know that it has evolved and changed, sometimes radically, in the past.

We know that opinions held by the Contact Commissioners in the past, have on occasion been altered or modified under new light and in new circumstances.

We know that the papers themselves, at the hand of their high creators, have been changed and amplified and made to evolve as our mortal minds were put to them.

We know that the Angels of Progress are not entirely pleased with what we have thus far done in contemplation of publication, protection and dissemination of the Urantia Revelation.

All of the above emboldens us to suggest that in this vital and pregnant period, the group mind of the Forum should be employed to analyze and appraise the potentials inherent in the coming months.

We believe the Forum people as a group should turn with the most earnest effort toward the consideration and development of as much sound groundwork as is possible in all the practical aspects of this Book's future.

Respectfully, but most earnestly, we request an opportunity to know all the facts in connection with, and all the provisions concerning, the Urantia Book and the proposed associated organizations as their plans exist today.

To this date, no group opportunity has been offered to study, to freely discuss or to examine charters, articles of incorporation, by-laws, et cetera, of the several contemplated organizations.

To this date, earnest Forum members, many with sound experience, judgment and ability, have had no opportunity for frank and full expression of opinions based on familiarity with these organization plans which have been brought to elaborated state by the Contact Commissioners and outside aides.

We believe legal talent is justifiably used in formulating certain instruments which implement the Urantia Book plans. But we do not feel that Forum people should be excluded from full and complete understanding of all instruments identified with the Book for which we have a grave and undeniable responsibility as individuals.

Our responsibility incurred through months or years as Forum members does not drop from our shoulders with dissolution of the Forum as a formal body. All of us will be affected vitally by the future of this Book—and in view of the responsibility we feel toward it, and which the Book imposes upon us, we feel we have a right to understand all the terms of contracts or of formal organizations which have grown out of our collective experience.

There have been no restrictions on our examining, handling and reading—individually or in groups—the Papers which must transcend all the man-created documents to which we have not had free access, and about which our fullest judgment has never been sought.

We believe it is relevant that our questions were sought in connection with the Revelation itself. Our judgments, we have reason to believe, were observed and weighed again and again in connection with matters of great importance to untold unborn generations of men. The Forum has been used as a sounding board against which revealing truths were tried.

We believe our group should be trusted with the very natural task of serving as a human jury in connection with some of the proposals about which we are not fully familiar.

We believe there is sufficient intelligence, experience, and good judgment in the Forum group to provide fair analysis and invaluable reaction in the grave matters of the foundation, the brotherhood, the publication plans, et cetera—which are, after all, the proposals of mortal men.

III

Respectfully we submit our opinion that it should be not only the privilege, but the unmistakable duty of the Forum group, to sincerely and prayerfully ponder what is projected in connection with the Revelation to which our hearts, our minds, our hopes and our aspirations have been dedicated.

We, the undersigned, deem it incumbent upon ourselves—and such others of our group as feel a responsibility toward the Urantia Revelation, but whose wishes we have not ascertained in the matter—to turn our attention now to friendly and sincere consideration, analysis and appraisal of the man-made plans for dissemination and protection of the God-made manuscript which is so dear and important to us all.

We propose, preferably with help from you, to follow our consciences and promptings in this matter. We seek your permission to discuss these organization and publishing affairs deliberately, without haste and by arrangements as our group may elect in terms of full meetings, committees, report-backs, et cetera—but in any event first as follows: (a) Forum Room, 533 Diversey Pkwy., (b) beginning Sunday, September 13th, 1942, (c) under the leadership of a chairman of our own choosing, (d) with the essential papers, charters, articles of incorporation, et cetera to be made available to a committee later.

We point out and commend to your consideration the following:

There is no need for—and there is great weight of solemn honesty and sincerity against—precipitant action under present circumstances in finally and formally closing up publishing and, or any organization affairs which have been forming for at least ten years.

Forum people cannot have been expected to assimilate from an annual reading the essential forms, many ramifications, connotations and potentialities in a formidable series of documents which legal talent and highly intelligent laymen took months and even years to formulate.

Morally and ethically, those whose lives may be affected profoundly by these organizations and arrangements are entitled to analyze what their years of interest, good faith and forbearance helped bring into reality.

Legally, those who provide financial support for any collective effort are entitled to a full accounting and understanding of the potentials of the corporate or other bodies their contributions are used to bring into being, or to which their contributions are entrusted.

Should this specific group be denied the privilege of deliberately considering and fully understanding these subjects because it is feared the group will disagree on details, fail to appreciate the problems involved, or disapprove of some phases of the plans—that fear augurs ill for the Urantia Book if ever it is launched into the world with such plans for its cradle.

We believe that unity, if not uniformity, should prevail in our small Forum group which has been so signally blest in this association. We believe that such unity should be achieved as a matter of deliberate accord—not through blindness, unawareness, or inadequate consideration. We believe that our unity should come out of frank discussion, magnanimous give and take and a fair humility toward the views of others.

IV

We do not question the sincerity, honesty or conscientiousness of any associated in this matter.

We do question the infallibility, the inviolability, the longtime perspective, the soundness and the validity of any complex set of legal plans destined to vitally affect the futures of men if such plans cannot stand the scrutiny, inquiry, examination and analysis of men.

V

Dear friend, may we have full and adequate enlightenment, your further confidence and your cooperation?

ABOVE: The Sherman family in 1941 en route to California. [L-R] Martha, Marcia, Mary, and Harold [UCA ARCHIVES]

LEFT: Harry Loose in his front yard in Monterey Park, California, 1941 [SHERMAN FAMILY PRIVATE COLLECTION]

ABOVE: 533 Diversey Pkwy., the home and office of Dr. William S. Sadler, where the Urantia manuscript was kept [Saskia Praamsma]

LEFT: The Cambridge Apts., 530 Diversey Pkwy., across the street from 533, where Harold, Martha, and Marcia Sherman lived from 1942 to 1947 [Ted Morrison]

ABOVE: Four members of the "Contact Commission" at 533 in the 1930s. [L-R] Emma L. ("Christy") Christensen, Lena Sadler, William Sadler, Bill Sadler
[WWW.URANTIABOOK.ORG]

RIGHT: Ruth Kellogg on the roof at 533 Diversey Parkway
[TICKY HARRIES COLLECTION]

BELOW: Anna and Wilfred Kellogg at one of the annual Forum picnics
[WWW.URANTIABOOK.ORG]

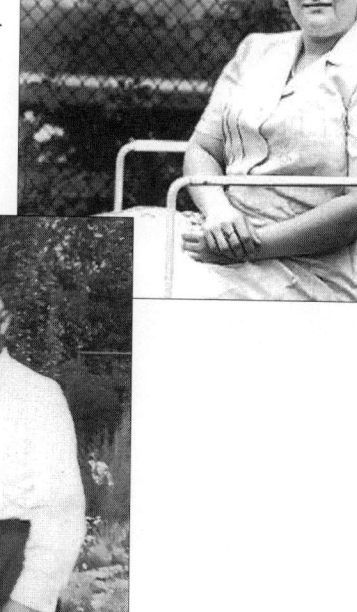

ABOVE: G. Willard Hales, Carrie Hales, and William Sadler at one of the annual Forum picnics
[WWW.URANTIABOOK.ORG]

LEFT: Rachel Gusler and her son Louis, circa 1942
[UCA ARCHIVES]

Sir Hubert Wilkins [UCA ARCHIVES]

Charles Francis Potter [UCA ARCHIVES]

H.C. Mattern [UCA ARCHIVES]

Clyde Bedell [C BARRIE BEDELL]

Bill Sadler and Bill Hales at the 1942 Forum picnic at the Hales home [URANTIABOOK.ORG]

[L-R] Marian Rowley, Martha Sherman, Alvin Kulieke, and Lucile Olson [UCA ARCHIVES]

[L-R] Lulu Steinbeck and Grace Palmer at the 1942 Forum picnic [UCA Archives]

[L-R] Art Born, Lee Miller Jones, and Charles Rawson [urantiabook.org]

[L-R] Ruth Burton, Martha Sherman, Lulu Steinbeck, Robert Burton, Mrs. Walton, Harold Sherman, Glenna Johnson, Grace Palmer, and Mildred Hoffman, at Grace Palmer's dinner party, November 15, 1942 [UCA Archives]

[L-R] Mildred Hoffman, Lulu Steinbeck, Glenna Johnson, Harold Sherman, Grace Palmer, Martha Sherman, Robert Burton, Mrs. Walton, and Ruth Burton [UCA Archives]

Part IV

Branded a Rebel

1

The Psychology of Fear

SIR HUBERT WILKINS to HAROLD SHERMAN

The City Club,
New York, September 3, 1942

Dear Harold,

Looks as if I won't be able to make Chicago on the 13th but hope the results of the collective efforts turn out for the best.

Several here at the Club and at the Rialto office (where I took some work to be done today) asked after you and send their best wishes.

Was glad to see you both the other day and hope it won't be too long before we meet again.

Best wishes & regards,
Hubert

FORUM CALENDAR *September 4, 1942*

Returned in eve (8:30) from Traverse. Met at door by Bucklins who report the petition has been presented to Dr. Sadler at 6 this evening. (Dent, Miss Baumgartner, Luther Evans)

DIARY *September 4-5, 1942*

In Traverse City from Aug. 31 till Fri., Sept. 4, to learn situation there and bring Marcia back. Returned at 8:30 p.m. to encounter the Bucklins in front of our apartment house the instant we stepped out of the car. This was an amazing occurrence since we had been held up by traffic 3/4 of an hour coming in on Lake Shore Drive past Soldier Field where the Army Show was in progress. Had we arrived earlier, we would have of course missed them. As it was, we found the elevator broken down and the Bucklins helped us upstairs with our luggage.

They reported tremendous activity and little sleep during our absence, and the securing of 48 names on the petition, which had been presented to Dr. S. by a committee comprised of Dent Karle, Luther Evans and Elsie Baumgartner this very evening at 6:15 p.m. The Doctor had received them and Dent Karle had presented the petition in a sealed envelope so the Doctor would not open and read it in their presence. He tried to do this, however, by breaking the seal and declaring, "I think I know what this is. Sit down. I think we can decide this right here."

Dent Karle declined by replying, "No, Doctor. We'd like to have you study this at your leisure and return to get your answer late Monday."

The committee members had shaken hands with the Doctor on entering, being ushered in by Mr. Kellogg who had asked them to wait a few minutes since the Doctor was seeing a patient. But now they filed out, leaving the Doctor gazing at the petition which he had taken from the envelope. As they passed Mr. Kellogg in the hall, he said, "Good luck to you." (The appointment to see the Doctor had been made by Dent Karle through Mr. Kellogg who had asked if it was to be "business" or "personal." When Karle appeared with two other Forum members, Kellogg could not conceal an expression of surprise.)

The Bucklins reported work into the wee small hours every night and incessant telephone calls and journeyings by day to contact and call upon every reachable Forum member. They told of Al Dyon cracking up badly and pleading to have his name withdrawn, as well as his wife's, then finally standing pat when he was informed that the only way this could be done would be for him to write a letter which would be affixed to the petition. Miss [Eva] Vincent and Miss Rowley, two old standbys, signed, as did a Mrs. [Rachel] Gusler, who was revealed to have been one of the members who wrote Dr. S. a letter criticizing organization plans.[1] This letter bore a startling similarity

[1] See p. 141 of this volume.

Russell Buehler
Mildred Buehler
Luther Evans
Mrs " "
5 Clyde Bedell
Mrs " "
Miss Githens
Mr. Al. Dyson
Mrs " "
10 Miss Rawley
Miss Vincent
Mrs Evans (2nd)
Martha
Harold
15 Elsie Karle
Albert Karle
Mrs Steinbeck
Mr. Steinbeck
Miss Jones
20 Mrs Gessler
Jim Hicks
Betty Hicks
Mr Kulicke (Sr.)
Miss Brown (Carolyn)
25 Miss Cook
Miss Baumgartner
Mr Robt. Burton
Mrs " "
Dr. Herbert Williams
30 Mr Lee Miller Jones
Mrs " " Jones
Mary Lou Hales
Mr Lavrentz
Mrs "
35 Miss Kemper

Petition as presented on Sept 4/42
42 signers

Partial list of the petition signers.

in its contents to the one Harold had written, and indicated again widespread Forum feeling with respect to developments.

The Karles approached the Haleses, calling first upon Bill and Mary Lou. They got Mary Lou's signature, who said she thought free discussion was a good thing. They then made an appointment to see Mr. Hales Sr. with Bill, and both explained that because of their peculiar personal relationship they could not sign the petition, but Mr. Hales said, "I'm with you people 100%, and while I can't sign I feel I can do more behind the scenes and after the Doctor receives the petition. I intend to have a talk with him. But let me say I admire your guts."

Difficulty was experienced in securing the proper woman member for the committee, and when Miss Baumgartner was chosen she was in a quandary as to why she should have been chosen since hardly any Forum member had ever paid any attention to her. She was finally decided upon her course of action by the reading of Harold's two letters to her (borrowed from Clyde Bedell) at the home of Luther Evans on Thursday night. The Evanses had permitted their home to be used on three different night occasions and were exhausted by the end of the week. The Lee Miller Joneses, on whom the Bucklins and Karles had counted, fizzled out badly along with the Dyons and the Rawsons, who were not even approached.

Al Dyon, in the course of the week, had become so upset that he had gone to Christy and told her of the petition and of his signing of it, and she had expressed great concern and told him, "It must be stopped." She then showed him a communication which she apparently interpreted as justification for their present actions and asked him to get in touch with the others and have them desist. Dyon was unable to convince Bucklin or Karle that this communication contained sufficient significance to be worthy of consideration, they stating that if the Sadlers were sure of their position, why should they be concerned?

Later Friday night, after the Bucklins had gone, Harold saw Miss Vincent and Miss Rowley leave the Sadlers, and we learned Saturday that they had been called in by the Doctor and influenced to withdraw their names.

FORUM CALENDAR *September 5, 1942*

Harold has lunch with Miss Baumgartner.

Harold asked to read letters at Mrs. Steinbeck's in evening. Those present—Leverentzes [*Ed. note:* Fred and Alice Leverenz], Miss [E. Virginia] Kemper, Bucklins and us.

DIARY *September 5, 1942*

Saturday a.m. it became known that Christy was phoning everyone but the apparent ringleaders on the list of 48 names and having them come in relays with the apparent intention of appealing to them, overawing or dominating them to the extent of having them remove their names from the petition. Members were seen during the day, including Mary Lou Hales, but the two Hales men were out of town for the weekend as was Mr. [Edmond] Kulieke Sr. Some members decided not to go when invited; others who intended to stand fast went for the purpose of determining Dr. S.'s attitude and method of approach. It seemed obvious that the Sadlers were afraid to face the Forum as a body and to bring these facts out in the open. That their feelings were running high was evidenced by a refusal on the part of Mr. Kellogg to let the Matterns read when they called around 10 a.m. Saturday. They were treated abruptly and dismissed with no assurance as to when they might take up their reading again.

At noon Harold thought it wise to have lunch with Miss Baumgartner, whom Harry Loose had spoken well of, and he called for her at her office in the *Chicago Daily News* building where Harry had formerly been stationed. Harold told Miss Baumgartner in confidence something of his contacts with Harry, and she said Harry had told her some years in advance of her being brought into the Forum that they [Elsie and Harry] were someday to be associated in a spiritual work together. She had not comprehended the full meaning of his prediction until Harold's letter to Dr. S. had been read to the Forum almost a year ago, when it suddenly dawned on her that this group to which she now belonged must have been the one to which Harry had referred. She wrote Harry a grateful letter upon making this discovery, which Harry showed to us while we were in California.

Harold told Miss Baumgartner how highly Harry thought of her and how glad he, Harold, was that she had consented to act on this committee. She explained that she really was suffering from serious heart trouble and could not afford to get emotionally upset. She wished this privately known so that her refusal to be too active in the work ahead would be understood. She said she had noted a growing tendency on the part of the Sadlers and certain members towards becoming religious zealots, and expressed alarm at their interpreting every little happening as having been circumstanced.

When Harold spoke of the Sadlers "playing favorites" among members of the Forum, Miss Baumgartner quickly commented that this was remarked upon by many members at the annual picnic when we and Sir Hubert were placed at the head table on the porch with Mr. Hales and the Sadlers and Christy. Miss Baumgartner said the meeting with Harold meant a great deal to her, and that as a member of the committee she was not going over to see the Sadlers as invited but would call with the committee when they returned for the answer on the petition.

Saturday night the Steinbecks invited us over, saying they wanted the Leverenzes and Miss Kemper to hear Harold's two letters. They apparently were deeply impressed, particularly Mr. Leverenz, who said he had noticed a growth of Bill's ego and said that it was the beginning of a "messianic complex." He asked Harold if he would be willing to repeat a statement made by Bill who said he would challenge Higher Sources if any orders came through contrary to his own ideas or interpretations. Harold said he would face Bill with his own statements, if this were found to be ultimately and absolutely necessary, but did not want to personalize the issues if it could be helped.

The Steinbecks were dated up to see the Sadlers at 7 p.m. Sunday, there apparently being a series of little meetings scheduled throughout the day. It was the opinion of Mrs. Steinbeck that it would be a good thing for the Doctor to meet some members whom he could not sway rather than those members declining his invitation.

Miss Kemper, in referring to the hazards of an organization setup and how it is apt to be regarded by the outside world, said she was in a chiropractor's office on Cambridge St. some months ago and the chiropractor said to her, "I've seen you going in and out of the Sadlers' place. Do you belong to that group who think they've got a direct wire to God?"

FORUM CALENDAR *September 6, 1942*

Karles stop for visit and supper (Isbell's) before going to evening interview with Doc.

DIARY *September 6-7, 1942*

Sunday 9/6 the Karles phoned early afternoon saying they were coming in and would stop at the Bucklins' and get in touch with us later. Martha phoned Mildred to tell her of this, and Mildred reported that Christy had just phoned, crying, saying there were many things that they (the Bucklins) did not understand and asked them to come over, and they were on the point of leaving. Mrs. Githens, Mildred said, had just arrived from seeing the Doctor and she [Mildred] promised to phone back after they had returned and tell us what had happened.

It was now known that the Doctor had been seeing the rank and file of Forum members on a worked-out schedule from Friday night, after the petition had been presented, through Saturday, and intended eventually to cover all Forum members with meetings of small selected groups going on throughout Monday also. The Doctor was reported to be reading a communication which inferred that this was another Lucifer rebellion with Harold the leader of same, and calling upon all members to withdraw their names from the petition or be classed as a rebel. This procedure was having dramatic and emphatic effect.

Late in the p.m., while we were wondering how the Bucklins had fared, the Karles arrived with a self-conscious, secretive air, simply stating that the Bucklins had returned and had been so impressed with the authority of the communication that they had withdrawn their names. Mrs. Githens, who had stood steadfast, now decided to withdraw her name also. The Karles themselves had arranged to see the Doctor at 9 that night after a call from Christy, who reached them at the Bucklins. They were to go in company with Mr. and Mrs. Lou [Luther] Evans and Miss Baumgartner, which, allowing for the two wives concerned, represented the original petition committee. Karle had said he wished to ask the Doctor certain specific questions.

It is reported that the Doctor said he had no intention of issuing a pamphlet, and there would be no Brotherhood organization for from 3-5 years after release of the book. These statements in themselves were a reversal of his former announced intentions, but though we waited into the evening after the Karles had left us from dinner for word from them or from the Bucklins, we got no call. This seemed exceedingly strange, since they had been in such close touch with us throughout all these discussions and activities. We saw them leave the Sadler residence at a little after 11 p.m. and go back to the Bucklins' but no word was forthcoming, although we learned later from an unexpected source that they remained until long after midnight discussing developments, and that Mildred had phoned Clyde Bedell and several others, advising them to get in touch with the Doctor and arrange to hear the communications, at the same time recommending that they withdraw their names.

It now became apparent that Harold was being made the special target of the Doctor and that all were being ordered not to tell him anything; that he was to be taken care of in a special and final way when all names had been removed from the petition.

When we came in from taking Mary back to Hull House, we found a call in our box from Mr. Steinbeck but did not phone him till the following a.m. When reached at around 10:30 Monday a.m. when we still had not heard from anyone, he stated frankly that Forum members were being told Harold was the instigator of "this uprising," but it was Mr. Steinbeck's feeling that no higher beings would have instituted such persecution proceedings. He stated flatly that this was the first communication he had ever heard which he could not go along with. He said he felt it unfair to Harold not to know what was being said about him, and had gone on record to the Doctor that he would sign the same petition tomorrow if it were presented to him.

Mrs. Steinbeck got on the phone and said there was no doubt that the Doctor was most wrathful concerning Harold, and had said that Bill would never forgive him, but that he supposed since he (the Doctor) had sponsored him, he would have to stand by him in the end.

The Doctor indicated that he still was willing to consider any new publishing ideas and would arrange to see Harold's publisher around September 14th. Why he should have mentioned any date we do not know. He possibly thought he would have everything under control by that time and handle everything himself by that time as formerly. Harold stated to the Steinbecks that, but for their kindness and consideration, we would not have known anything specific about what was taking place.

Mrs. Steinbeck advised that Harold phone the Doctor for an appointment, since others were now doing so as there was an announced "deadline" of 6 p.m. Monday night when everyone was supposed to have their names withdrawn or be classed as a rebel.

Mrs. Steinbeck further said that her sister, Caroline Brown, was to see the Doctor at 2 p.m. Monday (9/7/42), and, if there was anything further of interest to report, she would be in touch with him. Harold had talked with Miss Brown previously (at the Bedells') and found that she knew many of the "ismic" and "New Thought" leaders in New York City and was a confidante of the well-known Emmet Fox,[2] having schooled him in proper body posture, which is her profession. Harold referred to Fox's nervous breakdown and said that when he shook hands with him at the Psychic Forum where Fox had given a talk, he had received the impression that Fox's crack-up had been due to an emotional involvement with a woman. Miss Brown said, "That's most interesting. That's exactly what happened. He fell in love with one of his Jewess admirers, and his inner prejudice against the race prevented them marrying. The conflict in his inner self, coupled with his fear that a large portion of his audience would learn of his dilemma or that the woman herself might reveal it, brought on a physical illness."

Miss Brown commented upon the vulnerability of most so-called spiritual leaders, however inspiring their presentation, and said she feared that the Sadlers were approaching a similar crisis from the egoistic and lust-for-power standpoint.

After her appointment with Dr. Sadler, Miss Brown phoned Harold and said, "I feel you have a right to know what transpired since I was not specifically instructed not to tell you, although I think I would have told you anyway as I feel it is very unfair for you to be kept in the dark. There is no question but what the blame is being placed upon you. When we came in, Dr. Sadler said he was sorry he 'couldn't put on a scene for us' like he had for the earlier arrivals, as his wrath was now wearing off somewhat. He indicated he was acting on instructions by his method of procedure—*whose* instructions he did not say—they may have been his own. I asked him questions and feel that he sidestepped some of the issues, but he did admit that good might come out of this development when I said that the Forum members were now better acquainted and more aroused than ever before."

[2] Emmet Fox (1886-1951) was an exponent of New Thought, a metaphysical philosophy that taught positive thinking, meditation, and other ways of realizing the presence of God.

Dr. S. declared that he had known all along what was going on and once, by what he called television, had been permitted to see the meeting which had taken place at the Karles'. He said complete reports had been given him by higher intelligences of all that had been happening, and that he had even received a paper on Harold before he had come here, warning that Harold was a troublemaker. He did not read this paper. He scoffingly commented on Harold's dream, which Harold had related to the Kelloggs, and said that Harold had even tried to turn Ruth against her own parents and bring about a split between the mortal commissioners. He characterized the petition as a 7-point personal attack upon him, and read a paper on "Ideaists and Idealists," in which Gandhi was referred to as an idealist of the martyr type while Lucifer had been an idealist of the ego type. The Doctor said it was very bad in the case of the ego type, and he intimated that Harold was in this classification. He said Harold was a promoter who had come here in an attempt to usurp existing authority and run things his own way and to get commercial control.

The apparent recent communication had to do with the statement that the Urantia society must be organized to protect the Truth against other groups that might seek to appropriate it. Forum members were left with the impression that Harold was the evil influence and that a special punishment was being reserved for him. They were all pledged to secrecy and forbidden to contact Harold, and the apparent authority of manner and communication seemingly struck fear into all hearts because none save the Steinbecks and Miss Brown got in touch with us for any informative reason.

Harold, having heard nothing, phoned Dent Karle to ask what had happened, and Dent embarrassedly said, "I'm afraid I can't tell you a thing. You'll just have to wait." This was a complete turn about face from his former attitude and indicated something damaging was being said to all members about Harold. Dent seemed eager to get off the phone and asked if Elsie could talk to Martha, who said to her, "Well, Elsie, what goes on?" To which Elsie replied, "I tried to phone you earlier but couldn't get you." Martha said, "What about?" Elsie said, "Oh, just a friendly call. You folks just sit tight and everything will be all right." Martha said, "What do you mean by that?" Elsie said, "I can't explain but I'm sure everything will work out all right."

Harold then phoned Mrs. Githens and got a similar reaction from her, much to his surprise. She said she didn't dare quote anything for fear of quoting incorrectly; that she still felt her signing of the petition was the right thing to have done but that she removed her name because of what she regarded as a convincing communication and because the others were doing it. (Elsie Karle had said on Sunday, and this attitude was apparently borne out here, "If you doubt one communication you'll have to doubt them all.")

In the afternoon, Harold phoned Clyde Bedell, who had been to see the Doctor in the morning, and asked if Clyde could tell him anything. Clyde hesitated, and then in a very reserved voice said, "No, I don't believe I can tell you a thing. You'll just have to take your turn like the rest of us." Harold said, "Why the secrecy?" Clyde said, "Well, that's just the way it is, I guess." Harold said, "It's quite evident that the Doctor is centering his attack upon me," and Clyde said, "Well, you're probably right." Harold then went on to say, "I understand he thinks I have commercial designs upon the Book of Urantia." To which Clyde replied, "Yes, I think he does." Harold then said, "As a matter of fact, I'm not interested in taking a damn dime out of the Book of Urantia, now or at any other time." And Clyde said, "Well, why don't you tell him that when you see him?" There was a pause on the phone during which Clyde made no further comment, and Harold, noting his embarrassment, hung up.

Monday 3 p.m. Harold decided it was probably not good psychology to assume a standoffish attitude when others were phoning in for appointments, so he phoned the Doctor, and after the phone had rung for quite some time the Doctor answered. Harold said, "This is Harold Sherman calling," and the Doctor, taken unaware, said in surprise, "Oh, Harold!" Harold then said, "I understand you have received a new communication and we would be interested in having it read to us at your convenience. I hope you have not been too disturbed by present developments." The Doctor's reply was, "Well, I have been—terribly disturbed. We will call you." And he hung up.

At around 10 p.m. Mildred Bucklin called for the first time and asked Harold abruptly if she might speak with Martha. When Martha got on the line, Mildred said, "I meant to call you earlier today but I had to take a taxi to work this a.m. and worked all day. I just wanted to tell you that my feelings for you are unchanged by anything that has happened, and reporting for Mrs. Githens that she had meant to include her love to Martha in her telephone conversation with Harold in the morning." Martha, sensing this was all Mildred could say, thanked her, said goodbye and hung up. Apparently none of the men folks felt they could communicate with Harold at all and were letting their wives do this as a gesture of continued friendship.

The Matterns phoned, and Harold dropped over to see them and to autograph some books. He gave them a fuller explanation of what was happening, and Mattern showed him a letter he had received from Harry Loose which predicted this crisis and told H.C. that he was to add his strength to Harold's and give him support in his time of need. (Copy attached.)

[*Loose wrote:*]

Monterey Park, August 29, 1942

My Friend:-

You have already come to the realization of the need for your continued presence in Chicago for a period that is, for the present, indefinite. Your usefulness, and need, to H.S. in the approaching minor crisis is of import. He has present need, and continued need, of the added strength available from your well of force. He can draw upon this whether in your physical presence or not. He has relief in your physical presence and association, and perfect trust. He is attacking with great force an evil that threatens great harm to the Revelation. Positively do not believe that your part in what has been and what is yet to be is all an accidental happening. You will assume more in the not-far-distant future in cooperation with H.S. in his activities. You are now just at the beginning of things. You have a very long personal history—and are here for a purpose that was planned long ago. You will become more aware of this all as time advances. It may be my duty to talk informatively with you of these and other similar matters at some future time. I do not know.

Do not mention my name to anyone except H.S.

Avoid association in any way with the Haleses.

Do not allow anything to disturb your serene mental life. Accept with great gratitude that which you are learning. Discuss any matters needing clarification with H.S.

Keep mentally close to Mrs. M. and allow nothing to disturb the peace in your home.

I refer to the present as a "minor crisis" because there are others in the offing in continuance of this matter that promise greater impact.

I, too, am strongly depending upon your present and future strength to H.S. in his need.

Thank you both for your early but much appreciated telegram.

With all good thought,
Harry J. Loose

Mattern revealed he had been in the thick of the KKK fight, being personally responsible for its breakup in Pennsylvania, New York and New Jersey after discovering it to be an organization based upon evil prejudices and commercial rather than spiritual and patriotic motives—and being tried several times by fanatical groups of KKKs heavily armed who threatened his life. He had successfully defied them and said that Harold should stand alone if necessary, and that "one with God was a majority."

It was Mattern's feeling also, to which Martha has subscribed, that our name should not be withdrawn from the petition and that we should stand our ground in the face of our indictment and condemnation. Harold discussed the possibility of his taking the floor at the Sept. 13 meeting and answering the charges against him, and Mattern said he thought this was a good idea and that he would give him every support. It was heartening to have their counsel and faith at a time when we were practically standing alone.

At midnight we received a surprise phone call from Mrs. Steinbeck in which she said to Harold that she had had several talks with Mrs. Githens and that she was meeting with her the following a.m. in her office for the purpose of doing "some work for us." She said, "You know I have gone rather high in Science and Metaphysical things myself and we want to send you all the power we can. Is there any problem or matter you would like us to present to the Universal Father for you?" Harold said no, there was not, but that he did appreciate their kind thought and support. Mrs. Steinbeck said if they could be of any further service Harold should not hesitate to call.

HAROLD SHERMAN to HARRY LOOSE

Chicago, September 8, 1942

Dear Harry:

Amazing, incredible things have happened. It is hard to know how or where to begin.

We returned from Traverse last Friday night to find that a petition had been presented to Dr. Sadler and the other mortal commissioners, totaling 48 names—asking for free discussions of all Forum matters. I was in on the forming of the petition with Messrs. Bucklin, Bedell (who really wrote first draft), Evans, Wilkins (who dropped in here for one day and signed petition), and a man by the name of [Lee Miller] Jones (who later lost his nerve) as well as Dent Karle, one of the most active in getting names on the petition.

Things began to happen immediately. Dr. S. reacting as I had foreseen, hit the ceiling in fanatical anger. No attempt had been made to keep secret the fact that many Forum members had been meeting about at each others' homes, and some of them had run back with tales to the doctor that I had been reading copies of my letters to him to the different members who asked to hear it. I also reported to members the statements Bill and the Doctor had made to me with respect to their commercial objectives and personal ambitions. I did not attack the honesty, sincerity or integrity of anyone—keeping my points only on the principles involved.

Friday night, after receiving the petition, Dr. S. swung into action. He began phoning the rank and file of those on the petition, telling them that he had received a warning message about me before I ever appeared here—that I was a troublemaker . . . however, he had had faith in the higher beings' protection, and had let me "do my stuff" . . . that I was a promoter type . . . that I had come here with the idea of usurping his authority and making a commercial killing with the Book of Urantia . . . that I had tried to turn the Contact Commissioners against each other by talking to the Kelloggs and telling them of a dream I had had . . . and stating that this was really a LUCIFER REBELLION . . . and that I was influenced by Caligastia in taking the steps I had taken . . . and that if they did not withdraw their names from this petition, they would STAND CONDEMNED AS REBELS.

Employment of the PSYCHOLOGY OF FEAR has worked astounding results . . . taking the members in groups of from two to five or so, he has successfully beaten them down with a message apparently received from DEF, one of the Midwayers, in which the need of a Urantia Society is stressed (which sounds strangely like the statements Dr. S. made to me weeks ago) . . . there is another message having to do with the Ideaists and Idealists, which illustration he used to me weeks ago . . . in which he stressed that I was an idealist and I was right—but it wouldn't work . . . Gandhi was an idealist of the martyr type . . . Lucifer of the egoistic type . . . and it is inferred this is where I belong.

Your letter to H.C. Mattern and instructions therewith came just in time. He needed such recognition . . . he can be a tower of strength in what is to come. He revealed to me last night that he had joined the Ku Klux Klan, found it was rotten, and started fighting it from within . . . and, at constant threat to his life, with guns pushed against his head and stomach, he had broken up the Klan in Pennsylvania, New York and New Jersey. He was tried one night before a jury of 12 hooded Klansmen, each with guns lying before them . . . and threatened with instant death if he did not desist. He defied them. This is the kind of a man I need to face what is to come.

Dr. S. began calling in what he termed the "ringleaders in this rebellion" on Saturday and then strange things began happening. Martha and I heard no more from them. They were told prejudicial things against me . . . as though I were condemned by higher beings . . . and pledged to secrecy . . . until I should be taken care of in the manner designed to punish the leading rebel of them all. Martha and I are to be called in ALONE to face the fanatical wrath of Dr. S., who states that Bill will never forgive me for what I have done (according to reports). The doctor still has his eyes on my promise of a possible book publisher and financial backing, and intimated to some of the members that "he would consider all propositions, naturally" . . . so he apparently expects to CHASTISE ME . . . get me to CRAWL ON MY BELLY and, with my ears pinned back, appear at the first Forum meeting, thoroughly squelched, A SINNER FOREVERMORE and an ALLY OF LUCIFER in the eyes of all Forum members.

I have decided, when we are called in . . . we are to be the LAST, after all names have been removed . . . to DEMAND of the doctor that he clear up this attack upon my character and my motives . . . that IF HE DOES NOT, I intend to take what steps as are necessary to defend my own good name before members of the Forum. If the doctor refuses and is willing to let me stand condemned . . . then I intend to TAKE THE FLOOR at the first Forum meeting and make your birthday one long to be remembered. HARRY—BE WITH ME FROM THREE O'CLOCK ON, CHICAGO TIME, NEXT SUNDAY, for I will be needing you and all strength. MATTERNS will perhaps be my only standbys when I start.

The ability of the Dr. to dominate this group by his theatrical tricks, calling down the wrath of the Gods, etc., and the fear they have in standing up to him in a crisis, is beyond belief. I would never have expected that SOME of our friends would have SEVERED CONTACT with us under any circumstances . . . and it remained for some people we had just met, the Steinbecks, to phone us privately, in defiance of the order to isolate me . . . and tell us what has been going on and what members are being told.

First, it is apparent that NO CONDEMNATION of the Forum's action has come from the ANGELS OF PROGRESS and Sonsovocton, who have the Book of Urantia in charge . . . only from the Midway creature, DEF . . . at least this is my present knowledge . . . and I do not think I should take such purported messages too seriously . . . and should say that, until the ANGELS OF PROGRESS have spoken . . . I do not consider we have been condemned . . . that I cannot conceive of such INHUMAN METHODS of persecution being devised by HIGHER BEINGS . . . no mercy or justice being shown . . . and myself condemned in private when I had no chance to talk back or defend myself. This, to me, does not seem to be GOD'S WAY of doing things . . . I intend to tell the Forum members of how Martha and I have been punished, of the members who dropped away from us . . . who left us isolated . . . and point to this as an example of how people in the outside world are to be punished, when the Urantia organization is born . . . and ask: IS THIS GOD'S WAY OF PRESENTING THE TRUTH TO HUMANITY?

Then I may say that I have as much right to infer, under such circumstances, that Caligastia is inspiring the actions of the Dr. and Bill as they have to infer that those of us who signed the petition have been influenced by Lucifer.

Harry, I don't know what I will be called upon to do or say at this stage . . . things are happening so fast and we haven't been called in yet . . . I want to request that we are interviewed by ALL MORTAL COMMISSIONERS . . . I want to face them all so they can hear what is said to me and serve as witnesses later. I doubt if this will be permitted . . .

the doctor probably won't like such a request . . . but I will report what has happened at this meeting to ALL FORUM MEMBERS, if humanly possible, in any event.

It's terrible, Harry, that such a situation must be met. It is particularly trying on Martha from the human side but she is standing up with me 100 PERCENT . . . and even suggested, "Would you like me to stand by your side while you are defending yourself, since we both are condemned?" I haven't decided yet whether this would be wise, as I may be on my feet for quite a time . . . but I may call her up at the finish.

I'm enclosing a couple of special deliveries to add to your airmail as I need to hear from you before Sunday if possible.

I will try my best to keep you advised. Miss Baumgartner served on the committee of three, Evans and Karle being the other members . . . who presented the petition to Dr. S. . . . and I had a good long talk with her . . . but she has been squelched along with the rest . . . and all these Forum members will carry the wrong impression of me the rest of their lives unless it is CHANGED.

Harry, I am considering leaving a signed statement with the Forum members, declaring that I never had any intention of making one cent, either now or at any future time, on the Book of Urantia, nor of having my name connected with it, and then asking the Doctor and Bill if they would be willing to sign this same statement, since they state they are only the custodians and not the owners of the Truth! What do you think of this? Can you not petition the higher ones to be with me in my hour when I stand alone, in my human attempt to represent Christ and his Truth on earth?

DIARY *September 8, 1942*

This a.m., apparently after her session with Mrs. Githens, Mrs. Steinbeck phoned again to say that she wanted to clarify one point we might not have understood—that the Bucklins had been given a definite list of members to call and make dates with the doctor—but all on this list were our friends and we should keep up our courage. This seemed to indicate definite expressions of feeling underneath the surface.

2

"Nothing to Say"

DIARY *September 9, 1942*

Wed. Christy phoned around 9 a.m. to make an appointment for us to see the Doctor at 10 a.m. Thurs. Harold took the phone and asked if he could have all contact commissioners present as he had something he wanted to say to them. This request seemed to take Christy by surprise; she hesitated and apparently asked the Doctor, then said, "No, the Doctor just wants to see you and Martha."

HAROLD SHERMAN to SIR HUBERT WILKINS

Chicago, September 9, 1942

Dear Hubert:

I am sending a copy of this letter to Washington with the hope it may reach you sooner, one place or the other.

I regret to say that incredible things are happening here. The petition, totaling the surprising number of *48* names, was submitted last Friday night. No attempt was made to keep the free discussions of Forum members secret from the doctor. I told him myself, and Bill and the Kelloggs and Christy, that Forum members were divided in opinion and would soon ask to be heard. But NONE of them realized there would be so MANY.

The doctor, as was to have been expected, hit the ceiling and immediately launched upon the most fanatical reprisal plan. Armed with what he announced as a special communication (which I have not yet had read to me because Martha and I have still not been called) . . .

he summoned in Forum members in small groups from two to five . . . and literally *gave them the works.* He told them he had received a special message warning against me before I arrived here . . . that I had sought to divide the mortal commissioners . . . that I was attempting to usurp control for commercial purposes . . . and that I WAS A LEADER OF A LUCIFER REBELLION! Playing upon the fears of these members, who believe in the Book of Urantia (as we also do), he called upon them to withdraw their names from the petition or be classed FOREVERMORE AS REBELS! Even sane-minded, sound-thinking leaders such as those you have met—the Bucklins, Karles, Evanses, etc.—wilted under this attack. They were told not to contact US in any way, that a special kind of punishment was to be dealt out to us AFTER every Forum member had been given opportunity to WITHDRAW his name from the petition.

This morning we are standing ALONE, Martha and I . . . having been cut off from everyone but ONE SURPRISING SOURCE whom we do not know well . . . which has advised us what is happening. We have just been phoned that the Doctor will see us tomorrow morning at ten, when we are due to be severely chastised . . . and, if permitted to remain in the Forum, forever under indictment in the minds of Forum members as Lucifer allies.

All of the apprehensions I have had of the way things have been going on the human side are now justified. Ordinary human reason demonstrates that this is man-made persecution—NOT the act of HIGHER BEINGS, no matter how represented. Can you not see how fiendish would be the punishment of humans in any PUBLIC ORGANIZATION who dared to raise any question whatsoever pertaining to any human authority or interpretation?

Martha and I do not intend to remove our names from the petition. We signed it in good faith and with a clear consciousness and conscience of our being in the right. I am intending to go before the Forum next Sunday and demand the floor. No court in America would condemn a man without a hearing, and these charges made against me have been craftily given to Forum members in small groups so that I could not defend myself. Unless these charges are cleared up in the open, I will always stand condemned . . . and my further association with these Forum members blighted.

I do not know what will be your stand. The doctor does not dare let any of this become public, of course . . . and the time to fight this whole unhealthy thing out is in the privacy of this little group. It is amazing the hypnotic control he exercises over their minds . . . I do not doubt the revelation . . . but I do now doubt the use he is making of his position of authority. The people are placed in the spot of having to accept everything he tells them as instructions from on high or doubting the whole truth. They have forgotten the old Biblical advice: "By their fruits ye shall know them."

The doctor is even claiming that he was permitted a "television view" of our meeting at the Karles' home some weeks ago . . . and that a running account of our meetings was provided by the higher-ups. This was not necessary, since the doctor had many human informants to tell him of what was going on at all times.

I am going to present a sworn statement to the Forum members that I never at any time in the past, now, or in the future, have entertained the thought or desire or will ever take one cent for any services or talents I may offer to the Book of Urantia. I am then going to ask the doctor and Bill if they will add their signatures to this statement. I will be amazed if they do because I have evidence they are counting heavily on the financial returns they feel can be gained by the book and the organization setup. And no man can properly represent the TRUTH who has a commercial interest in the TRUTH. He will pervert it every time, sooner or later, for his own purposes. This has been the way of the world . . . and the Sadlers have constantly pointed out, "We are only the custodians, not the owners of this TRUTH." It is up to them now—to prove it.

I am sorry that this trouble has had to arise . . . this is not a pleasant situation to have to face . . . the doctor is a powerful protagonist who knows all the tricks in public speaking and debate. I will have to place my faith in God that proper words will be placed in my mouth when the occasion arises. I wish you were going to be here Sunday, for I have such faith in your own inherent fairness. I have no feeling of guilt . . . I know what is in my own mind and heart . . . I am answerable direct to God . . . I am not impelled by fear as other Forum members are . . . I am not moved by a human's raving and ranting . . . I see no wrong in asking respectfully for a free discussion of Forum problems . . . and I see no reason why Higher Intelligences should chastise Forum members for such a plea.

The Angels of Progress, who have this in charge, have not spoken . . . only DEF, as I understand it, a Midwayer . . . who is one notch above the human and not an authority. The statements the doctor is reading the Forum members as recent communications, he has mentioned to me in detail in past talks with me . . . and referred to these communications as having come through a year or so before . . . but *not* read to the Forum members.

He is bowling the Forum members over by the flat statement that he is acting on instructions from On High . . . and they do not feel that they can challenge this.

You've known me now for a number of years, rather intimately, and you've come to know my wife. I hardly think you would support any of the charges the doctor is making against us.

If we do not successfully buck the doctor at this point, I do not know how any of the Forum members can get out from under his bondage. I seek nothing for myself . . . no money, no glorification of my name . . . only the protection of the TRUTH from human prostitution.

I appreciate your having put your own name on the petition. The doctor may have written you his version and asked you to take it off. If he has, and you feel you can trust the knowledge with me, I would like to know what explanation he has given. I will need what help I can have to face what is to come . . . but if this is a TRUE REVELATION, as we believe it is, then ANYTHING we can do to protect and preserve it cannot be too much . . . untold millions will either lose or profit as the result of our efforts—measured by their degree of success.

My best to you in which Martha joins me.

Sincerely,

P.S. The doctor, nor any other Forum member, knows of my intended plan to take the floor next Sunday . . . and they must not know. This must come as a complete surprise.

HARRY LOOSE to HAROLD SHERMAN

Monterey Park, September 10, 1942

Dear Harold:-

Your letter arrived this morning and I am getting this back to you before Sunday by way of one of the Special Delivery stamps attached to one of the Air Mail. Your letter, though startling in its details, was not a surprise at all. It was certainly expected and anticipated. It made snappy and exciting reading at this morning's breakfast table.

Sadler knows a lot about psychology, medicine and surgery, this is granted, but he knows very little about law. In his assertions, as quoted in your letter, he has left himself wide open to suit by you. Such a suit, with all details exposed in Court, with various Forum members as witnesses, and the background subject matter thoroughly brought into the open, would be a terrific advertisement for the Book of Urantia and introduce and establish the Forum as a regularly constituted body, from whose members money was collected, and in whose name some $25,000.00 was on deposit. All of this would establish Court standing and jurisdiction by which the entire matter of the printing of the Book and the continued existence of the Forum, by that name or another, could be brought into and thrashed out in Court. This would place the present copies of the Book of Urantia in the position of being read into the Court records, by which avenue they would become available and accessible to newspapers and general public for examination, printing, and reading as a public record. This can all be done by way of Court action to which Sadler has laid himself wide open by his slanderous and defamatory allegations regarding yourself.

Let me assert STRONGLY that all the above is very far from the liking of or desire of either the Sadlers or the Haleses. The very possibility of the above to Dr. Sadler should bring a realization of the potentialities and induce a distinct and hurried change of present thought. Can you imagine Sadler on the witness stand under cross examination?? Or Hales?? And, of course, this all would bring in the recipient of the revelation. He would have to be named by Sadler, and others, or they could be sent to jail for contempt of court. By Sadler's action, as indicated by your letter, he has unknowingly and ignorantly placed you in position where you can bring the whole matter into Court with every reason to expect satisfactory results.

I am glad Mattern is with you. You need his strength and assurance. Joshua ben Joseph had the comfort of the association, the strength, the belief and assurance of his small intimate grouping. But even HE could not satisfy even this small grouping. There had to be a Judas. Did you really expect better?? Well, neither did you really expect all to go smoothly and without friction. Dr. Sadler is far from perfect in his mental reactions. You very well know this. Please recognize, too, that behind the scenes you will find the well-disguised but sinister Hales. An active advisor and participant. Much more deeply concerned than is apparent. There is too much to write in detail. You rather fully understand the situation, I know.

I just want you to know that I am with you, as always, and that I will be so close to you Sunday that your hand could touch me. Before you take the floor, if you are allowed to, be sure to take strong recognition of my presence and strength. And know NOW that this small tempest is but the beginning. There will be other, and greater, storms. Please know, in this, you will have other help but know, too, that there will be nothing to take all responsibility from you. This is YOUR fight. Now, however, is the time for you to flee the scene of the present battle if you feel faint of heart. Just disappear—and that will end it. I mean this very seriously and there will be no criticism.

Do you begin to see the "why" of the insistence of the need for the keeping of the Diary?? And don't forget to keep the Diary up to date.

I have had a long letter from Elsie Baumgartner in which she offered to report to me a summary of activities as they developed. I have answered her letter and accepted her proffer this week past. . . .

I am . . . glad for Martha's dependable strength—and for the Matterns. Remember, however, now is the time to flee the wrath of the present storm if you feel faint of heart. If not, be not afraid; you are advancing, you are growing, you may be fitting yourself for even greater responsibilities. But, please, just as your whole life of the past has been the surmounting of one difficulty after another, just so the continuation will be. This is just a polite way of saying, "Life in the past has been just battle after battle, and it will so continue battle after battle." Sadler understands much of psychology and he may read you that he has you licked by his present outburst—and that you will disappear over the hill and far away instanter. And he may be mistaken.

And now a personal favor, Martha. Years ago in the Walgreen drugstore in Chicago, there is a chain of them there, I bought a TYSON bath spray at less than one dollar. The metal head of the TYSON is set in a deep rubber cup which allows a directed spray instead of a scattered spray that waters more of the bathroom than it does of yourself. This sprinkler head is attached to a length of rubber hose which is pushed over the faucet when the spray is used. It is made for the convenience of the old-style plumbing, such as are in the older houses and flats. Anyway, with sundry repairs, our old TYSON has been usable up until a few weeks ago when it just HAD to be thrown away.

The TYSON was very evidently a proprietory article and owned by, or whose distribution was controlled by, the Walgreen drugstores. None of the drugstores out here carry the TYSON or anything similar and there are no Walgreen drugstores here. Martha, if it isn't too much bother, will you get one of these TYSON's at any Chicago Walgreen store and send it on to us here. We will both be very grateful and will immediately return the purchase price. Thanking you in advance.

Please keep me advised as you can, Harold, as to the progress of proceedings. Please do not forget my presence and strength on Sunday.

Much love to you both from Ma and I,

FORUM CALENDAR *September 10, 1942*

Appointment with Dr. Sadler (Christy) at 10 a.m. Harold and Martha. "Nothing to say."

DIARY *September 10, 1942*

We kept our appointment at 10 this a.m. with the Doctor who met us at the door and extended his hand in perfunctory manner. As we went into the living room, Christy met us with a worried expression she could not conceal. Her hands were cold and she kept moving them nervously during the short interview.

The Doctor began in an affectedly quiet way by saying that he was seeing us because he had promised so to do, but that he was not yet ready to talk to us. He said, "In my 67 years I have gone through many things and I've found that time is the great healer. I feel I would be better able to say to you what I want to say later, and you should be better able to discuss this situation with me. I think this is a time for prayer and not for discussion." To which Harold replied, "I *have* prayed, Doctor. I have prayed a great deal."

The Doctor said, "There is one other point I am turning over in my mind. Some time before Jo Davis even sponsored you I received a communication about you which puzzled me. I have not mentioned it to anyone, not even Christy, until now, but I think I begin to understand what it meant. Some day I may read it to you."

Harold, for purposes of emphasis, asked, "You say, Doctor, you have never mentioned this communication before—not even to Christy?"

The Doctor then repeated, positively, "No, I have not."

Harold then asked, "Who is the authority behind this communication?"

The Doctor said, "I cannot tell you."

Harold said, "My conscience is clear."

The Doctor said, "If I didn't think it was, I wouldn't be talking to you."

Harold further stated, "I am unafraid of anything this communication may say and I think it should be read to the entire Forum body."

"Oh, no," said the Doctor, "that will never be done, but I am glad you feel this way about it as it may have a bearing on what I will have to say to you later. However, I don't intend to argue with you now or even talk about this matter, but if you'd like to talk about the weather or the beginning of school or subjects like that, I'm willing to converse with you."

Harold said, "I'm not interested in the weather. I'm ready and willing to discuss everything fully and completely now."

The Doctor said, "I'm glad that you are. But you'll just have to wait until I feel the time is right."

Harold then asked, "Are you going to tell us what you've told the others?"

The Doctor, surprised, said, "What have I told the others?"

Harold said, "You know what you've told them."

The Doctor said, "No, I don't intend to tell you what I've told them any more than you told me what you've said to them about me."

Harold said, "Doctor, what I said to them I've already said to your face or am prepared to say."

To this the Doctor replied, "Well, this is not the time and there is no more that I can say unless you want to talk about the weather."

Martha then spoke, saying, "Then I guess there is no use in our staying longer."

The Doctor, with a little gesture, said, "I guess not."

We then got up, said goodbye and left abruptly.

After the interview with Dr. Sadler, Harold phoned Mr. Steinbeck and told him that the Doctor had refused to tell him anything, asking if he and Martha could come over and see the Steinbecks and Miss Caroline Brown and secure more information from them as to what he had said to Forum members. Mr. Steinbeck said he saw no reason why we couldn't get together, but would discuss it with Mrs. Steinbeck and phone us tonight. This he did around 10 p.m., saying that he and Mrs. Steinbeck had been discussing the matter all evening and that he was phoning as he had promised though he had been advised by a number not to do so.

He said that Mrs. Steinbeck had seen the Doctor around 6:30 this evening and he had told her it was better that no one talk to us and that this matter be allowed to quiet down, and that he would talk to us when feelings had become more normal. Mr. Steinbeck said, "I hope you appreciate our position, Mr. Sherman. Dr. Sadler has been our leader and mentor for so long that to go against him now is almost like going against our faith and the truths that have come to us through him."

Harold said, "I understand, but does it seem to you to be divine justice to isolate us from the fellowship of our Forum members and to single us out as special objects of persecution when we all acted in good faith and in all sincerity in petitioning for a free discussion of Urantia subjects?"

Mr. Steinbeck said, "No, Mr. Sherman, this is what Mrs. Steinbeck and I have been talking about most of the evening. It doesn't seem fair and right, and for the time being you people may have to be the martyrs, but out of this we think a great good may come."

Harold said, "Our consciences are clear and we have the courage of our convictions. We now stand condemned in the eyes of all Forumites. When we come to the meeting on Sunday we come as outcasts. We are praying for guidance. We do not know what we shall do as yet, but we feel we have a right to have the charges made against us brought out into the open so we can face them. This is only common justice. If we accept this situation by default then at no future time can any Forum member feel free or dare to express his individual opinion."

Mr. Steinbeck said, "We see your position, Mr. Sherman, and we sympathize with you though we know you don't need that. We want you to know, Mrs. Steinbeck and I, that you have our friendship and that we honestly feel we haven't met a finer couple in a long, long time. However, we've got to stick to our leader until it is proven that we need another."

Harold said, "I would not think of embarrassing you people. You have already demonstrated your friendship and human consideration beyond that of anyone else in the Forum. You may be sure we will not betray your confidence."

Mr. Steinbeck said, "Thank you, Mr. Sherman. Mrs. Steinbeck and I will be praying for this to come out all right, which we are sure it will, in time, to everyone's benefit."

Harold then said goodnight.

HAROLD SHERMAN to HARRY LOOSE

Chicago, September 10, 1942

Dear Harry:

This morning we saw the doctor and Christy, a strange meeting. He greeted us at the door of his own apartment on the third floor with a lifeless handshake, and Christy's hands were clammy cold. We sat down and the doctor and Christy sat across from us. Then he said he was seeing us because he had promised to, but that there was nothing he could say to us at this time . . . that he would have to decide for himself when that time would be . . . and that if we wished to talk about the weather or school or anything like that, okay.

He said there was one point he'd like to mention, however—that he had received a communication warning him about me before Jo Davis had sponsored me . . . but had not taken it seriously . . . however, he could begin to understand it now.

I said: "Such communication should be read to the entire Forum. I am unafraid to face any communication or statement. My conscience is clear."

Doctor said, "No, I won't read this communication. I haven't even mentioned it to anyone until now, not even to Christy." (And yet I have been told that he has told every member of the Forum that he had been forewarned on me—so he has told a deliberate lie.)

I said, "Doctor, are you going to tell Martha and me what you have told the others?"

He looked startled and said, "What have I told the others?" and I said, "You know what you have told the others" . . . and he said, "No, I'm not going to tell you that any more than you've told me what you told other Forum members about *me!*"

My answer was: "Doctor, I've already told you to your face what I've said to the others . . . and anything that I haven't told you, I'm willing to tell you direct. I'm ready to discuss this whole subject fully and completely now!"

But the doctor wanted none of this and reverted to the "weather," so we got up and walked out, abruptly. Christy was visibly worried during the short interview in which the doctor acted "aggrieved." (He should have been an actor, he knows all the tricks.) I do not hold any malice toward him . . . I am not forgetting his great service . . . but it is pitiful to see how he has fallen.

Doctor did not mention the petition or give us an opportunity to take our names off, which we would not have done. He may be saving a special kind of humiliation for us by giving us a chance to take our names off in the presence of the entire Forum on Sunday—with all other names already removed. I intend to take the floor and will have to be thrown out bodily before I will surrender it . . . demanding that charges be preferred against me before the whole Forum body . . . that he read me the same communications he has read to others. If he does not, I have had a report on them and will have to take a different tack, recalling them and depending upon the memory of Forum members to know what I'm referring to . . . particularly with reference to the charges which have been made against me. And then answering these charges, point by point.

The stage is set and I hope I am being spiritually rehearsed for my part, during the night seasons, as I will need great wisdom and love and guidance on Sunday.

So much has been happening, I've neglected to answer some questions or points you have raised in recent letters.

Under existing circumstances it, of course, would be unwise to bring the woman book publisher on to read the [manu]script, or her wealthy lady friend.

It has come to me a number of times recently that the last name of the subject or instrument is "BROWN." This seems like such a common name . . . could I be right? If I told the doctor privately some time that I knew the name of the subject, I think he would be paralyzed. If I am supposed to be entrusted with something authoritative to impress the mortal commissioners, I hope it is granted me. . . .

The Matterns are standing by, like rocks of Gibraltar, to "protect us" on Sunday. The outcome is in the hands of God. I will be doing my Father's work as I feel He would direct me. My constant prayer is, "Thy will be done."

The doctor will try every trick to get me off the floor and promise "another time" for considering such a matter . . . and I may get the ill-will of certain ultra-religious members by standing my ground . . . but if I don't face him down now . . . I see no chance in the future. He is really afraid to FACE ME before this first Forum meeting, wanting to keep me in the dark so I cannot confront him. By demanding that he make charges against me in public and that he read the communications to me, the only thing he can hide behind is that he is acting on "higher instructions" and cannot do otherwise. How much weight this will carry with the membership, I do not know. Certainly all are apparently COWED now, through FEAR of punishment from on high, unbelievable as this may seem. BUT, maybe something is smoldering there which will come to my defense when the meeting is on.

At any rate, this is the information up to date. I have sent a little package in remembrance of SEPTEMBER 13th . . . which will be a memorable day now—perhaps in the history of the planet Urantia. This is a CUP I wish could be passed from my lips—but I will drink it to the full, gladly, if I can be made the spiritual instrument to protect and preserve the TRUTH from human prostitution.

I will be thinking strongly of you this Sunday . . . and LOVINGLY of ALL . . . even my most bitter opponents. May I be given physical strength, spiritual courage, and divine wisdom on this day!

Our best love to Mother Loose and your own dear self.

HARRY LOOSE to HAROLD SHERMAN

Monterey Park, September 12, 1942

Dear Harold:-

Did you ever question what function Christy, the maiden lady, fulfills in the residence—and for such a long period of years?? And she cannot lay claim to even the distant kinship of being a third cousin. Something snapped with Dr. S before the death of his wife. Think it over. Others have. And questioned.

Instructions ("warnings") from higher intelligences are not blithely disregarded as Dr. S is supposed to have disregarded such regarding yourself. They are seriously followed out to the very letter instead. Do not believe this story of his. I can tell you very positively that he has had no such "warning" or "instructions" from higher intelligences. He would have fearfully followed them out to the very letter if he had. He deliberately lies if he states that he has had such.

All Caligastia's power to influence any other intelligence was taken from him many years ago. He is still capable of evil but not that to which the Doctor accredits him. The same, with small alterations, for Lucifer. Sadler refers to other quite similar but lower-degree intelligences whose name symbols he is not familiar with. His attitude, for these some years past, might indicate that he is acting under the jurisdiction of such intelligence. Particularly because of the continued close Hales tie-up. There have been some suggestions (not warnings nor instructions) to Dr. S regarding the Hales situation but Dr. S has chosen to disregard such on his own responsibility—and to his present, and eventual fuller, discredit.

You should receive my Thursday letter today. I hope that it helps to give you confidence for tomorrow. My birthday, of the flesh this Urantia year, may be a very memorable one—as per your letter of today. I cannot conceive of you fleeing from the wrath of Dr. S and being over the hill and far away today. And so I must tell you that you, and Martha, have accomplished much GOOD, and with very far reactions, in your program of the immediate past. Much more than you can presently visualize. Please believe me when I tell you that the "pillars have been shaken" and things will never be quite the same with the Forum as was in the long past. And, something else: instead of the Forum being "cowed" with fear, as per your letter, I can tell you positively that they were all being heavily "bulled" by Dr. Sadler. You may positively express to any such "bulled" Forum members that Sadler is NOT acting on any "higher instructions" at the present, as he may infer; and to fear any "punishment from on high" because of their differences of opinion with Sadler is an insult to the "higher intelligences." They can all give hearty belly laughs and deep and gusty Bronx cheers if he makes any such assertions.

I thank you both for the kindly thought of my birthdate as expressed in the cigarettes rec'd. I have made good use of them and placed them where they will be much appreciated. I do not smoke them anymore myself—not since July 24th. Please thank "H.C." and his wife for their appreciated birthday card. I am especially grateful this Sunday for small Martha and for both the Matterns, for Christy, for ALL the Kelloggs and a few others not here named for they all today will give you strength—and the blessed confidence and assurance of belief in you—though not outwardly possible of expression by all.

I have, long before, asked that, in the eventual, the name of the instrument be presented to you by some other avenue than I and that you also meet him face to face and converse with him. All of the above if, in the face of the movements yet to come, such would be wisest. It is very probable that if such does occur, the first contact would be with the wife of the subject.

I am today pushing my projection of strength and nearness with all my forces to you—draw heavily—and lean upon me.

Love, as always, to you both,

Harry

3

Taking the Floor

FORUM CALENDAR *September 13, 1942*

Resumption of Forum for fall. Harold attempts to talk. Mattern *only* visible supporter in group. Matterns stop reading as a result.

DIARY *September 13, 1942*

Clyde Bedell phoned at 2 p.m. to ask if we were going to the Forum meeting, a rather strange question since we have always attended; and unless we had actually been placed in a unique position with respect to the other members, there should have been no reason for anyone to imply that we would not be present. When Harold said we were going, Clyde said that was fine and that he was sure everything would work out okay. Harold said it seemed an example was being made of us, since no one had gotten in touch with us, and Clyde said, "Well, *I* have. I'm even calling you now." Harold said, "Yes, but you've told us nothing of what is going on and you won't tell us anything." Clyde said, "Well, I can't do that." Harold said, "Do you think this is fair?" Clyde's only answer was, "Sit tight and I think everything will work out."

We met the Bedells as they were parking their car outside our building when we were going over to the meeting, and Clyde again urged Harold to "take it easy."

(Harold's letter to Harry following the meeting covers essentially what happened at the meeting, and is attached herewith.) [*Ed. note:* The diary entry continues after Harold's letter.]

HAROLD SHERMAN to HARRY LOOSE

Chicago, September 13, 1942

Dear Harry:

What a HELL of a way to celebrate your birthday!

Sadler appeared before the Forum body himself and welcomed us as HIS GUESTS, which was my cue that he was taking no chances . . . the implication being that no one should speak out of turn if he is a guest.

He read the five different communications he said he had received through the years addressed to the Forum, being especially pious and courteous . . . and emphasizing any references to a Urantia Brotherhood or Association . . . and the fact that the Contact Commissioners have the book entirely in their charge UNTIL they turn it over to the TRUSTEES of the FOUNDATION. He also stated that jurisdiction had been removed from the Forum body and no higher authority was now maintained . . . but there was every evidence that he intended to retain control of it himself.

I waited until he got ready to dismiss the Forum members for the first-hour intermission, when I arose and said: "Dr. Sadler, at the start of this new epoch (which he had referred to) may I speak to the members of the Forum?"

He immediately bristled, and said: "No, not at this time."

I stepped out into the aisle from my chair and proceeded up front to stand beside him, saying: "I'm sorry, Doctor, but there are some things I *must* say to the Forum."

He said: "Sit down! And I'll tell you when you can talk to the Forum. You are a guest in my home. You have no right to speak."

I said: "I am a member of the Forum, Doctor, and Mrs. Sherman and I are here today as outcasts. We have been accused and we have a right to be heard."

Dr. Sadler repeated, "Sit down. You are not going to speak now."

I said, "Doctor, are you afraid of the truth?"

He said, "I repeat, you are my guest. Take your seat. There is going to be no argument here."

I stood my ground, and by this time other Forum members, as anticipated, were jumping up. Clyde Bedell, who had been a holdout before, but who capitulated along with the rest, grabbed my arm and said, "Harold, you are harming yourself taking this stand. The doctor is right in asking you to take your seat. We are all guests here. You wouldn't come into my home and do this, would you?"

I said, "Clyde, this is different, this is the only place a man may speak of these things and we stand accused, of all the Forum members. We have a right to defend ourselves."

Dr. Sadler said, "If Sherman wants to speak and will take his seat, I'll tell him when he can."

I said, "May I speak later today, Doctor? I want to speak today."

He said, "No, you will not speak today."

I said, "Will you be there when I speak?"

And he said, "I refuse to answer that."

Hales was now at my elbow, grabbing my coat lapels and telling me what a good fellow he had always thought I was, how he'd read lots of "stuff" I'd written, and how I was hurting my cause taking a stand like this—"losing respect of all the Forum members." He kept on talking in this vein, asking me why I wouldn't listen to Clyde Bedell.

Then Dent Karle, another "friend" who had been active in the petition work, tried to intercede, and still I refused to take my seat. Meanwhile, Martha was being high-pressured where she sat by women begging her to ask me to come and sit down . . . but Martha sat unmoved. And now Russell Bucklin joined the group around me, with the Kulieke boys, two strapping young men, excitedly asking the doctor if they should throw me out. The doctor didn't quite go for this suggestion although he would have liked to give the "go ahead." Bill Sadler began to edge down the aisle toward the group surrounding me . . . but H.C. Mattern left his seat and blocked the way, and tried to ask the doctor a question, saying: "Doctor, I'd like to ask you if you really believe in God?"

The doctor refused to answer, and Mattern said, "I am just a new member but I've known Harold Sherman for years and I . . . !"

Mattern was cut short by the doctor saying, "No one is going to make a speech here!"

Bedell then turned to Mattern and began to intercede with him while Hales kept after me. Mattern asked: "Do you people believe God is in this house?" and Bill Sadler, almost losing his head, exploded with: "I consider that an insult!" which was the only humorous remark of the set-to (although not so regarded) . . .

I still stood my ground with questions coming from the floor: "Doctor, do you want us to adjourn?" Some members, men and women, were crying; others were defiant. I think many felt sheepish that they had lacked the courage to take a stand and had left us to face things alone.

The cards were too stacked, Harry, as I sensed they would be, and as an inspirational reading of the Bible had indicated: See Ezekiel 33:30-33, and you'll have the picture.

I finally agreed to take my seat and managed to get in this comment to the Forum members, that we had respect for them and loved them all . . . which statement the doctor tried to prevent . . . but it got across. At the intermission, many gathered around to shake our hands and express friendship. Some meant it . . . the others, with a "better than thou" attitude, gave the usual lip service.

Dr. Sadler said, when I sat down, that he never permitted comments during the Sunday services but that the Wednesday night twice-a-month meetings which Bill supervises permit discussion, and if I had anything to say, I could say it before this group . . . to which anyone was privileged to come.

Under the present "loaded" circumstances, to accuse the doctor of dishonesty, etc., would accomplish no purpose as I can see it now. But a clear statement of my own stand with respect to association with the Forum, reading a sworn statement that I have no commercial ambitions, and "clearing my name" seems to be in order. After that, for the time being, SIT TIGHT and OBSERVE. What do you think at your distance.

Incidentally, if you hear from Miss Baumgartner about this, I will be most interested to get her outside viewpoint. Under NO CIRCUMSTANCES make any comment against Sadler to her as I now TRUST NO ONE outside of Martha . . . a terrible thing to have to say. The Haleses are in this thick . . . but I feel that I have taken a vigorous enough stand to have slowed them up for some time . . . and I hope the Higher Intelligences do not feel that I have failed them.

I feel absolutely free in my own conscience and do not see how I could have acted differently under the circumstances, although I know the doctor feels he has won a great victory, and Bill was laughing hysterically at proceedings, which indicates how unstable he is and would be as a leader. The doctor was visibly shaken when I did not immediately take my seat and held the floor for at least fifteen minutes or more. He poured on the syrup thick after the intermission and reread the last communication in which it said we must stand to prevent DISUNITY, which he emphasized . . . and I think most Forum members felt that I had demonstrated I was the rebellious member.

Clyde Bedell got ahold of me afterward and said, "Harold, I had a fine opinion of you until today . . . but if you let your ego run away with you after this and do not take a more humble position . . . and stop being IMPATIENT . . . your usefulness to the Forum will be entirely impaired. I think the next two weeks are going to decide your fate. I have had to eat humble pie because I get impatient and want to see different things done myself. . ."

I said, "Clyde, you are not in the same position as Martha and myself, or your viewpoint might be different. We were not even given an opportunity to withdraw our names from the petition, as you were."

He seemed surprised at this, and said, "I can't understand it, but I am sure you will be."

I said, "We have been singled out for special punishment and held with an indictment over our heads because the doctor has not made his 'peace' with us. What about his OWN EGO and STUBBORN PRIDE? Are we always to bow to it . . . is he always right?"

Clyde hesitated and said, "I don't know about that, but I do know that if you don't go along with the Forum, you'll lose all sympathy and you'll be out."

You should know by this time, Harry, that I am not moved by fear . . . I felt your presence today . . . and I felt a Great Presence. Clyde suggested that I pray to have the right guidance. I told him I did pray . . . and he said, "Well, you didn't pray right . . . you just let your mind and your ego tell you what to do. You're too sensitive, too impatient, you want to force things. Take it easy or you'll spoil everything, as I feel you can be of value to the Forum."

Apparently, I am being charged with trying to run things . . . actually, I have not been impatient; just the contrary, I have wanted to slow things up—to keep things from being done too fast . . . and thus to encounter serious mistakes. But the opposite picture has been painted to Forum members, together with my commercial ambitions.

In the light of this report, what is your own feeling that my procedure should be? I want to be so SURE that I am in the RIGHT. I hope I have not failed today, I repeat, in the eyes of those who are watching.

The doctor puts on such a disarming front, he is such an actor, that he wins ready sympathy. He started out once and said, "You can talk with him, but I won't." However, I stopped him by saying, "No, doctor, you stay here. Are you afraid to face the truth?"

I feel good tonight after the ordeal and thank you for your letter. No court action unless a very last resort. Love to you both.

DIARY *[continued]* *September 13, 1942*

During the intermission following Harold's attempted talk, some members gathered around to extend their hands and tell us they did not consider us to be outcasts. While Harold was on his feet and was being appealed to to sit down, Mr. Hales said to the Forum, "That's all right. Most of us are enjoying it." Harold challenged him on this. Martha, being besieged by different women around her to ask Harold to sit down, was tapped on the shoulder by Mr. Burton, who whispered in her ear, "You just sit tight."

Those who came up to us afterwards were Mr. Hill (who said he was on the other side but liked us just the same—by "other side" he meant he had not signed the petition), the Haleses and Bill [Hales] Jr., and Russell Bucklin, who spoke to Martha and said Mildred was literally sick over the whole thing and couldn't come to the Forum. He himself seemed deeply moved and on the verge of breaking into tears. Elsie Karle asked Martha if she would go across the street and have some refreshments (of course not accepted). Miss Brown turned about and patted Martha's hands. Betty Hicks was friendly throughout, and Miss Baumgartner shook hands and said she considered us friends. Mrs. Rawson came over with a warm smile and assured us of her friendly feelings. The Matterns also came to shake our hands and offer moral support and then left, not to return. Mrs. [Elizabeth] James talked quite a while with Martha, saying, "We must be patient and not try to move too fast." Mr. Kulieke Sr. had a nice handshake as did Mrs. Githens. Mr. and Mrs. Dyon came over separately and rather lamely greeted us over nothing in particular, as did the Kulieke Jrs. and Miss [Lucile] Olson. Mrs. [E. B.] Van Dorn came over and took Harold's hand and whispered in his ear, "You stay put. You're all right." Miss Vincent shook hands with us without comment or feeling.

Clyde Bedell got hold of Harold and took him to one side, and said, "Harold, I had a lot of respect for you until today, but you've gotten off on the wrong foot and this may cost you the friendship of many Forum members."

"What other course could I take?" said Harold. "We have been shut off from all human fellowship and not even given opportunity to take our names off the petition as all other signers have."

Bedell seemed a bit surprised at this, as though he hadn't known it. He said, "Well, Harold, you'll have to put aside your ego and face the Doctor in a humble spirit and ask his forgiveness."

Harold asked, "What are we going to do about the Doctor's ego and his stubborn pride? Will we always have to knuckle under to it whether we're right or wrong?"

Clyde said, "I don't know about that, but I *do* know you are not getting anywhere this way, and unless you make your peace with the old man you won't get very far with this Forum."

Harold made no commitment. As Clyde turned away he said to both Harold and Martha, "We'd like to have you a member of the Forum," acting as though this matter was in doubt.

We left the building. On the way out we passed Mrs. [Helen] Thurman, who spoke to us, and Leone, who shook Harold's hand. Bill was engaged in animated conversation with his "bodyguards," the Kulieke boys, who had offered to throw Harold out. Mr. Kellogg waved at us as we went by the office door, looking none too happy.

Out on the sidewalk we passed through an assemblage of at least thirty Forum members who were engaged in excited discussion. It looked for all the world like the group that gathers just before the coffin is carried out to the hearse, but we, perhaps to their regret, emerged looking like pretty live corpses and with even a smile as we passed among them and across the street to our hotel. Mr. Dyon reached out and shook Harold's hand, and Mr. Steinbeck called, "I'm glad to see that smile!" We encountered the Bedells and Evanses and Betty Hicks at their car, and they spoke as we passed.

Mary Mattern reported remarks she overheard while sitting in the annex (Bill's living room). One woman said, "Why, nothing like this has happened in the twenty-five years I've been here!" Another one said, "Who is that other man? (Referring to H.C.) They ought to throw those two ruffians out." Still another woman: "Oh, this is terrible—this is awful!" If those thoughts were felt around Martha they were not voiced, perhaps in deference to her.

Clyde Bedell phoned at 10 p.m. and in a concerned tone of voice said to Harold that he thought Harold should begin thinking objectively instead of subjectively about this whole matter.

He said, "After all, Sadler has been doing pretty well all these years—at least, he was until this fellow Sherman came along. But Sherman was a 'catalyst' and he stirred up a chemical reaction in the Forum members, so that all matters of discontent they had carried through the years were precipitated. I think this has had a salutary effect on Sadler. He is human as hell and I think he realizes now that he has neglected many members. I think he'd be free to admit that. Not only this, but he has neglected to refresh our memories on the communications we have received in different years. I think if he had read them to us and we realized how many points they covered I could never have written that petition. I feel now—*we* feel—that not having gone to Sadler after our doubts had been crystallized was a great mistake. We should have said to the Doctor, 'What communications are there?' But we didn't do that.

"Now the cards are stacked against all of us—against *you*. Sadler rides in the saddle, a position he has darn well earned through the years. If I were you, Harold, I'd go to Sadler. I'm sure you believe in the Papers. I'd go to that old man and I'd say something like this: 'We've been in a mess. I'm sorry. I want to do the right thing by the Book, etc. I'll do everything you say. I want to be right.' Harold, you can't be militant. Look what's at stake. If you go to the Doctor in this manner and he doesn't treat you right, then you place him in the position of being wrong, and I don't think the Forum members would stand for that; but right now he has their sympathy. I'd go to him right away—don't delay—and when the Wednesday night meeting comes up I'd fix it so that it can be announced that the breach is healed and that you are off your high horse."

Clyde went on, "Harold, you've got to stop being an egotist. That was my trouble. Are you more interested in maintaining your pride than finding out how things could be made amicable? You know, there's an old Greek proverb [*sic*]: 'Never attribute meaner motives to your enemy than your own!'" Harold reiterated that he had respect and affection for all Forum members and that he held no animosity toward the Doctor or Bill, but he did feel keenly about the principles involved and the manner in which Harold and Martha had been treated.

Bedell said, "Well, that's water over the dam now. What's done is done and you people face the future. That's the only thing that counts. What are you going to do about it? If I were you, I'd see the Doctor tomorrow. The sooner the better."

Harold thanked Clyde for his phone call and advice, and said he would take it under advisement but made no commitment.

H.C. MATTERN to HARRY LOOSE

Lincoln Park Arms,
Chicago, September 14, 1942

Dear Mr. Loose;

You may be interested in my viewpoint of the actions of a certain group of people here in Chicago at the meeting on Sept. 13, 1942.

Knowing Harold and Martha for several years before they went to California—we have and still believe their attitude toward the Truth is sincere and coincides with ours.

Then Harold was kind enough to bring you into our lives. When you gripped my hand, I have never before felt such a personality developed in any human being as was exchanged by your handshake and the gaze into your eyes—you certainly have an inner development that is beyond description.

Receiving admittance into the group by recommendation, we joined with the most interested and sincere attitude—and read the papers when time permitted. Of course, Mary and I knew nothing at that time of Harold's fight which was to take place. We had a rather strange feeling about the atmosphere around the place the second time we were there, and told Harold so. He then gave us the information about the petition which was being signed by many of the members. We had purposely not wanted to meet any of the members until after this thing had come to a head so there could be no feeling that Harold had brought us here in an antagonistic frame of mind. However, I had assured Harold if I could help him in any way, I was there to do the job.

At the meeting, Harold waited patiently for the Doctor to invite him, in vain. Just before recess time, Harold politely asked for an opportunity to speak. This was denied him. Still he insisted—no courtesy being shown him—in fact the Doctor was extremely rude—he even asked the members if they wanted Harold to sit down, and openly refused to give him a chance to speak. Five men attempted to silence Harold.

Then I arose and moved toward the front, asking the Doctor if he would answer one question: "Are these papers the revelations of God's or the Creator's?" He refused to answer—when one of those men who had gone after Harold grabbed my coat lapels and insisted that I had to sit down—which I refused to do—again I asked why not let us pray for Divine Guidance, this was refused. During the commotion, many said aloud, "Throw him out" and applauded every time the doctor spoke.

Our impression is that if this is a Divine Revelation, it is in mortal hands which, over the period of years, have become selfish, egotistical, domineering and are now using it for a cloak to create the impression they are a God Being and must not be crossed or doubted. In other words, they are creating a fear in the members which will, in place of setting the truth free, bind it up tighter than it has ever been on this earth before. Martha and Harold's friends have turned their backs because the Doctor told them they must not get in touch with them. What a tragedy to put such fear in the hearts of men.

It is not for us to judge whether the members are hypnotized, lack intelligence, or that they are not capable of making a real true investigation or decision.

The man who drew up the petition and led Harold and Martha to believe that they agreed to a frank, open discussion on the subject of organization—that it was the only thing to have to be sure this was all to be kept free—told Harold in front of all these people that, up until this time, he had respected him highly—but unless he sat down and did as the Doctor told him, he could not have that respect. Some tried to force Harold down, others used flattery, but Harold still stood. So did the Doctor. They finally escorted Harold to his seat. Then the doctor rather superciliously said, "There will be a meeting on Wednesday night and Mr. Sherman may say what he likes, in fact anyone is welcome to bring a soapbox." Intermission was given and Mary and I left.

On our arrival home, I predicted that very soon I would be given the name of Lucifer or the troublemaker, and before long they would be saying nice things to Harold. However, I frankly feel that Harold, under no conditions, can upset or influence these people now or later unless the Higher Powers lend him more assistance than they have up to this time—and this does not reflect on Harold's abilities, his motives, greatness, vision and sincerity—but rather that he is battling against a bunch of people who are not interested in bringing the TRUTH to the masses unless they and they only shine out before the public. The group is in the power of the Doctor and also those who stand to profit materially by that power. This is my honest opinion, which I have observed over the period of the four weeks we have been here.

You can see what a battle Harold is fighting, but he proved to the members that he was not under the spell of the Doctor and was not fearful of stating what he felt to be true.

Sincerely,
H.C. Mattern

HAROLD SHERMAN to WILLIAM SADLER

Chicago, September 14, 1942

Dear Dr. Sadler:

I am truly sorry for all that has happened and the way in which it has happened. Had you talked to us in the manner that you did the other Forum members when you called us over last Thursday, all could have been different.

But your first statement that you had nothing to say to us and would not discuss the situation, indicated plainly that we had been singled out for some special form of punishment as an example to our fellows. The fact that members had been instructed not to contact or talk to us, and that you had referred to us personally in your talks with them, further demonstrated that we alone were being made the "butt" of an action which 48 members signed in good faith and spirit, asking only the right of free discussion of matters which were and are to vitally affect, in time to come, all of their lives.

I can understand how you would have placed the responsibility at our door for this development and I will assume any responsibility which is mine, but a large number of those who signed the petition expressed to me and to their fellow Forum members the same criticisms and suggestions as voiced in my original letter to you.

I did not suggest the petition. It was felt by Forum members that a representative appeal must be made to you, for consideration to be granted, since it had been their experience in the past that you did not react well to suggestions, either written or spoken, and it was recalled how you had ridiculed in public the writers of letters to you.

I repeatedly stated to you my knowledge of the widespread differences of opinion which you discounted as coming from a small minority. I could tell that these members would wish to be heard on these matters for the purpose of clearing their own minds, and you had told me definitely that these matters would not again be taken up with the Forum, as they were a "closed book." I knew that many Forum members did not consider these matters as "closed" and told you this also, in the presence of Christy and Martha, on our ride up to Marion.

Because I knew that this appeal to you, however phrased, would be a shock, and yet felt with the others that the appeal should be made—I sought to prepare you for some such happening, and Bill, Christy and the Kelloggs as well. I mentioned these differences of opinion not once but a number of times to you all.

To the Kelloggs, I stressed the need of harmony in the time to come, and told them further I thought you were going to be greatly disturbed by the attitude of the members and that they, the Kelloggs, should understand it wasn't meant as a personal attack but was an expression of concern over book and organization plans and a desire on the part of these members to enter more fully into discussions and plannings for the future.

I said to Bill on one occasion that I felt different views would be expressed by Forum members and that he should be tolerant of their opinions, since they would be expressed in good faith. Bill said: "Harold, how could I be otherwise than tolerant, since others were tolerant toward me a few years ago when I felt keenly about some things?"

No effort was made to keep any meetings of Forumites secret nor to prevent you from knowing about such meetings if any members cared to tell you about them, which some did. Neither was there any organized plan of procedure; members were invited about to each others' homes spontaneously until the last planned meeting at the Karles', when many wished to sign the petition.

I was out of town that final week but had waited till the last moment to pick Marcia up and bring her back here for school, so I do not want you to think that I sought to avoid any responsibility for any part I played, through this absence.

My conscience is clear; I have acted in good faith, with no more personal feeling toward you than any other of the Forum members, and I am sure they have none. I have spoken my thoughts frankly and freely to those who wished to know my views and felt it was permissible to do so in the privacy of this group, since all others were giving free expression to their own views, and all with the best interests of the Book of Urantia and its developments in mind.

I repeated different remarks you and Bill had made to me from time to time because I felt these comments clearly indicated the need for free discussion. You yourself had reiterated that you had a "closed mind" and that these things had all been settled, and yet many of these Forumites stated this was not their understanding at all. I felt that it was dangerous at this juncture, for any of us to have "closed minds" on the human side and that free discussion would help all of us maintain a counter-balance, one with the other.

I know, because I am a late arrival on the scene, and because I have presented some new ideas for consideration, that you no doubt feel me to be a promoter; that I have been attempting to usurp or undermine your authority; that I am impatient and egotistically trying to push developments, motivated by commercial ambitions.

I regret that this has been your conclusion but I can understand how it would logically, from your viewpoint, seem to be so.

I asked for a hearing before the Forum because this seemed to be the only form of human redress left to me, and while you emphasized that I was a "guest in your home," this is the only place where the Forum meets as a body. The Wednesday night meetings are not meetings of the Forum proper, and since this was a Forum matter, the only place to make any statement was before the Forum, and the only Forum meetings, as you well know, are on Sunday, in your home. Therefore, I do not think I was out of order, if you consider the Forum to be a free body and if free discussion is to be permitted.

I have no interest, desire or intention of challenging your authority or in "running the show."

If you will recall my letter to you—in place of my being impatient, I have been concerned lest things progress too fast before the right publication and organization plans are conceived. I have counseled you to stop and reconsider present plans and to determine whether or not they can be greatly improved or changed for the better. I am *against* "pushing things" and I will gladly wait ANY LENGTH OF TIME, for the RIGHT things to happen.

I think the enclosed sworn statement, which I intended to present to the Forum on Sunday, to answer the charge that I have been commercially ambitious with respect to the Book of Urantia, should satisfy your apprehension on this score. [*Ed. note:* See opposite page.]

530 Diversey Parkway,
Chicago, Illinois.
September 10, 1942.

To Whom It May Concern:

I, the undersigned, do hereby declare that my sole and only interest with respect to the BOOK OF URANTIA is strictly spiritual.

I have not in the past nor do I now or ever desire, nor will I accept any moneys which might be forthcoming through any efforts of mine in connection with its publication.

By the same token, I seek no identification and glorification of my name in connection with said publication. The use of my name I will not permit, since I believe that this TRUE REVELATION must stand alone, unembarrassed and unencumbered by any human affiliation.

I do now take this occasion to declare and solemnly promise, under oath, once and for all, that no circumstances which can arise in the future can or will compel me to seek mercenary gain for any services rendered with respect to the publication of the BOOK OF URANTIA.

Whatever I possess that I can give in time and services in this work of the Kingdom is gladly offered to my Creator, to the Angels of Progress and to Sonsovocton, for the privilege of this service is beyond price.

Signed by me this tenth day of September, 1942.

Harold M. Sherman
Harold M. Sherman

Signed and sealed this 10 day of
WITNESSED BY: September - 1942 -
Betty Sherrard
Notary Public
Comm - Expires Sept 22 - 1943.

I feel, if you can take an objective, impersonal point of view with me, at this time, that much good and greater harmony and unity can come out of this Forum group than ever before.

It is not my nature to be a "troublemaker" or a "dissenter," as my entire life record will show. My one deep interest is in everything that will lead to the best presentation of this TRUE REVELATION to the world.

I have nothing to sell. If such ideas as I have are not considered worthy or right by the Forum as a whole, in free discussion, and by the contact commissioners, I do not expect any more consideration for them than the ideas of any other Forum member.

Now that these matters have been aired, I am willing to go along, in a co-operative spirit, toward the one spiritual end we all seek. It would be helpful and gracious of you if you indicated to the Forum that all was well between us, for I have no feeling against you, nor Bill, nor anyone else—and neither has Martha.

We subscribed wholeheartedly to the tribute paid you in the petition, and since the Forum body no longer was operating under higher authority, and was "on its own" as a human body, we felt it was fair and right to ask for free discussion.

I cannot conceive of any humans receiving spiritually decreed punishment for such an honest act. I will face my God any time, and have faced Him, through prayer, during these past days, and have called upon the Angels of Progress to examine my mind and heart and know that I have been sincere and well-intentioned in everything I have done.

We all have our human faults. I confess mine. Will you forgive me those as I forgive you yours? And let us all meet once again on an even firmer friendly and spiritual footing.

Sincerely,

HAROLD SHERMAN to JIM HICKS

Chicago, September 15, 1942

Dear Jim:

When Betty returns to you she will tell you of Forum happenings here in which I have been compelled to play an unhappy part. The doctor apparently has decided to make Martha and me the "goats" and is holding us under "indictment" before our fellows—which is not even human justice, let alone divine. Can you imagine what is going to happen when a public organization exists and any member raises a question which a leader may interpret as challenging his authority? The persecution will rival the days of the Inquisition.

Betty has told me of your continuing perspiration difficulties and I *did* send you some thoughts which I felt might be helpful. I am convinced it is a nervous reaction due to unconscious mental tension which activates the sweat glands. This probably was automatically brought upon you at some time when you went through a particularly trying experience and now it continues under associative "pressure conditions." If you could go back in your mind and recall what happened when this first occurred and what your mental attitude was then, you would have the key to the situation. By changing that mental attitude, which still exists in your subconscious (refer to my book, *Key to Happiness,* for technique) you will release the stimulus in consciousness which reacts upon your nervous system and the sweating will cease as quickly as it came upon you. Meanwhile, for what good it may accomplish, I will send you thoughts visualizing your regaining subconscious involuntary control of your sweat glands.

And now, Jim, I come to a painful part of this letter. Martha and I have taken a tremendous liking to you and Betty on short acquaintance and we want to deserve your friendship always—but what has happened at the Forum has affected our personal lives as well. For reasons we cannot now explain, we must keep ourselves absolutely free of any business association with any members of the Forum which might later be judged to have influenced their thinking or attitude concerning us.[1] If this BOOK is what we all believe it is, then the TRUTH it contains is worthy of every sacrifice and every effort to protect and preserve it.

Being placed in the position we are, we do not wish now or in the future to embarrass our association with the Bedells and yourselves. We think too much of you to permit ourselves to be connected on a business venture and have possibly differing views on the personal side, whereas, if we are free as friends, we can express ourselves frankly and with no involvement. I would not want it said that any support which might be granted to us had been prejudiced in our favor by a business alliance.

[1] Jim Hicks, Clyde Bedell's brother-in-law, had been seeking to interest Forum members in an investment plan.

I cannot predict what the future has in store here. Our attitude is friendly and it will be cooperative but we will not submit to unjust treatment for we do not believe the divine is unjust or that any unjust decrees have come from that source.

I hope you will understand how we feel and I am sure you will when you have talked with Betty. With things going as well as reported, you will easily be able to dispose of all stock.

We very much appreciated being given a chance to buy shares with your company and shall always wish you folks well . . . but just now other things on our horizon are far too important to jeopardize in any way.

Sincerely,

4

A Few Friendly Overtures

DIARY *September 15, 1942*

Harold received a surprise phone call from Robert Burton, attorney and Forum member, in apparent support of his statement made to Martha at the time Harold was on his feet asking the right to speak. He had said to her then to "sit tight," against the admonition of other Forum members to call upon Harold to take his seat. Mr. Burton, in his phone call, said he wanted Harold to know that he had the sympathy and support of most of the Forum members and that there just wasn't anything they could do at the present moment, as the message read to them by the Doctor, which was supposed to have come through on Sept. 4, dealt specifically with the points raised in the petition, making the petition unnecessary.

Burton said, "We did not realize before how completely under control and supervision this whole book and organization plan really was." Harold asked if the references to the Urantia society and the need for its existence were part of this message, and Burton said he could tell us more when he saw us personally, as he and Mrs. Burton wished us to come out for dinner soon and would be calling us to set a definite date. He said Mrs. Burton wished her regards to be sent to us and asked if Harold was going to speak to the Forum on Wednesday night.

Harold said he doubted if he would, with the present existing attitude; and Burton said that might be wise, that we'd just have to go along and watch things, that this was not the way he would have handled the matter in connection with us had he been doing it. He said he felt, among other things, it was a clash of personalities.

Harold asked if he saw any divine justice, or even human justice, in the treatment accorded us by the Doctor. Burton said, "No. But we'll just have to wait and see what he finally intends to do and then judge accordingly." The phone call indicated that some Forum members, at least, are doing some serious thinking.

HAROLD SHERMAN to SIR HUBERT WILKINS

Chicago, September 15, 1942

Dear Hubert:

On Sunday afternoon, at the reconvened meeting of the Forum, I asked Dr. Sadler for the floor, at the end of the first hour, and he curtly said, "No—sit down!" I was standing when I made the request and continued on up the aisle to the front by the blackboard and stood beside the doctor, declaring that I must ask that I be permitted to make a statement, since the action taken against Mrs. Sherman and myself made us "outcasts" in the eyes of the Forum body. Doctor cut in to say, savagely: "You are a guest in my house and I forbid you to speak. Sit down!"

I remained standing, not antagonistically, but appealingly, and now different Forum members who had been active in drawing up the petition—Clyde Bedell, Dent Karle and Russell Bucklin—followed by Mr. Hales, who grabbed me by my coat lapels, surrounded me.

"Sit down, Harold, you are doing yourself great harm appealing in this manner!" they counseled.

Every time I tried to say something, even to answer these men, the doctor, almost hysterically, cried out: "You're not going to speak. I won't allow it! I repeat—you're a guest here . . . you are all my guests . . . no one has a right to speak here!"

I said: "Doctor, this is the only place the Forum meets and the only meeting of the Forum body. This is the only redress I . . . !"

But he would let me say nothing, and now H.C. Mattern, a positive type of individual and a most unusual character, whom I had just brought into the Forum and who is here from New York with his wife, reading the book—became concerned as the two Kulieke boys said to the doctor: "Shall we throw him out?" and jumped up to come to my rescue. He tried to query the doctor but was shut up . . . and it now looked, for a moment, as though we were to have an amazingly fanatical outburst of religious hatred, bearing out my contention that once you try to ORGANIZE THE TRUTH and SET UP HUMAN AUTHORITIES, perversion and persecution begins.

I saw that it was impossible to make even a kindly statement, and I had no intention of being rough in the first place . . . but I would not leave the floor until I had been permitted to say to the Forum body, "I want you to know I have respect for every one of you and love you all."

At the intermission, many gathered around to shake my hand and to express guarded sympathy. They are having a hard time comprehending the doctor's order to isolate Martha and myself, and are baffled because he has let them think it is an order from on high. Today I had a phone call from Mr. Burton, who is the only attorney member of the Forum. He said, "Harold, there is something not right on the human side over there . . . and we want you to know that while we are forbidden to speak to you at present, you have more sympathy than you realize . . . and more support. We are placed in the position where, if we challenge the doctor at this time, he infers we are challenging the truth itself."

Hubert, my life recorder does not show me as a "troublemaker" or a "dissenter" . . . and you must know that I gave great deliberation before I took the step I did. It was by no means an easy thing to do. No one has ever faced the doctor . . . they have all backed down through the years . . . but he now knows that I do not fear him . . . and that I cannot be controlled through religious fear. He does not yet have a "corner on God" and can't shut God off from us . . .

Yesterday I wrote the doctor a letter and enclosed a sworn statement that I had no intention of ever commercializing my interests with respect to the Book of Urantia, which he has alleged, among other things, to Forum members.

He said, lamely, after I had sat down, that I could speak to the Wednesday night meeting, if I chose . . . "where we give people the soapbox occasionally, when they want it" . . . but this does not represent the Forum as a body and I will not be tricked into such a position, where I can be "shot at from the floor."

Having taken my stand so that the Forum knows there is one who will not back down when injustice is meted out in the way of treatment, I intend—IF the doctor will decide to "bury the hatchet"—to go along quietly and let Forum members think what they choose . . . and observe the human conduct of affairs from this time on.

We all have our faults . . . but, oh, Hubert—how weak is human nature . . . where greed, jealousy, ego, lust for power and these other elements are present. I am interested only in the principles at stake and the protection of this great TRUTH. I want no position or individual credit or money . . . whatever talents I have I gladly contribute, if they are usable.

To think that the minds of all Forum members can be so "controlled" as to follow mandates of the doctor's and to let fellow members be made the "goats." Fortunately, I have never been disturbed at what people have thought of me . . . I have proceeded always as I have felt was right . . . and if others have not understood, that could not be helped.

I have wanted you to have this up-to-date account. The doctor has not read me the messages nor does he intend to . . . because I think he knows I would recognize them to be messages which did not come through recently . . . but over a year ago, which he has told me of, and which he is now representing were just received, in order to score his points. This is the human side and indicates how anxious he is to maintain control of the Truth, despite his reiteration that he is only the custodian. I have faith that time will bring balance, plus help from higher sources. Our best!

HARRY LOOSE to HAROLD and MARTHA SHERMAN

Monterey Park, September 17, 1942

Dear Harold and Martha:-

I am answering Harold's letter mailed September 13th detailing some of the Forum activities of that very day. I am also answering both Martha's and Harold's letters—the envelope of which also contained the affidavit and the copy of the letter sent to Sadler by Harold. . . .

I have re-read the Bible references contained in Martha's letter of today and the lone reference in Harold's last letter and will be able to look them up in the Bible and read them fully shortly. I cannot get to it right away. I am pretty sure I know the gist of most of them, without being letter perfect, but will verify them a little later. Martha really writes a very full and descriptive talking letter and the feel of it is very definite—holding it in the hands gently, palm over palm, and it talks a great deal.

Yesterday, I went to the funeral of my old friend, Mr. Hindemarche. He died Sunday morning. He awakens today.

I hope that you can find the Tyson at the Walgreen drugstore, Martha, and that it is on its way out here. And don't forget to tell me the cost that I may return it to you at once. I feel all over soap now after my bath because I can't rinse myself with that spray.

I do hope that through all the present troublesome times, you have not failed to keep up your Diary. Can you not now more clearly see the reason for the book that you are to write. I won't be here when it's written but my name will be included in it and your name will be on it. An anonymous book on this subject would lack apparent verity and be useless. Neither could you produce such a thing with verity, or belief, if the sustaining characters were anonymous. You will find a lot of true names will be written in your book, as they should be, for the benefit of the many generations that will read it.

I am glad for your recognition and acceptance of the physical assistance. I would not have remarked it but for your acknowledgment of the good results.

There is so very much that the Book of Urantia tells—but there is much more that it does not tell. So much that is beyond the usual normal human understanding limit. Just think, it has taken you both, under exceedingly favorable circumstances, quite a while to finally reach where you are—and accept what has been so liberally laid before you. So very much of your own belief could even now be torn down by giving further information beyond your present limit. For instance, I would like to tell you more about Abner—and Andrew—and Cleodotus—but should I risk tempting your disbelief—now? Or would it not be better, and safer, after a further growth. You can grasp much more in a year from now. Sometimes I wonder if you have ever really realized how much has been given to you *both*.

To digress—is there anything further in regard to the farm?? Don't lose interest there. Don't lose the Jane Addams matter if you still value it. I personally have not much faith in its worth. There are other possibilities much more promising of returns for your time, talents and labor.

Something happened with Dr. S some years ago. There is something that had its beginning long before Mrs. S passed on. Witness

Christy. People not so prominent living in such association in a mere apartment would have had to change their relationship or move in a limited time. Kelloggs strongly disapprove. Do not forget for a minute that one of the several prolific sources for evil concerned here is the entire Hales grouping. Use extreme care and be on your guard ever. Please believe in your so recent operation, just closed, that you have not "lost face." You have "gained face" instead. Not alone with some Forum members, but with certain higher intelligences more understandingly concerned. Please do not believe that all that has occurred in the recent mild tempest was without form and void. There is a REASON—and a very good one.

I hold Martha's letter between the palms of my two hands and it talks much to me. There is so very much more in the letter than what was there written. I have had no letter from "H.C." and I have had no letter from Elsie Baumgartner.

I believe that you will eventually see and speak with the instrument. He knows so very little himself. His wife far more than he. Such eventual contact would not profit nearly as much as the knowing contacting of one of the Seven—a Forum member—and a resident in Chicago. In your recent writings you have not mentioned his name. However, both of the above meetings are very possible. I believe one to be very probable. You are growing—you have handled your first real assignment with decorum, wisdom, diplomacy and tact.

I get very lonely sometimes. It is so hard to always remember that one of the penalties of life in this dimension is the living always alone through it all.

I am returning herein the affidavit and the copy of the letter to Dr. Sadler. They are both admirable. There is more in these letters of mine to you than you get in a single cursory reading. I would advise a rereading. Please reread my last letter to you. It tells you so very much. Please believe me when I tell you that you are both of increasing value.

Much love to you both—and to Marcia too—

As always,

FORUM CALENDAR *September 17, 1942*

The Burtons and Miss [Mildred] Hoffman[1] invite us for evening talk.

[1] The Shermans alternately call her Miss and Mrs. Hoffman in the diaries.

DIARY *September 18, 1942*

We drove out to the Burtons', who live at 7400 South Shore Drive, and found Miss Hoffman, a retired schoolteacher, to be residing with them. She is also a member of the Forum. Despite the cordial overtures of the Burtons, they did not bring up the subject of the Forum until we mentioned it ourselves just before leaving. They seemed to feel that rather specific instructions had been received from higher sources with respect to book and organization plans, and said what a few other Forum members have said: "We think it will all come out alright in time."

Harold stated that he had no commercial interest in the Book of Urantia as charged. Mrs. Burton said, "Well, I think that sometimes when a man like the Doctor covets something himself he's apt to accuse another of coveting the same thing."

We were asked if we had been given opportunity to remove our names from the petition, and we said we had not. This seemed to surprise the Burtons, and Mr. Burton said again, "If I had been handling this matter I wouldn't have handled it this way."

Yet spending an evening with the Burtons indicated how weak-willed they are, regardless of how well-meaning. They reported to us, thus verifying once more, the fact that the Doctor had read them several communications which he represented as being received Sept. 4 but the contents of which he had told in detail to Harold and Martha as early as Aug. 10 when he said that these messages had come through over a year ago but had never been read to the Forum. The communications had to do with the expressed need for a Urantia society, since without it some fifty organizations would spring up in a few years' time.

There was also mention made of the "Ideaist" and "Idealist," all of which was recognizable to Harold as material referred to by the Doctor long before Sept. 4. This being true, it becomes quite evident why we have not been read these communications, for we would have recognized their earlier origin to the Doctor's very great embarrassment. It will surprise us now if under the circumstances these communications are ever read to us. Harold asked if his name was actually mentioned, and they said it was; and Harold asked if he was being held responsible for what had happened and they said yes, that this was definitely implied.

September 19, 1942

Jim Hicks, returned from Hot Springs, Arkansas, phoned in answer to Harold's letter and said he "understood" Harold's situation with respect to the Forum and his decision in not going through with purchase of stock. Jim said he had not yet talked with Clyde and did not know much of developments, but that what had happened should not interfere with our friendship. He hoped we would visit them whenever we came to Arkansas.

FORUM CALENDAR *September 20 & 27, 1942*

Harold and Martha continue to quietly attend regular Forum sessions and every succeeding Sunday.

DIARY *September 20, 1942*

FORUM—Paper 1: "THE UNIVERSAL FATHER"

After long deliberation, Harold and Martha decided to attend the Forum meeting to indicate to the Doctor and members that we had been unaffected by the events of last Sunday and had no personal sense of guilt concerned therewith. It seemed to us that the Doctor would have taken great satisfaction in our not appearing and that our presence there would demonstrate conclusively that we were unafraid.

When we arrived, we found the Doctor in the hallway on the second floor talking to Mrs. Hales as we passed. Mrs. Hales spoke and the Doctor said hello in an indirect way. We went through to our seats, which happened to be behind Bill Hales, who greeted us and made a comment about the weather. The Karles, two rows in front, turned about obviously to catch our eye and nod a greeting. Several other Forum members, whom we did not know by name, smiled at us and nodded. The Evanses came in and glanced askance at us as they passed by. Just before the meeting started, Clyde Bedell stuck his head out from the annex room and looked searchingly about until his eyes fell upon us. It was apparent that he was curious to see whether or not we had come. When he saw us he appeared a bit surprised and waved his hand.

Bill Jr. took the first hour in a reading of the first paper on God the Universal Father,[2] which impressed us as magnificent. We found

[2] This was most probably Paper 2: "THE NATURE OF GOD," since Paper 1 had been read at the June 21st meeting (see p. 47 of this volume), and Paper 3 was read at the September 27th meeting (see p. 276 of this volume).

for some reason that it meant much more, even with Bill's reading, and attributed it to the background we had gained from a reading of the entire book manuscript.

The Burtons had come in and sat beside us, showing the most friendliness of any members. Mrs. Burton even whispered that they had brought some watercress for us which they wished to give us after the meeting. She gave Harold a little note from Mrs. Hoffman, which was also intended as a little friendly gesture.

At intermission, Dent Karle dropped down beside Harold, obviously a bit ill at ease. His comments were guarded. Clyde Bedell stopped momentarily. He did not offer his hand but stood beside Dent Karle and nodded a greeting. His attitude was quite reserved. Elsie Karle came over to Martha and chatted about school problems. We were left almost completely alone by all other Forum members. Lee Miller Jones came over and gave Harold his hand. As Rev. Rawson passed out the door, Harold caught his eye and smiled at him. Rawson smiled back but kept going. Russell Bucklin did not venture near but stood in the aisle and nodded to Harold, an attempted cordial greeting but a hurt and almost fearful expression on his face. (Mildred Bucklin had been down to see her daughter Winnifred at Hull House, and told Mary Winnifred was leaving on a visit to relatives in Detroit, and Mary understood she [Mildred] had given up her job. This indicated the nervous tension she has been under.)

Dr. Sadler steered a careful course throughout the second hour but did emphasize, almost as though to justify his own human weaknesses, the fact that man has much of the animal in him and that the "mark of the beast" does not disappear until we have made considerable progress on the Morontia Mansion Worlds.

With the meeting over, few paid any heed to us. Martha said hello to Christy who was just outside the Forum door. Christy returned the hello and then spoke to Harold, who was following, and shook his hand. Martha then spoke to Mrs. Kellogg, who came out after her to the stair landing and gave her a firm handshake, and accompanied her down the stairs. Mrs. Burton had given Martha the sack of lovely watercress, and as we reached the first-floor landing, Harold saw Mr. Burton at the desk talking to Mr. Kellogg. Harold stepped inside to thank Mr. Burton for his wife's gift and extended his hand to Mr. Kellogg, who took it in an abrupt and what seemed to be a fearsome manner. Mr. Kellogg turned away and busied himself with other things, and Harold left to be met by Mrs. Van Dorn, who whispered to him as she shook his hand, "Well, I see you got back alright." The inference seemed to be that Harold had been forgiven by the Doctor and permitted to attend this meeting. Whether this is what most Forum members thought on seeing us there we do not know, but Harold made no reply to this comment.

Outside we ran into Mr. Hales returning to the building from having been out to his car. He was caught off-guard at running face to face with Harold, and extended his hand reluctantly as he passed, saying, "Hello." The whole atmosphere radiating from him was distasteful and unhealthy. We stood up under this unpleasant situation unusually well, it being apparent to us that it was much more of an ordeal to many others there, particularly Bill and the Doctor, who made every effort to avoid us and got out of the room and out of sight as quickly as possible.

HAROLD SHERMAN to SIR HUBERT WILKINS

Chicago, September 21, 1942

Dear Sir Hubert:

The enclosures tell their own story. I sent this letter and affidavit to Dr. Sadler this past Tuesday and have had no word from him.

Martha and I, after deliberation, attended this past Sunday's meeting of the Forum. We were greeted by a few of the Forum members but most of them are "afraid" to get in touch with us.

This is the most interesting "psychological" situation I have ever encountered.

It looks as though I would have to be in New York on business around October 1st or a few days later. I hope I can see you then and discuss developments here at length.

I am not concerned, basically, but the human side here is "quite something."

Watch the October *Coronet*, due on the stands the 25th of September, for your article.[3] I owe you your half of what was received for this adaptation, minus the agent's fee, or net $135.00.

Best to you!

---

[3] The six-page article was called "The Time I Tried Telepathy" and was derived from *Thoughts Through Space.*

HAROLD SHERMAN to HARRY LOOSE

Chicago, September 21, 1942

Dear Harry:

We were glad to get your letter today and to learn from you that we had handled our "first assignment" acceptably. It had not seemed to us that we had accomplished so much "on the surface" . . . but if higher intelligences are pleased, we are happy—because it has not been an easy experience, or a pleasant one, as you so well know.

The Burtons phoned us last week and had us out to their home on the South Shore Drive. He used to be an attorney, his wife a schoolteacher whom he met and married at the Forum. They are simple people but have shown us more friendliness than any other members . . . and the only ones who have really been in touch with us or invited us to their home since "the petition was presented to the doctor and he started calling the members in and putting the fear of God in them," etc.

Even so, the Burtons kept carefully off the subject of last Sunday and the doctor's attitude toward us, until we brought it up in leaving. Then, on questioning, they told in general of the communications the doctor had read . . . and I am convinced that one of the reasons he will *not* read these communications to us, is that they are not official . . . and were received *over a year ago*, and he *knows* he has *already told us* of these communications . . . and he has put them together and made them serve him at this present time, letting the Forum members think they were just received . . . and transmitted in direct answer to the petition matter!

Certainly, if the doctor has taken such action, he will be punished later for such unwarranted assumption of power . . . and for controlling the human wills of the Forum members, by making them think they have been dictated to by higher powers . . . and directed NOT TO GET IN TOUCH WITH US. It is pathetic to see the expressions on the faces of some of those whom we considered our close friends . . . they would like to open up but THEY DON'T DARE.

After long deliberation and prayer, Martha and I decided that we would ATTEND YESTERDAY'S FORUM MEETING, just as though nothing had happened. We would not offer to speak to anyone who did not wish to recognize or speak to us, nor would we offer our hands first, but we would go quietly about our business. We knew that Doctor, who had not acknowledged the last letter and affidavit, would be HOPING we would not have the courage to show up, after our "reception" last Sunday . . . and he and Bill gave us a wide berth when they saw us. FEW Forum members even spoke to us . . . some making elaborate attempts to avoid us, which were amusing. Bill read the first hour, the paper on the Universal Father; Doctor followed after intermission with comments on the Westminster Confession of Faith. He has been discoursing on different religions and how they will have to adapt themselves to the Urantia revelations, their points of disagreement, etc. Doctor mentioned, in his talk, that man had much of the animal in him and the mark of the beast was not removed until he had made considerable progress in the morontia worlds . . . (Was he trying to alibi himself, with a guilty conscience?)

Mrs. Kellogg went out of her way to give Martha a firm handclasp yesterday. I offered my hand to Mr. Kellogg who took it abruptly and turned away, as if afraid he would be seen shaking hands with me. I think the Kelloggs are economically dependent upon the doctor and are in a bad spot personally to express their real feelings or misgivings. We have noted the Christy angle and are aware of the doctor's physical attitude toward women. Christy is likewise in one "hell of a spot." She said, "Hello, Harold," and offered her hand to me yesterday. I grasped it but said nothing. She likewise spoke to Martha, who had said hello to her. Bill Jr., who has said he would "never forgive me," avoids us entirely. The doctor got out of the way so he would not have to face us, also. And Mr. Hales, running into us on the street after the meeting as he was coming back to the building from his car, extended his hand reluctantly. We came upon him suddenly and he was unable to mask his real feelings . . . we got a most distasteful and unhealthy reaction from him.

Martha has felt drawn to the senior Mr. Kulieke, whose big, strapping sons offered to "throw me out" last Sunday. He is a most pleasant man who says nothing, just looks on.

We cannot imagine who the "one of the Seven" is . . . as most of the members seem to have fallen by the wayside at present. I would certainly like to be making "*knowing* contact" at the right time.

This "mild tempest," as you call it, has certainly shaken things up and enabled us to get an illuminating gauge on many Forum members. It seems incredible that all could have been bowled over this way . . . but the threat of being removed from contact with the Book of Urantia has been more than any could stand . . . also, they were horrified at the suggestion that they had "unwittingly participated in another attempted 'Lucifer rebellion.'"

You should have had a letter from H.C. Mattern by this time, giving his account of the Sept. 13th meeting, although he addressed it to Monterey Park.

Harry, we've come a long, long way—and we feel that nothing now could disrupt our faith. We've been pretty severely tested ever since being in Chicago . . . and you now know how we have persevered despite all obstacles. I am hungry to know more of Abner, Andrew and Cleodotus, when you are ready to tell us. Remember, I have always sensed that there was something to "reincarnation" . . . it has always seemed real to me . . . and if it applies in my case, then it is even easier to comprehend why these feelings have been strong within me. . . .

Strange that you should mention your feeling about the Jane Addams proposition . . . that is exactly mine at the moment. I can't make myself do any more work on it just now . . . and FEEL other, more vital, important, worthwhile and productive things will be coming to me. I will NEED it pretty soon, for we have devoted practically full time to the development across the street since coming here.

Indeed we have not forgotten the farm. I have made two payments on it and another is due November first, when the tenant farmer is supposed to move off. I would like to be able to send Arthur down there by then . . . and will if financial matters take an upward turn for me. World conditions are getting progressively worse and we may have a financial crack-up in this country again . . . so I don't know how long any of us will be able to make money.

You should now be able to bathe without getting a soap hangover, as the Tyson arrangement should have reached you this past weekend.

I may have to go to New York around October 1st, to attend a hearing on my MARK TWAIN CONTRACT. Harry, wherever money is concerned, friendships and all other fine things in life usually become involved. Clara Clemens Gabrilowitsch, whose estate is being managed by Charles T. Lark, has undertaken the financing of some 20 Jewish refugees and has spent much more of her money than she should . . . and NOW is contending that she did not GET ENOUGH from the Mark Twain deal . . . and is trying to CUT IN on what I am receiving. In other words, she is blaming Lark for having made such a contract, when my DRAMATIC WORK was what made the Twain material valuable . . . and it looks as though I would have to FIGHT to hold and retain what is coming to me . . . in addition to going to the expense and trouble of another trip to New York.

But I am holding no malice toward Clara . . . she is just an emotionally unstable woman who is being ill-advised by some Jewish lawyers and who has turned ungrateful, under the pressure of need for more money. I am holding the right thought and hope and pray that WHAT IS MINE WILL NOT BE TAKEN FROM ME.

I have counted on this bigger payment this fall, when the [Twain] picture is to be released as we need it for living and for the farm. With it, we can accomplish much and be able to devote much more time to spiritual work. Perhaps my New York trip will open up other channels . . . I may be pulled there by this for other reasons, too. I am trying to maintain a constructive attitude toward the whole development.

Your letters mean a great deal to us and we hope you and Mother Loose keep your usual health. We would like to get back out on the coast and be able to see you again before too long. I want to keep contact with Wanderman, Potter and Ronayne . . . and to consider the lady publisher and her wealthy friend, as you mention. Am glad none of these were here when this happened, as it would not have made a good impression on them—the human situation.

Here are a few more airmails . . . Our love and our gratitude for all the HELP you have sent our way . . .

DIARY *September 21, 1942*

Miss (?) [Mrs. Henrietta] Swanson called this a.m. and identified herself as a Forum member, saying she was going to California for the winter and she had a house she would like to rent us. We had a postcard also from Miss [Edith] Harrington, Dr. Sadler's secretary, herself a Forum member, now on vacation, who evidently wished to indicate her friendly feeling.

September 23, 1942

For some mysterious reason Clyde Bedell phoned to have another one of his "sounding out" conversations with Harold. He said he was calling to see if our status quo had changed any during the week, and Harold said no. Clyde said, "Have you done anything to help matters along?" Harold said he had sent a written statement to the Doctor which should have clarified the situation and left the door open for the Doctor to contact him. Clyde said, "That's fine. I was glad to see you at the Forum last Sunday and I thought the attitude of the Forum members indicated they were friendly."

Harold said this present situation was not disturbing us in the least as we had no feeling of guilt, but that we had been hurt by the attitude of aloofness on the part of Forum members we had considered our friends. Harold said that Clyde himself would have been hurt had such an attitude been directed at him and his wife. Harold further stated that he could not consider such an attitude as a part of divine instructions and preferred to interpret it as a human mandate of Dr. Sadler's.

Clyde said, "I'm inclined to agree with you there. The Doctor is an old man and terribly human. He was greatly hurt by this petition, and since he has received communications to indicate that the subjects of the petition were not to be handled in this manner, there was nothing for us to do but withdraw it." Clyde continued, "When I was phoned by certain Forum members and told to get in touch with the Doctor, I called Christy and let her know that I had no intention of defying higher Intelligences, so she knew my attitude was friendly before I came in."

Harold said that he likewise had phoned in and got the Doctor on the wire and had spoken to him in a friendly spirit asking for an appointment, and the Doctor had said abruptly, "We'll call you." Harold said, "When we were called, expecting finally to be treated as the others, we were greeted by the Doctor's statement that he had nothing to say to us at the present time. This indicated to us that we were a 'marked couple' and were being held on probation or under indictment." Harold intimated the Sunday 13th episode might never have happened had consideration been shown us the previous Thursday.

Clyde said, "Well, probably the Doctor is giving you both a chance to cool off."

Harold said, "We hold no resentment toward anyone and have held none. Our only hurt has been our being ostracized from those we considered our friends, and this attitude we cannot understand."

Harold said he was going to New York sometime next week and that he was still willing to be helpful in the publication matters if the Doctor wished, but that he had no commercial interests whatsoever and had made a sworn statement to this effect to the Doctor.

Clyde said, "I wish you hadn't done that," which was directly counter to a statement he had made shortly after his own session with the Doctor when he said, "I think it would be a good idea to let the Doctor know you have no commercial interests. I don't believe you have, but I think it might help your situation with him." Clyde now stated that he did not remember the Doctor's inferring that Harold had any commercial ambitions with respect to the Urantia Book. He reiterated that he thought things would work out in time.

Harold said he must appreciate that it was not the easiest thing in the world to attend Forum sessions under present conditions, but that we had not been told to stay away. Clyde said he could understand that, but that he hoped to be seeing us next Sunday. He did confess that he knew different Forum members had asked the Doctor if they should not be seeing us, and the Doctor had indicated that it might be just as well for the time being.

On hanging up, we suddenly remembered that it was the Wednesday evening when the Doctor had declared that Harold was privileged to bring his soap box and address the Forum members, and that many had perhaps come expecting some fireworks. Clyde's call may have been inspired because of his wonderment as to what our next move might be, but as proof that we had erased this situation from our minds we had completely forgotten about it.

HARRY LOOSE to HAROLD SHERMAN

Monterey Park, September 26, 1942

Dear Harold:-

I am acknowledging receipt of yours of September 21st with the enclosure of the three airmail stamps and the thrilling story of your brave return Sunday last to the scene of the so recent battle between the forces of truth and error. It was a courageous return both for you and for small Martha.

If you can mentally visualize Mrs. Sadler as the balance that kept the doctor in the straight and narrow way—that kept the weight of the *right* in the doctor's mental status—you will have a much clearer picture and better understanding of the calamity of the collapse of things since her very much regretted passing. And Christy resided there even then—and before. Mrs. Sadler was the offset of the weight of commercialism, and more, of the Hales full grouping, headed by the elder male Hales, of course. The greatest continuing, and active, and present, evil behind the throne is still the Hales influence. Sadler has contributed greatly himself to his continuing fall by his great exaggerated ego, the "king can do no wrong" complex, and his accepted way of life—which you and others have observed.

Both of the Kelloggs have kept the faith with far greater sincerity than has Sadler. Kellogg is not a physically well man—serious stomach ulcers—extremely nervous—and, in a way, the Kelloggs are financially dependent upon Sadler. They do not recognize that they are just as valuable to him as he is to them, really even more so. They have believed the other so long that it would not be possible to convince them of anything else—even if it was so desired—which it is not—they must come to their own conclusions.

You have probably reasoned out all that I have remarked of Sadler to yourself without any assistance, or indication, from me. If it were not for Sadler's present physical possession of the Book, there would be a much different perspective by the entire Forum grouping. You very probably recognize this also. As you also know, yourself, he twists the truth to suit his best interests—as witness the rearranged communications. Please know that you are the first ones not to stand in awe of him. You are the first one not to "yes" him. You are the first one to dispute his infallibility. You are the first one not to be afraid. To have a reasoning mind of your own regarding all these things. To express clearly and to the point with truth and without mental reservations. Of a truth, the continuing development will be exceedingly interesting to observe.

Sadler knows that he is in the wrong—he knows that very well—when he listens to his "inner self"—he knows, too, that you know he is in the wrong, and others know also. I can tell you with the greatest of sincerity that adjustments will be made—but how—when—or by what avenues—I have no knowledge. I may have some information later—but I have no surety of that. The whole continuing matter is entirely outside any furthering active interest so far as I having any responsibility. As I have said before, you are entirely "on your own"—or, perhaps more truthfully, in cooperation with other intelligence—whether it be but full co-operation with your "other self" or a distinct intelligence, I do not know. You are but groping now—but soon the path will be more plain.

I must not fail to acknowledge receipt of the Tyson which arrived last Saturday morning very safely. It was a very clever and sweet little maneuver of Martha's to make an advance birthday gift to Ma. I did not anticipate that—and expected to pay for it. And now I must express from Ma to Martha her appreciation for the advance remembrance—and I express "many thanks" for myself also.

I also want to tell you that I rec'd a nice letter from "H.C." written by Mary Mattern for "H.C."'s signature—and a nice note enclosed from Mary Mattern herself. . . .

Glad that you have not forgotten the farm.

I hope that your attendance at a hearing on the Mark Twain Contract in New York is not necessary. I do not believe that you will suffer loss. She was in a position to accept or not accept the Contract—and she did accept. Unless she can prove that her New York agent was dishonest, it would not seem that she has anything to stand upon. If she has to be present in N.Y. at this hearing, she may stop over in Chi and see you—to your benefit.

Hope *Thoughts Through Space* brings a good return—and soon. Don't let Bill Sadler's attitude bring you any annoyance. The hurt is really his—and his is the loss.

Sure wish that I could be with you this coming Sunday afternoon at the Forum—and to go from there over to your apartment and have one of Martha's biscuits—or maybe two. But "if wishes were horses, beggars might ride" and so, unless something unexpected turns up, I won't be seeing you there. . . .

The Alexian Brothers Hospital is about 4 miles from your present residence. West and South. It is easier and plainer to get directions as to how to drive there from inquiry at your hotel. I don't believe that I will impose on you by continuing. I was going to ask you to make a visit there for me but I believe that it would be best to wait a little time. I will write in some letter later on regarding the matter.

Well, folks, Ma and I again express thanks again for the Tyson—and come out clean from the tub now—no soapy aftermath. And with every good thought and MUCH love and confidence to you both,

As ever,

DIARY *September 26, 1942*

Miss Brown phoned Harold to say she was leaving for New York to close up her apartment there and come back here for the duration, and that she would like to see us before she left. This being our anniversary, we made a date to see her Monday evening, September 28.

Harold hung up on her call and the phone rang back with Mrs. Steinbeck on the wire, sister of Miss Brown, who said she had wanted to speak to Harold. She said, "I just wanted you to know that you haven't lost the esteem of the Forum members and that they are doing a lot of thinking since you got up and asked to speak at the September 13 meeting. We didn't know before, for instance, that we were 'only guests' in the Doctor's home. We have found out since that he said different things to different people, and this does not seem to be in accordance with what was supposed to be divine instructions. No one is clear as to where his own human attitude leaves off and the 'divine instructions' begin. I had lunch with Elsie Baumgartner today who said she would like to see you, as certain things the Doctor has said and done don't seem to jibe."

[She continued:] "I was over at Sadler's today with my sister (Miss Brown) to do some reading, and while there my sister, because she was leaving town, wanted to make her donation to the book publication. She spoke to Mr. Kellogg about it, who said, 'I'm sorry. We can't accept any donations right now. But if you'd like to subscribe for some of the books, that will be okay.' This indicates to me that the Doctor, if he has received some instructions from higher up, has been advised not to publish the book himself but isn't saying anything to us about it. Either that, or he's afraid to proceed after the questions we have raised in the petition. We have observed four or five points that he has backed down on already, and we feel much good has been accomplished. But there's a lot of things that aren't right yet. At the Monday night meeting of the Seventy after the September 13 Forum meeting, Clyde Bedell, Russell Bucklin, Dent Karle and Luther Evans went upstairs to see the Doctor to put in a plea for you (Harold). I don't know what was said but we could hear it going *hot and heavy* for half an hour. Do you mean to say," she added, "the Doctor hasn't been in touch with you yet?!"

When Harold said that the Doctor had not, but that he had written the Doctor and sent him a sworn statement that he had no commercial interest in the Urantia Book, Mrs. Steinbeck said, "That's fine! What you have done has got the whole Forum body wondering. When you got up and asked to speak and were turned down, the members who didn't know what it was all about immediately wanted to know. What explanation Doctor has given I don't know, but they've heard plenty from others.

"I really think it's too bad that he's not a spiritual person, and as president of the Seventy I can say that we're not learning to live Urantia. He's begun to order us around now and to give us things to do in the Seventy meetings which don't make sense to me, and which indicates that he's trying to keep us busy so we won't think so much about what's going on. Mrs. Bucklin broke down completely and Doctor advised her not to go to the Forum meetings for four or five weeks. She came over to my house and practically collapsed, and stayed with me from 4:30 until 8 p.m. shortly before she left town.

"I have never been definitely told not to see or talk with you people, but I *did* phone the Doctor the time you wanted to come over, to ask if I should see you, just to see what he would say. He did not tell me in so many words that I could not, but left me to infer that he would rather I wouldn't. We decided with things as they were for the time being to regard his inference. I know that he has told quite a few others that he would prefer they not see you and has led them to believe this is by divine decree. Of course we have our own judgment about that, but I'm going to keep my eyes and ears open and will report to you from time to time. In fact, I'll plan to see you and Mrs. Sherman soon. We know your interest to be the same as ours—you're dedicated to the right spiritual presentation of this book. It's unbelievable that the Doctor would treat you in this way."

Harold told her of our one meeting with the Doctor, the Thursday before the September 13 Forum session, in which he stated that he had been warned about Harold in a communication which he had never mentioned to anyone before, not even Christy. Mrs. Steinbeck said, "Why, he did too mention it! I told you about that after I had my little meeting with him and he told Miss Brown the same. That's just plain lying."

Harold said that he demanded the Doctor read this communication to the entire Forum body, but the Doctor said he would not.

Mrs. Steinbeck said, "I'm glad you people are continuing to come to the Forum meetings regardless. That shows you are not afraid of the Doctor for anything he may say, and is leading many members to feel that you are right and he is wrong." Mrs. Steinbeck went on to say that she had talked with Mrs. Githens, who said to her that she hoped Harold would not speak at the Wednesday night meeting since this did not represent the Forum and he couldn't reach the people he would want to reach. Mrs. Steinbeck said to Mrs. Githens that she did not think Harold would speak, as he would know this was the Doctor's attempt to avoid any real presentation of Harold's views to the Forum. Even so, Mrs. Steinbeck reported, there was an unusually big crowd at the Wednesday meeting that the members thought Harold was going to address.

5

The Open Discussion Meeting

DIARY *September 27, 1942*

FORUM—Paper 3: "THE ATTRIBUTES OF GOD"

Tom Woodrow [*Ed. note:* Wideroe] read instead of Bill this time. His voice, once accustomed to it, was pleasant; and because he stuck to the text and did not try to interpolate his own remarks, we found we could get more out of the chapter. Bill Jr. was not in evidence. We sat near Miss Brown, who told us she could not see us Monday night after all but hoped to see Harold if he came to New York.

At intermission Dent Karle came back and sat near Harold, and asked if he was coming to the next Wednesday night open discussion meeting. Dent said that he had been made chairman, and that the first things that they were going to discuss were the foundation and organization charters. At the close of the meeting, Harold asked Dent who was attending such sessions, and Dent said, "all the group of us who are interested in these developments." Harold said he had not decided whether he should attend or not as yet, since we had not yet had our talk with the Doctor. Harold explained that we were still technically on the banned list and he did not care to embarrass any of the other members by our attendance and participation in any further meetings until matters were clarified.

Dent said, "Well, use your own judgment, but I consider this project bigger than any personalities or individuals."

Harold said, "It undoubtedly is, and we have come here under the strange circumstances which exist in our case and conducted ourselves as decently as we know how, and yet we have not been treated the same as the rest of you. If you were in our place, I think you would feel differently, too. I certainly would, were conditions reversed and you and your wife were occupying the position *we* have been placed in."

Dent had no reply to this. He simply said, "Well, we're meeting on Wednesday night, and if you care to come we'll be glad to have you."

Dr. Sadler had written a schedule of meetings on the blackboard which Harold copied as follows:

No. 1—Forum, Sundays 3-5 p.m.
No. 2—Seventy, every other Monday night (class)
No. 3—Bill's class, every other Wednesday night (next meeting Oct. 7)
No. 4—Open discussion meeting, every other Wednesday night (next meeting Sept. 30)

This last listed meeting indicates that the petition has had this much effect at any rate, but whether open discussion really means *free* discussion in the last analysis, even with Dent Karle in the chair, is still to be determined. As we went out, the Evanses, Christy, Steinbecks, Rev. Rawson, Mrs. Rawson, Mr. Jones, Mrs. Hales and Mr. Kulieke Sr. spoke to us, the latter emphasizing he was *very* glad see us. Mrs. Evans said to Martha, "Bring Marcia over some time. I mean it."

HAROLD SHERMAN to HARRY LOOSE

Chicago, September 28, 1942

Dear Harry:

It was nice to get your always fine letter in the Monday mail.

We attended the Forum meeting as usual, Sunday, but most of the members give us a "wide berth." They are still observing the doctor's mandate not to contact or talk with us . . . in other words, we are still on the "banned list," and he has let them think this is a divine decree. They have been prohibited from telling me what he said about me to them, and while I have left the door open for him to "patch things up" in my last letter to him (I sent you this letter with affidavit) without compromising my own position or kowtowing to him, he still evidently does not want to face me. He takes care not to be near the door when we come in or when we go out . . . and Bill was not there yesterday. Tom Wideroe read in his place. It was pleasant to be able to listen to someone who did not try to interpolate his own "wise comments" or "facetious remarks" to the sublime material being read. It was the third chapter, on "God the Universal Father, His Attributes," etc.

Mrs. Steinbeck phoned several days ago, in a surprise call. She is now president of the Seventy group which meets every other Monday night. She said, "Mr. Sherman, I want you to know that most of the Forum members are *for* you, but we can't do much about it right now. However, lots of us are doing some real thinking . . . and your stand against the doctor September 13th, and his saying we were only *guests* in his home, was an "eye-opener" to us. Do you mean to say the doctor hasn't gotten in touch with you yet?"

When I told her that he had not, and that when he *had* called us over it had only been to tell us he had nothing to say, etc. . . . but that he had been warned against us in a communication received before we arrived, *which he had not mentioned to a soul, not even Christy,* etc., Mrs. Steinbeck said, "WHY, MR. SHERMAN, THAT'S A LIE . . . THE DOCTOR TOLD US ALL HE HAD BEEN WARNED AGAINST YOU!" She had given me this information before . . . being one of the few who would tell us anything of what had transpired. I told her that I had demanded of the doctor that he read this communication to the entire Forum body, but he had refused. She said, "I think he should, in fairness to you, but I'll bet he never does it." Then she added, "Mr. Sherman, I regret to have to say this, but Dr. Sadler is NOT a spiritual person."

We have observed many things, Harry, and we remark again at your wisdom in letting us find these things out for ourselves before you made comment. What a PICTURE you have had of what is going on here and how BLIND, emotionally and intellectually, the OTHER Forum members are! How little real GUTS and REASONING powers they are now exhibiting. We had been told by many members, weeks ago, that things were so different since Dr. Lena had died! They trace the entire change of Doctor and Bill from that time!

Mrs. Steinbeck went on to say that the doctor takes CARE not to let us know where *divine* instruction leaves off and his *human* instruction begins. He wants to let us believe that most of what he does is by "divine guidance." But it is Mrs. Steinbeck's belief that the doctor got some word from higher authorities which he is embarrassed at giving out to the Forum, censuring him, and acting upon some of the points raised in the petition.

At any rate, every other Wednesday night has now been set aside as Open Discussion night, and Dent Karle has been appointed chairman, as was requested in the petition, and I was approached by Karle who asked if I would come this coming Wednesday. I said I would have to think it over as I was still on the "banned list, with Martha" as the doctor had not talked to us yet and read us the communications he said he had received. Karle said, "Well, use your own judgment—personally, I think this development is much bigger than any personalities or individuals."

The indifference to the position Martha and I have been placed in was amazing to me. I said: "That is TRUE, Dent . . . but the doctor is the one who has been getting personal in this entire matter by setting Martha and me aside and trying to punish us in the eyes of the Forum. If YOU and YOUR WIFE had been placed in the position Martha and I now find ourselves in, do you think I would have been sitting on the sidelines, letting you remain in this position?" Dent made no reply to this, simply saying, "Well, if you'd care to be there Wednesday night, we're going to start by reading the charters of the Foundation and organization . . . and discussing them."

How much really FREE discussion is actually going to be permitted, remains to be seen. But this is a roundabout concession to the petition by the doctor, who has let the Forum members infer, by his interpretation of past communications, that an ORGANIZATION is NECESSARY . . . so, they are kept from discussing the merits or demerits of the existence of an organization . . . and are confined to trying to improve the present charter, if they can.

I told Dent I did not care to "embarrass" the other members by my presence if I had not been actually taken back into the "fold" by the doctor, since he had accused me of being a "promoter." (Incidentally, Harry, I came across a magazine article in the October *Your Life*, which has to do with "You Can Be Sued for Gossip." It states in one paragraph: "For example, to call a man an 'accelerator' or a 'promoter' has been held by the courts to be slander . . . ," so your statement that he had left himself open to a suit on several counts is certainly valid!)

I am wondering whether I *should* attend these meetings or let the others wrestle with these problems for a while, since I have stated unequivocally to many that I consider the present charters commercially and fanatically inclined. I'm not trying to back down, but I don't want the Forum members to get the impression I am a constant "dissenter" . . . and they might, since they do not clearly see the evils, as yet, as I see them . . . and I would have to go on record against them if I were present.

Maybe the actions of the Sadlers and Haleses will speak louder than words a little later, and the members will then recall my warnings, without my having to take part in discussions at present. I have not yet made up my mind on these points.

God knows—what plans are made are of vital importance . . . but it's still quite a little time before the book itself is to come out. However, they could set up the Foundation or organization incorporation any time. I'm inclined to believe they've been slowed up considerably by what has happened, however . . . BECAUSE Miss Caroline Brown, sister of Mrs. Steinbeck's, asked Mr. Kellogg the other day whether he would take a donation from her toward the book publication cost, and he said, "No, we can't do that now . . . but if you'd like to subscribe to some copies of the book, you can." Heretofore they have taken money. Doesn't it look like they're a bit worried on this score?

I hope I receive more direct light on what action to take in the future. I also hope I do not have to go to New York but am afraid this may be necessary as I got a long-distance call last night, while I was not at home, from Mr. Lark—perhaps with respect to the time of the hearing, when Clara will have to be faced. I hope and pray that I will not have to suffer loss because of such proceeding. . . .

Glad Ma liked her birthday present and that you could enjoy it too. . . . Just now the doctor will consider no other proposals of mine . . . the Matterns made a bad impression, supporting me, after they were well received by the doctor and Bill. They haven't gone since . . . but they'll do a different kind of job later for the book, I am sure. I know they'd appreciate word from you. . . . Sorry about the death of your friend in the previous letter. Time catches up with us all in this life, sooner or later.

I am eager to get back on the radio in my own philosophic program . . . also back into the writing swing, after this battle here . . . I want to keep contact here but am wondering if, with exception of attending Sunday meetings, I shouldn't remain quiet for a while. Our love—

SIR HUBERT WILKINS to HAROLD SHERMAN

Washington, D.C., September 29, 1942

Dear Harold:

Your batch of letters outlining recent events was received today upon my return from Dayton, Ohio.

I felt conscious on the 13th of some disturbance but of course could not "see" the details clearly. Thank you for keeping me posted. I have received no communication from Dr. Sadler since I was last in Chicago. Not knowing if, or when, the petition had been presented, I could not send the Doctor the letter I intended to send immediately after the petition had reached his hands. Now, although I have no typewriter here, I think that a copy of this letter, sent to the Doctor, will let him know my attitude.

The refusal to let you speak bears out in a measure what was intimated by those present when the petition was being prepared. That was—"they" could not expect to individually get a hearing and if they did, no result satisfactory to them would be obtained.

However, as I said at the meeting, my personal approach in the matter would have been a simple request to have an opportunity to leisurely study the proposed Charter. Then, after careful examination, to comment specifically upon any article which in my opinion was likely to lead to trouble.

It was because it was the opinion of those present that such a simple request would take time and lead to an unsatisfactory result, and because it was believed that the Charter might be immediately and irrevocably registered, that I signed.

It was quite apparent that such a petition would be looked upon by the Doctor as a vote of "no confidence" to some extent, and perhaps exhibit the reverse of what perhaps he had believed to be the condition.

It is impossible for me yet to know—and, probably you do not know—how far the Doctor has responded to the tenor of the petition. But it seems to me that if the Forum members are to be for all time associated with the whole plan, they *should* be given the privilege of knowing the whole procedure—at least the right to peruse and comment on the human activities as they have had selectively the privilege of commenting on the revelations.

I feel certain that neither you nor the others at the meeting I attended acted in bad faith—all were entirely without base ulterior motives.

I have always been reluctant to take action on the say-so of others and wonder how far others you have contacted have said to you what they would *like to do* and what they would like to have done, rather than what they would willingly do individually. Of this you must judge.

From my personal observations, I do not believe that Dr. Sadler, Bill, Mr. Kellogg, or any others I have contacted in the group have desires to reap worldly profit—monetary or otherwise—from association with the material as is, or published. Their years of patient, loyal work is sufficient proof of that.

I think you have shown laudable qualities in standing forthright and openly upon your convictions. Few modern humans do so. I query only the advisability of forming an opinion and taking such a positive action after a comparatively short association with and a short-term knowledge of the material.

I am inclined to think that your affidavit is, in a measure, like the "petition," a "denial of the non-existent," so to speak. Time will prove, and would have proved in any case, that points regarding your desire for identification, for glorification, and mercenary gain will not arise in you.

Those of us who sense the "divinity" of the revelations must have conceived a trust in them that we may not be willing to express in regard to our human associates, and while association with contemporary world affairs induces a reluctance to refrain now and in the future from preventive action, I think, in *spiritual affairs* where time is so relative, cure is probably more in keeping than prevention—witness the presentation of the Revelators at this late hour.

We have already experienced a privilege of tremendous proportions. I hope that we all can carry on in friendly relationship with the Doctor and all associated with him, *and at the same time* feel free to exhibit and exercise the right of personal appraisal.

I feel sure that the disturbance has brought to light an attitude never before so openly expressed in the presence of the Doctor, and I hope that the eruption will be cured by full and free cooperation.

With best regards,

Hubert

P.S. Am sending your letters etc. back under separate cover. Hope you have good luck in New York. I may be up there for the weekend but doubt it, am terrifically busy here and might have to start off anywhere at a moment's notice.

Oh. Forget what you call my share of *Coronet*. It is all yours. You did the work.

DIARY *September 30, 1942*

Open discussion meeting 9/30/42. We were undecided until the last minute about attendance at this meeting, and Harold observed that few people were going in at the Sadlers'. He phoned Mrs. Steinbeck to ask about the meeting and she said it had been the second one that was held—the first one with Dent Karle having an attendance of 28 people, including Mr. Hales. This was the meeting (we figured back) which Harold had been "given permission" to speak at, which probably accounted for the big turnout. Mrs. Steinbeck said she was not going tonight and knew nothing about the meeting, which had not been widely heralded, but she was sure Dent Karle and a few of the members at least must be there. She said she would gladly tell Harold more if she knew anything. It was then about 8:15 p.m. and we determined to go out and see if we could observe any particular activity across the street.

As we were walking along the side of the Sadler building, we were hailed from the second-floor-rear darkened windows by Billy and Patsy,[1] who had apparently gone to bed but were keeping alert watch in order to have seen us.

"Hello, Martha Sherman," called Patsy, followed by a similar greeting from Billy. As we answered and continued walking toward Diversey, the children crossed the room and looked out the front (north) windows, calling out after us. We decided under such circumstances that we *would* go in. It was around 8:30 by this time.

When we were admitted after pressing the bell, Mr. Kellogg, who had let us in, acted actually startled. He nodded at us and disappeared in haste down the hall. (*I love you!*) We stood in the entry way and saw Miss Vincent in the waiting room doing some reading. We asked if there was a meeting, and she said, "Yes, upstairs."

We went up to the second floor and found thirteen members present, including Dent Karle, chairman, the majority being women. A partial list is as follows: Dent Karle, Mr. [Ernest] Pritchard, Mr. Steinbeck, Clyde Bedell and Ark Pettie. The women were Miss[es]

[1] Two of the three children of Bill and Leone Sadler. The third was Charlie.

Baumgartner, Cook, Rowley, Thuerck [?][*Ed. note:* Florence or her sister Clara Thuerk], and four others unknown to us. They were in the process of reading the charter. As we sat next to Mr. Steinbeck, whose presence at this meeting Mrs. Steinbeck had not intimated in Harold's earlier phone conversation, we were amused at this. Written on the blackboard was the following:

Order of General Business
1—Discussion of organization plans
2—Defraying maintenance expense of Forum room

(This last order of business struck us as incongruous since the Doctor had emphasized at the first reconvened meeting that we were "guests in his home." Now we are apparently expected soon to pay for this privilege.)

Clyde Bedell had a front seat and was seemingly trying to steer the discussion with sugar-coated comments on almost every clause that Dent Karle read in answer to questions or objections raised. Miss Baumgartner queried a clause referring to one of the purposes of the foundation, "to disseminate the teachings and doctrines" etc., and said, did it mean that someone was going to formulate doctrines from the Book of Urantia? Clyde Bedell spoke up and said the best way to tell was to look the word "doctrine" up in the dictionary; that he was sure it only pertained to the doctrines in the book itself. By consensus of opinion, however, a question mark was placed after this clause.

Karle continued reading and covered clauses referring to the exclusive power of the trustees to handle all monies and make all manner of investments at the risk of the Foundation but at no risk to themselves. Harold asked if he was right in interpreting that bad investment judgment on the part of the trustees could jeopardize all holdings of the foundation. Dent Karle as chairman agreed that this was so. It then was brought out that *one* trustee holding a majority of proxies from the other four could vote to make any investment or business transaction he desired, and furthermore that no trustees of this foundation were to be limited or governed by the statutes of any state or states, and that they had the right to act on behalf of any interest in the Book of Urantia "as if they owned it."

Harold asked if those present felt it was wise for the book to be jeopardized by the possible bad judgment of trustees given such power when they were self-appointed and could elect their successors to office.

These clauses were question-marked for further discussion. It had been Clyde Bedell's expressed desire that the charter be read through without comment and any clauses discussed at a later time, but he himself found there were certain things he wished to question as the meeting proceeded.

When the meeting was called at 9:30, which apparently is the designated closing time, Karle was only halfway through. The next meeting is two weeks hence.

At the conclusion, we greeted Mr. Steinbeck and Miss Baumgartner, the latter saying she had intended to phone us. Clyde Bedell slipped out without speaking to us, though he had nodded to Harold on our arrival, but we did not hasten away and he could have shown us the courtesy of a personal greeting had he so wished. We spoke to Dent Karle momentarily as we went down the stairs, and Harold said he was glad to see they were giving such close attention to the charter clauses; that it was his opinion that a spiritual project such as this was should see to it that its financial handling was made more specific as to the nature of investments, management and control. Dent said, "I'm inclined to agree with you."

As we reached the first-floor landing, Mr. Kellogg was at the reception desk and nodded to us with an obviously worried expression. Neither Bill Jr. nor Dr. Sadler had been in evidence. We left with the impression of an emotionally upset household, it being increasingly evident to us that Dr. Sadler not only is afraid to face us with the presentation he gave the others, but that he doesn't know what to do about us. We meanwhile are actually not fundamentally disturbed or nervously on edge, and are even able to see occasional humor in the embarrassment of others when in their proximity.

Clyde Bedell's prize remark of this evening was his assertion that he had often thought it would be better for the Book of Urantia if none of those originally associated with it prior to its publication were alive when it came out. He inferred, however, that other humans, who lacked the background appreciation of the book, would no doubt identify themselves with it on publication and that we probably, under such circumstances, would be better fitted to protect the truth of this Urantia revelation than these new enthusiasts who were basically strangers to it. We recognized one of Dr. Sadler's pet arguments in these comments of Bedell.

HARRY LOOSE to HAROLD SHERMAN

Monterey Park, October 1, 1942

Dear Harold:-

I am answering your very illuminative letter of September 28th.

Sadler and Hales expect you to attend the Open Discussion nights. For that very reason, my personal reaction would be not to attend. In addition, no benefit could accrue by placing yourself, and small Martha, in a position which would leave either or both of you open to mental examination by the unfriendly. It would cheapen you both. No more could be added to what you have already delivered. Personally, I would refrain, for some time at least, from placing myself where I could be injured. I would not walk into any trap with eyes wide open. I would, however, continue to be very regular in attendance at the regular Forum meetings on Sunday. As an observer, watchfully waiting, with all good at heart and in mind for the Book. And for this also, that your courage and belief in the right of your stand be evident to other Forumites. That neither the Sadlers nor the Haleses can point their finger and smirk—and boast that you had been "run out" by Divine intervention. Evidencing your continued belief in the rightness of your beliefs by this continuing attendance at the Sunday Forum would bring only respect from friendly, or doubting, Forumites. I hope that what I am trying to explain is clear to you.

I would not remain in Chicago solely for the purpose of attending the Sunday Forum meetings if you could be employed profitably, and to your best financial interests, elsewhere. I hope that this is understandable to you. Meaning that if there are other and further activities in addition to what you have already accomplished regarding the Book and the Forum, circumstances will so evolve themselves without any effort or knowing intention on your part that will bring you back to Chicago again—should you go away.

Attention please. In addition to the foregoing paragraph, do not take this as a recommendation, or suggestion, from me to make a change of residence. I personally believe that there are plenty of opportunities for radio work, or other activities, in addition to writing, in which your letter suggests you might want to become active—right in CHICAGO. Surely, you could not live anywhere else any more comfortably or any more reasonably in expense.

I am enclosing a clip from last Sunday's paper regarding Wilkins.[2] In his present position, would it not be possible for him to arrange some advantageous activity for you in connection with war work. Something that would give a salary and that would allow you to continue to live in Chicago—give you time to do some writing—and attend the Forum also. The government wants people in war activity like yourself—people who can do publicity work—who can write—who can talk from the platform—who can talk on the radio. Turn this over in your mind.

Yes, there is much that you have seen and also much that you have "become aware of." (There is much for you to do in Chicago.) But there is a great deal more that you are not yet aware of. You may rest assured, however, that the Sadlers and the Haleses, and several "Charlie McCarthys," have had a terrific shock and that things will never be the same with the Forum again. You, and small Martha, have done a very satisfactory job so far—and I know present results are highly satisfactory—but the end is not yet.

"Obtaining Money By Means of a Confidence Game," the same by "False Pretenses," the same by "Conspiracy," the same by "Fraud and Deceit." Somebody has talked to someone who knows, and no more cash contributions are solicited or accepted if offered. Yes, indeed, you can surely be sued for "Gossip."

Harold, I would give much to be able to give you the background of this whole activity. Its intent, its ramifications, its connections, its abuse, its betrayal. It is all so very wonderful and so humanly unbelievable—and yet so very true. Commercialism, Egotism—the greed for earthly values—the earthly things that enter in—lust—lies—liars—twisters and obfuscators of the truth—the whole gamut—what a story—what a story.

I hope that you do not have to go to New York on that matter—but, if you do have to go, be of good heart—and, while there, accomplish as much as possible—Wanderman—Ronayne, etc. . . .

I have other avenues of information and I do not like to impose and so did not conclude my remarks regarding the matter I remarked my interest in in my last letter [*Ed. note:* the Alexian Brothers Hospital]—thinking that you might make a call regarding another matter and another location. A word picture that I would like for my own

[2] This clipping has not been found.

observation. I may include such request in my next letter or the one after that.

I am mailing a letter to "H.C." by regular mail at the same time that this one goes to you.

No word from Elsie Baumgartner as yet. And I really do not think that I will ever hear from her.

Love to you both as always,

6

An Amazingly Revealing Interview

FORUM CALENDAR *October 1, 1942*

Dr. Sadler reads paper purporting to be communication regarding Harold and Martha received before we entered Forum membership. Christy witness.

DIARY *October 1, 1942*

Last night after retiring Harold did not go to sleep immediately as usual, and when Martha asked him if anything was disturbing him, he said, "No, but I feel that new things are getting ready to happen." Martha asked him, "Good or bad?" He said, "I can't tell *what* they are, but I feel they are good."

In the morning at eight Christy phoned to ask Harold if we could see the Doctor at 4 p.m. today, which we agreed to do. Christy's voice seemed strained. We are wondering if our presence at the open discussion meeting last night has placed the Doctor under further pressure and caused him to feel he must either make peace with us or try to stop us. At any rate, we are going over to see him in a friendly spirit.

We devoted the entire a.m., Harold having developed an idea for a new book under the title "The Great Adventure of Your Soul," to rereading the messages received from Ara while in California.[1] As Harold started reading them, an inner voice directed, "Read as of *now*." We did so and were greatly moved and held spellbound by the predictions contained and the application of contents to our present situation. The messages seemed to substantiate the impression Harold had last night with respect to new developments in the offing. (During his reading of the Ara messages, a title for another book came to Harold's mind, "Little Talks with Your Soul." Harold felt that this could be inspirational in nature and partake of some of these rewritten messages.)

Today we received a fine letter from Sir Hubert giving support to Harold's stand and also a cordial note from Jo Davis expressing appreciation of Dr. Wanderman and asking us what we now thought of the papers across the street. Evidently by the tenor of her letter she knows nothing of what has transpired.[2]

Fresh from what proved to have been an amazingly revealing interview with the Doctor, we herewith set down the facts. We were sent up to the third floor as usual and were met at the door cordially enough by Christy who refused to shake hands because she had a heavy cold (probably why her voice had sounded strange over the phone).

We were ushered into the living room and Christy brought in the Doctor, who shook hands with us. He was carrying some yellow note paper, and after an exchange of meaningless pleasantries declared that he could only go so far today; there was something he wanted to get out of his system. He said he had been in a turmoil for two weeks not knowing whether to present this to us or not, but had finally reached a decision last night.

He said, "I'm referring to the communication I received which I feel pertains to you people. Since this message came through during one of my personal talks with a midwayer when no one else was present, which is the only way they would carry on personal conversation with us, it represents the notes I made that night and wrote out in full the next morning. As nearly as I can figure the time, this came through about a week or two before Jo Davis phoned me and introduced you to me from Marion, Indiana. This is undated as we were

[1] Vol. 1 includes several of these messages. The book, *The Ara Messages* (Square Circles Publishing, 2016) contains them all.
[2] Jo Davis's letter has not been found.

not permitted to date such messages or to identify from whom they came. I have now determined to read this communication to you on one condition, that you permit Christy to hear what is said here and that you say nothing to anyone about this message."

Harold said, "Just a minute, Doctor. We have heard from a number of sources that you told Forum members you had been warned against us by a communication before we came here. If you have, this has naturally prejudiced people against us and that's why, when you told us about this message at our previous meeting, we said we felt in fairness to us it should be read to the entire Forum."

The Doctor seemed disturbed at this and said, "Well, I don't think I mentioned it, but tempers were running pretty high and several people were pretty outspoken. Several members wanted to talk to me personally about you but I refused to do this. I always had one of my associates present. One man in particular phoned and insisted on talking to me about the Shermans. I told him I would see him if he brought another member and allowed me to have someone in attendance. Then I prepared a statement concerning you people which I read to him and I refused to say any more. I'll read this same statement to you later."

The Doctor then got down to a reading of the message he said he had received, giving not a warning, as he put it, in attempted denial of his statements as reported to us, but a "pre-enlightenment." There then followed the most obviously contrived and fictionized psychoanalytical report on us, based on certain fragmentary knowledge that the Doctor and Bill and the Kelloggs and Christy might have put together out of conversations with us—said report attempting to answer and refute certain attitudes we were known to have with respect to the field of psychic phenomena which were foreign to the Doctor, and other stands we had taken with respect to book and organization.

While our names were not specifically mentioned, the message purported to refer to a couple who would soon seek membership in the Forum by telephone. Upon this flimsily conceived cue, the Doctor saw fit to interpret that the couple described was *ourselves*. He claimed that he had not thought of this communication at the time we came in and it had not re-occurred to him until August of this year when Forum members were developing split opinions on Forum matters. (This is entirely inconsistent since, first, if such a message had been received, our phoning a week or so after would have caused him to recall such a message and cause him to wonder about us. He would have not forgotten, *could* not have forgotten or disregarded so recent a communication. Then, too, we were received so cordially and it was announced by the Doctor that we had been "circumstanced." Bill told us that we could not have come with better credentials, and he thought we might even be members of the Reserve Corps of Destiny.)

The message went on to say that the man of this couple was of a highly nervous type with an unstable nervous system, but highly energetic and alert; that he was unusually versatile by nature and did not stick to anything for long, and that he mistook his versatility for knowledge and ability when they were merely cleverness. This man really had an ordinary mind, but an engaging personality and a cleverness which accounted for such success as he had attained. Among other things he was an egotist and an idealist with certain practical slants, but his temperament was that of one who liked to try to dominate any individuals or groups with which he associated. He was interested in psychic matters and also in dreams, and thought he had some evidential experiences, which he had not. At least three times during the past decade he had been on the verge of losing his mental balance through delving too deeply into elemental conditions, but had always just managed to save himself by cutting it off short. (This was a garbled attempt at covering a story we had told to Bill about our experience with automatic writing when we had decided suddenly to abandon it twenty years ago![3])

This man [the message continued], because of his nervous tendency, could not stay at any one job long and the best thing he could possibly do would be to find a home for himself and family and settle down for the next five years. Both this man and his wife were sincere but misguided. The wife, being solicitous of her husband's ill-health and suffering from a cleverness inferiority, was greatly impressed by her husband's versatility and gave him credit for being much more accomplished than he was. If this couple could read and accept the Book of Urantia it would no doubt stabilize their lives, but they might be concerned over lack of mention of the psychic matters they thought they had experienced. Actually the Book of Urantia was for the world, and not to answer the specific questions of a couple like this who had

[3] Harold told of his and Martha's experiences with automatic writing in Vol. 1, pp. 30-34.

become involved in such phenomena. It would be up to the Doctor if they applied for membership to assume the responsibility of accepting or rejecting them. This man had a certain dramatic ability but was impatient to get things done and liked to promote things, as he was the promoter type. However, if the Doctor chose to take in this couple, the supposed midwayer would go along with him on the decision.

When the reading was finished, Harold looked at Martha and said, "Do you wish this read again?"

Martha said, "No!" and then, addressing the Doctor, said, "This can't apply to us in any way. It is inaccurate and untrue. Any intelligence that was behind this couldn't have been referring to us."

Harold substantiated Martha's statement and said, "If a midwayer sent you that message, and since midwayers are only a step beyond the human, he must have been a prankster or prevaricator as we are told some of them are."

The Doctor sought to deny this, but Christy reminded him that Harold was probably referring to many of the midwayers who had "fallen."

Harold went on to say, "Doctor, I'm astonished that you would interpret such communication to refer to us; and if you mentioned, even by inference, this communication to any of the Forum members, you've done us great and unwarranted damage. Have you ever been warned against any other Forum members in this manner?"

The Doctor would not say that he had.

Harold then said, "It's highly dangerous to attach the names of *any* Forum members to such a communication and brand them because of it. This does not represent us at all, and if you have felt that it does, you had best disabuse your mind of it right now."

The Doctor said, "Well, I have been disturbed by it, and you can see how I might, with things developing like they have." Harold said he could see how the Doctor's interpretation would have prejudiced him unwarrantedly against us, but it was hard to understand why the Doctor would have made such an interpretation. Harold indicated that the purported message covered several subjects that we had discussed with the Doctor and Bill pertaining to psychic matters, but he did not charge the Doctor openly with fictionizing the whole message, which it is our definite conviction he did so.

The Doctor, obviously anxious to avoid further questions which Harold was in the process of asking him, said he had gone as far as he could today except for reading us the written statement he had made concerning us which he had read to certain Forum members. This statement was an apparent attempt of the Doctor's to avoid possible legal entanglements and to soften certain verbal statements he had previously made against us which had aroused the resentment of a few members. When pressed to prefer charges against us, he had resorted to this carefully prepared written statement, which said in effect, "I have nothing personal against the Shermans. I'm only interested in clearing up the misrepresentations and misstatements that have been made concerning myself to the Forum members."

When Harold asked him point blank if he was referring to misstatements that *we* had made or [that] other Forum members [had made], the Doctor said, "Well—both."

Harold then said that he would own up to any statements he had made about the Doctor if they were repeated to him and he found they were directly quoted.

The Doctor said, "I don't intend to discuss that at this time—those things will have wait till later, but I'm off the side track onto the main track now since I've gotten this message off my chest. I've had specific instructions as to what to do in your case but have been held up because of my uncertainty as to whether to read you this message I interpreted as being about you. In about ten days to two weeks I'll see you again."

Harold then asked his most pointed question: "Doctor, was it by divine decree that we have been segregated from our fellows?"

The Doctor's answer was, "I can't say as to that now," but he refused to deny that such had been the case either through his own human action or a purported message from on high. He said he had known all along what was taking place from higher sources, and that the day before the petition was presented he received instructions as to what to do and started acting upon them immediately after the presentation.

The Doctor said he had more trouble with those whose names were not on the petition, many of whom felt we should be removed from the Forum. Harold said that it was unfortunate this development had been reduced to personalities and that we, personally, had the same human feeling of affection for all concerned that we had had before. The Doctor had nothing to say to this but shook hands as we left, and Christy put her arm around Martha, saying to us at the door, "I love you both."

(One of the last questions Harold asked the Doctor, now just recalled, was: "Doctor, in the light of our statements in respect to the communication you have just read us that it in no way applies to us, are you ready to withdraw your interpretation of its application and relieve your own mind on it?" The Doctor said, "No, not yet. You'll have to wait until our next meeting. Meanwhile, you think over what was said here today.")

HAROLD SHERMAN to SIR HUBERT WILKINS

Chicago, October 1, 1942

Dear Hubert:

Thanks for your well-considered letter concerning the goings on across the street. There is much I could say to you personally and will say when we meet . . . which could be around the middle of this month, for I may have to come to New York at this time . . . and hope you can join me there.

What has been uncovered is amazing beyond belief—nothing at all to discredit the wonderful revelation . . . but much to throw light upon the Doctor and how he has "cracked up" mentally the past few years since the death of his wife, Dr. Lena.

The lengths to which he has gone to try to forestall a free discussion of questions and to discredit Martha and myself would seem unbelievable if we did not have the evidence. It is not the doings of a normally balanced individual, however pleasant he has seemed "when he has not been crossed." He is Dr. Jekyll and Mr. Hyde when aroused, and will stop at no subterfuge to score his points against those who oppose him.

While on the surface your evaluation was right—that we might have taken a longer time to take part in precipitate action since we were new here . . . and had only had an opportunity for reading the papers through once . . . ACTUALLY, we had a greater knowledge of what was going on and the whole setup (BECAUSE we had been taken in so hospitably by the Sadlers and all), eclipsing that of almost any other Forum member regardless of their length of service.

We needed no longer period of time to see where things were heading . . . and when many other Forum members expressed the same concern and were even more outspoken against the doctor and certain personal plannings, we felt that this action should be taken NOW. We were not alone in this, remember . . . nor did we canvass one single member . . . the canvassing was done by the old members . . . we simply took part in the discussions and stated our opinions frankly. I had already gone directly on record with the doctor as to how I felt, in the letters you saw, so I said nothing to his back I had not already said to his face.

Hubert, I and other members had had opportunity to read the charter; many had not asked to read it, but we knew enough about it to know it should be severely overhauled. And when you read it, I am sure you will agree. Nothing constructive could have been accomplished by the procedure you suggested . . . any criticisms would have been politely pigeonholed . . . as previous suggestions all *have*. Even now—with the deliberate lies the doctor has told and with a deliberately FICTIONED psychoanalytical message PURPORTING TO HAVE BEEN RECEIVED BY THE DOCTOR BEFORE WE WERE SPONSORED BY JOSEPHINE DAVIS, HIS COUSIN, IN MARION . . . *WARNING* AGAINST US . . . which have prejudiced many members temporarily against us . . . it is doubtful what can be accomplished at the moment!

We were called over this afternoon and this amazing "document" was read to us. Our names are not mentioned, but the doctor has seen fit to interpret that it means us, in the light of developments. I KNOW he wrote this himself and represents it as having come from a Midwayer, in "personal conversation with him." He took the talk down in notes and wrote it out in full the next morning, so he says. It is a complete attempted "defense against the points we have raised" . . . and is actually libelous in its delineation of qualities it is inferred we possess, etc.

We said it "could not have referred to us because it was untrue and inaccurate throughout" but did not openly accuse the doctor of forging it . . . since we are trying in every way to be tolerant and to "go along," having FAITH that Higher Intelligences will protect the TRUTH and take care of the doctor for his deviation from fair dealing, in due course of time.

We are still "on probation" but have continued to attend Sunday Forum meetings, without invitation. He has not dared tell us we could not come. An "Open Discussion" night, every other Wednesday (last night Sept. 30th), has been set up . . . and a small handful are reading the charter and commenting on it. But they are under the doctor's dominating influence again and are "pulling their punches" . . . so this won't mean much. We dropped in on this meeting last night, and Dent Karle, greatly subdued, is acting as chairman . . . but the FORUM, as a body, is not in on this discussion . . . and it does not represent the vital action and consideration so badly needed.

The Haleses are the sinister influence behind the doctor. Of this I am sure . . . they clinched this evidence in their treatment of me on the floor Sept. 13th . . . and their interest is decidedly commercial . . .

Hubert—your query as to whether the other members have said to me "what they would like to do and what they would like to have done—rather than what they would willingly do individually" is well put.

NONE OF THEM HAD THE GUTS TO STAND BEHIND US . . . we were left standing ALONE when the doctor threatened to take their "religion away from them" . . . and insinuated that they were parties to an "attempted Lucifer rebellion." Can't you see how dangerous such interpretations will be in a PUBLIC ORGANIZATION, the minute someone raises an honest question . . . and how fiendish will be the persecution . . . if this is a little private sample?

Eventually we may have to take a protective stand. Now Martha and I feel we have done as much as we can . . . and while we will not permit ourselves to be compromised, we will not challenge the doctor on many inconsistent and untrue points which we could. It was not easy for us to stand as we have in the face of such feeling as has been expressed . . . and such prejudicing of the minds as has been deliberately accomplished against us . . . but I am sure the RIGHT will win out in the end . . . and this was NECESSARY to begin to clear the atmosphere over there. I have great respect for you and your judgment . . . we need to keep friendly contact with *this*—for the future good we can do.

My best always—

HAROLD SHERMAN to HARRY LOOSE

Chicago, October 2, 1942

Dear Harry:

Last Wednesday night we went to the "Open Discussion" meeting of the Forum, where a corporal's guard of members were gathered, with Dent Karle as chairman, to listen to a reading of the charters of the Foundation and organization. Most of the members are even afraid to attend such a "permitted meeting," as they think the doctor may feel they lack confidence in him if they question anything! Clyde Bedell, who drew up the petition (he's advertising mgr. of the Fair Store), has gone over to Sadler's side, and sits there volunteering an explanation of every clause in the charters which is questioned, even faintly. [*Marginal note:* Also there was "Ark" Pettie who suddenly put in an appearance after being away for a long time—a former beau of Christy's!] Most of the members don't dare to speak to us as yet since our "indictment" has not been lifted . . . but we attend the Sunday meetings just the same . . . and the fact that we even showed up at the Open Discussion meeting finally brought initial action from the doctor . . . because yesterday Christy phoned and dated us to see him at four o'clock.

Harry, the lengths to which the doctor has gone to defend his position are pitiful and shocking. He has deliberately FAKED a message, purporting to have been received from a Midwayer, BEFORE we were proposed by Jo Davis of Marion, in which we are CASTIGATED. He told us, before he read it, that we would have to keep it secret, as he was ONLY READING IT TO US, even CHRISTY hadn't heard it before . . . that it came to him during a PERSONAL VISIT with the Midwayer, when everyone else had to leave the room, as was sometimes done, and he had taken notes himself and written them out the next morning!

I stopped him and said, "Doctor—we have heard from many Forum members that you have told them you had a message warning against us before we came here." He acted startled at this and said he didn't know how this could be . . . but he wasn't going to read the message to us *unless we promised not to discuss it with anyone!*

Then he read us this amazing FICTIONIZED DOCUMENT in which we are discredited, and about every question we raised is answered *against* us—so that, IF HE READ THIS COMMUNICATION to FORUM MEMBERS and represented it as having come from Higher Sources, it must have sounded MOST AUTHORITATIVE and simply bowled them over. They look ASKANCE at us now, and with a sickening "tolerant sympathy" as though we are well-meaning but "touched in the head," emotionally unstable, etc. It is all "hush-hush" about what was told them as far as we are concerned because they wouldn't "think" of embarrassing us further . . . any more than they would think of telling a neurotic that he or she was a paranoiac or dementia praecox case. We enter the Forum room as "outsiders" or "untouchables," and most give us a wide berth as though afraid they may become contaminated. Of course they have been ordered not to talk to us about what he said to them—or even get in touch with us!!

The highlights of the so-called communication are to the effect that the doctor would soon be *phoned* by a couple who would seek entrance to the Forum. (He explained that this communication was not dated as no personal conversations with a Midwayer were permitted to be dated . . . but, as nearly as he could remember, it was a week or so BEFORE JO DAVIS PHONED FROM MARION AND INTRODUCED ME OVER THE PHONE.) He claims he never thought of this communication again UNTIL *this* August when things began to happen among Forum members, resulting in the petition . . . and then he got it out and INTERPRETED IT as referring to us. (Our names were not mentioned.)

The message goes on to give what is called "pre-enlightenment" on this couple . . . and states that the man is a highly nervous personality, engaging in manner, with a "certain cleverness" and very *versatile* . . . but he MISTAKES HIS VERSATILITY FOR KNOWLEDGE . . . he actually doesn't begin to know what he thinks he knows . . . He is sincere but emotionally unstable, and has dabbled in psychic phenomena; he has had dreams, too . . . but none of these experiences have been genuine. On THREE DIFFERENT OCCASIONS in the past DECADE, he almost lost his balance completely, delving into psychic matters and JUST CUT THESE SHORT IN TIME. His wife is a charming person but, being solicitous over her husband's health which is not of the best, and suffering from a "cleverness inferiority," she is dazzled by her husband's versatility and rates him much higher than he is for he really has an ORDINARY MIND. This couple have never had a real home as the husband has never stuck to any one thing very long . . . and, if they should join the Forum and BELIEVE in the BOOK OF URANTIA, the Doctor, being a psychologist, might help this man recover his balance . . . and the BEST THING for this couple to do would be to settle down and make a home for their children somewhere for about FIVE YEARS. The man is an EGOTIST and an IDEALIST, with a more or less practical turn . . . but he likes to DOMINATE and he will not work well in any group as he is a *promoter* and will try to put over his own ideas.

When Doctor had finished reading this obviously *phony* message, Martha and I looked at one another, then she exploded: "Doctor, there is not a word of truth in this . . . it definitely does not apply to us and I do not see how you could possibly interpret it as applying to us." I added my denial, refusing to ever answer any of the points raised as being too ridiculous. I did not charge the doctor with FORGERY but told him that if this message was sent by a Midwayer, he was a prankster or a prevaricator. I went on to say that any Higher Intelligence who would give such a purported "psychoanalytical" report on anyone should certainly have specified their NAMES to have avoided any possible mistake or misinterpretation . . . if it had been important enough to issue this "warning" in the first place. I declared it to be highly dangerous for the doctor to interpret anyone's names as fitting this warning . . . and that he had done untold damage to us in the minds of Forum members by letting them know of the contents of this communication. He did not admit that he had done this—but looked worried.

I think the doctor really thought that this supposed higher attack on us would BOWL US OVER and SCARE US, as it had the other Forum members—and that we would ask forgiveness, etc.

When we did not react this way, it had him stumped. He said he could "go no further with us today" but for us to "think it over" and he would have another get-together in ten days or two weeks. That he KNEW what procedure to take from now on as he had "instructions," but he had read this personal message to him, to us, on his "own authority" as he thought we should know about it.

I said, "Doctor—was it by *divine decree* that we have been *segregated* from the other Forum members?"

He said, "I cannot answer that now."

I then said, "Doctor, in the light of our denial that this communication applies to us in any way, are you willing to withdraw your interpretation that it does?"

He said, "No, I am not—you'll just have to wait and let things work out. This is all I can say today."

Whenever I would try to press things home, he would start talking—an old psychological trick to AVOID HEARING WHAT HE DID NOT WANT TO HEAR.

I feel Christy is sitting in on a GREAT LIE and is SCARED TO DEATH but is privately pulling for us. Maybe I am wrong . . . but it seems so.

Incidentally, Harry, she is a mortal commissioner also. Should we wait until she dies, as well as the others, before any writing?

Dr. S. is using his position SO WRONGLY NOW, and SO PERVERTING THE MINDS OF FORUM MEMBERS, that I wonder how much longer he will be permitted in control? I am wondering if he received specific instructions to turn the book over to someone else, whether he would do it or not. He is FIENDISH and apparently will stop at nothing. BUT—he has so captivated the Forum members and so prejudiced them that for us to make an appeal or to make charges would now be regarded as the work of "unbalanced minds."

We are perfectly willing to stand on our own judgment when the time comes, Harry . . . but it seems that this whole situation is too rotten and too serious to PERMIT THE DOCTOR TO GET AWAY WITH IT. If we subside and accept this indictment and he does NOTHING TO CORRECT IT, then we are forever BLIGHTED in Forum minds and our usefulness is impaired. Martha and I are wondering if, at the proper time, we should not BRAND this communication as a FAKE and DEMAND that the doctor tell the Forum he has decided it *does not apply to us* (GIVING HIM THIS MUCH CHANCE TO SAVE FACE) . . . and, IF HE REFUSES, to say that this communication is LIBEL and DEFAMATION OF CHARACTER and we will be required to go to court to protect our good name.

As you said in a previous letter, he would make an ASS of himself trying to make this message STICK IN COURT. And none of the Forum members would like to be dragged into a public trial and forced to testify. Many of them would fanatically perjure themselves, and I think the doctor would destroy the communication beforehand.

It is SOME SITUATION. I neglected to mention that Bill gives us a wide detour . . . he and his father did not attend the Open Discussion meeting last Wednesday . . . but I am sure reports are carried to them of everything that goes on.

We are a THORN in their sides at present and a BIG ONE. The Haleses hate us as do other members . . . but a goodly portion who are doing quiet thinking must be WONDERING at many things. At least, I hope they are . . . I hope there is something left to build on there some day. (The Haleses are, of course, friendly to our face when not caught off guard.)

IF future leaders of any Urantia movement, which the doctor has told all Forum members MUST BE ORGANIZED, are permitted to HOLD SWAY as the doctor now does, religious persecution will reach new highs throughout the world!

I am sure the doctor's attitude against certain forms of psychic phenomena has CLOSED IT OUT of the book or any references to it. At one time Christy made a strange suggestion to me when I asked why an explanation of so-called spiritualism and other elemental forces was not given, since the book constantly referred to higher powers . . . Christy said: "Well, Harold—why don't you WRITE UP WHAT YOU THINK IS THE RIGHT EXPLANATION AND LET US SUBMIT IT AND SEE IF THE HIGHER UPS WILL ACCEPT IT FOR THE BOOK?" I was astounded. Can it be possible the doctor has tried to rewrite some of this book and submitted it for consideration? This is DANGEROUS. I know that he wrote a PREFACE which the Higher Intelligences REJECTED and put in their own. WHAT DOES THIS SORT OF BUSINESS MEAN?

Harry, there is plenty to be done in Chicago all right, but I'll have to begin to give attention to my own economic status pretty soon . . . although Bible references constantly reassure us by saying, "Take no thought of the morrow," etc. We have been doing no worrying . . . but are relying more and more upon our TAs and our meditation periods. Martha is WITH ME 100% and I wish you could have heard her talk up to the doctor yesterday. I was proud of her.

If this case were taken to court and it was brought out that the communication was from the Doctor and not from Higher Sources, would it not destroy confidence of many in the BOOK OF URANTIA. As Elsie Karle said, "You've got to either believe ALL the communications or NONE," and this is the terrible whip-hand control the doctor holds . . . they don't dare NOT TO BELIEVE for FEAR IT WILL DESTROY THEIR FAITH.

Harry, HOW could Higher Intelligences permit such a MESS? I know they don't interfere with HUMAN WILLS, but this TRUTH means so much to the world. I pray for more enlightenment and the WISDOM to act rightly in this most important matter.

Our LOVE to you and Ma Loose—who now must be as clean as the "driven snow" with the Tyson on the job.

P.S. What say you now?

7

Over a Tough Hurdle

DIARY *October 4, 1942*

FORUM—Paper 4: "GOD'S RELATION TO THE UNIVERSE"

As we entered the Forum room, Harold deliberately looked at Christy and then the Doctor, who both greeted him. Bill was already reading. Both he and Christy had heavy colds, perhaps brought on by the nerve tension of the past few weeks. Try as we may, we cannot get much inspiration from Bill's readings because of his smug, self-satisfied, benign manner and his facetious remarks which take one out of the spirit of the papers. He is obviously avoiding us and always exits through his own living room rather than through the Forum entrance which he used formerly.

At intermission, Mrs. Steinbeck, who sat behind us, leaned forward to whisper that a lot of funny things were happening in the Seventy meetings. She said, "You know we've been instructed to get three spontaneous speakers to talk during a half-hour period on the Urantia papers each session. This is extremely difficult to do, as most people don't want to talk at all and have had no experience. I think it is a deliberate attempt to embarrass us since we asked for greater participation in our petition, and this is a means of punishing us. It doesn't make sense to us." (It is plain to us that this is a move on the Doctor's part to attempt to show how little the Forum members actually know and to indicate by comparison how great a grasp he and Bill have of the papers.)

Mrs. Steinbeck said that they, the members, were at a great disadvantage since they did not have the papers to refer to in order to prepare their talks. She said, "You just can't get up there and discourse at random on subjects like these. Besides, we're not given any clue as to what to talk about or to what purpose." Mrs. Steinbeck promised to spend an evening with us as soon as her husband was finished with the convention this week, when she would tell us more about what was going on. She asked Harold if anything more had happened in our case. Harold said yes, and she said, "I'll bet it was good. I'd like to know about it."

The Doctor took up the second hour, as usual, carrying on with his comments on the Westminster Confession of Faith. He pointed out the difference between this "confession" and the Truths revealed in the Urantia Book; and while Urantia undoubtedly contains a great spiritual revelation, the religious manner in which the Doctor extolled it and the unfavorable comparisons with respect to other religions indicates how hidebound and prejudicial is to be the human presentation of this book to the world.

We met Mrs. Kellogg and Ruth on entering (downstairs), who greeted us enthusiastically. Ruth was cordial and sat beside us at the reading. She said pointedly, "I'm *very* glad to see you." Mrs. Kellogg was also cordial.

At intermission, Russell Bucklin came up to shake hands with Harold. He said Mildred had resigned her position and was feeling better, but that he himself had not been feeling too well. He acted as though he were afraid Harold might get on a vital subject but Harold only said as he turned away, "It's nice to see you, Russell."

As we were leaving, we ran into Clyde Bedell at the Forum doorway. He greeted us reservedly and did not extend his hand, which attitude we had noted on previous occasions. He is making an obvious effort to establish himself in the forefront of the Sadlers' affections after having been classified for years as a "rebel."

The attitude of all the Forum members, with the exception of the Burtons and the Steinbecks, continues to be guarded and reserved. We have observed that Mrs. Githens, who has been such a loyal and regular attendant through the years, has not been present for the past two Sundays which has either been because of indisposition (unlikely) or her own reaction to what has been taking place. Mildred

Bucklin is also remaining away from the meetings. A few members nodded to us perfunctorily but no one else spoke.

Dr. Sadler, in making side comments on the Urantia papers during his discussion of other religions, suddenly checked himself and said, "But I mustn't talk about that here. That's a subject for the Seventy. You Seventy members remind me and I'll tell you about it there." This indicated that he considers those who are members of the Seventy to be in a preferential position to the other ordinary members of the Forum.

October 11, 1942

FORUM—Paper 5: "GOD'S RELATION TO THE INDIVIDUAL"

To our surprise we were greeted with almost old-time cordiality by Dr. Sadler who, seated in his chair by the door to the Forum room, extended his hand to us as we passed. This indicated one of two things—either he was in unusually good humor or else he is relieved in mind concerning us since the last interview. His warmer attitude does not, however, blind us to the existing inconsistencies.

We sat next to the Burtons again, who even considerately changed their seats with us to another row when we offered to move because there was one seat shy for Mrs. Burton. Martha then gave her a copy of Harold's poem, "Eternity and I," which she had requested. She was obviously pleased and said she intended to frame it. The Steinbecks spoke to us as usual, and Mrs. Steinbeck came over to tell us her sister, Caroline Brown, had decided to stay in New York since she had landed a new client in the person of Ganna Walska,[1] whom she had met and who seems to be devoting her time and money pursuing one psychic fad after another. Miss Brown, in her letter, mentioned having encountered a friend who remembered hearing Harold talk before Harriet McCollum's psychology class[2] over ten years ago in New York. We realize how much ground Harriet has covered as we run into more and more people in different parts of the country who have taken her course at one time or another.

Harold asked Mrs. Steinbeck what had become of Mrs. Githens who had not attended Forum meetings recently, and she said, "Oh,

[1] Ganna Walska (1887-1984) was a Polish-born former opera singer who was married at the time to Yoga guru Theos Bernard. Bernard is mentioned in Vol. 1, p. 237.

[2] See Vol. 1, p. 22.

Mrs. Githens has been taking a 'mental vacation' from the Forum along with a few others such as Elsie Baumgartner and Mildred Bucklin. Miss Baumgartner and Mrs. Githens are having dinner together at O'Connell's tomorrow (Mon.) night, and Miss Baumgartner said if she had time they intended to drop in and see you folks. I told them they'd better wait until they could stay longer. I suppose I'm out of turn in telling you this, but I thought it wouldn't hurt for you to be expecting them. I'm having a heck of a time lining up people to speak before the Seventy. I spent an hour and a half reading up on the papers yesterday so I could give a talk myself. I don't know how this business is going to work out. We'll be seeing you soon and I'll tell you more about it."

Bill read Paper No. 5 in his customary manner but, despite this, all papers now seem more intelligent and inspiring to us than upon our first reading.

At intermission Elsie Karle turned around and spoke to us, and said that Dent was leaving town on a business trip this Wednesday, which meant that he would not be acting as chairman of the open discussion meeting that night. (We presume his substitute will be Clyde Bedell.) The Evanses, who sat on the other side of us, spoke as usual but had nothing to say. A few of the members nod when they see us looking at them but make no attempt to contact us. Russell Bucklin entered the room avoiding our gaze and went into the annex, and did not emerge until after we had left. We greeted Christy still suffering from her cold and told her to cut out citrus fruits as a possible aid, which she promised to do. Mrs. Hales went out of her way to shake our hands. If the Bedells or Rawsons were there we did not see them.

Mrs. Palmer, Mrs. Steinbeck's sister, said she wanted to have us over for a buffet supper some time around November 1st and mentioned the Burtons as other possible guests. This is the most show of hospitality extended to us since the Burtons' invitation to their home following the September 13th episode. Harold had the impression that the tension was a little bit eased today for some reason, and there seemed to be evidences that some of the Forum members are getting ready to get in touch with us. Doctor himself was more affable than at any other time, and in his second-hour talk was full of funny stories.

As we returned home and were entering the Cambridge, Lee Miller Jones, who was just getting into his parked car fifty feet away, saw us and came running over to extend his hand with a friendly air, saying (having almost bumped into a passer-by), "I almost stopped traffic but I wanted to shake hands with you," which he did with us both while Mrs. Jones waved to us from the car, as did some other members whom we could not recognize. This gesture, which was not necessary, seemed also to be somewhat significant.

Dr. Sadler, in side remarks on the forces working in the human minds, spoke of the influence of "fear" and how people could be driven to do things as well as be disciplined by fear. It was as though he was revealing his own technique for keeping Forum members in line. He referred to religionists as "trembling from the threatenings of God."[3] And while he intimated that this was not Urantia interpretation, still he emphasized the power of fear which compelled the early races of earth (Old Testament) to hew the moral line. This led us to observe, privately, that the Doctor had played upon the spiritual fears of the Forum members in turning them against us, but his attempted exercise of fear as a weapon directed at us had failed completely.

Mrs. Githens and Miss Baumgartner did not get in touch with us as planned.

October 16, 1942

The Steinbecks, as they had promised, invited us over this evening. It was evident, however, from almost the very moment we had arrived, that Mr. Steinbeck was intent on keeping the conversation off Forum matters. Each time Mrs. Steinbeck brought the subject up he kept talking to Harold, and once definitely said, "Let's not talk about that business tonight."

Even so, Mrs. Steinbeck managed to convey several things of interest. She said that Miss Baumgartner had phoned after the last Wednesday open discussion meeting to report that only eight had attended, with Dent Karle as chairman, but that a number of important questions had been raised which they intended to take up at the next meeting. (Dent had remained in town to handle this meeting after all, leaving later that night.) We had decided not to go and took the girls to see *Yankee Doodle Dandy* instead.

[3] Chapt. XIV ("Of Saving Faith") of the Westminster Confession of Faith includes this passage, which Sadler probably was quoting or referring to: "By this faith, a Christian believeth to be true whatsoever is revealed in the Word ... yielding obedience to the commands, trembling at the threatenings, and embracing the promises of God for this life, and that which is to come."

Mrs. Steinbeck remarked that they had been seeing quite a little of the Bucklins recently, that Mrs. Bucklin had had what amounted to a nervous breakdown and had been advised by Dr. Sadler not to put in an appearance at the Forum until after New Year's. Mr. Steinbeck stated that he had never cared much for Mr. Bucklin, but on better acquaintance had become quite fond of him. It seems Mrs. Bucklin does not wish to be left alone, and when Russell was called from the city on short notice and Mrs. Bucklin had dinner ready to serve, she phoned the Steinbecks and begged them to come over and help her eat it and keep her company. This they did. Mrs. Steinbeck reported that Winnifred came in that night all worn out, and was put to bed and remained overnight. She did not feel well enough to go to work in the a.m. but her mother insisted on it.

Mrs. Steinbeck further said, referring to the Seventy group, that she was having trouble getting members to stand up on their feet and talk about the Urantia papers. She said they were supposed to tell how they would present the Urantia truths to the world. Mr. Leverenz had the idea that an effort should be made to get the endorsement of the world's learned men. Clyde Bedell refused to speak, begging off until later, but Mrs. James, to everyone's surprise, made the best talk of all. Mrs. Steinbeck did not state what Mrs. James's views were.

Mr. Steinbeck then showed us home movies of the Forum picnic of two years ago which he said the Forum members had not evidenced much interest in. He said the same was true of the "still" pictures he had taken from year to year, even though he had been willing to supply interested members with sets of these pictures free. This indicated to us very little warmth of feeling or interest between individual Forum members or towards the Forum as a body, a rather surprising fact when the devotion of many of them to this spiritual project is considered. We did not press the Steinbecks with any questions, and left around 12:30 after what might be termed just an ordinary social evening. It is our impression, however, that Mrs. Steinbeck, if given the opportunity, would talk quite freely and frankly.

October 18, 1942

FORUM—Paper 6: "THE ETERNAL SON"

Attending the Forum as usual, we noted that Mr. Kellogg jumps and runs like a scared jack rabbit each time we put in an appearance. Why he should so obviously try to get out of our sight whenever he can is a bit difficult to understand, since many members just don't bother greeting us right to our face. Christy spoke to us as we came in, as did the Doctor (both busily talking to someone else). We sat in the row with Dent Karle and his daughter, Ima May [*Ed. note:* Ina Mae]. Dent, beyond a hello, had nothing to say. The Steinbecks behind us were cordial, both expressing appreciation of Harold's book *Your Key to Happiness*, which he'd given them on Friday.

Edith Cook was the reader today. She was a trifle nervous and read a little fast though distinctly. It seems to be the present plan to alternate with a reading by Bill one week and a Forum member the next. We marveled at how much more we seemed to understand from our own first reading.

At intermission we sat for most of this time without anyone coming near us and then, to our surprise, a Mrs. [Jennie] Allen came over to speak to Harold and was joined by Mrs. Blanche Webb who said, "Mr. Sherman, a group of us were out at the Burtons' the other night, and Mrs. Burton read us a perfectly wonderful poem you had written ["Eternity and I"]. She said you didn't ordinarily write poetry, but I think it's the finest poem I've ever heard." Harold said he was pleased that she had liked it, that he did not make a practice of writing poetry, and that this had come to him during a period of meditation. Mrs. Webb said, "Well, I can believe it was inspired. It bears reading over and over again. I was amazed when Mrs. Burton said you had written this before you knew anything about the Urantia papers. I did not see how this could be possible for you to describe the soul's entire progress ending with 'the embrace of the Father.'"

Harold said yes, he had realized on reading the papers that this was true and he would be glad to give Mrs. Webb a copy of the poem if she wished it. Mrs. Allen spoke up and said she'd like to have a copy also. Harold promised them both copies, saying we were happy to share it with anyone who appreciated it, and that it was one piece of writing he didn't wish to place commercial value upon because of its spiritual nature and the manner in which it had come to him. We could, for the first time, feel a good force working through the expressed interest of these two women in the poem. Few have read it who have not been profoundly impressed. It is possible that this little poem which was given to Harold may prove most influential in breaking down the reserve that has been shown us through the influence of the Doctor. Heretofore Mrs. Webb had remained cool and distant though speaking.

After Dr. Sadler's discourse on the Westminster Confession, which is apparently boring and uninteresting to many members and even resented by a few, Harold was approached by a Mrs. [Catherine] Trent, who said she had been a member for about five years and whom we did not remember having seen before. She explained that her husband had serious eye trouble threatening his sight but that she was eager to bring him into the Forum, and Dr. Sadler said he could come in if someone could be found to read to him. She said he was a construction engineer and had a good mind, but that the pain caused by his eye trouble had almost driven him mad. She said she felt he needed this Urantia knowledge to help sustain him, and that she had told him what she permissibly could but that she felt he would have more respect for a man's point of view. She asked Harold if he was now doing any reading, and if he was, that her husband join him and have the papers read to him and also get an opportunity to discuss them.

At this point Harold introduced Mrs. Trent to Martha, explaining that we had finished our readings for the time being and that Harold might be called to New York soon on business, but that he thought it should be possible to start a small reading group later which could include her husband since there must be a number of people interested in making a closer study of the papers.

Mrs. Trent showed every evidence of being nervous, high-strung and under pressure herself, and we sympathized with her. She said, strangely enough, that she had come to Harold because she felt he had the type of mind that would interest her husband. What could have led her to this conclusion, apart from the many other men members whom she must have become acquainted with during the five years, we cannot conjecture. This little experience served to emphasize the rather "unapproachable" atmosphere radiated by most Forum members who are rather selfishly and self-centeredly interested in getting what they can from the Urantia papers and going on their way without exhibiting any real personal interest in other Forum members.

Mrs. Githens was present for the first time in several weeks, but so far as we could see did not even look our way and went without speaking. Russell Bucklin spoke but kept his distance. Dent Karle, in answer to a direct question of Harold's as to whether they had found anything worthy of consideration in the reading of the charter, said, "No, nothing in particular. We just finished reading through it and next time we're going to take it up clause by clause." Mrs. James came over to speak to Martha while Harold was talking to Mrs. Trent, and when Martha told her she had heard Mrs. James had made the best talk at the Seventy meeting, tears came to Mrs. James's eyes and she replied, "Well, I think sometimes when we need help badly, we receive help."

Leone [Sadler], who had seated herself in our row during the second hour, spoke pleasantly to us both as we were leaving and said they had no contagious disease in their house at the present time. (Since we have been here, the family has had a run of contagious diseases such as mumps, whooping cough and measles, and have made no pretense at keeping quarantine, the Doctor even going down to Marion with us and confessing on the trip that he himself had whooping cough. Despite this he kissed various Forum women members freely and even jokingly remarked to Harold, after stating that more people died of whooping cough than any other contagious disease, that it would be a good thing if Harold would contract it before he got any older since it was progressively more dangerous with age. This attitude on the part of a physician was as incomprehensible as it was reprehensible. The Doctor in his discourses repeatedly refers to the imperfections of human creatures and their inability to do much about it in this life as though he were subconsciously confessing and excusing his own misconduct.)

For the first time none of the Haleses was present today.

Sir Hubert Wilkins is apparently scheduled to speak to some club in Oak Park Monday night (19th), as several Forum members have mentioned it. We, however, have not heard from him and are wondering if he has gone direct to Oak Park and located out there until after his talk. It is possible that the Haleses may make overtures since he is going to be in the vicinity, and the Haleses have shown a particular interest in this scheduled lecture for some time back.

October 19, 1942

Sir Hubert arrived in town this a.m. and stopped at the Rienzi as usual, and phoned Harold asking him to come over in the morning which was the only time Hubert had free. He was interested in getting an up-to-the-minute report of Forum developments, and when Harold had finished, said that the "human element" in no way abrogated the spiritual validity of the Urantia papers. He said it was most regrettable that lust for power and commercial gain had entered in after the fine work the Doctor and his associates had done through the years. He said he *did* feel that the book should be protected by copyright and a foundation be set up to care for all monies received, but not for private gain. He said he would have no time to see the Doctor or anyone this trip as he had to be en route back to Washington immediately after the lecture. He stated that the Haleses had invited him to stay at their home on this visit here since he was to speak at Oak Park but he had declined. This confirmed Martha's own feeling.

Referring again to the matter of the petition, Sir Hubert said it was clearly apparent to him at the luncheon meeting he attended with Clyde Bedell, Dent Karle, Russell Bucklin, Luther Evans, Lee Miller Jones and Harold that all these men felt as strongly as Harold, some even more so, that these steps should be taken. Sir Hubert reminded Harold that he [Sir Hubert] questioned the clause in the petition referring to the financial contributions made by the members, saying he thought this would particularly antagonize the Doctor. Clyde Bedell immediately defended the paragraph saying that this would indicate to the Doctor that we considered we had a vital basic interest in the whole enterprise. He was supported by the others present, and Sir Hubert said, "Well, you men are on the ground here and you've been members much longer than I, so I will accept your judgment."

HAROLD SHERMAN to HARRY LOOSE

Chicago, October 19, 1942

Dear Harry:

The joke is on us both. We have been waiting for a letter from YOU! And wondering why we had not heard. I could not feel that you or Ma Loose were in much different health or that I should be concerned in this way. I thought maybe you might be waiting for me to report another possible meeting with Dr. S. before writing me again—but Dr. S. has put off seeing us since reading us the purported "warning message" about us. I should appreciate your rereading my last letter to you and commenting about it. Remember I mentioned that Christy was a Contact Commissioner . . . also Bill. Must we wait until they are both gone, too, before writing anything . . . or just until the "older contacts" are gone?

Nothing of any particular note has happened here in these past two weeks you mention.[4] The Forum members still give us a wide berth. We did not attend the "Open Discussion" meeting this past Wednesday, following your suggestion . . . and have been keeping up our one-hundred-percent attendance at the Forum, however. This past week, Edith Cook did the reading of the paper in place of Bill . . . and several weeks ago, Tom Wideroe. Bill reads on alternate Sundays now . . . which is an attempt to kid the members into believing they are "participating." Dr. S. and Christy have greeted us as we have come in, the past two Sundays. I think he feels he has gotten over a tough hurdle with us . . . and thinks we will cause him no more trouble. But I am sure some of the Forumites are wondering . . . several have been made actually sick over this development and are not attending Forum meetings. They are all afraid to talk to us until given the "green light" by Dr. S., which is the most fiendish kind of human torture, so intended . . . but it doesn't bother us a bit because we have no feeling of guilt . . . our consciences are clear and we are "right with God," through our TAs. But the other members, if they have any consciences left, must feel "lousy." How they can ever face us again and really explain their "desertion of us all this time," is incomprehensible. We would hate to be in their shoes.

It looks like necessity for my New York trip is off . . . that the Twain matter may be straightened out without my having to be dragged in. Meanwhile it is soon going to become necessary that I line up something profitable to do, and have been hoping I could get on the radio again in my own philosophic program. I am letting the Jane Addams matter rest for the time being, also as you suggested . . . and agree with you conditions may change for the better later but it might be wasted time at present.

Never feel, if you do not hear from us, that it is for any personal reason. We look forward to word from you from day to day and have missed your letters more so, perhaps, than you have missed reports from us. We wish we could drive up in the car for one of our good old visits . . . or could travel there in spirit to see you and Ma Loose . . . We're giving thought and making plans to get the farm in readiness to live on it and get Arthur set, as soon as money comes in. LOVE TO ALL AND WRITE SOON!

---

[4] Loose's letter has not been found.

DIARY *October 21, 1942*

This a.m., while marketing, Martha ran face to face into Mildred Bucklin, who greeted her with a kiss and then plunged breathlessly into a detailed account of her near mental breakdown of recent weeks which was caused, she said, by assuming just too many responsibilities. First Russell's struggle (financially, we presume), then her job after twenty years away from office work, worries over Winnifred, and finally her mother's illness, plus her laundry and housework at home. She did not mention the Forum or petition activities. She had given up her job, taken her mother to Detroit with a brother, and had just been relaxing at home. She related in detail her constant weeping spells, her calling Dr. Green in Washington and visiting Dr. Grimmer here (both homeopaths), and how Dr. Sadler had finally given her the best advice, to plunge into a family washing; that she was not tired physically but mentally!

He had also advised her to stay away from the Forum meetings, only one of which she had attended this fall—the first Wednesday night meeting of Bill when he had read a new paper on the mansion worlds, or rather, a revised paper on it, which included some of the former apocrypha. Martha just listened quietly, making only one comment, that she didn't see why the Forum should upset her (Mildred). Just then Leone (and Charlie) appeared, and Mildred hastily said goodbye and was on her way. She gave the impression of trying to keep her story going at high pitch to prevent questions, and had a sort of wild, indirect look in her eyes.

We are wondering how she will stand the news of Winnifred's elopement the first week in September and the knowledge that a baby is already on the way. Both Russell and Mildred have opposed this young man (a Mexican, and a year younger than Winnifred) from the beginning. Mary has told us the story and has had Winnifred's permission to tell us. We suggested Winnifred put the story of the marriage in a letter to her father *first*, as a *personal* telling of it would blow them all up with possibly many unkind things said which would later be regretted. This Winnifred apparently intends to do and has already put herself in the care of their family doctor, Dr. Grimmer, following our suggestion.

8

Mrs. Gusler and the Dictator

FORUM CALENDAR *October 21, 1942*

Mrs. Gusler ventures her first call on us in evening.

DIARY *October 21, 1942*

We were going out the lobby tonight to take the car and visit Mary at Hull House when we were hailed by a woman who had been calling us on the house phone. She identified herself as Mrs. Gusler and said she had thought to have a half hour's visit with us before going over to Bill's meeting. We felt immediately it was important to see her, and assured her we could delay going out. We returned with her to our apartment, and Harold had Marcia slip into the kitchen and close the door so that Mrs. Gusler would feel free to talk.

Mrs. Gusler said that she didn't mind missing Bill's first half hour from 8:00 to 8:30 as Bill was now holding an examination period, quizzing his members on what they remembered of his last week's comments and readings of the papers. She said they were permitted to take notes but had to leave them on the premises, and could come early and refresh their minds on them if they wished. She indicated that this practice was not being received with any enthusiasm, Bill having free access to all this knowledge and they being so limited. She said she could hardly wait to get the published book away from across the street and in her own hands for study.

She said that her husband and two sons were no longer attentive, and that she didn't know quite why they had lost interest. We kept the conversation on generalities in accordance with our decision to let others approach us first. It was evident, however, that Mrs. Gusler wished to speak of what had occurred, because she brought up the subject herself by saying, "I have never been so upset in my life as I have over what has happened. I took my name off the petition but I'm even sorry now that I did that. I still see no wrong in what we asked for in that petition, and I can't understand the reason now for our having been ordered to remove our names. This whole affair has left us all bewildered. Of course we've all been associated with the Doctor for so long (she came in in 1935) and we felt the only thing we could do was to abide by what he had told us and let time throw some light on just what it was all about."

Harold, after this frank statement, said to Mrs. Gusler, "I appreciate your speaking as you have. You are the first person, since the presentation of this petition to the Doctor, who has even dared to come and see us. We believe as wholeheartedly in the truth of the Urantia papers as you people do. We were not given opportunity to strike our names from the petition but we would not have done so if we had. We have no sense of guilt whatsoever, but it has been baffling to us why we should have been singled out and boycotted as we have."

Mrs. Gusler said, "Well, we were practically ordered not to talk to you or see you, and were led to believe that the Doctor was going to take some kind of action in your case, but we thought this would be done and straightened out long before this. We just can't understand what is going on at all."

Harold said, "It has been difficult for us to understand how we could be treated as we have by either divine or human decree, and why those members we considered good friends should have forsaken us as they have."

To this Mrs. Gusler replied, "They are just as good friends as ever but they have been placed in a most difficult position. The Doctor has made certain statements which they either have to challenge or accept, and this almost amounts to doubting the authenticity of past spiritual messages if he is challenged. The members are simply waiting to see what comes of this whole matter and withholding their judgment."

Harold said, “We have sympathized with the position members have been placed in and we have felt that despite what has happened real good will eventually come out of it.”

Mrs. Gusler said, “That’s just the way we have tried to feel, but just at present we are all quite confused.”

Harold said, “We have felt that something pretty strong must have been said against us by the Doctor to have caused the members to have taken the stand they have. In fact, we have heard that the Doctor has told members he had received a communication warning him against us.”

Mrs. Gusler looked surprised. “Oh—so you know about that,” she asked.

“Yes,” said Harold, “the Doctor himself told us he had received such a communication.”

This seemed to let the bars down insofar as Mrs. Gusler was concerned. She said, “I would not have felt free to mention this had you not brought it up.”

Harold said, “Mrs. Gusler, perhaps you can appreciate now why I appealed for a hearing before the Forum. I told the Doctor that if he had received such a communication, he should read it to the entire Forum body and I would publicly face any charges made in it. I could see that I was never going to be given an opportunity to answer the charges made against me unless I took some stringent action.” (Harold then explained the Matterns’ connection with the September 13th episode, ending with the reference to the Doctor’s reminder that he was welcoming us as guests in his house. Mrs. Gusler said, “Yes, this was a shock to me. He had been instructed that all Urantia matters were to be conducted in the Forum room and not upstairs in his own home, and we felt this Forum room belonged to us as much as to him. But since he termed us as only ‘guests,’ it implied that he considered that he owned the papers.”)

Mrs. Gusler said, “May I ask you a frank question?”

Harold said, “Feel free to ask us any question whatsoever and we will gladly answer.”

She said, “Would you mind telling me what you said to Ruth Kellogg?”

Mrs. Gusler seemed to be under the impression Ruth had been over to our apartment for dinner. We told her we had taken the Kelloggs Sr. to Isbell’s for dinner one evening and had the Kelloggs and

Ruth over one evening, but she specifically said, "No—didn't you see Ruth one time alone?"

Harold said, "Yes, we did, but before I tell you what we said to her, I should explain that we purposely and repeatedly told the Doctor, Christy, Bill and the Kelloggs of differences of opinion among Forum members, thus hoping to prepare them for the requested open discussion of Forum matters we knew was coming. This occasion, when we saw Ruth alone, was to tell her frankly that we might have to take a stand with these other Forum members, and we did not wish Ruth or her parents to misunderstand our attitude; that we knew the Doctor and Bill would be much disturbed and we thought her parents might be most helpful in stabilizing matters. We told Ruth that since she was not a contact commissioner but was so close to the situation, we felt she could explain it to her own parents, and that they would realize the members were not antagonistic toward the contact commissioners but simply wanted free and open discussion of Forum plans."

Mrs. Gusler interrupted to ask, "But Mr. Sherman, didn't you suggest to Ruth that her parents could seize the plates of the Urantia Book from the Doctor and Bill and that you would get them copyrighted, and that Ruth was destined for a high place in the Urantia work?"

We were both astounded. Harold raised his hand and took an oath before God that he had never said any of these things.

Mrs. Gusler looked at us and shook her head, and said, "Well, I never! That's what the Doctor told us! I think I'm correct about the plates. I will have to check with the Bucklins. They saw the Doctor the same time I did." She then went on to say, "You know, Mr. Sherman, it's awfully hard after all these years to be finding these kind of things out about the Doctor."

Harold said, "We must learn to distinguish between the spiritual and the human. Nothing that has happened or can happen will alter the truth of these papers."

Mrs. Gusler asked, "But didn't you tell Ruth that the Kelloggs weren't invited to the Sadlers' after the (Jesus) birthday meeting August 21st?"

Harold said, "I will have to go back in time to explain this remark. When I first wrote my letter of criticism to the Doctor, he came over to our apartment and asked me to write two new letters, putting my criticism of the organizational plans in one, saying that this was a 'closed book' and that he did not want to present the letter in its present form to the Kelloggs or the Forum members as it would tend to antagonize and prejudice them against us. I asked Ruth if it was not the policy for all contact commissioners to be consulted on matters pertaining to the Forum plans, and she said yes, that she thought so; and then I told her of this instance which seemed to surprise her in which her parents were not consulted. I mentioned also the special courtesy shown us at the Haleses' picnic when Sir Hubert and ourselves were invited to dine on the porch with the Haleses, Dr. Sadler and Christy. I then mentioned the special affair to which we were invited after the Christ birthday meeting. The Kelloggs were in neither of these groupings. I told Ruth we felt no better nor any more entitled to special consideration than any other Forum members despite our appreciation of the hospitality extended."

Mrs. Gusler again shook her head. She said, "Well, it's been intimated that you have been influenced by that minority of midwayers who do not agree with present plans."

Harold said, "Yes, different members have reported to us it has been inferred we were leaders of an attempted new Lucifer rebellion."

Mrs. Gusler laughed and said, "The Doctor calls it 'the Sherman rebellion.'"

Harold said, "It's practically the same thing. The Doctor read some messages to you people, I understand, concerning the Ideaists and Idealists and also stressing an apparent necessity of having an organization. He intimated that anyone opposing these messages was a rebel and classified me as an idealist, in which classification are Gandhi and Lucifer."

Mrs. Gusler said, "Yes. The Doctor said we can't argue with an idealist because he's right, but despite the fact he had been warned against you, he still felt he could handle you."

Harold said, "I've been accused of having a commercial interest in the papers and have sent a sworn statement to the Doctor that this has never been my intention, and that I would not even permit my name to be used in connection with any service rendered."

Mrs. Gusler said, "Yes, I've heard about that, and the Doctor said you had written a letter saying you were sorry for the trouble you had caused."

Harold said, "I have never retracted one statement I have made nor *will* I."

Mrs. Gusler replied, "Some of the members said that they supposed you *were* sorry that things had turned out as they had, but not necessarily sorry for what you had done."

In referring to the messages the Doctor had read to the members, Mrs. Gusler said he represented them as having been received about six months ago. Harold said that the Doctor had told us of these same messages in detail early in August and stated at that time they had been received about a year and a half ago. Mrs. Gusler seemed disturbed at this and Harold asked her about the recent message, tying in with the time of the petition, that he was supposed to have received.

"Oh, you mean the one making him the Dictator?" she said.

Harold, astonished, said, "Dictator?!"

"Yes," she said. "You know he was relieved of his responsibility in the message read at the Haleses' picnic, but this control was given back to him at the time of this rebellion and he was made a Dictator to handle matters."

Harold said, "Does this sound like a spiritual decree?"

Mrs. Gusler said, "No, it doesn't. That's what has us all wondering."

Harold then asked Mrs. Gusler to try and picture the inhuman position we had been placed in, and said he had told Dent Karle that if Dent and his wife had been placed in a similar position, he, Harold, would not have stood for it.

Mrs. Gusler said, "What did he say to that?"

Harold replied, "He dodged the issue and simply said we would have to wait and let time work things out."

"You see," said Mrs. Gusler, "they all hate to disbelieve the Doctor, even though there's lots that doesn't seem right. Why, he's even denied what he has said to one group, to another; and what he has done lately and his treatment of you people has cost him a great deal of respect and confidence. You know, he had to take a great deal of criticism while he was interviewing these members and a lot of them were outspoken against Bill—Dent Karle and his group particularly. Why, I remember Bill saying to us some time that he was going to buy all the copies of the Urantia Book he could at $5 per and sell them at $7.50 and make a lot of money! But most of us feel the book should be sold at a popular price so that the Truth may be within the reach of all."

Harold said, "It *must* be done that way. This was one of the criticisms I made against the book's high price. I suggested a popular priced edition as well, and I suppose this was not in accordance with their commercial plans. I regret to have to say it, but I feel the Doctor and Bill have developed a lust for power and they see a chance to make considerable money out of this development. Doesn't it stand to reason that if we were interested in making money with them, we would not now be opposing their plans?"

Mrs. Gusler said, "Yes, but you are accused of trying to get control of the book and its copyright so you can handle the picture rights and everything else."

Harold said, "That is a lie. I insisted that the copyright should be held by the foundation and all rights protected so that none of them could be perverted or distorted by wrong adaptations in any field. I have offered to put the Sadlers in touch with a publisher who might have been able to bring in as much as a million dollars for the publicizing of the book and do whatever else I could, all without any thought or suggestion of remuneration by myself. How many Forum members would have come here from California at a cost of several thousand dollars in expenses and other possible contracts and given the attention we have to these Urantia papers? The Doctor is afraid to face us and prefer charges in the open against us because he knows we will make him out a liar."

Mrs. Gusler said, "When the petition was presented, Bill said, 'How could people like Sir Hubert and the Shermans do this to us?'" Then she asked, "Do you know what Sir Hubert thinks of this now?"

Harold said, "I saw him this last Monday when he was here to lecture in Oak Park."

Mrs. Gusler said, "Yes, I went to the lecture with Miss Baumgartner, and about eight other Forum members were present, including the Haleses. Sir Hubert gave a fine talk on Alaska as a strategic base for military operations. I'd like to say I've read your and Sir Hubert's book, *Thoughts Through Space*, which Miss Baumgartner loaned me and which I enjoyed very much."

Harold, in answer to Mrs. Gusler's previous question, said that Sir Hubert had expressed faith in the Urantia papers but regret over the Doctor's present attitude.

It was now about 9:15 and she had stayed much longer than intended. When she arose to go, she said she would like us to come over to dinner soon and would phone us suggesting a night. She said she wished to read us a letter she had written the Doctor, and to hear the letter Harold had written. She said further that she had not liked the humorous and rather biting remarks the Doctor had made to the Forum about the letter she had written, and that he apparently could not take any form of criticism. Harold said, as she was leaving, that he was convinced that the communication the Doctor said he had received warning against us had been made up by him, and that when the Forum members used their reason they would realize that such treatment as we have received could not be by divine decree.

Mrs. Gusler replied, "It certainly does not seem so. Why, Christ treated even Judas more humanly than you have been treated. There has been much discussion among Forum members and many are not satisfied." She left giving us the impression that she intended to speak to other members, particularly the Bucklins, about what we had discussed tonight and the absolute denial of the charges made against us.

HARRY LOOSE to HAROLD SHERMAN

Monterey Park, October 21, 1942

Dear Harold:-

I am acknowledging receipt of yours of Oct. 19th.

Yes, Christy is a "Contact Commissioner." She became so originally because of her shorthand ability and the necessity of such in taking down voluminous conversations between different high intelligences in the presence of the sleeping "instrument." This was away back in the beginning—before it was recognized what was in prospect—before anything had been routined—before there had been any planning as to reception. Christy was originally hired for this purpose—and because the "calls" would come more often in the night, which necessitated hurrying to the bedside of the instrument by taxi or private car from all parts of Chicago in response to summons by way of telephone, Christy was given a room at Sadler's to be "on hand" when these calls would come. The call from the home of the "instrument" by the wife was only one call by phone—that phone was direct from her to Sadler's home phone, and it lay between Christy and the Kelloggs to go through the phone lists of the "Contact Commissioners" and call them and tell them to hurry to the home of the "instrument." That was Sadler's first contact with Christy.

Dr. Lena was a "Contact Commissioner"—Bill Sadler is one—*Mr. Hales,* etc. Originally there were 17. By deaths, this number has been reduced from the original. Christy will be alive—so will Bill S—so will Hales—and others when you write. Dr. Lena has gone—Mrs. Kellogg will be the last of the immediate grouping indicated in the writing—others of the original 17 will still be here. Both Sadler and Kellogg will precede Mrs. Kellogg in passing. I am very nearly positive that your writing will occur *before* the passing of Mrs. Kellogg. I have reasons to so believe.

Your writing will raise a terrific "dust" amongst many of the old Forumites. Many will be in perfect accord.

You will appreciate the "farm" before then and even more so after that time. For your own sake, and that of small Martha, please do not broadcast the farm—or its location. You will appreciate this later.

I am needed in the physical in Chattanooga, Tennessee, for two weeks at least and should be present in the physical in Chicago for a like period. Do not yet know what will result from the above—nor how it is to be accomplished.

Make no peace with the powers of darkness. Retain your mental *selves* under your own jurisdiction and do not make the mistake of allowing hypnotic directed thought. There are those who are now, and long have been, under the spell. "This too, shall pass away."

Christy and ALL the Kelloggs are very strongly WITH you, but, as you must recognize, they are most peculiarly situated.

Hope the necessity for the N.Y. trip is definitely off.

Did the suggestion that Wilkins might indicate government employment register?? Of course Wilkins backs you up. Your way is right—he knows it—and is in no fear of S or H.

Sadler is very well acquainted with the human mind and its activities and reactions—he well knows the corroding action and effect of "fear" on the physical body—he uses this mental weapon much—it is a wrong and cowardly thing to do—mental pain is much more deep and lasting—and repetitious—than physical suffering. S is a little disturbed because you have not reacted as he anticipated in the present, and past, crisis. I tell you most positively, "Be not dismayed nor afraid. Be of good cheer and filled with courage." S has more reason to fear you than you have to fear him. I do not guess—I know. You have strongly the upper hand and must surely know it—whether he recognizes this fact fully or not. Also, whether you believe it or not, whether you recognize it or not, you have been, and so continue, an active agent for good—and are operating under the guarded suggestive direction of a higher enmissioned intelligence—this with the acceptance of and cooperation of your TA co-enjoined with your own intelligence and ability to reason.

As long as the Sunday Forum is available to you, be a very regular attendant thereat. Retain your contacts with it and any cautious Forumite who may shed the "fear" that has been placed upon him, who may evidence continued interest and friendship with you.

Don't be annoyed or dismayed by the symptoms of horror because of your presence—nor the smirks—nor the "holier than thou" attitude of the Sadlers—the satellites—the "Charlie McCarthy's," etc. Obtain much silent amusement thereat. Remember, "This too shall pass away." Remember, also, that many are strongly with you—even some who were not of the original 48 of the petition.

With the passing of S and Mr. and Mrs. K your book should be in the publisher's hands. Mrs. K will be the last of these three to be here—and I am nearly positive that your book does not need to await her passage.

Write when possible—hold to the faith—and the faith will hold to you—if I do not hear from you, I will know that it is because there is naught to write about of change in the complexion of things—but know, too, that both Ma and I haven't much else here now but watching the development of the approaching crisis. We, too, wonder at many things—but our knowledge is so very limited.

I wonder if I am going to be able to really make it to Chattanooga and to Chicago or not.

Love from us all to you both—and the girls too,

HAROLD SHERMAN to HARRY LOOSE

Chicago, October 22, 1942

Dear Harry:

Things are commencing to crack open here by degrees, at last . . . and we are mindful of what you said in a previous letter—intrigue, scandal, lies, etc., etc. WHAT A STORY! . . . WHAT A STORY!

Harry, it is INCREDIBLE, what the Doctor has told the members about us!

To our great surprise, as we were going out the lobby to take the car and run down to Hull House to see Mary last night, an elderly lady who was on the house phone, trying to phone us, called to us. She was a Mrs. Gusler, Forum member, who had dared write a letter to Dr. Sadler a year or so ago, criticizing in a kindly, constructive manner his conduct of affairs. Dr. Sadler had lighted on her unmercifully, and several others, for writing such letters, intimating that they were "paranoiacs." We had never seen Mrs. Gusler privately before . . . and she was calling last night on her own volition.

Sensing the importance of this visit, we changed our plans and went back up to our apartment with her. She had come in to attend Bill's Wednesday night meeting, and had half an hour to spare . . . until 8:30, but stayed until 9:15.

It was apparent to us, after the usual talk on generalities, that Mrs. Gusler's mind was disturbed and she wanted to find out our side of the story. She finally came out with it and said she just couldn't believe the things said about us were true . . . and that, if we didn't mind, she'd like to ask us some very personal questions. We said, "By all means—ask us anything you wish to know." And she said: "Tell me, did you ever tell Ruth Kellogg to get her father and mother to SEIZE THE PLATES from the DOCTOR AND BILL . . . and did you tell her that you thought she was destined to play a big part in the Urantia developments . . . and did you tell her that, if her parents SEIZED THE PLATES, you would get the book COPYRIGHTED IN YOUR NAME . . . and see that it was sold to the movies for a big price, etc.?!"

Harry, we were ASTOUNDED. We knew the Doctor must have said some dastardly things about us, but we could not believe he would dare go this far. He had sworn everyone to secrecy . . . had told them that the HIGHER BEINGS had enabled him, through SUPERNATURAL MEANS, to SEE AND BE PRESENT at the Karles' home when many of us met out there to discuss Forum matters. That he had been kept advised of every movement but had been told to wait until our petition was presented before taking action. The MESSAGE he then received made him a DICTATOR, to crush the SHERMAN REBELLION . . . Sherman had come under the influence of the group of Midwayers (in the minority) who were opposed to the present plans . . . probably those who went astray during the Lucifer rebellion and who were still at large.

Harry, this is the working of an ABSOLUTELY PERVERSE and DERANGED MIND . . . Under the influences he and Bill are now operating, they will lie and FRAME ANYBODY and ANYTHING TO ACCOMPLISH THEIR PURPOSES.

Dr. Sadler has not had us in to see him again after reading us this "warning" he claims he received about us . . . and he is afraid, I know, to read us the messages he read to the other Forum members. Martha and I had about decided that we would "take," up to a certain point, what he might hand out, for the sake of temporary harmony, and let him eventually hang himself, in the faith that the HIGHER POWERS would intervene . . . but after this last REVELATION, which has come to us through Mrs. Gusler, it is so ROTTEN and we have been placed in such a BAD LIGHT, that it may take a LAWSUIT one of these days to CLEAR OUR GOOD NAME.

While these weeks have been flitting past, I have tried to reorganize my own creative mind and get some work out which might bring me an income, as I am getting low in cash again. But perhaps we will be cared for as we were so miraculously in Hollywood . . . for MUCH REMAINS TO BE DONE IN CHICAGO . . . and I know the Doctor would love to get rid of us! I don't see how we can take what he would interpret to the Forum as a "run-out powder" now.

Mrs. Gusler assured us, as you have all along, that many Forum members have lost respect for the doctor . . . and are STILL OUR FRIENDS . . . and that they are simply waiting, giving him every chance to TREAT US RIGHT, before they decide what steps to take.

Mrs. Gusler herself is greatly upset; her faith in the doctor has been shaken, but not in the TRUTH.

Harry, we thank God we have been given the COURAGE and the FAITH to go through this human ordeal . . . and NOTHING could make me retract one statement I have made to or about the doctor. He is afraid to meet me in OPEN HEARING, for I will make a liar of him and seriously embarrass all contact commissioners.

Why do you suppose RUTH KELLOGG told this story? She said some frank things about Bill, as you will see if you will refer to my report to you of some time ago . . . and acted as though she hoped changes could be made over there. Was she intimidated? Mr. Kellogg runs every time he sees me coming as though he is afraid to face me or that I may say something to him. Mrs. Kellogg alone remains as friendly as ever and goes out of her way to say, "I'm awfully glad to see you." Even this is guarded, when the doctor is not in hearing. I think Christy is terribly afraid, but a soul in absolute bondage. Bill stays out of my way completely but is burning up with hate. Their plans have been stalemated for the time being.

Sir Hubert was through here on Monday to give a lecture and is WITH ME. As a man of the world, he has seen how undependable the human creature is . . . and what happens when Greed and lust for Power enters in.

The way I feel now, when the doctor calls us in next time and tries to whitewash the whole thing, leaving us still condemned in the eyes of the Forum and posing as a charitable dictator who has "forgiven us our sins," my inclination is to brand what he has told the members as a pack of lies and call upon him to clear this up or I will be compelled to take action.

Harry, that man would not stop short of murder to try to eliminate me, with what I know, if he could . . . I am convinced of this side of his nature now. I have no fear . . . I can face him right to the teeth because I am armed with the TRUTH. If I ever came to a REAL ISSUE with him, I would turn a sealed envelope containing the whole story over to an attorney and say to the doctor that if anything happened to me or any member of my family, proceedings would be started against him immediately.

You remember the last letter I wrote him, which certainly was FIRM. He has now told some of the members that we have said we were "sorry for the trouble we caused," as though we were asking forgiveness. This is a vicious attempt to justify what action he has taken against us and to intimate that we have pled guilty. How in the world can this man be brought to justice and the papers protected. I wish some direct illumination and guidance would come to us.

Doctor told us, one time, he had hypnotized the subject on several occasions and experimented with his mind to try to prove the genuineness of the messages. Has he hypnotized the subject's wife at any time also . . . and could he in any way get control of this man's mind now . . . to further his own purposes? Of course, these messages he has read to the Forum he claims came to him PERSONALLY . . . that he had to take his own notes . . .

My—to think that the TRUTH would fall into such hands . . . or that there should be such a fall from grace on the part of the CUSTODIANS who are now, in their own minds and hearts, THE OWNERS!

It would seem to me that these PAPERS should be taken from the Doctor's custody for their own protection, at the right time, IF he does not change his ways. And how can we hope he will, until he is faced with TERRIFIC PHENOMENA of some kind which puts THE FEAR OF GOD in his soul?

I would not want to face what he will one day have to face, either in this life or the next.

Let's not make a BONER like we did this last time and not write each other. Life is short and we want to keep in close touch.

Our love to Mother Loose and yourself. It's cold here today and we yearn for the wonderful Hollywood weather you should be having now.

HARRY LOOSE to HAROLD SHERMAN

Monterey Park, October 25, 1942

Dear Harold:-

Your letter came in yesterday's single delivery of mail. One delivery on Saturdays only. I have just come back from taking Ma and little John down to Sunday School. I leave in an hour to take Auntie down to join Ma at Church and to bring little John back home here. I have hustled home so as to sit down here to the old typewriter and see if I can knock off an answer to your letter so that I can mail it when I take Auntie down. I ought to be able to finish some sort of a letter in the hour—anyway I'll do the best that I can. If I make any mistakes you'll understand the reason why—from the above explanation.

Your letter was sure shocking—but not surprising. I would not like to answer for the sins of omission and the sins of commission, committed and in process of being committed by Sadler and Bill, the Haleses and a few others regarding this great revelation any more than you have remarked in your letter. Both Ma and I feel, and have long felt, that when Dr. Lena passed on, something happened that was not for the best. It was Dr. Lena that kept Sadler balanced.

Higher Intelligences move in mysterious ways. Witness Mrs. Gusler as a minor instrument. There are others. Mrs. Gusler may be an ex-patient on whom Dr. S may have a long case-card history of symptoms and treatment. Because of this, she might not be a witness in good standing in Court, if necessary—depending on whether she was a patient for mental treatment or physical. This is true of several Forum members, Mrs. Hales and others. Mrs. Gusler was not one of the 48 petition signers who deserted, I know. Could she be a messenger from Dr. S, seeking information and leaving inaccurate data behind—to learn friendly contacts by locations where a repeat of the inaccuracies appeared. If Mrs. Gusler is on the square, she is a very good contact and surely knows other Forumites who have her same opinions. If she will honestly cooperate with you, she will be of great value in many present angles and some to further develop.

A sort of hypnosis really has played a part in furthering certain situations regarding this whole matter—this is perfectly true—but in ways and at times not under discussion in your letter—which Sadler mentions to you—or has mentioned in past contacts. And this peculiar sort of hypnosis is a mental something beyond what is here known as hypnosis in that it operates without the consent of the subject—and in which the possession of the human "will" is not taken over by the operator. It is a much higher form of what is here known as "hypnosis." Sadler understands the methods of the process of hypnosis very well BUT HE DEFINITELY *IS NOT* AN OPERATOR. He could not hypnotize and explore the mind of the "instrument," as he has said that he has done. And, because he is not an Operator, he could not hypnotize the wife of the instrument either. He LIES if he states that he can personally use hypnosis—I KNOW. He violates one of the very first rules of hypnosis in telling what he did about hypnotizing the "instrument"—*NO* Operator of hypnosis can impose his hypnotic "will" upon a subject without the subject's knowledge and free consent—unless such practice has been a prior oft-repeated willing operation. The "instrument," the subject in the present case under discussion, would never be a "willing" subject to such. This could not be allowed by Higher Intelligences having the present operation in charge. Believe me when I tell you that both the "instrument" AND HIS WIFE are very definitely protected in their privacy against such mental intrusion. Surely you can see the great wisdom in the thus insurance of their mental safety.

This revelation may be lost entirely to this generation unless there is some adjudication of the present mess. I have no authority for that statement, but I do know that ALL the papers can fully and completely dematerialize—as they did IN FULL at one time—and were only returned, and contact re-established, on a sort of "probation," as it were. That dematerialization has been taken from the memory of all but a very select number. GUARD AND KEEP UP DATA IN YOUR DIARY.

The story about Ruth Kellogg does not ring true to me; I do not doubt but that Sadler told it, though. I cannot conceive of Ruth saying what is credited to her by Sadler. I can far more readily believe an entire untruth by Dr. S or "much made from little" by him. It will take more evidence than just Sadler's word to make me fully believe what he has said of Ruth.

You have been, and will continue to be, under severe mental attack (you know this even better than I) but you have had protection—both mental and physical. You do not need to fear. You evidence NONE, and because of this you have Dr. S a little unsure and guessing. He feels that you represent some authority but he cannot place it.

Has *Thoughts Through Space* given you any profit yet?? Won't there be a payment from there soon which would relieve the financial pressure to some extent????

If Sadler was present at the Karles' home as an observer, unseen by all, he was in what is termed the "Astral." Yet, in one of your letters, Sadler denied the possibility of the "Astral." How come the change of opinion.

I wish that I could indicate something to you regarding the present financial worry, but I cannot. I do not know anything—except that the best barometer for judging the future is by what has happened in the past. With the increased cost of living, you can recognize the problem here with what is available for all living expenses.

I also have need, in an important matter to do with this whole picture, to be physically present in Chattanooga, Tenn. soon—and the very same angle calls to Chicago—but I have no way to accomplish this under present financial conditions. I have found, however, that these things finally are adjusted in the end by circumstances that just seem to fall into place at the right time. What a spot for the activities of a philanthropist—even a quite small one—right now.

I am reading your letter and commenting as I read along. For what has happened, for which you have proof, you have sufficient information for the issuance of a "Psychopathic Warrant" for examination as to sanity—with plenty of witnesses and much publicity.

Reread the following because it is important. At the proper psychological moment, in perfect sincerity and truth, you could leave with Dr. S. a cryptic and knowing sentence or two to the effect that you had direct authority for your past program and still have such authority. Let it drop with this cryptic knowing sentence or two and definitely give no further information that no matter how questioned would bring illumination further. This would give S something of a shock—and something for him to mull over in the night silences.

Remember that I wrote in my last letter: "Christy and ALL the Kelloggs are very strongly with you but, as you must realize, they are most peculiarly situated." I still believe you will eventually find this to be the truth. "It is a long lane that has no turning."

I am glad that the N.Y.C. Twain matter has come to a conclusion without your presence needed there.

From your letter, there seems really nothing further that Sadler can do, or say, to more belittle and discredit you.

Sadler does not want any publicity beyond that of the Forum. Just the thought of such publicity as any Court procedure—or civil suit—would be a terrific shock that he would do almost anything to avoid. Just the mere threat of such would take all the lies out of him and he would frantically start waving a large olive branch in all directions.

Don't get scared—don't take any "run-out powder"—there is much for you to do in Chicago—even though you have already accomplished a great deal. My hour is up—will mail on my way down.

Love to ALL—

DIARY *October 25, 1942*

FORUM—Paper 7:

"RELATION OF THE ETERNAL SON TO THE UNIVERSE"

Entering the Forum room, Harold spoke to Christy asking her how her cold was. She replied with what seemed to be her usual smile, "Much better, thanks."

We sat in our customary place about three-quarters of the way back. The Burtons seated themselves beside us. Mrs. Steinbeck was in the row behind, and also Mrs. Gusler and Mrs. Trent. To the latter Harold gave a copy of his *Key*, thinking it might be of help to her ailing husband. Mrs. Steinbeck reported that *her* husband had been ill with bronchitis this past week. We were introduced to a Mrs. [Jessie] Hill, who has been a member for the past fifteen years, and who said she was glad to meet us and would like to get better acquainted since she had heard so much about us. Since she has been away for some months this may not mean so much, as the majority still give us a wide berth. Rev. Rawson shook hands with Harold as we came in, since we ran into him at the door.

Bill read the paper today and departed from the reading several times to interpolate his remarks. He made the astonishing statement that his Wednesday night group was memorizing the names of the different orders of celestial Beings even though this was not supposed to be done.

"Actually," said Bill, "according to Urantia these papers were written, in so far as possible, in such a manner as to keep us from crystallizing in our minds the exact nature and character of these celestial Beings, so that we can spiritualize our concept of them rather than intellectualizing them. But we're intellectualizing just the same and, while I admit it's a dangerous thing to do, we're trying to get a mental grasp of these Beings."

Bill indicated by a further explanation that he felt he could control this intellectual process so that he could obtain a spiritual result at the same time. However, it has been our observation that both the Doctor and Bill have been doing nothing but intellectualizing the entire Urantia Book and communicating or instilling very little of its spiritual values to Forum members. The Doctor's analytical comments on the creeds of various religions demonstrates again the intellectual approach, since he is filling the minds of the members with distorted interpretations of the truth, the very thing many humans are trying to get away from. How much more worthwhile it would be if this time were devoted to an attempt on the part of the Forum members under someone's spiritual direction to make the Urantia truths a vital part of their lives.

After the meeting, Harold asked Mrs. Gusler if she had checked on the "plate seizing" accusation. She said her illness of the week (a cold) had prevented her doing so, but she would soon and get in touch with us. Harold told her how much we appreciated her call, and she said she herself would have appreciated such a call had she been placed in our position, and that she had faith that justice would eventually come out of this.

Mrs. Allen came to Martha for the copy of the poem ("Eternity and I") and tried to sell us on sharing an apartment with a friend of hers. (These offers are becoming common, almost as though someone were on a "fishing expedition" to find out how long we intend to stay in these parts or to try to get us to move from our present "overseeing" location.)

Mrs. James came up to purposely greet us and shake hands. Clyde Bedell came through and avoided looking at us. Mrs. Bedell, who sat behind us, passed close by down the aisle and nodded at Martha. On the way out the front door, the former Miss Penn [Mary Esther Boike] stopped us in the doorway and said she was just recovering from a serious operation. She kept us there prepared to go into all the details, and Mrs. Githens, who has apparently been afraid to meet us, was compelled to pass us. She shook hands with Harold and started on out the door, when he said to her that he occasionally got downtown and would like to have lunch with her some time. She hastily said she never had lunch as she had to be in her office at 1:00 p.m. but that she'd like to see Harold some time. Harold told her when she was free to let him know, but it was evident that she is highly nervous and fear-stricken despite her Christian Science background.

Russell Bucklin came down and walked out to the corner with us but spoke of nothing but Winnifred and a new (secondhand) coat she had bought. He could have made some more vital comments had he chosen but seemed glad to be on his way. And so the Bucklins, despite our former close association, remain strangely aloof.

FORUM CALENDAR *October 26, 1942*

Matterns leave Chicago.

HARRY LOOSE to HAROLD and MARTHA SHERMAN

Monterey Park, November 1, 1942

Dear Martha—and Harold:-

Thanks, Martha, so much for your letter of Oct. 27th.[1] We do get more from them when they are written in pen—they are—of course—so much more personalized, so written, and it is easier to really visualize the writer and to seize the mood and tempo of their thoughts. It gives for better and fuller understanding. Even the *feel* of the letter is different. This "seizing the mood" is much harder to do with the typed word.

We very well remember the snappy, exhilarating fall days in Chicago. They made you walk briskly—and, maybe, whistle a tune. It is invigorating for you young folks. It probably would not be so much appreciated by us older people now. Walk a bit in beautiful Lincoln Park and see the colors of the fall leaves—and along the lakefront there—you'll come home hungry.

---

[1] This letter has not survived.

For 5 years and 9 months, I was a police officer in Lincoln Park before joining the police department of the City of Chicago. I was in citizen's clothes the greater part of this period doing detective work. It was much smaller in those days, and began at North Avenue and ended at Diversey Boulevard—now called Diversey Parkway. The whole south end of the park was once a cemetery—that is, south of Center St.—and when they put in, or changed, the water or sewer systems, or made other improvements—where the earth was disturbed—many of the old graves were found—and had to be moved a little to one side—or buried elsewhere. A young woman—with an infant in her arm impressed me much—this was one of the disturbed graves—and you could look through the glass over the faces in the old-time casket. Both bodies were perfect—they looked like they but slumbered. But the glass had been cracked in the discovery and handling and the air entered and reached the bodies and, as you looked, they disintegrated before your very eyes. It was fearsome and uncanny to several of the other bystanders and workmen.

Yes, I very well know that the situation across the street has been exceptionally trying. Martha, the whole future will continue to be "trying." But you will be satisfied with your upward climb and progress as you mentally turn and look backward. But, Martha, just to mention it, you have had a "trying time" for many years—not particularly because you, individually, had much to do with making it so—but your role in life has much to do with it. The "relations" and the "in-laws," the "children" and this so "very different" man that you have—so gifted and so talented—so "crabby" and hard to live with at times—with his moods and sensitiveness—his seriousness and the need for humor—his great need for you—his leaning—just 12 years old sometimes—just a small boy who has to be comforted—and then again, an old old man—he needs *all* that you give him—a wife—a mother—a sweetheart and a mistress—a comforter in time of stress and then a "Father confessor"—this man, pulled this way and then that way—subject to the torment of the shrieking mental winds that tear at the very soul—and that disturb not or are even heard by the vegetable human. What a terrible whipping this man's ego has been subject to these past weeks!

Would you think that a normal mind could so perform? Martha, if I could only tell the whole story—what an escape mechanism it would be for me—not alone to tell the story—which you have been so recently and presently observing—but more and added of similar, or worse, mental garbage—in the whole history and entirety of the very small portion of the whole with which, and of which, I have the knowing. I somehow feel that, in the eventual, permission will be accorded to join the whole, or part, of this story to that which Harold will eventually write. I only *feel* this, I don't know it of a surety, but I cannot help but feel also that all this added data—so illuminative of the reasonings of the human mind—should surely NOT be irrevocably and entirely lost to a seeking posterity.

No, Harold has not written to me of the speaking dates—or the subjects—at Marion, December 9th. Your mention of such was interesting quite. I have been hoping to hear that he had a sponsor for radio talks along the psychological—like the ones in N.Y. His Marion titles [*Ed.note:* the titles Harold was considering for his lectures] sound interesting. I have neither criticism nor recommendation. Harold has a good mind and I have more confidence in his choosing than I would my own—in any field—except one. . . .

Was slightly startled when I got so far in your letter where you mention the Chattanooga and Chicago possible trip. I had no idea that you folks would jump to the idea that I was suggesting in a sort of back-hand manner that you could help me with the thing. Nothing was further from my thoughts—though I do confess that I would not hesitate a bit were the same interest displayed by someone who would not miss the expense. I made a terrible mistake with the Tyson and you so very gracefully covered it by making Ma the recipient of a birthday gift a long way in advance. I must be more watchful in the future of my writings. I do not want to so transgress.

You will come to know eventually that there are many more besides Mrs. Gusler—who have been—and now are—questioning themselves and one another.

How very valuable that Diary is eventually going to be. My—my—my.

I may hear from the Matterns when they arrive in L.A. They are VERY different people from the usual. I never saw them but that little time over at your place—but they both made a very fine impression with me—and I am so glad that they are so very devoted to you folks. There are not many such in this war-weary world.

I would have to hear Ruth Kellogg herself before I would believe what has been said. I do not believe the story. Ruth would not tell the cruel and heartless lies entailed. Do not believe—unless you hear Ruth retell what has been accredited to her. You never will, I am sure.

I surely would not remain in the Forum during the "second half"—but I would be sure to be in attendance regularly during the first half.

Love to All of your very dear ones, and that comes from Auntie—Jo—Little John—Ma [illegible]—Harry

FORUM CALENDAR *November 1, 1942*

Evening at Mrs. Gusler's & Mr. Gusler.

DIARY *November 1, 1942*

FORUM—Paper 8: "THE INFINITE SPIRIT"

It was a bad rainy day when we stepped across to the Forum. Bill was reading as we entered and nodded a greeting at Christy, who sat by the door with the Doctor. His face wore a troubled expression. We found Mrs. Githens and Mrs. Gusler in the row just ahead, both of whom recognized us in a friendly manner. Bill's superior manner of discoursing between paragraphs irked us a bit more than usual. He poses so obviously as the ultimate authority.

At intermission, Mrs. Webb came back for her copy of "Eternity and I." She said to Martha, "I appreciate this more than I can say, and I am making copies to send to some friends of mine out of town. Please tell Mr. Sherman how grateful I am." Mrs. Allen also came up to thank us for the copy we gave her last week, and said, "I just want to tell you how wonderful I think your poem is. It's something I want to read over and over again." Then she asked, "Did you believe in transmigration at one time?" Harold said, "No—I felt intuitively that life evolved much as indicated in this poem, but the poem itself came to me in a moment of inspiration and we consequently feel toward it as you do." Mrs. Allen remarked upon the poem containing the entire story of the soul's evolution as told in the Urantia Book, and expressed wonder that it could have been written before we had any knowledge of Urantia. Harold said he felt that our TAs had the power to bring us individually the truth if we sought it, and Mrs. Allen agreed that this was probably so.

The Doctor, continuing on the Westminster Confession (which seems to be endless), got off on a discourse about marriage, divorce and adultery. He then jumped to hygiene and eugenics, and remarked that this was about as far afield as he had ever gone in comments since the reading of the papers began. He seemed disturbed about something and not quite himself. Bill, who remained in the Forum room for the first time during intermission, stayed also for his father's discussion and interjected intended humorous remarks from time to time which did not seem funny to us.

Mrs. Palmer invited us to her house along with the Burtons and possibly several other Forum members two weeks from this Sunday evening. (She is Mrs. Steinbeck's sister.) Neither the Haleses nor the Karles were present, probably on account of the bad weather. On the way out we were approached by a Mr. Krumbaugh [*Ed. note:* George S. Crumbaugh], whom we had seen but not met, and who expressed appreciation of the poem which Mrs. Webb had shown him. He said, "She is going to make me a typewritten copy. Do you mind?" Harold said, "No. I'll gladly give you a printed copy next Sunday." Mr. Crumbaugh made the statement that he had felt as that poem expressed for the past twenty-five years, and he believed that the real truth existed in us if we could only learn how to become aware of it.

We could seem to feel a force operating in the Forum today, almost as though some of the Forum members were getting tired of waiting for the "ban" to be lifted from us. We noted that neither Mrs. Githens nor Mrs. Gusler remained for the Doctor's half of the afternoon.

As we were having dinner at 6:30, Mrs. Gusler phoned to say that she had gone over to the Bucklins' home to have a talk with Mildred during the second hour, and that Mildred checked with the statement that the Doctor intimated that we had tried to influence the Kelloggs, through Ruth, to have the book plates removed from the Doctor's care to us. Mrs. Gusler asked if we could come over to her home in Oak Park in the evening in spite of the bad weather, and we agreed gladly to go.

We arrived around 8:30 and found we had met Mr. [Carl] Gusler before, though we weren't acquainted. His interest in developments was quite dispassionate since he had not been regularly attending recently. They got almost immediately to the point, and Harold reviewed for them our activities and attitude with respect to the contact commissioners, the Forum matters, and members since our arrival here. Mrs. Gusler read us the letter she had written Dr. Sadler some weeks before this year's annual picnic and which he had spoken disparagingly of before the Forum. The letter pointed out some of the same inherent organization weaknesses that Harold had stressed, and Mrs. Gusler promised to give us a copy.[2]

Harold then read the two letters he had written the Doctor, and Mr. Gusler remarked that they were a finely considered summary of the entire book and organization problem, in his estimation. He said he did not see why the Doctor should have found fault with the contents of these letters if he really were interested in bettering his own plans. He went on to say that it had been apparent to him for the past two or three years that the Doctor, perhaps actuated by the fact that he had been in control of this work for so long and because of his own ego and developed personal ambitions, had allowed his human desires to dominate in the assuming of a proprietary attitude.

Mrs. Gusler said, "Now that I reflect on it, I don't know why I ever removed my name from that petition. It wasn't because of fear but mainly, I guess, because of the communications which were read and the fact that the Doctor said he had been made dictator and all the rest were removing their names. If I had stopped to think I wouldn't have done it. I'm sorry now that I did. The Doctor spoke of the penalties we would all be under if we did not take our names off, one of the penalties being he would return the money we had contributed (although I don't see why that should be a penalty to us—rather one to him).

"He said that all Forum organization activity had been 'frozen' for the time being. He characterized this as a 'Sherman rebellion' and declared he had instructions to deal with you separately. We've been waiting ever since, and wondering as we've waited, for final disposition to be made of your case. We all feel that his action is not in keeping with the spirit of the Urantia papers and we cannot understand it. But I decided recently not to wait any longer, to use my own reason and see if I could get at the bottom of this. I felt it wasn't right to keep you people shut off from everybody as you have been without even knowing what accusations had been made against you. That is why I came to you as I did and told you, frankly, what had happened and asked you point-blank questions. Now that you tell me there is no

[2] The letter has not been found.

truth to the accusations, it makes things worse than ever. Please tell me, Mr. Sherman, did the Doctor ever read you the communication he said he got warning him against you?"

Harold admitted that he had, and asked Mrs. Gusler if she knew whether this purported communication had been read to any Forum members. She said, "Not that I know of, but they all know about it." Harold then said that he wouldn't reveal the details of the communication except to say it was a vicious attack upon his character and that it did not mention him by name. This amazed Mrs. Gusler, who said that the Doctor had certainly led the Forumites to believe that this communication had been specifically about us. When Harold further explained that this was not received as a written communication but was delivered verbally while the Doctor took notes, she expressed further surprise. She was shocked when Harold stated that the Doctor had said he had never mentioned this communication to a soul—not even to Christy—which made him out a positive liar.

Mrs. Gusler said one of the most damaging points used against Harold was the accusation, reportedly made by Ruth, who had withheld this information some three weeks after seeing us, to the effect that we had tried to split the contact commission and to get her parents (the Kelloggs) to seize the plates of the Urantia Book for him. Harold branded this as a total untruth and said we had simply called Ruth over to tell her of the existing differences of opinion among a wide number of Forum members and that we might have to take our stand with them; and we hoped she and her parents would understand that we did not feel unkindly toward them nor the Doctor, but that we felt certain vital issues were involved. Harold said he referred to the letters he had written Dr. Sadler and the Doctor's statement that he had not shown them to the Kelloggs. Harold asked Ruth if all contact commissioners were not supposed to pass upon questions affecting the book, foundation or organization, in anticipating the coming demand for free discussion. Harold said he felt the Doctor would be considerably disturbed, since he did not realize the great number of Forumites who felt the need for fuller participation, and Harold hoped the Kelloggs and Ruth could help keep harmony in the face of the action to come.

Mrs. Gusler said, "Well, that's certainly at variance with the story the Doctor has told, and he calls your action unforgivable, which I think it would be if true."

The high-handed manner of the Doctor's dealings with the Forum members was indicated in Mrs. Gusler's telling of how Mildred Bucklin was tearfully petitioned by Christy over the phone to get in touch with certain specific Forum members and have them make appointments with the Doctor, that something awful would happen if she didn't. This type of threat had its desired effect, and Forumites practically fell over one another trying to make amends. All members were called in by small groups, whether they had signed the petition or not, and all were filled with venom concerning Harold. As the women removed their names, the Doctor said he had been instructed to tell them that he was to signify their being taken back by a kiss.

Mrs. Gusler declared emphatically that Harold was unmistakably made out as a criminal, an actual Judas, and since he was referred to as the leader of a rebellion it was implied that any who refused to withdraw their names were also rebels. She said, despite this, the Doctor was forced to take a lot of criticism from members on his and Bill's egotistic and autocratic ways. She said he was constantly being caught up in statements that did not check from one group to the next. And in telling Russell Bucklin how he had been present in the spirit at the luncheon meeting and other meetings, he said he had seen Sir Hubert sign the petition far down the list, when in reality Sir Hubert had signed it first (at the luncheon meeting), placing his name three-quarters of the way down the page, saying he felt his name should not be among the first because he was such a new member. The "money paragraph" in the petition seemed to offend the Doctor most, and Harold pointed out that this clause was put in by Clyde Bedell and okayed by the other members.

Mrs. Gusler explained that Christy said she would rather the members would not get in touch with us as it would make it easier for the Doctor to deal with us. She said the Wednesday night Harold was supposed to talk there was a big turnout, and that Mr. Kellogg was a terribly worried man. She said his relief was obvious when the evening was over and Harold had not appeared. Mrs. Gusler agreed that this was no meeting or occasion to have corrected a grievance, and that the Forum body proper was the only one to have appeared before.

Mrs. Gusler said some of the members were remarking about some good coming of the petition, referring to the temporary suspension of organization plans and the fact that open discussion was now permitted, but she admitted that most Forum members were afraid to raise their voice for fear of incurring further disfavor and that the open discussion meetings had already dwindled to only a few members—herself, Dent Karle and Russell Bucklin being all that were present on the last Wednesday night. However, many points worthy of discussion were raised about the charters.

In commenting on one of the open discussion meetings, Mrs. Gusler said they got to talking about the power inherent in the organization charter to expel anyone who differed in opinion and who was disposed to argue these truths. The discussion was brought home by consideration as to whether the Forum members would vote to expel any such member who developed argumentative tendencies or diverse views, and Miss Edith Cook spoke up declaring she would certainly vote to remove such a person. Mrs. Gusler replied that she thought such a power to expel members was dangerous since the truth should be free and a member's views should not be placed under any compulsion. She went on to say that there are many things in the charters which need study and questioning, but she is afraid these open discussion meetings are going by default because of the intimidation of most of the members.

Mr. Gusler said he felt the human side of Dr. Sadler had gotten the best of him, and that he was now so involved he didn't know how to get out. He said he imagined the Doctor was stalling for time in the hope we would move from the city or that he could quietly adjust matters without raising any more of an issue. This same opinion, Mrs. Gusler said, was held by some Forum members, and she added, "I hope you don't have to leave. I hope you stay for several months." Mr. Gusler added that perhaps the Doctor had worked alone in his own field for so long that he did not know how to work in co-operation with others.

Harold made it clear that we did not intend to let this attack upon our characters stand and were simply waiting until everything was revealed that the Doctor held against us before taking some course of action.

Mrs. Gusler said, "Well, I don't see why it's fair for you people to keep on carrying this burden, and I'm going to do what I can to help clear things up. I'm going to speak to some of the members and tell them you deny the charges and that I think a wrong is being done you by the Doctor."

She went on to say that the indictment was almost entirely against Harold, and that he had openly taken charge of this rebellion at a meeting at the home of the Steinbecks. Harold, of course, had done no such thing. Mrs. Steinbeck had asked Harold to come over and asked him to bring his letter to the Doctor.

Referring to the communications Dr. Sadler had read, Mrs. Gusler said they were not actually communications but notes that had been taken at different times, purportedly about six months ago, during conversations the Doctor had had with the midwayer D.E.F. Harold stated emphatically that he was positive the communication the Doctor represented as being a warning against him was a creation of the Doctor's entirely and not from any higher intelligence—that it was a deliberate human attempt of the Doctor to discredit him and turn all members against him. Mrs. Gusler said she wondered if the Doctor had not reached the point where he felt he was receiving impressions directly himself, and she wondered, if he did receive any instructions from on high contrary to his own humanly determined plan of action, whether he would now respect them or even recognize them.

Harold said we could understand why Forum members would feel compelled to believe in Dr. Sadler's word for the time being or commence doubting the truth of any and all of his statements, but Harold declared all accusations to be false and said he was ready to face all accusers before the Forum body at any time.

We left the Guslers with the feeling they had been wholly frank and unreserved with us, and that at last we had been given a comprehensive and true lowdown on what had been happening.

[*Marginal note:* Mrs. Gusler was admitted to the Forum in 1935 by midwayers.]

HAROLD SHERMAN to HARRY LOOSE

Chicago, November 2, 1942

Dear Harry:

Your much appreciated letter addressed to Martha arrived this afternoon.

We are going through one of those strange and trying waiting periods just now, which we encounter occasionally . . . waiting for the next assignment or activity to develop. I have sought to sell my services on the radio again and have two programs under consideration but no word as yet.

I have interested Kiwanis International in a community cooperation project to band the leaders of all organizations in every locality together, in what might be called a Home Front Command . . . so that every community may be truly UNIFIED for the war effort. The Board of Kiwanis International happens to be meeting this week in Chicago and if they pass favorably on the idea, it can be launched in 2800 towns and cities simultaneously, and I can make the initial talk and introduction of the project in Marion, before my former "adopted home town" Kiwanis club, December 9th. The details of this We Americans plan are too much to relate here but one of my ideas is to enable millions of Americans to make their WILL and VOICE known, overnight, as to what they desire their leaders to do about problems in their home community and in the nation. . . . Sometimes, Harry, you almost lose heart and say to yourself, "Why should I sweat blood to try to save humanity from itself?" because you get so little thanks for any efforts you put forth . . . and yet, if a few of us don't even try to help matters, there's a frightful pay-off coming. It may come anyway . . . but, at least, we'll have done our best.

Mrs. Gusler phoned us last night to ask if we would come out to see her husband and herself. They live in Oak Park, and we accepted promptly though it was a cold, rainy night. We drove out in the car, of course . . . and she immediately launched upon the Forum situation as a subject for discussion. She said she had checked with the Bucklins, and that the Doctor had told them, as he had all, that I had plotted to seize the plates, through getting the Kelloggs to act for me . . . or urging them to, by my approach to Ruth in a private talk we had with her. We feel the same way you do—that Ruth herself will have to tell us she reported this about us before we'll believe it. Mrs. Gusler said, "There's no doubt about it, Dr. Sadler made you out a crook, a criminal, someone not to be trusted or associated with . . . and what could we do? If we did not accept what he told us as gospel, many of us felt we would even have to begin to question the papers themselves."

Mrs. Gusler then went on to say that quite a few Forum members were still waiting to see what disposition Dr. S was going to make of our case before they arrived at final judgment . . . but they were doing a lot of wondering. She said, as you have declared, that we had many more friends than we realized, despite the fact they have not been in touch with us . . . that everyone feels our treatment has not been in the spirit of the Urantia papers.

The little Open Discussion meetings, "allowed" each alternate Wednesday, have now dwindled to only three people in attendance this last week, Mrs. Gusler reported. The doctor, of course, wants them to die out . . . he wants no serious questions raised about his Foundation and organization plans . . . and he has intimidated many of the members to the point that they are afraid to risk his wrath again, by making any suggestions or criticisms.

You read the last letter I wrote the doctor, in which I stood by my guns . . . and told him I was sorry the scene had to occur on September 13th, which would have been unnecessary had he taken a different attitude toward us, etc. Now the doctor is telling different Forum members that I have written him I am sorry for what I have done and am apologizing for it . . . IMPLYING that I have ADMITTED MY GUILT. Meanwhile, weeks continue to go by and he does not see us again . . . but I know he is AFRAID TO DO SO. He doesn't know how to wash this mess up, since he feels we won't stand for a WHITEWASH . . . and if he tries to slide over matters, without clearing our name, he instinctively senses I will DEMAND REDRESS. I am turning over in my mind what I will do when the time comes. In the Doctor's and Bill's desperation, if they find they are going to be revealed for what they have become, I think they would stop at nothing.

Bill told me once he would challenge any message which came through if it seemed not to be in accordance with his own convictions. He also said, "I am answerable to no human being!" Dangerous talk. Mrs. Gusler said, "I'm not sure now, with the Doctor being in so deep, that he would recognize or follow any message of reprimand and instruction he might receive. He would talk himself into believing that such a message was from evil sources, so he could disregard it and maintain his selfish hold on things."

Harry, could all the papers be dematerialized and placed in the custody of someone else, if necessary? Something drastic may have to be done, in time, to protect and preserve this great work.

I certainly wish you would be permitted to give us the "rest of the story," sordid as it might be, to file away with our gathering record. Yes, the Diary is already invaluable. How well you knew what was to come! Do you feel now that you can tell us more of our own experiences back in the time of the Master? I am sure I could accept it now . . . and with real inspiration and some insight.

I pray every night, as does Martha, that we may do the will of the Father, and I hope I may be gainfully employed again soon in a spiritual as well as commercial capacity, while still caring for the situation here.

DIARY *November 2, 1942*

Harold attended the "block meeting" of Chicago's Civilian Defense at the Belair Hotel this evening and ran into Mr. Steinbeck on the way out who had also been present. Harold told him, strangely enough, that he had been thinking strongly about him and his color movies [*Ed. note:* of the 1940 Forum picnic] while the Civilian Defense pictures were being shown, and was quite surprised to get up and encounter him. Harold again stated what a pleasant time we had at their home, and Mr. Steinbeck said Mrs. Steinbeck was sick tonight with a bad cold, and being a Christian Scientist made it worse. Harold said that when she recovered he intended to ask them over, and Mr. Steinbeck replied they would be glad to come. Then Harold was impulsed to say, "You tell your good wife when you get home that we at last know the full details of the charges made against us and that we brand them as lies from start to finish."

Mr. Steinbeck looked at Harold for a moment and said, "Well, it doesn't surprise me, and I want you to know that you and Mrs. Sherman have won the admiration of the majority of the Forum members by the manner in which you have conducted yourselves through this whole unfortunate affair. The way you have come in at each Forum meeting and quietly taken your seats, keeping your place and speaking to no one unless spoken to. This has made a deep impression upon Forum members, who are doing plenty of thinking about the way you are being treated. They don't know just what to do about it yet but, I assure you, there is much favorable comment going the rounds about you. As for me, this development almost cost me my faith in the Urantia papers; but perhaps what has happened, even though it's too bad that you two have had to bear the brunt, will be all to the good. It should teach us the lesson to be able to distinguish between the human and the divine."

Harold said that we were shocked and amazed when we finally learned the full accusations that had been made, and that we still couldn't believe the Kelloggs could have been a party to it; but that we were standing up under this all right and only hoped and prayed that its ultimate outcome would not cause any members to lose faith in the Book of Urantia itself. Harold further stated that we intended to maintain the same attitude until the proper steps might be shown us, but that we could not permit these lies to go unchallenged in the ultimate. Mr. Steinbeck said, "No, I don't think you should. We can't figure out what's going on over there but some things certainly are not right."

A friend of Mr. Steinbeck's then approached him and cut off this conversation as he and Harold were walking up Diversey on the way home. Harold was also able to say to Mr. Steinbeck that the Doctor had told him in front of Christy that he had received a warning in a communication against Harold which he had not mentioned to a soul—not even Christy—but that Harold knew then that he had mentioned said purported communication to other members, the contents of which were also a lie. Mr. Steinbeck shook his head as though this kind of business was beyond him.

It seemed strange that Harold should have been impulsed to attend this "block meeting," and that Martha had also urged him to go, for we had no thought that he might meet anyone he would know.

9

Mrs. Gusler's Analysis

FORUM CALENDAR *November 2-9, 1942*

Harold and Martha decide to remain at Forum for reading of paper only and not for Doctor's discussion on religions.

DIARY *November 3, 1942*

This p.m., when we returned from downtown where we attended a movie with Marcia (Elec. Holiday), we found there had been a phone call from Mrs. Gusler. Martha phoned her back and Mrs. Gusler asked if she could drop in to see us tomorrow evening concerning some notes she had made on the present situation. As we were to have company (Martha's cousins) Wednesday night, we suggested, this being a beautiful fall day, that we could drive out to see her this afternoon. Mrs. Gusler said she would be very happy to have us.

We arrived around quarter of four and could not get away until 7 p.m. We found that Mrs. Gusler had set down on paper her analysis of what had happened in an attempt to reason out why she had been prevailed upon by the Doctor to remove her name from the petition and also to determine the true facts actually involved based on the evaluation of what had been told her by the Doctor and our own refutation of his charges. She read us the outline of her own reasoned thinking, stating that she was trying to get her mind out from under the spell or influence exercised by the Doctor and to see things as they actually were so that she could judge them accordingly. She explained that so long as she had accepted the apparent mandate of the communications which were read she, nor anyone else, had been capable of doing their own thinking. The outline she then read us proved to be a remarkably clear and penetrating crystallization of the fundamental points involved, and gave us reason to hope that if other Forum members commence evaluating the factors involved in like manner, the true state of things will be revealed and justice brought about.

As nearly as we can recall, her "thinking out loud" (as she called it) was as follows: "Do I believe that this fiendish attack of the Doctor's in casting aspersions at those who wrote letters of well-intentioned criticism and his equally fiendish manner of treating the Shermans was sponsored by spiritual sources or by his own human liabilities? Should I not, in order to judge fairly and without influence what has happened, separate my belief in the Urantia papers from identification with the Doctor and consider him on the basis of his human acts alone? What bearing did what the Doctor have to say to me, when I was called in and asked to remove my name from the petition, have to do with the points raised in the petition?"

Mrs. Gusler explained that she could now answer this question by saying it was the apparent authority of the communications which were read, one of which stated that an organization was necessary. She did not feel at that moment that she had the human right to go against a message from higher sources. Now, on reflection, she cannot understand why she removed her name. She said there seemed to have been an influence present, and when she left the first time without withdrawing her name, the Doctor said to her: "Remember in the Lucifer rebellion how some went back and forth and could not make up their minds. You had better not wait too long."

That night she had returned to remove her name, and Dr. Sadler said he had been instructed to welcome all those women, as they took their names from the petition, by bestowing a kiss. This little ceremony did not take place with her, but she said it did in the cases of the younger women, notably Miss Baumgartner, Elsie Karle, Mrs. Luther Evans, and Mildred Bucklin. This seemed a strange procedure to her, as she put it, "as though we were being returned to grace and taken back into the fold after our purported rebellion."

She again said that the Doctor referred to this as the "Sherman rebellion," as though this would go down in history alongside the Lucifer rebellion of centuries ago. Undoubtedly, this inference that the Forum members had been party to an attempted rebellion influenced many to act through fear rather than reasoned judgment.

In removing their names from the petition, all were required to draw a line through their signatures and then attest to their act by affixing their initials. Those who might not withdraw their names were warned that any money they had contributed through the years would be returned. This threat obviously made the members feel as though they would become outcasts, and since they had given their money in a free spirit toward a revelation they wholly believed in, it would make them to have now appeared as disbelievers to take a stand against the Doctor by refusing to withdraw their names. None of them, however, could really understand what connection existed between the demand that they strike their names from the petition and the points raised by the petition itself, and many so stated as they took their names therefrom, complying largely at the Doctor's request and because they did not wish to challenge his authority.

Mrs. Githens, of all the members, held out the longest against the removal of her name and only capitulated when she found everyone else was taking this action. Even so, Mrs. Gusler reported, the Doctor was compelled to take a barrage of criticism from many members who unloaded their pent-up feelings which had been repressed by his attitude through the years. When Mrs. Gusler herself removed her name she made it clear to the Doctor that she was not recanting at all from the spirit of the petition, and similar statements were made by quite a number of members. As of today, Mrs. Gusler cannot comprehend why the Doctor should have taken such extreme methods because of this petition presented in such good faith by such a large representation of members unless he, with a choice few, have some set plans which they do not wish to discuss with, or have upset by, the Forum membership.

Mrs. Gusler continued with her outline: "The Doctor told us that he had received a communication warning against the Shermans, but the Shermans now state that, not only is the communication and its charges wholly untrue, but it does not even refer to them by name. Furthermore that this was not a written communication, as any official communications have been, but that it was verbally received by the Doctor who jotted down notes on it and wrote it up the next morning. At the time of its receipt, the Doctor stated to the Shermans that he did not interpret it as applying to them but recalled it at the time the petition was presented, got it out and reread it and then realized, according to him, that it had been written about the Shermans."

Mrs. Gusler said to us that the Doctor explained to them, despite his receipt of this warning communication before we had arrived as members of the Forum, that when we did appear he felt he could "handle us" and had taken us in and let us remain. This is an obvious misstatement, since by his story to us, if he really *did* receive this communication and did not write it himself, he did not think of it as applying to us until the time of the petition. Therefore his feeling that he could "handle us" from the moment we became members, or even his knowledge that we were the ones warned against, does not apply. Mrs. Gusler said that he specifically stated and led them to believe that the Shermans had been mentioned by name in his communication and that he knew in advance that they were troublemakers but had felt he could control them. This coupled with his accusation that we had tried to plot, through the Kelloggs, a seizing of the plates and a splitting of the contact commissioners, must have seemed most diabolical and shocking to Forum members.

Mrs. Gusler raised the question in her own mind in her outline: Can the Doctor have misinterpreted this message as applying to the Shermans? Harold stated frankly and positively to Mrs. Gusler that he believed this so-called message which took the form of a psychoanalytical condemnation of us to have been written by the Doctor. She said she was not quite ready to believe this, and Harold said, "Mrs. Gusler, I do not think you could or would attribute what was contained in that so-called communication as coming from spirit sources, could you have heard it as we did. If we could ever get it read to the Forum membership, I feel they would recognize it to be of human origin: It does not stand to reason, in the first place, that any spirit intelligence would have gone into such minute detail concerning the character delineation of two people who were being warned against unless he mentioned them specifically by name."

Mrs. Gusler said, "This throws a new light on things. I think it was a great mistake for the Doctor, if he received a communication which did not mention you by name, to have interpreted it as applying to you. Of course you have read it and you feel you cannot at this time reveal its contents, but I believe your statements to me; and when you say it is entirely untrue and that it does not mention you by name, as the Doctor indicated to us, that is enough for me."

Her outline continues: "It now appears that the Doctor was not acting wholly, if at all, on instructions from higher sources on the action he took on receipt of the petition and in his treatment of the Shermans. He has been a lone wolf all his life, accustomed to dominating people by the very nature of his profession. He has never had the experience of working in association with others. Can it be possible that he is going through the stage which so many religious leaders have experienced wherein his human liabilities have gained the ascendancy over his spiritual nature? When he says he has been made 'dictator,' in place of this having been a spiritual mandate might this power not have been given him to so act by the other contact commissioners? Could he have come to believe he has been receiving messages and instructions direct from his own TA? Could this in any way account for what seems to be his confusion with the spiritual and his acting, as we feel, not after the spirit of the Urantia papers?" (Mrs. Gusler declared that practically all Forum members felt the Doctor's attitude and actions in no way reflected the spirit of the Urantia papers, and this had shocked and disturbed them as much as anything.)

Her outline continues: "It would seem to me that the foundation should exist only for the purpose of enabling its trustees to guide the destiny of the Book of Urantia in the publication, translation to other major languages and distribution of the volume. I feel that the functions of this foundation should be restricted, and the investment of monies and the power of the trustees to perpetuate themselves and to vote themselves incomes, etc., should be eliminated. I think that an organization such as the Urantia Brotherhood will someday exist through developed public interest in the Book of Urantia, but I am opposed to any structures being set up and superimposed upon the people at large. I feel that this truth should be free to all, and I would be happy to introduce all my friends to it on my own individual endorsement rather than as a member of any existing organization, and let them interpret it for themselves.

"I feel that an explanation to the effect that this revelation came through a human instrument, under observation of a medical group, [should be] made and identified with the book." She said to Harold, "Of course you don't believe that any explanation of the book's origin should be made, and that is where we differ." Harold said, "I wish to make clear that I have no set ideas and that much depends upon the exact manner in which it is done. If an explanation is made of the book's origin without involvement of personalities, I can conceive that this might be productive of much interest. But I *am* against Dr. Sadler's issuance of a pamphlet and putting his own name to it and thus personalizing the whole matter, which I feel would be pulling this great book down to a human level and subjecting it to ridicule through the Doctor's psychiatric background and his association of many neurotic in tendency. Please do not feel that because I have had some definite ideas on publication and organization, I would consider them final. I have felt, however, that the entire Forum should seriously consider and submit and pass upon any and all ideas which might relate to the perfecting of the right human plan for publishing and presenting the Book of Urantia to the world."

With respect to the selling of the book, Mrs. Gusler said that members were to be permitted to buy it at $5 a copy, but if they sold it to others the price must be $7 a copy. Bill stated to his group one night that he intended to buy as many copies as he could at $5 and resell them at $7 and make a lot of money. In this connection Mrs. Gusler said she wished to ask Harold a frank question which had been raised by her husband and which many others might raise: "Could Harold have any possibility of making a profit out of the publication arrangements he had proposed through the publisher in question?"

Harold answered emphatically in the negative, stating that he had told the Doctor if he were interested that he, Harold, would bring the publisher here to Chicago and turn him over to the Doctor. Harold further stated that he had heard intimations that the Doctor had implied he, Harold, was commercially interested, and that he had sent a sworn statement to the Doctor denying this charge, declaring his services to have been offered free and without any cost whatsoever; and furthermore, that he did not seek nor would he permit any use of his name in connection with any service which he might render in connection with the publication of the Book of Urantia—that he neither sought financial credit nor personal credit. Mrs. Gusler said that she was glad to clear up this point.

Following the reading of her outline, she ended with the written statement that the Doctor, by his attitude, his actions and his statements, had put himself on the spot—that he had definitely defamed the character of the Shermans and that she hoped the Shermans would hold him accountable and would take such steps as were necessary to clear their names. Having read this, Mrs. Gusler turned to us and asked, "What if the Doctor should refuse to clear this matter up? Could you take legal action against him?"

Harold said, "We definitely could and we may be compelled so to do. What he has said against us is slanderous and libelous. I predict now that if we brought suit his so-called communication warning against us would mysteriously disappear. He would not dare have this read in court. We can collect serious damages on these charges which he can in no way substantiate."

Mrs. Gusler said, "Well, this is a terribly confused situation but I'm at last free of the influence I believe we were all under, and I'm tremendously relieved that I can now think and reason for myself. Do you have any objections if I see some of those who were closely associated with you in the Forum and quote to them what you have said to me?"

We assured Mrs. Gusler that we had no objection whatsoever and would gladly answer any questions of any Forum member at any time. Furthermore, we were prepared to face the Doctor and Bill and the Kelloggs or anyone on any and all charges that had been made against us. We told her again how heartening it was for us to at last have been given a full picture by her of the nature of the accusations against us.

In an earlier reference to the announced intention of the Doctor to place the two Bills (Bill Sadler and Bill Hales) in charge of the foundation and organization with their seniors managing the enterprise from behind the scenes, Mrs. Gusler remarked that the Haleses really tried to live the Urantia life in their homes. She particularly commended Bill Hales Jr., and Harold also complimented his likable personality, but of course we are not well acquainted with them and have no way as yet of personally evaluating their attitude.

It was now around a quarter of seven, and as we got up to go Mr. Gusler came home. We were invited out to dinner but declined, and when we told Mr. Gusler how helpful his wife had been in giving us the full perspective on developments, he said, "Well, my wife usually reasons things out pretty accurately, and I hope this matter is cleared up for your sakes as well as for the good of this revelation. It is evident there are some things there that need correction, and I think they would have eventually come to the surface whether you people had appeared on the scene or not. It seems quite evident that the Doctor, and a little group of his selection, had developed personal ambitions which they felt were being jeopardized, and they have taken these steps in an attempt to defend them."

As we were leaving, Mrs. Gusler followed us to the door and said she would finish formulating her own thoughts and would then see some of the Forum members and would be in touch with us. It was after 7:30 when we arrived home.

November 4, 1942

To be sure we had properly quoted the Doctor's comments to us to Mrs. Gusler, Martha phoned Mrs. Gusler this a.m. and read from the records of October 1st the Doctor's *introductory* remarks to the communication purporting to be about us, his indecision about reading it to us and his intentions of seeing us in ten days to two weeks following this date, on further instructions. Mrs. Gusler said that was substantially as she remembered it, and added that she still felt her idea for an introduction to the Book (e.g. "received through mortal sources from the divine") was not out of keeping. Martha remarked that she thought either the whole story or none at all would have to be told, but that it would eventually have to be the *whole* story, as many people, who had been considered by the Doctor and told the facts, had not cared to pursue the subject further and, feeling no responsibility therefrom, had made derogatory and derisive remarks over the "pink angels," etc., to others. Also Miss Kemper's remark regarding the group with "the direct wire to God"[1] indicated that in the neighborhood, at least, comments were going about. Mrs. Gusler added, "Yes, and there were many who attended the Doctor's 'philosophical' discussions on Sunday afternoons for years before they were told to keep it a private matter." Mrs. Gusler is also continuing to favor some sort of organization, as specified as natural in the picnic communication.

[1] See p. 212 of this volume.

10

"The More We Find Out, the Less We Know"

DIARY *November 6, 1942*

Mrs. Gusler phoned at 9 a.m. to tell us that the Karles had visited her home on Wednesday night (11-4-42) from 6:45 to 10 o'clock, and that they had discussed Forum matters together because they [the Guslers] felt the Karles were as level-headed as any of the Forum members. Their conclusion had been that it would be better if no forced action or ultimatum were given. Mrs. Gusler said that she and Mr. Gusler had perhaps urged us to see it out, but the Karles felt unusual loyalty to the Doctor over long years of association. They had decided that, after all, the Doctor had been the leader and they, not being able to see clearly, felt they'd better follow along for a while. Even though we (Shermans) had every reason personally to press action, they felt we should wait until a conclusion or final action had been made on the Doctor's part.

Mrs. Karle still felt that either one had to believe the whole revelation or none at all. (This bears out Harold's contention that the identity of an organization leader becomes so intertwined with the idea itself, that if the leader's integrity is doubted, the idea also is doubted. The reaction of the Forum members to what has occurred indicates they are not living the truths of Urantia or they could discriminate and choose between the Doctor's human acts and statements and the revelatory matter itself. This dilemma they are in demonstrates that they have been intellectualizing the truth rather than spiritualizing it. The Doctor himself has not spiritualized this truth as is evidenced by his extremely unspiritual attitude and conduct.)

Mr. Karle said he had been so perplexed over the whole thing and thought perhaps unwise things had been said on both sides. They were trying to rationalize the whole situation but had noticed a very decided change and different attitude from the Doctor during the past year and a half. They couldn't understand why something affecting the whole Forum should not be discussed in the open in the Forum. They felt we had done our part in attending the Sunday Forum and in our attitude, but owing to the setup over the years they felt it better to wait than to push. Martha stated that we had no intention of pushing this matter unduly but were waiting until something definitely happened to point the way and until, in our time of meditation, we had decided upon a plan for procedure. (In this connection the past two nights Harold has opened the Bible to Habakkuk 2:1-4, inclusive, and we knew we must wait.) We felt the real issue was to be sure the Book of Urantia was properly presented and not our own personal issue. Mr. Karle also said that he felt a certain amount of fear was developing among the members even in discussion in the Wednesday night meetings.

Mrs. Gusler said there were other things she could say to us in conversation but not over the phone, and that somehow she believed "you people." She added that she had read Harold's *Key* and found it an interesting and helpful point of view, but she felt he had changed his views somewhat from the theosophical by now. She had just phoned us to let us know of her talk with the Karles. As far she herself was concerned, the situation could rest with the reading of the picnic communication (wherein the Doctor had any authority other than a regular Forum member removed).

HARRY LOOSE to HAROLD SHERMAN

Monterey Park, November 7, 1942

Dear Harold:-

I am replying to your letter of November 2nd, which arrived safely. Glad to know of your continuing contact with Mrs. Gusler. More comforting and confirming data will reach you as time goes along.

You wonder at the evil existing here amongst the knowing in high spiritual places. You would think that surely the succeeding dimension would be entirely free from such—but it is not. Just the passage from this particular dimension into the next does not change this picture, either. The succeeding dimension is not free from all evil. Such exists there too. There still continue many traits that existed in the physical. It is a long struggle upward and onward. Neither is all joy and gladness there. There are problems there, too. Remember that there is nowhere complete peace and freedom from responsibilities—from sadness—from the trials of progression—until much further progress is made than the succeeding dimension. Neither is it a place of sweet repose and laxity. The Devil will still find work for idle hands and minds. I speak figuratorily when I spoke of the Devil above—but you know what I mean. You would not be happy here with a life of slothful ease and idleness—and the real "you" will be not a whit different there. You are still the very same "you" as when you left this present flesh. Individually, you will be much more knowing because of your long past history.

The entire revelation may be completely dematerialized—and even taken from the minds of but a few here. Your Diary may eventually be the only record of such ever happening. I therefore advise you to keep it as detailed with information as possible. If this revelation is finally so disposed of—because of the reasons you so well know, it surely will be the crime of the ages. None greater than that—not even the Iscariot. I sincerely hope that this does not have to occur. However, if this does happen, your Diary will be the only true history extant. On your shoulders, by way of this diary, may fall the only story of this great happening.

O it is all too confused to try yet to translate. In my desire to acquaint you with much more of the matters of which you ask in more detail, I sometimes transgress. Please believe, it is not I withholding these things from you of my accord. It is because I have not permission so to do. I am not a free agent acting of my own volition. I am very limited in my actions—and am restricted in my mental activities to very prescribed limits. I may, in truth, tell you the following: "If it so happens that there occurs the dematerialization of the revelation, for the reasons you now know, and others that may yet be added, your book so named 'The Diary' and with fitting descriptive words following, will not be published until after your release from this planet.

The title and position of the author will be given authoritatively in the short preface."

There is a period of adjustment now in process concerning my path, immediate activities, and future, and I am under great strain. Please believe me unquestioningly—and unremarked—until I am able to explain more fully—and then you'll quite understand. And so forgive any lapse—of any kind—that may occur during this request.

Harold, for you there will always be the unsatisfied restless questing for peace—and release from responsibility—the same melancholy in the background. As long as you are in the flesh, there is no escape for you in this dimension. However, you will never return here—to be tormented by fragments of partly remembered prior earth experiences and episodes. I, too, hope that the day soon comes when you are ready to receive more—and permission is so granted.

Love from Ma and I,

November 8, 1942

FORUM—Paper 9:
"RELATION OF THE INFINITE SPIRIT TO THE UNIVERSE"

We greeted Christy cheerily as we entered the Forum room today, who stated that she had now recovered from her cold. The Doctor was not yet in his accustomed place beside her. Harold had seen him this a.m. bundled up in a heavy winter coat and upturned collar while his three grandchildren played around him. The weather was mild and he looked incongruous so attired, and *very* old.

Mr. Gusler followed us into the Forum room and slipped in our row ahead of us where his wife was already seated. We were hailed by Jim and Betty Hicks sitting just behind us who were in for the day from Arkansas. Jim looked drawn and thin and said he had just recovered from the flu, having lost 14 lbs. They were cordial as usual.

The Karles seated themselves in our row on our other side and were the most cordial they have been since "the happening." Dent stated that he expected to leave in about ten days for Alaska to be gone at least for nine months. He was eager to get in touch with Sir Hubert who was returning here in three days beginning November 10th for lectures in the vicinity. Harold promised to see if he could arrange a time for Dent to interview Wilkins and get information he desired about Alaska, so he would know what to wear and take with him. Harold asked Dent pointedly if he was to be at the next Wednesday open discussion meeting, and Dent said he was not sure at the moment but hoped to be. Harold intimated that we might attend this time.

The Steinbecks and Mr. Burton spoke to us. Mrs. Steinbeck said to Harold that she was having "one dickens of a time" getting speakers for her Seventy meetings (three speakers each time about ten minutes each), and still had two to get for Monday night's session. She said she wished she had Harold in the group to help her, which, under the circumstances, brought an amused chuckle.

Bill read, illustrating his reading with blackboard diagrams. While the material is wonderful, he lends it no human warmth or personal application in his presentation. We had decided that we would leave after the first hour today, since we are getting nothing from Dr. Sadler's dissection of other religions during the second hour and cannot see that it serves any vital purpose as concerns the Book of Urantia.

We found Mr. Crumbaugh just leaving O'Connell's during the intermission and gave him the copy of the poem "Eternity and I" he had requested last week. Mrs. Kellogg, seated at the desk downstairs, had nodded her cordial greeting as we left, with Mr. Hales slapping Harold heartily on the back as we came down the stairs.

The day was so nice that we went out for a walk through the Park, and on the way back we encountered Leone Sadler with her three children. We stopped to chat with her and the children who were eating Crackerjack for the first time in their lives and seemingly enjoying it. Little Charlie was so full that his eyes popped. Leone was her usual friendly self and said it was great to have everyone well for a change, but even so it was quite a job taking care of three kids. This was a subject we could all agree on. We told Leone that we had only stayed for the first hour and had felt we needed an outing so had left at intermission. She said she could understand how we felt and wasn't the day perfectly wonderful, which it was. It is nice to be so free in conscience as to be unconcerned over what anyone may think relating to anything we may say or do.

Mary reads each Sunday afternoon for two hours and sees various members who are all friendly to her and whom she greets cordially. She is getting much from the papers which are about Jesus and his life (papers 120 on to 197 [*sic*]).

HAROLD SHERMAN to HARRY LOOSE

Chicago, November 9, 1942

Dear Harry:

I think we should try to keep in touch during these stressful times as much as is humanly possible, without burdening each other . . . and it is certainly never a burden for me, however busy, to give time and thought to *you.*

You have heard us mention the Dent Karles before. They have been among the most steadfast and loyal of the Forumites and took a prominent part, as reported, in rounding up signers of the petition. They were bowled over by the doctor's action, and felt that they must "go along" for the time being and observe his actions and attitude and use their reason and judgment as best they could, in order to gain the proper perspective.

Mrs. Gusler, after her conferences with us, called the Karles in and told them we had denied all charges. Mrs. Karle, while she had not felt that she could inwardly believe the accusations made against us from the start, nevertheless now felt that "if she were to disbelieve the doctor, she would have to disbelieve the Urantia papers also." This DEMONSTRATES the terrific MINDAL hold the doctor has gained on otherwise sensible, normal, decent people . . . and how he has to INJECT his personality into the papers . . . when the TRUTH should have been kept separate and apart from any human interpretation or authority. The doctor is, by way of this, showing how TERRIBLE would be the situation if this Book of Urantia were published under CONTROLLED conditions. Worse religious persecution would exist than has ever come to pass before on this planet.

The Karles told Mrs. Gusler that the Shermans had made a fine impression, coming quietly to the Forum meetings every Sunday and not speaking to anyone unless spoken to, despite the accusations held over them. They counseled against precipitate action, hoping we would wait until the doctor had taken such action as he had PROMISED Forum members he would take—in punishment of us, acting on "purported instructions from above." The fact that the doctor has not disposed of our case in all this time has the entire Forum body wondering and growing in doubt.

In seeking wisdom as to what attitude to take ourselves, I was moved to turn to a passage in Habakkuk and received this apparent answer, Chapter 2:1-4: *"I will stand upon my watch, and set me upon the tower, and will watch to see what he will say unto men, and what I shall answer* when I am reproved . . . *And the Lord answered me, and said, 'Write the vision, and make it plain upon tables, that he may run that readeth it . . . For the vision* is *yet for an appointed time, but at the end it shall speak, and not lie; though it tarry,* wait for it; *because it will surely come, it will not tarry . . . Behold, his soul which is lifted up is not upright in him; but the just shall live by his faith.'"* Doesn't this sound to you like explicit instructions?

Mr. Karle told the Guslers (her husband is a peach, too, a clear-headed thinker) that FEAR was developing among Forum members, and that the Open Discussion meetings were dropping down to nothing . . . few had the courage to raise any question as to organization plans or clauses in the charters, for fear of material and spiritual punishment and the renewed wrath of the doctor.

Yesterday, for the first time, we got up and left at the intermission, as the doctor was about to begin his discourse upon the Westminster Confession of Faith, which he has been dissecting now for weeks, as an indication of HOW the Urantia truths could be adapted to the Presbyterian and kindred faiths . . . WHICH IS ALL WRONG from my viewpoint. Our job is not to try to impose a GRAFT of the real truth upon the falsities of the past. Especially when the whole story has been told, correcting the errors . . . but the doctor's idea is that we must go out like Paul and compromise and bargain for acceptance of the Truth by existing organizations, in whole or in part. The whole attitude is so cockeyed and so obviously at variance with the spirit of the papers that it is not worth discussion.

It was a nice day and Martha and I walked through Lincoln Park . . . only to run smack into Leone Sadler, Bill's wife, with her three children. She has been, on the surface at least, the same as ever toward us. We were glad she saw us and could report back that we had simply left the Forum to take a stroll and not because of something important. This will get back to the doctor who will know that we have not been staying through fear of him, to his hour . . . and that we feel entirely independent, capable of doing what we please.

Mr. Karle is leaving for Alaska, according to his present plans, to be gone for nine months. He wants to see Sir Hubert who is returning here for three days next week, November 10th, to make some lectures in the vicinity. I am sorry to see Karle go, as he is one of the most potentially strong members and had been placed in charge of Open

Discussion meetings (which, while they have not amounted to much, have at least kept a spark alive). I am wondering if I should not have a frank talk with him before he departs. I do not care if it gets back to the doctor that we now know—and are denying, all charges. *He* is on the spot; we are not.

Mrs. Steinbeck, present chairman or president of the 70 group, told me yesterday she is having "one dickens of a time" getting speakers to express their views from among the members, and what they would do in presenting the truths of Urantia when the book is out. This is an order of the doctor's, to have three members speak ten minutes each, at every 70 meeting . . . supposedly a free expression of their views. It is to LAUGH. Mrs. Steinbeck said she thinks he has done this in an attempt to embarrass them, as most of the members have never spoken on their feet in their lives . . . and that, by urging them to do so, he is further inhibiting them. She has been quite outspoken through it all . . . and got a laugh out of me when she said, "I wish you were in the 70, so you could help me!" Can you imagine how welcome I would be in this group?!! Incidentally, if this is to be Karle's last week here, because most members are intimidated, Martha and I are planning to attend the Open Discussion meeting, to show the doctor and others we are not afraid. I think it very important to demonstrate absolute fearlessness during this period, to give courage to other members who are suffering tortures with respect to their own consciences.

If material might be dematerialized, WHY would it have to be destroyed? Why could it not be given over to the other group, in Omaha, Nebraska,[1] with instructions for them to take up from this point and carry through to conclusion? The contact commissioners here know of the existence of this group, and if they got authoritative orders and their NUMBERS were read off to them, it should absolutely paralyze them. Of course, in the doctor's present state of mind, if he received any REPROOF from on high, he would interpret it as evil influences and refuse to accept it. I have no doubt that he has received instructions now which he has not interpreted as applying to him and his conduct.

Why could not certain PROVED members of the Forum be designated to carry on, and the papers taken away from the doctor and his group?

[1] The Omaha group is mentioned in Chap. 6, on pp. 118, 120, 122.

I suppose, as we were admonished to do in another inspirational opening in the Bible, we will have to "Wait on the Lord." I agree with you—it would be the CRIME OF THE AGES to have this TRUTH withdrawn after all this supreme effort to enlighten mankind.

Harry, a statement made to me by Christy was shocking. A long while ago . . . it seems long, last June. She was having dinner with us and I was remarking that the Book of Urantia dealt so authoritatively with SUPERNATURAL phenomena of a high order . . . why wasn't there something in the book explaining many so-called "psychic happenings" which millions of people have experienced. (I knew that the Doctor had a CLOSED MIND on this subject and had come to feel that he had INFLUENCED, by his attitude, all data of this nature from coming through.) Christy agreed that it would be good for a chapter on this subject to be in the book, and then she said: "Harold, you know a great deal about these things. Why don't you write up a statement as to how you think they can be explained and we can submit it and see if the Angels of Progress will okay it for the book?"

WHAT COULD SHE HAVE MEANT BY THIS? Has the doctor dared to write up HIS IDEAS of different subjects and submitted them for an OKAY. Have some discrepancies crept into this amazing document through the doctor's attempted interjection of his OWN IDEAS into this spiritual revelation. If so, he should be eventually banished, someone else placed in touch with the "instrument" as a contact commissioner, and any false writings replaced by the TRUE ONES, and any MATERIAL which should have been in the book, BROUGHT THROUGH, to the end that the Book of Urantia finally exists as intended.

This question of Christy's disturbed me no end for a while, though I was positive these Urantia papers were not the product of the doctor's mind. But why should she ever have made such a proposal to me—IF something was not right over there? I hope many of these points eventually clear up . . . Christy could tell plenty were the way ever opened up.

Our best thoughts are with you at all times . . . *Thoughts Through Space* has not sold too well yet . . . price too high, $3 now.

FORUM CALENDAR *November 10, 1942*

Sir Hubert morning talk re Forum situation.

DIARY *November 10, 1942*

This morning we received a letter from Mother Sherman in Marion, Ind. Harold is to speak there December 9th to the Kiwanis and Foreman's clubs. Martha is not planning to go because of Marcia. Mother Sherman reported having met Josephine Davis, cousin of Dr. Sadler, last Friday, and said, "She was talking about your coming and wished Martha could come, too." I said, "Oh, she can't very well because Marcia is in school." And then Jo said, "Sure she can! I have it. Marcia can stay across the street with Christy. I'll begin to work on the idea!"

This gave us the first real laugh since this strange series of events across the street began to happen. We could imagine how welcome Jo "Miss-Fix-It" Davis's suggestion would be to Dr. Sadler and Christy at this time! This places them somewhat on the spot, as Jo has probably written them by now. Since they are under obligation to the Davises for entertainment and to us for having taken them on the trip to Marion, they will almost have to reveal to Jo what has happened here or invent some alibi as to why they are unable to accommodate Marcia. They will know, through Jo, that Harold is going to Marion on December 9th and this should cause them to desire to clear up matters with us before that time. Otherwise they should be apprehensive as to what Harold might report to the Davises when he sees them. We will await further developments with interest.

About the middle of last week, Miss Penn (married name forgotten), who works as proofreader for Dr. Sadler, was encountered by Harold in the lobby of our apartment hotel inquiring after a room which was soon to be vacant. Harold learned from Mr. Mitford (desk man) that she had mentioned our name as reference, which was done, of course, without our knowledge or consent. This was a bit surprising in that people usually ask permission of others, particularly if they are not well acquainted, before giving their names as reference. She was undecided at the time Harold met her as to whether she would take the apartment or not. She did not mention to Harold her purpose in talking to Mr. Mitford, and simply exchanged greetings. Now, today, we learned from Delia, our maid, that Miss Penn is moving in on the sixth floor. Delia said she heard her speaking to Mayzie (the housekeeper), going down in the elevator, and asking, "Which floor do the

Shermans live on?" It is a coincidence that someone so closely associated with the Doctor and the Urantia papers should be coming to live in this house at this time. It is possible that Miss Penn is unaware of exactly what has happened, since she was absent from the Forum for some weeks due to a serious operation.

Harold had been told by Sir Hubert that he was returning to Chicago on this date for lectures before the Evanston Women's Club and the Chicago Geographical Society. Harold phoned him at the Rienzi Hotel at 10 a.m. and found Sir Hubert just had time to drop over for half an hour from 11 to 11:30 a.m. We told him of the charges we now knew had been made against us as revealed by Mrs. Gusler, to the effect that we had tried to plot through the Kelloggs to seize the plates of the Book of Urantia. Sir Hubert indicated the charges were incredible and said Christy had written inviting him to have dinner with the Doctor on this visit but time would not allow. However, Sir Hubert said he would try to arrange to come through here and see them next Monday night (November 16) as he returned from Lincoln, Nebraska.

When informed by us that the Doctor was making these charges to everyone, first enjoining them to secrecy, Sir Hubert said, "If he makes this request of me, I will tell him that unless I am free to exercise my own judgment, I do not care to have him make any statements at all. I see no reason why anything that is above board should be kept undercover and treated in this manner. It would seem to me, if the Doctor had any doubts about your attitude or conduct, his first step should have been to have called you over and face you with the charges, and settled the matter once and for all. I wish to hear both sides of this difficulty and come to my own decision, and then determine whether I can be helpful in ironing things out. Certainly no human acts, however reprehensible, should have any influence whatsoever upon the acceptance of the truths contained in the Book of Urantia. I believe that the book itself should stand on its own, unrelated to any human personality or interpretation. On this basis it is then up to each individual to derive spiritually what he can from the book, and any failure to gain inspiration and enlightenment from it would be his own loss. This present disturbance clearly demonstrates the troubles which might arise if too-close human association is permitted with the book after publication."

Referring to the material details of publication, Sir Hubert stated that he felt some people might have to receive a revenue from the book's earnings in order to afford to give their needed services. Harold brought out the fact that as matters now stood, Sir Hubert's and our names were the only ones remaining on the petition, and that in the light of the Doctor's human attitude we would probably always be thankful that this was the case. Harold said that we were patiently biding our time awaiting final action to be taken by the Doctor for determining what our next step should be.

We all reiterated our faith in the contents of the Book of Urantia, and Wilkins declared that he felt no human explanation of its origin was necessary—simply the statement that "here it is," and leaving it to the judgment and appraisal of individual readers to evaluate its spiritual and revelatory authenticity. In this connection he further declared that he had never liked this "spiritual mystery and secrecy" anyway, and did not think it was in keeping with the intent of higher spiritual beings and the vital interest they must have in the destiny of human creatures. Wilkins wondered if this attitude were not for the most part a plan of the Doctor's, but it was hard to believe that the Doctor, after his years of devotion to this work, should have gone so far afield as he apparently had at this time.

Harold told Sir Hubert that Dent Karle wished to communicate with him for information regarding Alaska, and Sir Hubert took his phone number and said he would call him before he left.

Harold phoned Dent Karle at 2:30 this afternoon to inquire if Sir Hubert had reached him, and Dent said that he had and was much appreciative of the information given. Harold asked him if he intended to be in charge of the Wednesday night open discussion meeting as usual, and Dent said he was not certain as yet but that the meetings would go on just the same. He said if he left for Alaska his departure would be next Monday, and Harold said, "If you are to be gone for nine months I would like to have a little chat with you before you go. Our heart and spirit interest in what happens to the Book of Urantia is just as strong now as it ever was, and a lot can happen in nine months."

Dent said, "Yes, I know, and as a matter of fact I've been planning to see you people and the Bucklins before leaving."

Harold said, "We feel just the same toward you now as we always have." And Dent said, "I am sure of that, and the same goes for us. If I don't see you tomorrow night I'll be in touch with you."

November 11, 1942

Not having attended the "open discussion" meeting since our last session with the Doctor, we felt he might construe our absence as indicative of a developed fear after his reading to us of the purported communication of warning. Having learned also that this would perhaps be Dent Karle's last conducted meeting due to his contemplated Alaskan trip, we thought it wise to attend.

We were admitted to the Sadler residence by Miss Vincent, who sat at the desk and was doing double duty, rendering a service and reading some of the papers at the same time. We found upon reaching the Forum room only four members to be in attendance, including Russell Bucklin, who was acting as chairman in the absence of Dent Karle. The other three were Mrs. Gusler, Miss Baumgartner and Mr. Steinbeck. They were in the process of discussing clause by clause the charter of the proposed Foundation but all greeted us cordially as we came in, and Russell Bucklin was particularly friendly in his replies to Harold's questions and comments throughout the evening.

The little group was discussing the money setup. It was brought out that around $20,000 had been originally subscribed through voluntary contributions but that an attempt was being made to raise an additional sum of $25,000 to set up an office and publish the first edition and cover expenses for one year's operation. This campaign is still going on and pledges have been taken, but since the organization plans have been "frozen" it is possible that contributions have been temporarily held up, since Caroline Brown was not permitted to pay in her money when she volunteered shortly after this petition matter came to a head. Russell Bucklin said he understood Bill Hales was soon to make a financial statement to the Forum, something which had been intended to take place at the first reconvened meeting (on Sept. 13) but for Harold's upsetting of the program through his appeal from the floor.

Russell continued his reading of a clause covering the stated purposes of the Foundation and which contained the declaration of the intended fostering by this Foundation of a "religion, cosmology and philosophy." Everyone present challenged this declared purpose,

Miss Baumgartner saying she had never understood that a new religion was to be formed. She went on to say that she hadn't thought the power to disseminate the Urantia truths was to be contained in a Foundation but rather that this function would be one of the duties of the Urantia Brotherhood. She said, "At this rate the foundation has all the power and we have none, and the Brotherhood is just a slave organization, nothing more than a rubber stamp."

The others seemed to concur, and it was brought out that the trustees, who would probably initially be comprised of most of the present contact commissioners, possessed absolute powers of administration and also the power to perpetuate themselves in office or to elect any new trustee to office. The trustees were to be limited to five in number, and from indications and comments made to us by the Doctor the first five trustees would likely be the five "Wills" (i.e., William [*Ed. note:* G. Willard Hales] and [his son] Bill Hales, Dr. William and Bill Sadler, and Wilfred Kellogg). Miss Baumgartner pointed out that no time limitation had been specified wherein the trustees must vote to replace a deceased or retired trustee, and that those remaining could remain in power by exercise of proxy rights on behalf of absent trustees or by failing to appoint anyone to take their places. Even two trustees, or one, under such circumstances could exercise full and absolute power.

This caused Mr. Steinbeck to make a humorous but pointed comment: "The more we find out the less we know." In response to this, Mr. Bucklin said, "I think every Forum member should personally read and appraise these charters. As matters now stand the organization plans have been 'frozen,' but I feel it is our duty to continue studying this setup in the faith that, if we persevere, the questions we raise will eventually, either through the mortal commissioners or direct, reach the Angels of Progress and enable us specific instruction as to what course to pursue."

Mr. Bucklin went on to say that the articles of the charter were too "lengthy and cumbersome" to permit of intelligent Forum body discussion, and that he felt that the contribution of our criticisms and ideas would have to be made on an individual basis. Both Mr. Bucklin and Mr. Steinbeck said it was impossible to grasp the meaning and points through a simple straight reading to the Forum body. Miss Baumgartner felt there was a value in discussing the points with others, as sometimes points were thus clarified. Harold then asked if it would not be possible for this little discussion group to draw up a list of their own recommendations and submit them to the Forum body, which might serve to arouse the interest of other Forum members in making an individual study of the charters.

Russell said, "No. The Doctor will not permit it."

Miss Baumgartner spoke up, saying, "I don't know whether this might be considered out of order but, as I see it, there are three types of Forum members: (1) those who are ambitious to be teachers and who are not at all interested in the organization and financial plans but only in the spiritual truths; (2) those who are definitely afraid to question the plans as outlined, who have said to me that they would consider it wrong or sinful to do so; (3) those, like us, who are interested in studying and questioning the foundation and organization plans—but they are very much in the minority."

Mrs. Gusler asked, "Has an actual mandate ever been issued that we originate and set up an organization?"

Russell Bucklin said, "No. But after we had done so, a communication was recently received saying an organization was absolutely necessary." He stated further, "I personally don't think it is, but since there has been such communication I think we've got to go ahead and have as strong a foundation as we can to protect it. Even so, it won't be any more powerful than the Catholic Church."

Harold said he hoped not, and Martha added that with all the power the Catholic Church possessed it ruled its followers more through fear than love of God. Harold then asked point blank, "Can you say, Russell, how recently these communications were received? Did they refer to the 'ideaist and idealist' attitude toward spiritual dissemination of the truth, and did the communication further state that if no organization was established, within five years more than fifty unauthorized organizations would spring up?"

Russell said, "Yes. That was the substance of the communication. It was purported to have been received a short time before the presentation of the petition, and I think of course we should follow these instructions."

Harold said, "Russell, I feel I must state to you people here that these messages were reported in detail to me by the Doctor early in August, in attempted answer to some of the questions I had raised on organization matters. He told me at the time he had never read these communications but said they had been received by him a year and a half ago." Russell or anyone else made no reply to this statement. Harold did not press the point.

Mrs. Gusler offered the observation that she had always thought the Forum members were a vital part of this spiritual development, but now she had come to think that we were only in continuance through the "graciousness" of the commissioners. Miss Baumgartner said, "If this is so, if we really have nothing to say, then what's the use of spending our time deliberating on these matters since no attention will probably be paid to what we may think or recommend?"

Russell Bucklin answered, "I feel it is my duty to make known my judgment regardless."

Miss Baumgartner said, "I get your point. If the Angels of Progress are to be in charge of this work for the first hundred years, perhaps our questionings may draw some enlightenment from them. I guess I'll accept it as a personal duty even if nothing comes of it."

Points brought out in the charter in sections II and III were that the duty of the trustees was to preserve the purity of the Book of Urantia in translations, etc.; that they had absolute control and custody of all funds to expend in any manner they alone deemed necessary; they controlled the trust estate, funds, money, increments and profit therefrom, to invest, reinvest, buy and sell property, being authorized ("by whom?" interpolated Russell) so to do according to their sole discretion, "as though they owned it" in the United States and elsewhere, with no restrictions whatsoever and no personal liabilities in case of loss.

Harold remarked that the charter granted such freedom to speculate with the funds received that a series of bad investments, or mismanagement, could actually jeopardize the existence of the Book of Urantia itself.

Miss Baumgartner supported the statement, saying, "Yes, and if the foundation ever got in serious financial difficulties, it could be sued; and, since the book and its plates could well represent the only basic value or asset left, these could be seized for payment of debt."

Harold emphasized that the job of publishing, translating and distributing the Book of Urantia was big enough to command the best thought and attention of the trustees without their handling the financial investments. He said he would feel better if the management and direction of the book were completely divorced from any financial manipulations and transactions in its behalf. All seemed to agree that they would feel more satisfied if the handling of the book were not placed on such a commercial basis and particularly if no references to the "fostering of a new religion" were made in the charter.

An interesting comment was made by Miss Baumgartner to the effect that some blank pages had been left at the front of the book, which inferred that some important revelatory material was yet to come through, perhaps shortly before publication, to fill these pages.

After this session we invited Mrs. Gusler and Miss Baumgartner to have some hot drinks with us at O'Connell's. They accepted, and Mrs. Gusler let us read from her notebook the address she had given to the Seventy on the subject of how she would present the Urantia truths to the world. It was a well-considered statement, a copy of which she has promised to give us.[2]

Harold said privately to her that he thought the Doctor and those across the street were wondering how long we intended to stay in Chicago; that we had had indirect queries made and offers of apartments but had given no indication of how long we would remain. With Marcia in school, they have probably decided we will stay until the end of the first semester. If we left without our personal status being cleared up, we feel the Doctor would indicate to the Forum that he had been instructed we would soon be gone and that he, charitably, had let us go our way, leaving the members under the impression, however, that we had been guilty. Harold made plain to Mrs. Gusler that we would not leave Chicago without bringing this situation to a head, for the good of the Book of Urantia and the peace of mind of all Forum members.

She said she had not spoken, as yet, to the Bucklins and thought it wise not to speak to many, but the Bucklins may have heard through the Karles of our denial of the charges.

Miss Baumgartner said again that she was convinced the Doctor would not consider *any* suggestions made by Forum members, and unless the Angels of Progress took action she had no hope of any changes being made. When she got up to go, she said she had not written Harry Loose a report of happenings as yet because she had been too confused and had not settled things in her own mind.

[2] See Appendix D.

Mrs. Gusler took Harold to task on one point, saying, "You committed a faux pas, didn't you, when you said that you didn't think the Doctor should give his talks on comparative religion, because this procedure was approved of in the last official communication read at the Haleses' picnic."

Harold said, "Regardless of this, it is my feeling that the discussion of the book publication and organization plans involving the destiny of this spiritual revelation is much more important for consideration than listening to any talks on different religions." Harold went on to say that both the Doctor and Bill seemed to be more interested in the intellectual appraisal of the Book of Urantia than its spiritual appreciation.

Mrs. Gusler said, "I don't know as to that. Have you ever heard the Doctor at the Seventy meetings? He's wonderful!"

She then went on to say that beginning Sunday, November 22, the Monday and Wednesday night meetings are to be added alternately to the Sunday afternoon meetings in order to conform to the gas rationing edict.[3] The Sunday Forum meetings are to start at 2:30 and continue to 4:15 including the reading of one paper, however long, and the Doctor's talk on religion, with a five-minute recess between. Then from 4:15 to 5:30 the regular meeting of the Seventy or Bill's class will take place as the case may be. Miss Baumgartner said she personally couldn't sit this long and that she would begin coming at 4:15. This was quite a stretch for any of the members, and it will be interesting to see how they hold up under it.

ARA *November 12, 1942*

Listen now in the night seasons, for a voice is soon to speak to you.

This Voice can only be heard in the stillness of your inner temple wherein I, Ara, reside, to watch over the child that is your evolving soul.

"Except ye be as little children, ye cannot enter the Kingdom of Heaven," Christ Michael said, when on earth.

A child looks up to his human father without question and with all faith. You must become conscious of the child of your own spirit which your life experience is creating within you and

[3] U.S. President Roosevelt had issued a bill which allowed most car owners a maximum of four gallons of gasoline per week. This measure went into effect on December 1, 1942.

have faith in me, who am acting for the Father as we work together to conceive a soul and give it embodiment for our joyous journey through the worlds of time and space, to come at last to the Home which the Father of all has provided for us.

The Father is mindful of your prayer, "Thy will be done." And yet, with you, as with many, the flesh is weak. "Of myself I am nothing," the sages of ages have said. And they have drawn from the night seasons, through close communion with those on High, the wisdom and sustenance so needful to great earth accomplishment.

Surrounding you and your dear one are a battery of powerful intelligences awaiting the earthly hour when you are to be called to the true work of the Kingdom.

Be not too disturbed during this trying waiting period. The planetary turmoil is upsetting to all human life and will be more so. But guidance and protection will be accorded you in moments of real and pressing need.

Meanwhile, give increasing spiritual ear to the instruction that is to come—and know that all is really well and the opportunity you seek will come.

Relax and feel my presence for I am truly with you. I am working in closest cooperation with him who indwells Martha for your destiny is as one and you will move forward together. Be of good cheer.[4]

HARRY LOOSE to HAROLD SHERMAN

Monterey Park, November 13, 1942

Dear Harold:-

Yours of November 9th arrived okay and I haste to get this back to you.

The stench and tempest across the street grows worse. You and I are not the only horrified observers—and I do not refer only to those of the Forum that refuse to submit their wills and reason. Amongst other things, there has been some personal interjection—in addition to some purposely mistranslated matter now appearing in the record. The removal of Mrs. S is responsible for MUCH. I warn you again that the Haleses are concerned. Avoid them as you would a pestilence. Christy knows much—is much involved—innocently—the in-

[4] In Harold's November 17th letter to Harry Loose (see pp. 388-390) he recounts the "unusual experience" he had following the reception of the Ara message.

nocent bystander that sees the crime committed—entrapped. This, in addition to other things. Her very soul is sick. What a story she could tell. BUT she is filled with FEAR—deadly—horrible—shaking fear.

The group at Chattanooga—the Omaha group—and the other Chicago group—are most peculiarly situated—wholly unable of explanation—only to say that none are as far advanced as 533—none are prepared to receive such transfer as your letter suggests. The furthest advanced—and oldest—is Omaha. If there does come dematerialization, the whole structure will fall—nothing will be left.

I most certainly would unburden the entire matter to Wilkins. He has a present share of responsibility—and more later. He should know everything you can tell him of the setup. I surely would have a full talk with Karle also—if you have confidence in his intelligence and ability to reason.

When you think it is the proper time, I would surely get word to S that you are still waiting for absolvement—or sentence. In your talk with Karle, you could drop a hint of possible legal action being very justifiable. This would return to S naturally—with sudden and surprising results. I would also surely continue with attendance at the Forum—and not lose touch with the Guslers—or any others reachable—they would be needful in any future serious operation. In attending the Forum, show absolutely no fear—be completely at ease—and perfectly calm—remember that both you and Martha are very fully protected.

Yes, I would accept your Habakkuk as a directed message. It is so clear as to be hard to understand otherwise.

How often have I told you that the next dimension is NOT free from evil—sorrow—and a death much similar to that of this earth—that there is sadness—and melancholy—and FEAR existent there—very much the same as is known here.

(I wish that you would have Martha read slowly to you the ENTIRE 14th Chapt. of St. John. Read it when least likely to be disturbed—and preferably at the close of the day. Just "let go" and absorb it all.)

I beg you please to believe me when I tell you that this whole "experiment" has been under very interested observance by many higher intelligences. The whole revelation is so very much needed in this sad and sick dark world. It is so badly needed—without any additions or explanations by erring humans. I, too, cry that it should not be lost to a soul—ill humanity struggling here for more "light." What a most awful crime if it is taken away and naught left (but your writing of a Diary—as a remembrance of what the whole world had lost)—because of a very small group of a selfish, greedy few, seeking their own aggrandizement and pecuniary profit. O if Dr. Lena had but only lived—how different all would have worked out.

I warn you once more—do not get entangled in any way with the Haleses. Do not even sit near them in the Forum if it is possible to avoid. I warn you. Can you visualize Bill S going down in history—or the other Bill either—in the prominence of another Matthew—Mark—Luke—or John??? I cannot. What a mockery—what a mockery.

There has been much interference with my reception this past period. Confusion—lack of power—partial full reception with much fading of intelligibility. I have had periods similar to this before but never over so protracted a time-space. I have been unable to definitely ascertain the cause—and contacts ignore requests for aid in adjustment. Keep me advised. Love to all—from all—

DIARY *November 14, 1942*

Dent Karle phoned from our lobby at 6 p.m. to say he and Elsie would like to come up and see us if it would not interfere with dinner. Harold told them to come ahead. Dent announced he was leaving for Alaska Monday night, and said he guessed he owed us an apology for their not having gotten in touch with us sooner but there had been so much fall work to do around their yard, etc., together with other social obligations in Oak Park,[5] that this had not been possible. Elsie declared they had seen little of any of the Forum people except possibly the Bucklins, they having had Mildred out one weekend almost threatened with a nervous collapse. Elsie said Mildred could not stop talking, and Dent said, "We didn't see how Russell had stood up under it, as Mildred had almost lost her mind over these happenings."

Dent went on to state that he had decided not to let these developments affect him personally or to let other members of the Forum see that he was disturbed. He felt this was necessary to help maintain the morale of the group in the interest of the Book of Urantia, as most members were frankly puzzled over the Doctor's reaction to

[5] The Karles lived in Elmhurst.

the petition and his manner of treating us. He said, "Don't think a lot of us took this thing lying down. We talked back to the Doctor and told him just what we thought, and he handed out considerable abuse to us. He has done this from time to time through the years, so a number of the members are accustomed to this attitude. Apparently he simply cannot tolerate any interpreted challenge of his authority. Having experienced such an attitude over the years, I am convinced that no suggestions or recommendations any of us can make can ever change his plans or intentions. Our only hope is that the Angels of Progress will answer our plea and our best thought through the questions we raise, and issue specific instructions for such changes as must be made to protect the Book of Urantia in its presentation to the world."

Elsie Karle said they were confident things would adjust themselves in time and admitted that the Doctor had told Forum members not to speak to us, implying he had received instructions for dealing with us in a special manner and that they should hold off any contact with us until after this was done. Dent Karle said it was obvious now that the Doctor was at a loss as to how to dispose of us and that many members were not inclined to believe the charges made, but were simply waiting to let time and events determine the final real status of things. He said he was sure we had more friends and more sympathy among Forum members than we realized, but that many of them were actually superstitious and deathly afraid of going against the Doctor's mandates or doing wrong in any way. He said, "Of course, there was a smaller group, old-time women, almost idolatrous worshippers of the Doctor and Bill, who would accept anything unquestioningly that they said or did."

Harold remarked that he regretted to observe that very little spirituality was being gotten out of the papers in the manner presented, and that few of the members seemed really inspired to try to make these truths a part of their daily lives. Dent said yes, that this was true, and that he was really appalled at the attitude of many in the Forum. Martha pointed out the danger in a public organization if the minds of a small, supposedly spiritual group like this could be influenced as they had, and stated that we were taking a stand against this conduct, not just because of ourselves, but for the ultimate good of the Book of Urantia and its representation.

Dent said, "Yes, this is a serious situation and I don't see, now, how it is going to be corrected. It is evident that the Doctor and Bill are in charge and intend to keep control at all costs. There are many things about the charters for foundation and organization that I don't like, and I hope they are never established in this form. It's possible, I don't know, that world conditions may require such dictatorial handling as outlined but I would not like to believe it. Personally, I intend to offer my criticisms and suggestions and put them on file against the time when the plans may be 'unfrozen,' at which time I hope the Angels of Progress take a hand. I think a Brotherhood will come along eventually but that the Book should be issued on its own at first."

Harold said that we appreciated being reassured that many of the members had not condemned us as had the Doctor, and Dent said that a few of the members must certainly have gotten in touch with us, Clyde Bedell for one. Harold said, "Yes, Clyde did phone after making his own peace with the Doctor and inferred he believed the charges against us, and urged me to go over and see the Doctor and to humbly ask forgiveness and ask to be reinstated under peril of being removed from the Forum. We, of course, refused to do any such thing since we had no sense of guilt." Dent said, with apparent disgust, "Yes, I know. Clyde's that way. That's the way he does things." Harold said, "He's wishy-washy," and Dent laughed and said, "Yes, I guess that's it."

Harold referred to the charges purportedly made by Ruth Kellogg that we were trying to plot to have her father and mother seize the plates of the book, and said these accusations were so incredible we could still not believe the Kelloggs had made them. He said also that the purported communication warning against us, which the Doctor had read to us, was absolutely untrue and fictitious. Harold asked Dent if he knew of the Doctor reading this communication to anyone, and Dent said he thought not, but that the Doctor *did* say he had been warned against us by a communication. Elsie and Dent both admitted that this statement, coupled with the Doctor's charges, had made a strong impression on Forum members, and that many did not see how the Doctor would dare make such charges if they were not true.

As we learn more and more of what really happened, we can understand and sympathize with the terrible quandary all Forum members have been thrown in. We can also appreciate that some members who took a leading part in getting names on the petition have been chastised by other Forum members fanatically loyal to the Doctor as well as by the Doctor himself. This whole situation has actually shaken the Forum body, so to speak, from end to end.

Dent said, on leaving, that he hoped to see Wilkins in Alaska and asked if Wilkins had been called in by the Doctor with the request that he remove his name from the petition. Harold said no, but that Wilkins was planning to be back in Chicago Monday (the 16th) and was going to see the Doctor but that he was reserving the right to use his own judgment with respect to anything the Doctor might tell him. We assured Dent that our only interest was in the best possible development for the Book of Urantia and that we would act accordingly no matter what happened.

11

Mrs. Palmer's Dinner Party

FORUM CALENDAR *November 15, 1942*

Guests of Mrs. Grace Palmer for Sunday evening supper. Also Burtons, Steinbecks, Miss Hoffman, 2 relatives Palmer.

DIARY *November 15, 1942*

FORUM—Paper 10: "THE PARADISE TRINITY"

As we entered the Forum room Christy smiled and greeted us, and the Doctor raised his hand and said, in a voice almost cheery, "Hi." We passed on in and took our seats. Mr. Crumbaugh called to Harold to tell him how much he appreciated the poem and that he had almost committed it to memory. None of the Haleses were present, and Mrs. Githens and Mrs. Gusler were absent as were the Karles and the Bedells. The attendance had dropped off sharply.

Bill, who read as usual, was more generous with his comments and drew geometric equations on the blackboard to illustrate different spiritual statements made in the papers. His comments and illustrations were involved and non-understandable, tending to reduce these spiritual concepts to the mathematical. According to Bill's explanation, you have "to distort the truth in order to comprehend it." Actually, if members were permitted to listen only to the papers, without the interposing of Bill's own personality and views, they would be enabled through the aid of their own developed knowledge and the guidance of their TA's to perceive the truth for themselves. This opportunity, however, has never been given them through all the years that Bill and the Doctor have had control of the Forum body.

Bill took time out to emphasize that the Trinitized Deity—Father, Son, and Infinite Spirit—never sat in judgment upon any of their creation. Bill said, "Remember this, some of you, whenever you are tempted to sit in judgment upon any of your fellow humans." This was an amazing statement in the light of the lack of justice and mercy and human consideration shown us by Bill and the Doctor, and indicates how blind they are to their own faults and practices as measured by the spiritual principles revealed in the Book of Urantia.

This paper ended with an inspired reference to the Finaliters, a high order of spiritual beings whose ranks we are ultimately destined to join, if we survive physical death, and [the message] that the children of time who qualify are destined for an unimagined great service on behalf of the Father in the outer space levels beyond the present Grand Universe where new worlds are even now being formed. It was a breathless glimpse into man's possible eternal future, and concluded by stating that even though we pursued our Godward quest for an eternity, it would require an eternity to comprehend God. This brief mention of the contents of this paper indicates again the transcendent quality, knowledge and inspiration it contains.

We left at the intermission as we have now decided to do, and were told by the Steinbecks to meet them in the lobby of their apartment house at 5:15 p.m., that they would drive us to the home of Mrs. Steinbeck's sister, Mrs. Palmer, also a Forum member, who had invited the Burtons, Mrs. Hoffman, the Steinbecks, Mr. Steinbeck's sister, Glenna Johnson, a Mrs. Walton and ourselves for dinner.

We found Mrs. Palmer to be occupying one of the largest and most attractive apartments we have ever been in[1] and sat down to a really sumptuous and most delicious turkey dinner. The conversation was not on Forum matters except that Harold remarked on the big words Bill had used in his attempted explanations of the papers and Mr. Steinbeck said, "Yes, he used one ten-cent word and one fifteen-cent word!" Mrs. Hoffman spoke up and said, "Well, I can't understand what he's talking about lots of the time, can you?"

[1] Mrs. Palmer lived at 2130 N. Lincoln Park W.

After dinner, Mrs. Steinbeck was able to say to Harold that the Dyons had proved to be the big troublemakers and that they were the tattlers who had gone to the Doctor with big stories about different Forum members and that now, with things turning out as they had, the Dyons were lording it over some of those who had taken active part in the petition.

She said, "The Dyons don't even speak to me but I don't let that bother me. They seem to think they have a special stand-in with the Doctor and that they are superior to a lot of the rest of us. One of Mrs. Githens's friends of long standing has been turned against her by the Dyons. They are doing a lot of hobnobbing now with Miss Douglas and some of her friends. There's a lot of feeling under the surface, and the Doctor himself, I understand, has admitted to a few intimates that he feels he 'acted like a damn fool' during this period. He told so many different stories on you people to different Forum members that he's all balled up, and I think he's gotten in so deeply now that he doesn't know how to get out.

"Just how this is all going to turn out, I just don't know, but I'm sure having one heck of a time getting three speakers every other Monday night to express their views on what they expect to do for the Book of Urantia when it comes out. Lots of them don't know what they would or could do; some are afraid to express their opinions; some just aren't interested; and quite a few don't like to speak in public. I don't know what the Doctor is really trying to accomplish in the way he's going at it, or whether he is just trying to embarrass us and demonstrate that we really aren't competent to make any plans or take any action on our own. It doesn't make much sense to me, but I'm doing the best I can and hoping we'll come out somewhere. Lots of members are wondering a great deal about why he doesn't do something one way or the other about *you* people, and some of us are deciding he just doesn't know what to do." Harold was interrupted and no further discussion was held on the Forum subject.

We spent the most delightful and unrestrained evening that we've ever spent in the company of any members of the Forum, and both felt that the attitude of Mrs. Palmer, the Burtons, Mrs. Hoffman and the Steinbecks was unmistakably cordial and genuine.

12

Sir Hubert Investigates

FORUM CALENDAR *November 16, 1942*

Sir Hubert again Chicago. Morning talk re Forum followed by lunch at Adventurers Club guests of John Matter.[1] Sir Hubert interviews Bedell 3:30 p.m. and has dinner with Doc and Christy in evening. Reports to us 10 p.m. to midnight.

DIARY *November 16, 1942*

Sir Hubert phoned around 10 a.m. having made the trip from Lincoln, Neb., where he had lectured last night, for the express purpose of devoting today to seeing if he could get at the bottom of the things that had been happening at 533 Diversey by interviewing Clyde Bedell, who wrote the petition, and then seeing the Doctor and Christy at dinner in the evening. Wilkins dropped over to see us and we finished telling him all that we knew of developments, and he said he now wanted to get the story from the "other side." He asked that he might read again a copy of the petition, and when he had done so, said, "I see nothing objectionable in it which should have caused the Doctor to act as he has. I might have expressed things a little differently myself but the requests made in the petition seem reasonable." We all remarked again upon the great accomplishment of the Doctor through the years and expressed regret at his present conduct.

[1] A friend of the Shermans from Marion, now living in Chicago.

Wilkins said he hoped that he would be able to effect some sort of a reconciliation by suggesting that all concerned get together with the mortal commissioners and talk their differences out. Harold said he would be greatly surprised if this suggestion were welcomed by the Doctor, as he had refused Harold's request for an airing of the charges against him before the contact commissioners. Wilkins felt nevertheless that he should make such a proposal after listening to what the Doctor had to say and give him the chance to straighten things out. Harold urged Wilkins to learn what he could and to make up his own mind about the status of things, we all agreeing that the destiny of the Book of Urantia was the all-important factor in this controversy. [*Marginal note:* Wilkins stated that he couldn't believe the higher powers would let two men such as Bill and the Doctor stand in the way of the proper presentation of this truth to the world.]

Harold then took Wilkins to the Adventurers Club of Chicago, where they were guests of John Matter for lunch, and met and talked with some of the members. Wilkins then went on from there to call upon Clyde Bedell at the Fair Store.

At a little after ten tonight Sir Hubert phoned from downstairs and came up to see us. He had just left the Doctor and Christy but reported first upon his visit with Clyde Bedell. He said Bedell declared Harold had taken an aggressive attitude toward the Doctor and stated that his [Harold's] conscience was clear, intimating that Harold had seen the Doctor alone on this occasion. The Doctor, in the face of this attitude, had refused to discuss matters with Harold and decided to wait until things had cooled off. This entire report, however Bedell got the idea, was untrue as our previous records will show. Bedell's story agreed in general, according to Wilkins, with the account we had given him of developments. Bedell admitted that the Doctor had said he had received a communication from higher sources warning against the Shermans, and also that the charge had been, through the Kelloggs, that we had tried to plot for them to seize the plates. The few Forum members that we have been able to speak to and query about the two above points have had a knowledge of them.

Bedell's interview apparently added little to the picture Wilkins already had of developments, but Wilkins' session with the Doctor and Christy tonight cast some real illumination. Wilkins reported that the

Doctor said he could not forgive Harold for quoting to Forum members statements made to him in private, although he admitted Harold may have thought he was acting in good faith. Both Bedell and the Doctor emphasized that they did not think the petition would have been presented had it not been for "Harold's forceful personality and organizational ability."

Wilkins told the Doctor he could not believe, knowing Harold as he did, that Harold would ever have plotted to seize the plates. The Doctor said no, that he didn't believe that either. This was an astonishing turn-about-face, since this was one charge that we have substantial evidence was made to most, if not all, Forum members. The Doctor went on to say that as far as he was concerned he was saying no more about it and intended to let time heal the situation. He said the Shermans could go about and talk to little groups and eventually straighten things out.

He said that he and Christy were sorry the Shermans had not come over to read any more papers following this disturbance, and yet they had hardly known any two people who apparently believed any more thoroughly in these papers on short notice. (Of course it is obvious, though perhaps not to Sir Hubert, why we have not either felt in the mood or free to do any reading. The attitude of all at 533 Diversey has not suggested that we would be welcome.)

Wilkins said frankly to the Doctor that if the petition, when presented, had been proved to be unnecessary, he had hoped the Doctor would be magnanimous enough to have so explained this fact to the Forum members and then torn it up. Wilkins implied it was regrettable that so much fuss had been made over this matter. The Doctor avoided direct comment on this but said his greatest difficulty had arisen from Forum members who had not signed the petition who wanted to fight with those who had. He said six people had come to him and asked to have their names taken off the petition and the rest had finally done so.

(At the start of this discussion, Bill Jr., who had been present, walked out on the Doctor, Christy, and Wilkins, saying he had work to do and wanted no part in this. The Doctor remarked that Bill had said he would never forgive Harold, but that the Doctor and Christy did not feel that way. He said the Forum members resented the favoritism that had been shown Harold and the hospitality extended, and that while the Shermans were as free to attend the Forum meetings and read the papers, they could never again occupy the same close social position.)

The Doctor went on to say that he still would like to consider some of Harold's publication ideas, but he wanted to forget these [other] matters and have the Forum forget them. He claimed that he never discussed such problems of business before the Forum body and would not permit its being done. This did not seem consistent with some of the matters that, we know, from time to time have already been presented to the Forum as a whole. Wilkins asked the Doctor what he thought might be done in the way of an adjustment, and the Doctor intimated that he himself was going to do nothing but let time work things out. This would mean that he intends to let the untruthful statements made against us remain as they are, and to never face us with them or give us a chance to directly deny them. If we are shown to have been taken back into the Forum with nothing having been said by the Doctor to the Forum body, the implication would then be that our probation period was now over, that we had done sufficient penance, and that we had been taken back into the fold through the grace of the Doctor.

Wilkins, who has been misquoted in a public way many times, seemed to feel that we should make our peace if it could honorably and consistently be done, and let acquaintance with increasing numbers of Forum members give the lie to the accusations. Wilkins felt also that if wrong steps were taken by the Doctor or Bill at some future date, they would then become apparent to all, and action might be taken to correct them.

It now becomes shockingly clear that the Doctor's method of telling various stories about us and making different charges to successive little groups of Forum members has created great confusion and bewilderment, and it has become difficult to determine just what is what. The fact that the Doctor instructed no one to get in touch with us and refused to deal with this whole situation frankly and simply in the open certainly indicates some hidden personal motives. Since he said he would get in touch with us again himself when ready to see us, we feel it his move, and intend at this writing to wait him out unless other definite steps should be plainly indicated.

We thanked Wilkins for his efforts to clarify the situation. He said the Doctor was looking much older than when he had seen him a few months ago. It is evident from Wilkins' report that the Doctor does not dare to face a showdown with us on the charges he has made, and hopes they will die out with time.

After this writing and getting ready for bed, Harold reached for the Bible and opened up to Job 20:15-29, inclusive.[2] This seemed to be an answer to our questioning as to what our attitude should be from this point on with respect to the Doctor. The indication seems to be that the Doctor will be dealt with by higher forces at the proper time.

HAROLD SHERMAN to HARRY LOOSE

Chicago, November 17, 1942

Dear Harry:

When things happen here, they happen in bunches! I wish I could use telepathy like we use the telephone and make a two-way connection with you.

Sir Hubert was here yesterday, arriving just as I received your letter wherein you said I could tell him everything. This I proceeded to do before he went downtown to interview Clyde Bedell at the Fair Store, where Bedell is advertising manager. You see, Bedell drew up the petition and Wilkins wanted to get his story before having dinner with the Doctor and Christy last night.

About 10:30 last evening Wilkins came direct from Dr. Sadler's to our apartment and gave us his report. He said Bedell told about the same general story that we had told him about developments, with the exception that we had gone over to see the doctor in a defiant mood, "stating our consciences were clear, that we felt no guilt," etc., and that, when the doctor found we were so antagonistic, he refused to talk to us. This is definitely not so. The doctor told us the minute we came in, after he had sent for us that first time, that he had "nothing to say to us, unless we wanted to talk about the weather, or school," etc., as we previously reported to you. It was after he told us of the "warning communication" and I had demanded that he read it before the entire Forum and we would face any charges, that we said we had no feeling of guilt. So, you see, the Doctor has juggled his account of this interview to suit his own ends.

[2] The verses begin: 15 He will spit out the riches he swallowed; God will make his stomach vomit them up. 16 He will suck the poison of serpents; the fangs of an adder will kill him. 17 He will not enjoy the streams, the rivers flowing with honey and cream. 18 What he toiled for he must give back uneaten; he will not enjoy the profit from his trading.

Naturally, Dr. S. would be on good behavior with Wilkins, who will probably never see the side of him the other Forum members have seen. He told Sir Hubert that the thing that hurt them most was our violating their confidences in telling Forum members what they had said to us in private. But their statements indicated their "wrong attitude toward the Forum matters" and we felt that these declarations should not be kept secret. I had already told Dr. S. that I would gladly repeat to the Forum body any statements of his which I had passed on . . . and said that he should be ready to stand on anything he had told me about his plans for the Book. But the Doctor did not want me to prove that he had made these statements to the Forum . . . any more than he wants me to challenge him before the Forum on the lying statements he has made about us!

Wilkins said, "What about the charges that the Shermans were trying to plot with the Kelloggs to seize the Urantia book plates? I know the Shermans well and I know they would never think of such a thing." The Doctor said, TURNING A COMPLETE BACKWARD SOMERSAULT, "No, I don't believe that they would, either!" And YET, the Doctor told this very story to ALL the Forum members, as he sent for them in twos and threes, and poured out his venom! I think he knows now that these charges made against us are DANGEROUS, and he did not dare admit he had made them to Wilkins, who would have made a fine witness against him.

Wilkins asked what could be done to straighten matters out, and the Doctor said that, as far as he was concerned, he was not going to do anything . . . that time would heal things . . . and that we had the same rights as any other Forum members although we could never occupy the same friendly relationship we had borne before . . . and that *we could tell our side of the story* to any members we met, or to all of the Forum members, in little groups, if we chose . . . and that gradually things would clear up and people would forget . . . but he would never permit matters like this to be brought up before the FORUM as a BODY.

MAGNANIMOUS OF HIM, eh, what???? Having scared the living daylights out of most Forum members, putting the fear of God and higher spirit forces in them . . . having blackened our reputations . . . he would like to put us in the position of trying to pit our story against his, knowing full well that it would put us in a bad light, as though we are trying to undermine the Doctor by branding him as a liar, etc. . . . while they would *continue to believe* HIS STORY anyway!

I think it is fiendish of him to be willing to drop this now . . . and *never clear us* of the charges . . . He said further to Wilkins: "The Shermans haven't done any more reading of the papers and we thought they were so interested." This implied that our interest had not been so spiritual; but not many members of the Forum do extra reading, so it wouldn't have been unusual for us not to be reading, except as we read so much when we first came here until we had read the papers through once. (Personally, I have got to devote my time to trying to earn some more money QUICK.)

Anyway, the Doctor SLYLY would like to encourage us to begin reading and making close contact there again, so he could indicate to the members that he had "forgiven us" . . . and that our period of probation and punishment was over . . . but leaving Forumites with the impression we had been GUILTY, just the same.

He'll have to be cleverer than this before he can get us to fall for things like this. I know he'd like to have everyone forget this mess he has stirred up because he doesn't know how to get out of it.

Wilkins, while he of course believes us, is not so concerned as we are because he has lived a public life wherein he has been often misinterpreted and maligned . . . and has learned to overlook much of it. But SPIRITUAL THINGS things are at stake here . . . and we feel the situation is UNIQUE and MUCH DIFFERENT.

We intend to let the Doctor know, through Forum members, that we are WAITING for him to make disposition of us . . . as you suggest, either clear us or condemn us. Mrs. Gusler phoned today, and when we told her what the Doctor had said to Wilkins, she said, "Things get worse and worse. The Forum body will never be the same . . . it is badly shaken because of his conduct . . ." (Just as you had said in a previous letter.) Mrs. Gusler thinks we should quietly STAND PAT, which we intend doing.

Harry, I had an unusual experience several nights ago for the first time in a long while. As I was sitting relaxed, on the sofa, a voice inside my consciousness seemed to say:

> "It is I, John, who have come to be with you during the work ahead, to help you keep burning the torch handed you by Abner."

I was impressed that this was John, the Potter, described in the Apocrypha papers, across the street, as one of the 24 elders in charge of this revelation. I called to Martha and had her write down what was "coming through." It continued:

> "The fire for this torch comes from God, the Father, and is the eternal-urge-heavenward ablaze in the heart of man. It is this fire which eventually consumes all things of the flesh and releases the evolved soul of man from the ashes of his otherwise binding earth experience. You have asked for the true meaning of fire. *Physical* fire destroys all temporal forms; *spiritual* fire transmutes. Without it there can be no illumination. As you progress you will yearn to be more and more consumed in it, for only in this manner can your higher self be forged."

As if in verification, I was then impulsed to get the Bible *and* the dictionary together. Opening on inspiration I turned, in the Bible, to the following (2 Kings 2:11):

> "And it came to pass, as they still went on, and talked, that, behold, there appeared a *chariot of fire*, and parted them asunder; and Elijah went up by a whirlwind into heaven."

In the dictionary, I found, in looking up the word "fire": " . . . to change by the action of fire, as in the making of *pottery*" (John the *Potter?*); and that the synonym for the word SPIRIT is *FIRE.*

How close did I come to an understanding of the word or true meaning of FI-RE?

That same night, while about to drop off to sleep, an unusual verse was given to me. I called to Martha: "Quick, get up and write this down." Then I spoke what was "coming through" to her and added the title next morning, as follows:

SONS OF GOD

Hands he had not;
  Nor mouth, nor head, nor heart.
For in his world
  No form we know became himself a part.
And yet, a man he was—
  Another son of God—
Who lived and died as you . . .
  (A planet known as Od)

The form is not the man;
 The man is not the form,
And worlds no end with creatures swarm
 The wheel of life to run,
As led they are by light within
 Cast by Eternal Son.

Isn't this unusual? Where does it come from?

Fortunately we were unable to accept invitations from the Haleses when they tried to get us out to their place earlier this year . . . so we are not involved with them at all. Someday I would like to know their background better and just HOW tied with this they are. (Forum members are at present sold on the Haleses and claim they live the Urantia life in their home!)

Martha is going to read me the 14th Chapter of St. John a little later tonight. *JOHN?* Why did you mention *JOHN?*

I would not doubt that the doctor has taken some liberties with part of this book, now that his conduct is revealed! WHAT WILL HE HAVE TO ANSWER FOR!! I suppose it is far too much to expect him to change his ways now. He would have to have a personal visitation from a high authority that he could SEE to impress him . . . and would probably, as I have said, try to misinterpret any true message if it did not agree with his set plans and human ambitions.

I still hope and believe that any dematerialization of the papers can be averted . . . and am praying that things will develop here so we can STAY IN CHICAGO indefinitely and watch over this development. There is interest in my radio program from several sources in Chicago and I may sell it before too long.

It does not look like I'd have to go to New York until after the first of the year now. Still hoping Clara decides to let things go.

No more word on Twain but it will be coming along in January or February, I suppose. I've sent the Addams play to Lasky and if he will make me an offer for the movie rights, instead of going through any more grief with the Hull House crowd (Miss Carr, etc.), I will see if Schwartz and Mrs. Bowen will accept a picture sale . . . and believe I could do business if SOMETHING WAS ON THE LINE. Meanwhile, I'm staying away from them . . . until I can make a good impression . . . and "talk turkey."

I'll make a financial "killing" again one of these days . . . and then you'll be able to make the trip to Chattanooga and here. Money is only to be used for RIGHT SPIRITUAL PURPOSES ANYWAY . . . and if I had any, you should accept it.

Our love to you and Ma from us all. Someday please give me more of a knowledge of my own background, etc.

DIARY *November 17, 1942*

As Harold and Martha were talking about Mrs. Gusler and a possible dinner engagement, Mrs. Gusler phoned to ask if Sir Hubert had given us a report on his meeting with the Doctor and what his conclusions were. Martha answered that Sir Hubert had seen not only the Doctor but Clyde Bedell, the latter reporting practically our story except that our attitude had been very antagonistic when we were called to see the Doctor the first time, and that we had stated bluntly, on entering, that we were guilty of nothing and had clear consciences and showed no spirit of cooperation or humility, which was, of course, not true.

Martha stated Sir Hubert felt the whole situation had assumed such proportions because of the "he said," "she said" and "somebody told me" stories that were circulating. Being a figure in public life, he himself had had many wrong things said about him but he had learned to dismiss them more readily. He said the Doctor intended to let time wear away the situation and was going to do nothing more about us. His chief criticism of us was that we had betrayed personal confidences in discussing his statements to us regarding the organization and Foundation plans, and that the fault he was finding now was that we were failing to read any more of the Urantia papers.

Mrs. Gusler gasped, "Why, I just don't understand the Doctor!" Martha said he had told Sir Hubert that we could tell our own story to small groups and clear matters that way, and Mrs. Gusler was amazed. She said, "I don't think the Doctor realizes *how shaken* the Forum actually is! Things just aren't the same anymore. I'm so confused over his attitude."

Harold then took the phone, and Mrs. Gusler said that by our going around and talking to little groups of Forum members and telling our story we would be doing just what the Doctor had done. She said she felt that such an act on our part would be most unbecoming and undignified, and she couldn't comprehend why the Doctor would suggest that the matter be cleared up in this way.

Harold told her of how amazed we were to have Sir Hubert report that the Doctor *now* said he didn't believe we would have plotted to seize the Urantia plates, after his making these charges about us to Forum members. Mrs. Gusler said, "I just can't understand it!" Harold said we had decided to let different Forum members know that we were still waiting for final word or action from the Doctor so that he would realize we do not consider this situation a "closed book." Harold further stated he thought the Doctor was afraid to bring things to a head and face us with these outrageous charges. Mrs. Gusler said, "I've decided that he is, too. You know he was able to say some pretty unkind things about the writers of those letters of criticism by not mentioning their names, but now he has made charges directly against you two people and has gotten himself into deep water by your stand and doesn't know how to get himself out."

Mrs. Gusler asked if the Karles had seen us, and when Harold said that they had, she remarked, "Oh, I'm so glad. They are such fine, sincere people, and I know they've been terribly upset about this whole affair. I hope it makes you people feel better for having had a talk with them." Harold said that it had been reassuring to learn at last what some of the leading Forum members really thought. Mrs. Gusler said she just did not know what could be done since the Doctor and Bill exercise such control at present. She said it was her husband's best thought that we should continue to "sit tight" and let the move be up to the Doctor, and see what happens. This seemed to be essentially the judgment of the Karles and also that of Sir Hubert.

Harold reported that we had gone to dinner at the home of Mrs. Palmer with the Steinbecks, Burtons and Miss Hoffman present. Mrs. Gusler said she was happy we were beginning to have a chance to see some of the Forum members, as she thought this would do some good. She then asked if the Bucklins had been in touch with us as yet, and Harold said they had not. It is evident from Mrs. Gusler's continuing interest that many of the thinking Forum members are more concerned than they have as yet admitted.

ARA *November 18, 1942*

And fire it was that destroyed Cleodotus as he rushed in to save the records of the burning church in Philadelphia.

Rampant were the non-believers of this day, bent on plundering and killing. In this church were the treasures of the believers—a rich store of wealthy goods to serve those who sought to keep alive the truth. There, also, was the prized wine flask which Cleodotus had raised to the tortured lips of Christ Michael—prized at the thought that it had touched the flesh of Him who had died at the hands of his own created beings.

This, and the priceless recorded words of the crucified Creator Son, Cleodotus vainly sought to rescue and preserve. He died pressing the bottle to his own lips, feeling close to Him whom he had succored on the day of His trial and betrayal.

Thus did Cleodotus, in league with Abner, pledge the new and final service which was to carry them down to this present day to stand guard again that no second betrayal of the true revelation of God, the Universal Father, should come to pass.

How seemingly alone has been the journey of those two and yet, few there are on earth today whose footsteps have been more lovingly guarded and guided.

Is it not fitting that they, who stood fast in that far distant day against the host of those who would have bartered the truths of Christ to personal gain in the market place, should now stand fast again to prevent the return of this great and truth destroying evil? Far greater is this present crime, for the truth was never more hungrily yearned for by mankind!

Urantia trembles in the balance of a mighty cataclysm or a mighty spiritual Renaissance. The worlds of Nebadon look on in prayerful awe and anguished hope. They stand powerless against the rule of human will in the lives of men. This will must, of its own free choice, give way to the will of the Father or the ultimate certain destiny of the planet Urantia will be advanced into the centuries of time.

Stand firm, Cleodotus! You are not alone! She who is with you has been with you before. You have been tested in service and have not been found wanting. Much is soon to be revealed. Be of good cheer.

Ponder on the "ar" contained in the names Harold, Martha, Mary, Marcia and the name I give you—

-ARA-

13

Peaceful on the Surface

FORUM CALENDAR *November 18, 1942*

Mrs. Gusler our dinner guest here. Mary and Marcia eat out.

DIARY *November 18, 1942*

Mrs. Gusler came to dinner at 6 p.m. and we had Mary and Marcia eat out in order to talk uninterruptedly. She said that Dent Karle had talked back to the Doctor and had told him frankly that many members didn't like the egotistical way Bill was acting, quoting statements Bill had made and also describing actions indicative of this undesirable tendency. The Doctor sought to allay this criticism, but Christy gave support to Dent's declarations. Dent asked the Doctor point blank what made the Doctor consider this a rebellion. The Doctor said he had interpreted a statement from a higher source as referring to such when it said, "If you permit a free discussion on these organization matters there will be a *real* rebellion." Mrs. Gusler stated that the Karles and herself were wondering if this purported spirit message could not be interpreted as an actual warning to the Doctor. With a free discussion permitted, might it not have meant that the Forum members, when they had learned the details of the organization plan, would have strongly rebelled against them?

Mrs. Gusler asked Harold if he thought the Doctor had any psychic ability himself which would enable him to appear at the other members' homes and gain a knowledge of what was happening there.

Harold said, "Absolutely, no! The Doctor has told me on a number of occasions that he does not believe in telepathy, as such, and that he has never had even *one* personal experience, and that the phenomena attendant upon the production of the Book of Urantia are the only genuine phenomena he has ever come across. And now, at this late date, when he has felt himself to be challenged, he suddenly represents himself to have been given supernatural powers enabling him actually to spy on Forum members! It is inconceivable that any higher spiritual beings should have collaborated on such a low enterprise." This statement on the Doctor's part helped accomplish his purpose however—the further scaring and intimidating of many Forum members.

Mrs. Gusler asked, "What about the dream you were purported to have had concerning Ruth Kellogg, to the effect she was one day to play a great and leading part in the Book of Urantia project? Did you read her such a dream? And do you believe in dreams?"

Harold said, "I believe that we are sometimes guided by a higher power than our own minds through dreams or visions while we sleep, in answer to a conscious desire or prayer for the solving of some earth problems. I never, at any time, read Ruth any dream while alone. I did, however, read her and her parents what seemed to have been a dream received the night of August 14 while we were on a trip to Marion, Ind., with the Doctor and Christy. This dream had already been read to Christy, who had appeared to be impressed by it, and I had promised to send it later to the Doctor. Returning to Chicago, I showed it to Clyde Bedell, who said it was unusual but advised against letting the Doctor see it, as he felt the Doctor would accuse me of thinking I had been 'inspired.' Later, with the Kelloggs and Ruth over to spend the evening, and after I had told them that I felt there was much discussion going on between Forum members, and differences of opinion on Forum matters, I decided to read this dream as representative of my own feelings relative to the proposed organization. The Kelloggs were so interested that they asked me to read the dream to them twice."

Harold then turned to Martha and asked her to get a copy of the dream in question so that he could read it to Mrs. Gusler and let her judge for herself whether it said anything about "Ruth and the part she was to play in the Urantia movement." After reading "Battle Plans for the Book of Urantia," Mrs. Gusler said, "Why, I agree with the points raised. As to dreams, I used to dream the answer to many of my problems, especially in mathematics!"

Harold went on to say that he had told Ruth that she would probably have a part to play in the later developments pertaining to the Book of Urantia, as he believed *all* Forum members would, but he made no suggestion of his belief that she would play a bigger or more outstanding role in proportion to anyone else.

Mrs. Gusler then asked, "What do you think about an organization? Don't you think we should have one?" And Harold said, "Not at the start. A simple little Foundation designed to care for the book's publication, translation and distribution is all that I feel is necessary, and let the public reaction to the book determine the time and nature of any organization which may come to pass as a result of the book."

Mrs. Gusler then read us a copy of the talk she had given to the Seventy, defining the manner in which she personally would attempt to interest others in the Book of Urantia when it was published. She described how she would explain the book and its origins to her friends and invite their reader interest. She took for granted that no organization would be existent at this time of the book's publication, and said it was her feeling that all organization matters should be left in abeyance until later. She said she wished she could know the Sadlers, young and old, much better personally, as she understood that they, including the Hales family, had actually been living the Book of Urantia. Harold said he wished Mrs. Gusler could observe their personal lives more closely, as this might enable her or anyone else to judge more accurately between the human side and the divine.

Mrs. Gusler seemed to think, and some other members are under the impression, that Mr. Hales, with his knowledge of corporation and organization setups, had much to do, together with the lawyer, in drawing up the charters. (Wilkins said that Hales told him, at the annual picnic, that it was easy to make money—anyone could do it if they only went about it right—and this would indicate that he feels sure the provisions made in the Foundation charter will enable substantial money to be made from investment of its funds and donations eventually receivable on the Book of Urantia.)

Mrs. Gusler asked just what the apocrypha papers were, and were they open to the Forum membership as a whole. We replied that the Sadlers apparently did not consider it so, although they had not instructed us not to tell other members what they had read to us. Only a comparatively few selected ones who are considered to be in the inner or favored circle have been privileged to hear any of these papers read, and usually as they have been guests in the Sadler home. We told Mrs. Gusler a little about the recorded Tabamantia visit and she was thrilled, although a little perplexed when we informed her that a section of the apocrypha, which had to do with a TA's addressing the subject of his indwelling, had been interpolated in the book.[1] Mrs. Gusler stated that changes had been made in the papers through the years, including deletions, one of them being the fact that Lucifer and his rebellious associates were now imprisoned on the moon.[2]

A telephone call came in from Mr. Burton, who had been attending Bill's meeting across the street. He asked Martha if we would come out and see them this next Sunday with some other Forum members, and Martha accepted, it being our feeling that we should respond to all invitations extended during this strange period. Mrs. Gusler left to make a call upon Mrs. Bucklin, whom she was going to tell that we had denied all charges made by the Doctor.

November 19, 1942

Martha phoned Mrs. Steinbeck this a.m. to inquire for Mrs. Palmer's unlisted phone number to thank her for our most pleasant Sunday evening. Mrs. Steinbeck remarked that she had gotten over to Mrs. Bucklin's Wednesday after Bill's lecture and found Mrs. Gusler there, so there was much discussion of Forum matters. It remains to be seen as to how many members this reaches. We have decided to tell one and all that we are still waiting for the Doctor to make a move to clear us and call us over for a further talk as he had told us he would do.

November 21, 1942

Mrs. Gusler phoned Harold during the evening to tell him she had just completed reading *Your Key to Happiness* and she thought it was perfectly fine. She said she understood from Martha that Harold had changed his point of view with regard to reincarnation and was going to alter several pages in the next edition,[3] but that the book was excellent anyway and had done her a great deal of good. She told

[1] See Ed. note on p. 120.

[2] See Vol. 1, pp. 107 and 110, where Loose mentions the moon as a detention world where Lucifer was being held.

[3] The two versions are displayed in Vol. 1, pp. 402-404.

Harold she had had a very satisfactory talk with both Mr. and Mrs. Bucklin and Mrs. Steinbeck last Wednesday night, which she would tell us about later. She said the only purpose of her call was to express her full appreciation of the book, which she was going to recommend to all her friends. She said her husband was ill again and had been postponing a needed operation for rupture.

November 22, 1942

FORUM—Paper 11: "THE ETERNAL ISLE OF PARADISE"

Entering the Sadler residence we ran into Christy coming out who smiled and greeted us cordially. We passed Mr. Hales and a small group of men with the Doctor at the Forum room door. He [Hales] spoke to us but the Doctor did not see us. After we had been seated further back in the room than usual and the meeting had begun, the Doctor deliberately leaned around the curtains from his seated position outside to see if we were there.

Mr. Pritchard did the reading of the paper on God's abiding place, "The Isle of Paradise," which is an amazing document. This paper, in describing the central Isle of Paradise, stated it is motionless and non-spatial, having three levels (sections): the upper surface, the periphery, and the nether surface. The upper surface has to do with personalities; the periphery with conditions and things neither personal nor non-personal; and nether Paradise with non-personal force and energies and the source of origin of pervaded and unpervaded space.

It was brought out in this paper that pervaded space is now about at the midway point of the expanding cycle which lasts for a billion years and extends in a horizontal position from the Isle of Paradise, while unpervaded space extending in a vertical position from this same isle is maintaining universal equilibrium by the act of contracting. At the end of this billion-year cycle the respiration of pervaded space will have reached its outermost limits and a contraction then begins. At this same moment, unpervaded space will commence to expand, and in this manner new worlds of time and space and new ultimate universes will one day come into being.

In the end of this process of infinite creation, the eternal presence of God the Father at the Isle of Paradise maintains forever the stability of all universes as they revolve around this central ellipsoidal (1/6th longer N and S than E and W) isle. Since all lines of force and energy center in Him, the force of gravity operating from the nether side of Paradise holds all the worlds of time and space in its grasp like beads upon an endless string. Space is not force or energy or matter and is not influenced by gravity, but rather serves as the cushion for the functioning of this magnetic gravity pull else the hold of gravity upon the planets would be jerky and uneven.

The location of the Isle of Paradise is in a definite fixed place and could as certainly be reached by the children of time, having survival value and the proper spiritual development as well as guidance and means of transit, as any human, capable of navigation, could set a course for New York or London or Singapore on earth.

On leaving we spoke to the Steinbecks and Mrs. Palmer and Elsie Karle, who said Dent was in Seattle en route to Alaska. Miss Cook shook hands and spoke warmly with Martha. Mrs. Hales came up and purposely extended her hand to us both, engaging Harold in a short conversation, telling him about their closing up most of the home to save fuel. Asked if they were going south for the winter she said, "Oh, no. There's too much to do here this time of year—the opera, the symphony and other interesting activities; then, too, my husband is a member of eight different boards which keeps him too busy in a business way to get away." Leone spoke to us both as we were leaving, and Russell Bucklin nodded and smiled as did Mrs. Githens. We departed after the first hour as has been our recent custom. Mr. [Alvin] Kulieke Jr. and Miss Olson were standing outside having a breath of air and exchanged pleasant comments as we passed. The general attitude, however, remains definitely restrained and few of these approaches or greetings are spontaneous.

We drove out to the Burtons to keep our dinner appointment tonight and were welcomed at the door by Mrs. Hoffman, who stays with them. As we stepped in, we encountered Ernest Pritchard and wife [Louise] who were obviously surprised to see us. Apparently the Burtons had neglected (perhaps purposely) to tell them who their other dinner guests were to be. We learned that the Al Dyons had been invited and Al had pleaded illness. Since the Pritchards and Dyons have been old standbys of the Doctor, we doubt if the Pritchards would have come had they known we were to be there; and since Mr. Pritchard made a statement later on in the evening, that it sometimes frightened him to contemplate that celestial beings might be invisibly present, we are wondering if he is not worried tonight lest some of them may have seen them associating with us. Apparently superstition plus the Doctor's emphasizing of his utilization of psychic powers to put down "this rebellion" has struck fear in the hearts of many Forum members.

Mr. Pritchard remarked that Al Dyon was so nervous, he seemed headed for a nervous breakdown, and that his wife wasn't helping him any. The Burtons and Mrs. Hoffman had been invited by Christy to have tea with the Doctor before last Sunday's Forum meeting, and this indicates Dr. Sadler is making a late attempt to be more sociable with all Forum members, taking them little groups at a time. Even so, Mrs. Hoffman said, in a still injured tone, that she had tried to tell him of a dream she had had, and he had cut her off because he was interested in having someone more important speak.

Mr. Pritchard had exhibited an ingenious model he made of the entire cosmic scheme, including the Isle of Paradise, at the earlier afternoon Forum meeting following his reading of the paper. Harold now remarked upon it and Pritchard said he had to put ideas or concepts like this into some physical form before he could comprehend them. Complimented by Harold on his intelligent reading of the paper, Pritchard said this particular subject interested him greatly, much more so than the papers on personalities, many of whom he felt were changing and uncertain. But the forces and energies operating on definite universal laws were not.

It seems to be Pritchard's thought that the truths of Urantia are eventually going to be expounded in an evangelical manner, since he suggested that he'd like to have the Doctor prepare one good sample representative talk on the Book of Urantia, which would serve as an introduction, and then follow up with a course of five evangelical lectures explaining or setting forth these truths.

Mrs. Burton said, "Did you say *evangelical?* I wouldn't want that. We don't want to make a religion out of this."

Pritchard seemed a bit taken aback, but Mrs. Pritchard spoke up and said, "I think a foundation to protect the book is necessary, but I don't see any need of a Urantia Brotherhood and I doubt if I'd join one if it were set up."

Harold said that he felt as she did, and that a Urantia Brotherhood would be classified as a religion and would intensify resistance on the part of all other churches and peoples to the truths contained in the book. He said he did not think we should ever attempt, on the basis of the knowledge we might have acquired or which the Doctor might have given us with respect to comparative religions, to tell other people how to adapt their faith to ours. Harold felt this should be left strictly up to the individual whose Spirit of Truth and TA would be functioning to open up a greater realization of the truth as people of all religions made contact with the book.

Mrs. Hoffman spoke up and said, "I agree with you. The Doctor, in his talk on different religions, particularly the Catholic Church (she is Catholic) has made statements that offer interpretations of this religion which are not true and which, if he tried to use them on any Catholic, would so antagonize them that they'd throw him out of their home." Mr. Pritchard was thoughtfully silent during all these comments and looked at his watch as though he were anxious to call it an evening.

Harold had opportunity to tell Mr. Burton, alone, that he now knew the full charges made against him, all of which were untrue. Mr. Burton styled as fantastic the charge that Harold had tried with the Kelloggs to seize the plates, and shook his head and said the whole thing was incredible.

Mrs. Hoffman read some more of her sonnets, one of which was a humorous takeoff on the Doctor for not letting her tell her dream and telling about his dream experience instead. It has been the Doctor's contention oft repeated that dreams have little or no significance beyond revealing your sinful thoughts. He tells the story to illustrate, saying that he had offered this explanation of dreams to a minister who doubted him and he then said to the pastor, "All right. I'll tell you the worst dream I ever had and you tell me your worst dream and we'll compare notes!" The minister blushed and called the proposition off.

The Burtons and Mrs. Hoffman are definitely and unreservedly trying to be friendly; we made no effort to clarify our situation with the Pritchards, and what they may think after this evening is a conjecture.

When we arrived home we found a phone call had been received for us from Mrs. Merrill Davis of Marion, Indiana. If Jo Davis is in town, and has been seeing the Doctor, we are wondering what he has decided to tell her (perhaps as usual with the stipulation it must be held in confidence). Now that he knows Harold is going to Marion, the Doctor must be concerned at what Harold himself will say. [*Insert:* A letter received from Jo several days later indicated she had not had time for any visiting with the Doctor and apparently is still unaware of the developments here. Harold will be able to determine whether Jo has been informed on his Marion trip Dec. 9.]

HARRY LOOSE to HAROLD and MARTHA SHERMAN

Monterey Park, November 26, 1942

Dear Harold and Martha:-

Today is Thanksgiving Day—Nov. 26th—and when I turned on the radio this morning, the announcer was just introducing the President in Washington who was to read today's Thanksgiving Day Proclamation at the meeting held in the Blue Room at the White House, where there was prayer and singing and a half-hour religious service. It began at breakfast time, 8 o'clock, and we sat here, with the grate fire going, listening to it all during our eating period. The thermometer was at 33 above this morning when I ran across the street to pick up the morning paper from Jo's porch. Her husband brings it with him when he comes home late at night, and after he reads it, he leaves it out on his front porch for me to pick up when I get up in the morning. It saves me the expense of a morning paper—and is always there when I go over for it. The wood fire in the grate heats things up swell—and is so pretty to look at—and then the sun starts warming things up—and is a great ball of fire to the east—and I look to the north and there are the mountains—"from which cometh my strength"—and they are beautiful—with their dark blue color of morning. I guess that you folks miss the mountains back there in the middle east. . . .

I am answering your letter of November 17th—which arrived safely—with its news of more caperings—mental caperings—of Dr. Sadler. Glad of Wilkins' visit to Sadler and his immediate report to you of the evening with him. From Wilkins' long public experience, he should be able to read pretty well and truly the people with whom he comes in contact. However, Sadler is a pretty smart bird in that particular himself. You are a very good intuitive reader of people—and better than most folks—for you have had more practice—and more interest—in such. Yet see—did Sadler fool you at all—or just a little—or a lot??

Hope that you folks have a real swell Thanksgiving Day dinner—and a beautiful day to go along with it. Hope that you are all together—small Martha cooking some kind of a bird—maybe a big chicken—with small soda biscuits—and Marcia home from school—and Mary up from Hull House—and that afterwards the weather will be such that you can all take a walk down Diversey to the Park—and then south for a ways—maybe down to Fullerton Ave. and then back home. I very often think of our dinners together over at your house—and small Martha's biscuits. Miss the physical association of you folks very much—and wonder, sometimes, if I will ever really see you in the flesh again. . . .

Gasoline rationing starts on December 1st—and you will be restricted with driving. Glad that you have such good streetcar and elevated connections—and so close and convenient to your present address. Four gallons a week won't take me very far and I'll be much handicapped for transportation by way of bus here in California, and especially in Monterey Park it is very far from the best. I have an old baby buggy with no top to it to get groceries and vegetables in. It's quite a distance from the house here to the grocery and vegetable places, too.

Before I forget to remark it, I want to get this in very positively. If it is a possible thing to dispose of the Addams matter to Lasky with no further work on it, I very strongly advise you so to do. But be sure that you have some sort of authoritative permission so to do from Bowen, Schwartz, etc. so that you won't run into a snag there after doing a lot of work on it. I hope that you will push this whole thing.

Although I am writing this on Thanksgiving Day, I don't expect that I will be able to get it mailed today unless Jo and her husband go to the show this afternoon—for I won't be taking the car out until tomorrow morning at the earliest—and the Post Office here is much too far to walk over to it for mailing.

You have very good understanding of your whole problem there with Sadler, and from your letter's reading, there is nothing that I can do but to agree with your program of procedure. You have a very fine mind there to advise with in addition to your own thinking—I mean small Martha.

Cling to Mrs. Gusler—and the others that may be gathered to you through her or through other sources or contacts.

Harold, fire is the greatest element that there is—next to that which we term electricity—and it, too, like electricity (or FORCE), is very

very little understood. It, too, is both physical and spiritual. The duties, the make-up, the control, the usage, the physical possibilities, the spiritual truths, of fire, together with the thousands of ramifications of the element, would require a book fully as detailed and at length as the Book of Urantia. No scientist of this earth understands FIRE—any more than they understand the force that is titled Electricity—most scientists think of FIRE as a destroying element only—when it is a matter of fact that it is a great builder—just pause Harold and contemplate the fact that FIRE is the father of ALL gases. And that the word "fire" does not express what the element is at all. It merely indicates in the language that we speak the presence of an element of which we generally know but one activity. The list of its activities are not so limited—they are practically limitless. The element that we know as FIRE and the FORCE that we call electricity are the great builders, under jurisdiction and guidance, that form the dark islands of space that eventually become new worlds. The whole thing is too immense to even try to discuss here. Of greater import by far than the small history of Urantia as written, how would it be possible to condense such into a few paragraphs of typewriting.

You are much tormented—and entertained also—and mystified—by the fragments of the long long past that intervene in that mystery called sleep. Don't be disturbed by them—nor frightened at all—they have a definite and absolutely true background. Someday you will very fully understand. Such full understanding is not needful now. Be patient.

If possible, your place is in Chicago—to watch over the development you see with your own eyes unfolding. . . .

In my last letter to you, I remarked about confused contacts, etc. They are fully cleared, and reception is very clear and fine—with much strength and definiteness.

If you have a large collection of magazines that you have finished with—and the express or parcel post isn't too excessive—send them along.

Well, Harold and small Martha, I'll stop for now—with the very best of thought—and much love to you ALL,

As always,

My period of strain has not ceased. I expect to be able to write you of it all eventually.

DIARY *November 29, 1942*

FORUM—Paper 12: "THE UNIVERSE OF UNIVERSES"

As we reached the second-floor landing, we met Dr. Sadler face to face who extended his hand first to Martha and then to Harold and simply said, "Hello." We passed on in, exchanging a greeting with Christy who was seated by the door. We took our usual seats and were soon joined by the Burtons, Mr. Burton removing Harold's coat and hat from a chair so they could sit beside us. Mrs. Burton thanked Martha for the little note she had written thanking them for the pleasant evening a week ago. She said, "It was an awfully sweet note—just like I would have thought you would have written."

The Burtons held each other's hands frequently during Bill's reading of the paper, which indicated a warmth of feeling between them which, from the standpoint of human relationships, means a great deal to us. Mrs. Steinbeck and Mrs. Palmer sat just behind us and were friendly as usual, Mrs. Steinbeck reporting that her husband was home again ill with the flu. She said he was being given homeopathic treatment, which was the same as saying that they had been seeing a great deal of the Bucklins, since the Bucklins are strong advocates of homeopathic medicine and the Steinbecks lean toward Christian Science.

Bill's paper was extra long, requiring an hour and a half of almost steady reading. It had to do with the order and nature of the Universe of universes from the Havona worlds out to and through the seven superuniverses, to and including the four outer space levels and still beyond where observers have detected evidence that God's creative forces are even now in motion.

We left at intermission and learned from Elsie Karle that Dent was about to fly on up to Alaska from Seattle. Harold encountered Mr. Hales and thanked him for the Christmas greeting which arrived this past week and asked if Mrs. Hales and he had composed it. He said no, that Mrs. Hales had picked it up through some friend in Canada, and Harold said it presented quite a remarkable and authentic picture of Christ as we had come to know him through the Book of Urantia. To this Mr. Hales agreed.

The attendance seemed not so large as usual, with the proportion of about three women to one man. It will be interesting to note whether or not gas rationing greatly reduces this number. Mrs. Githens and Mrs. Gusler were not there today. Miss Baumgartner arrived just as we were leaving and greeted us most cordially—calling Harold by his first name.

HARRY LOOSE to MARTHA SHERMAN

Monterey Park, November 29, 1942

Dear Martha:-

This is the Sunday after Thanksgiving and I am sitting here in the old front room smacking away at the old typewriter keys and at least getting a letter to you started. I don't know whether I will be able to finish before I start down to Church with the car. It was cool last night—and cool this morning—the thermometer stood at 33 above when I started out to get the paper from Jo's front porch. That's the way that it runs all winter, however. Anyway, when we sat down here to our small breakfast table, I lit the wood fire in the grate and it looks awfully pretty and the warmth is fine. The day is fine and the great ball of brilliant sun is coming up and the middle of the day will be around 80 above. . . .

I mailed a letter just the other day to Harold which I hope arrived safely. In it I very selfishly asked that you send me the magazines that you have read by mail, parcel post or express. That is, if the expense was not too much. I don't buy any magazines and they are too good reading to be thrown away until someone gets some more usage out of them. However, I don't do any package mailing and have no knowledge of the cost of expressage and after I read my letter to Harold out loud to Ma, she said that I should not have done it as the parcel post on a bunch of magazines and *Digests* would be prohibitive. So I haste this letter off to you ahead of the time that I would have usually answered so as to tell you NOT to do this. And to apologize for making such a request. I get the *Saturday Evening Post* every week anyway.

I want to thank you for the enclosures of Harold's beautiful impressions.[4] He surely is a master of words and phrases and he mingles much truth in his writings. It is a mental escape mechanism that is very good for release from what goes on—particularly across the street. When he gets fully occupied mentally with something constructive, he will still have these moments when these things will

[4] Harold had continued writing poems after "Sons of God." See Appendix E for the other poems he wrote in 1942.

force themselves to expression, so be very gentle with him and accept them as they come and give thanks for his release. . . .

Thanksgiving evening around 8:30 the phone bell rang and I went to answer it. It was "H.C." Mattern—and he had a very hoarse voice—explained that he had a bad laryngitis and was hardly able to talk and that his "pal" would have to take the phone for him. So Mary got on the phone and explained that she believed that he had caught the cold the night before on the train coming down from Oakland. Anyway, they were leaving Los Angeles the following morning and stopping at Houston and then New Orleans, and then would be "home" by Christmas. She talked but little of the reading at 533 and the difficulties there, but said that things were very unhappy there. That they had expected to be able to see me when they arrived here but that they only stayed over one night and then left for Houston. Suppose that you will have heard from them yourselves and that they will repeat what I have just remarked.

I wish that I was informed as to the continuations, and the final end thereof, of the caperings across the street. But I do not know. If such is given me, I will surely write you of it.

Wish that Harold was occupied at something productive there in Chicago. Surely there must be place for him there. He should be there to watch the developments. Old as I am I have not learned patience myself—and I get so anxious when I see things developing that I have no jurisdiction over—and no knowledge of their eventual ending. Just about like Harold I guess.

Thanks a lot, Martha, for your nice letter and the enclosures too. I appreciate them. Forget about the magazines.

Wish that I could walk in on you in the flesh today—or meet you at the Forum this afternoon.

Love from Ma and I to you ALL,

HAROLD SHERMAN to HARRY LOOSE

Chicago, December 1, 1942

Dear Harry:

Chances are, by now, you have seen the Matterns, who are at present in Los Angeles, and have received from them a "blow-by-blow" account of the famous battle of Sherman-versus-Sadler on that memorable day, September 13th, made more memorable by the fact it was Mother's and your birthday.

At this writing, all is peaceful on the surface, while underneath smolders unrest and uncertainty. It is evident that Doctor is at a complete loss as to how to close this situation, and is hoping we will make the first overture so he can let it be known that we have sought a "return to grace." We are going to indicate that we are still waiting to "hear from the doctor," pretty soon. All meetings have been condensed into Sunday afternoons, due to the gas rationing, which makes a pretty strong diet for those who belong to Bill Jr.'s class . . . or the doctor's "70 Group," who remain on after the regular Sunday meeting, which begins at 2:30 . . . and do not leave until after 5:30. We are leaving now after the reading of the paper, and do not wait to hear the doctor dissect "*other* religions." This procedure seems to have him wondering.

We thought of you strongly on Thanksgiving Day and were interested to learn that you were writing us on that day, giving us a vivid picture, incidentally, of your actions . . . and particularly of the wonderful mountains from which, truly, "cometh strength." Remember? How can we ever forget? Our stay in California and our associations with you and Mother Loose will be a treasured memory as long as we stay in this dimension. And after that, we will be "looking you folks up," the first thing, on our *arrival!*

Martha's dad and the new Mother Bain, who is very nice, were here over Thanksgiving. We had some of Martha's biscuits and wished you were here to help eat them. It would have been interesting competition between you and Dad Bain for top eating honors, as he likes them, too. . . .

I note your suggestions with regard to Jane Addams script and will follow it. Lasky writes the material will make a fine movie, but he cannot handle it because of previous commitments . . . however, he suggests that I submit it to other studios at once. . . .

I am glad to get your comments on FIRE . . . these are most helpful.

Will be interested to learn what you think of the poems which are commencing to come through. Martha and Mary think they explain the great truths much more simply and understandably to the lay mind than the much more profound sections of the book. There is going to be a great problem properly presenting this BOOK to the world—and they are ASLEEP AT THE SWITCH across the street . . . fiddling away their time when SO MUCH of a constructive planning nature could be accomplished. Perhaps, at the right time, all human obstacles will be blown away, and right leadership for the big public steps placed in charge.

John Matter, Chicago friend of mine, whom I formerly knew as a resident of Marion, Indiana (he comes from one of Marion's oldest and finest and also wealthiest families), is taking me around and introducing me to advertising agency people and other contacts here . . . with the hope that I can sell my radio program and several other ideas and STAY in Chicago. He is also interested in my raising capital and starting a play-producing company, with business never better in the theatre line in this city.

I have reached a temporary low point in finances again and am doing my utmost and exercising my faith, with no money available to meet current bills as the first of the month arrives. I feel we will be cared for, but these are tough tests and I had hoped we would not have to face them again . . . since this has been a part of my life experience, off and on, for some years. The next Twain payment should take us out of the woods for some time to come, but it will not arrive until the picture is released, and what date that will be is not yet known—Lasky says maybe not until spring.

We are collecting the magazines and you will be receiving a bundle one of these days.

It is fine that "reception" is again good. We would like to share knowledge of happenings insofar as it is permissible.

I am enclosing a couple more airmail stamps for your use. In these stressful times, when regular mail travels even slower than usual, it is nice to get your letters while they are still warm.

December 9th I go to Marion to make the two talks I reported to you . . . one before the Kiwanis at noon, the other before the Foreman's Club at night . . . subjects, respectively: "Where Do We Go From Here?" and "It's Up To You!" It should be an interesting experience.

I am enclosing another poem, which you do not need to return as these copies are made just for you.

OUR LOVE AND OUR BEST THOUGHT ALWAYS . . .

14

"Through Death"

DIARY *December 1, 1942*

Martha phoned Mrs. Gusler this afternoon to inquire about Mrs. Gusler's absence from the Forum on Sunday and how Mr. Gusler was, as Mrs. Gusler had indicated on her last visit that he was not well and had been putting off an operation for some time. Mrs. Gusler was momentarily overcome by her emotions but was able to say that she had just returned from the hospital about an hour and a half ago. Mr. Gusler had been there under observation and tests for a week, and the conclusion today was probable cancer of the lower intestine. Martha asked if we could be of any service whatsoever, and Mrs. Gusler said, "Only your prayers." She said Mr. Gusler was to undergo an operation early tomorrow morning. Martha offered what consolation she could and Mrs. Gusler promised to keep us notified.

December 2, 1942

Martha again phoned Mrs. Gusler at 10 p.m. to learn how Mr. Gusler had come through his operation and was told he had eighteen inches of the colon removed under local anesthesia (probably to avoid as much nausea as possible, as he had been so sick for four or five days). He had suffered a great deal, but was optimistic about the outcome. He is possibly unaware that a second operation is to take place in four days and another in two months. Mrs. Gusler is being very courageous.

December 3, 1942

Philip Gusler, son of Mrs. Gusler, phoned at 10:30 tonight to say his father had passed on at a quarter of seven tonight. Funeral at 3 p.m. Saturday. Upon receipt of this news, Martha immediately wrote a note of sympathy and enclosed Harold's poem, "Through Death,"[1] which had come through inspirationally at one o'clock that very morning, it being Harold's feeling even then that the first mission of this poem was to be its delivery to Mrs. Gusler. Martha had the same feeling although neither spoke of it until news of Mr. Gusler's passing.

December 4, 1942

Mrs. Steinbeck phoned this a.m. to tell us of Mr. Gusler's passing. Finding that we knew of it, she said the custom of the Forum was to send a floral wreath for which Miss Baumgartner would take small contributions (usually about 25 cents per person) next Sunday.

Then she went on to say that last Sunday, after the reading of the paper and intermission, the entire class periods, including Bill's and the Doctor's talks, were given over to a discussion of the war. Referring to the 34th Regent (Tabamantia), the Doctor said this war was one of materialistic selfishness and would be allowed to run its course, that nationally and internationally the world was to be purged. Combining Urantia with modern historians such as Stuart Chase (*World of Travel* and *World After Research*),[2] he stated that "humanity had folded up its tent and was on the march to future destiny;[3] that the world would never return to its former state and that the scuttling of the French fleet marked the beginning of Hitler's downfall and the end of his regime."[4] All the statements were discussed in such a way that it was difficult to tell which authority was which.

We are wondering why this particular subject matter was brought into the Forum, as the final admonition from the Angels of Progress

---

[1] See Appendix E.

[2] Stuart Chase (1888-1985) was a prolific writer and advocate for economic reform. The book or books cited above seem to be a garbled retitling of Chase's *When the War Ends: The Road We Are Traveling 1914-1942.*

[3] Sadler was paraphrasing a statement made in 1918 by South African statesman J. C. Smuts, in reference to the newly formed League of Nations: "There is no doubt that mankind is once more on the move. . . . The tents have been struck, and the great caravan of humanity is once more on the march." A variation of this quote appears twice in the Urantia Book, in 71:8.15 and 99:1.1.

[4] On November 27, 1942 Vichy France scuttled its fleet at Toulon to avoid its capture by Germany. In retaliation the Germans turned Vichy France into a puppet state of Germany.

(33rd Regent) in the paper read at the picnic stated that, as far as the Forum was concerned, the war did not exist and apparently was not to be part of Forum discussions.

December 5, 1942

Today (Martha's birthday) we drove out to the Kampf's Funeral Parlor, 318 North Central Avenue, to attend the funeral of Carl Gusler. We found a fairly large chapel about three-quarters full and saw only one other Forum member in addition to ourselves, Mrs. Pritchard, to whom we nodded in greeting. Mrs. Gusler was seated in the front row between her two sons and apparently their wives. We sat toward the rear and did not go forward to the coffin which was placed in the central alcove amidst a mass of flowers.

An organ was playing soft meditative music, and at 3 o'clock a surprisingly young man took charge of the services, opening with prayer and referring to "that shore from whence no traveler returns." He then followed with some well-read excerpts from scripture, including the 23rd Psalm and several verses from John 14 (1-4), after which he read three short poems on the subject of death. Then he stated that he would like to quote from the pages of an unpublished book, *Reluctant Earth*, which he inferred Mr. Gusler himself had written, he being a great lover of nature. The characters, father and son, in this story, in discussing spiritual things, God, the heavens and earth, had been made to quote fragments of different favorite scriptures of Mr. Gusler. The man conducting the service stated that we could best gain an appreciation of Mr. Gusler's character and faith from these selections of his, and the simple, well-delivered presentation of them proved most effective.

This was quite a departure from the usual funeral ceremony, wherein the deceased's earthly merits and affiliations are extolled. No attempt was made to exploit the activities of the physical man, Carl Gusler, but rather to dwell upon the elements of spirit which we now believe have survival value. The short, for the most part unemotional but effective ceremony was closed with prayer—a prayer wherein those who came to pay the departed their last respects and honor were themselves invited to gain a spiritual value from the life he had lived and the faith he had exercised.

The casket was wheeled out the side entrance, and those going to the cemetery also left by this door while the organ was softly playing

"Going Home." We stopped to sign our name on the registry of sympathy and then went out the front entrance. Harold remained bareheaded as he saw the hearse and following cars drawn up in the alleyway and extending across the sidewalk into the street along which we must pass to get to our own parked car. We decided not to cut through between the hearse at the curb and the limousine carrying Mrs. Gusler and immediate relatives. Instead we went out into the street and around the front of the hearse and back onto the sidewalk, and continued for about a block until we reached our car. As we did so we saw the hearse and procession of cars approaching.

Harold removed his hat and we stood sorrowfully watching the hearse pass when, to our surprise, a rare little occurrence took place. As the limousine containing Mrs. Gusler drew abreast of us, she happened to be seated on our side looking out. From the expression on her face it seemed immediately evident that she was searching for us, and when she saw us she waved and kept her eyes on us as long as we were within her sight. We raised our own hands in sympathetic gesture and felt a most unusual spiritual exchange. It seemed to us, in that moment, that Mrs. Gusler was taking this occasion to let us know her appreciation of the note of sympathy we had sent, including Harold's poem "Through Death." It struck us as a supreme demonstration of thoughtfulness for Mrs. Gusler to have considered us in such a manner at such a time and affected us deeply.

It is strange, among many strange experiences in our life, that she of all Forum members who might have come to us, should have sought us out and to have given us opportunity for meeting and having several visits with her husband shortly in advance of his own departure from this planet. This, too, must be for a purpose, and we truly hope we can be of some service and comfort to a woman as courageous and fine as Mrs. Gusler has shown herself to be.

HARRY LOOSE to HAROLD SHERMAN

Monterey Park, December 5, 1942

Dear Harold:-

This is Saturday night and I am answering yours of December 1st. The evenings here at this time of the year are pretty cool and, with the war blackout that is strictly enforced out here now, it's pretty drear when you go out the front door of a night and leave the lights behind you. Because of the strict gas rationing there are very few cars on Garvey Boulevard and the street lights have been cut down to half power and all the street lights have a cap on them to prevent light being thrown upward. I don't suppose that there is any of such back there in Chicago. You folks are not in a "combat zone," such as this is out here, back 150 miles [*sic*] from the Coast.

I go for a short constitutional of an hour's stroll every night, starting at 8:30, and make a leisurely walk around several blocks and arrive home very glad to get in and sit down. I carry a cane with me. Not for support but because of dogs that come out and cause annoyance by barking at my heels. The cane I carry is a bent hickory stick that I used when I came from the Michael Reese Hospital in 1903—39 years ago. It was a "cowpoke" from the Union stockyards, [the kind] that were sold at the newsstands at that time to stockyard "buyers" and to visiting farmers or stock raisers that came in with a carload—or a trainload—of cattle for sale. A plain hickory stick with a bend at the top for a handle. They cost 10 cents at that time. It has not been possible to buy one for years now. I had been months in the hospital—with a portion of the omentum—or "apron of the stomach"—cut out and also seven feet of intestine—and the city paid the hospital bill and the costs of the operating surgeon. Anyway, I was in a plaster cast for quite a time and limped some and I carried that old hickory stick—which was a big help to me. I have had it since then—and have used it, too—on occasions—and I am now using it again. It is so aged and weathered and hardened by drying out and by age and so very smooth that it makes quite a respectable stick.

Martha has before now received my letter in which I told of the Matterns calling me by phone Thanksgiving evening. . . .

Do not neglect attendance at the Forum proper. No matter what happens. You are very fully protected.

If it were not for the "mountains" whence cometh my strength, I could not of myself generate the fortitude to stay here. I do not mean just in this particular location—but in this dimension. Glad Martha's Dad and Mother Bain were with you this Thanksgiving. They were undoubted good company for you ALL. He is such a solid citizen. . . .

If you can possibly find a market for Jane Addams as a movie, I strongly advise you to sell it. I am so interested in such a sale that I advise you spending some time and endeavor to so do. I emphasize the foregoing. But sure of your ability to deliver such should you get an offer. . . .

Yes, "reception" is now fine—and so is "contact." I so very hopefully look forward to your early advancement too.

Fire should continue to give you much thought. There is so very much there. It is the second mystery element. The primal builder. The father of gases. Less is known here of or about this element than is known of "Force" (Lightning. Electricity). . . .

There IS a place for you in Chicago if it can be found. John Matter may be the contact to assist.

I will be much interested in the results of December 9th at Marion.

The poem you enclosed is a beautiful thing—as, also, are the ones enclosed in Martha's last letter. A weaver of words and of phrases, of visions and peoples beforetime, a builder of castles with thoughts as the bricks and the mortar, of truths in no manner distorted but softened and gentled for seasoning, the more for digestion by humans, that seek and are frightened by greatness, that fear the immenseness of life. O weaver of words and of phrases, O weaver of dreams and of visions, O weaver of scenes and of peoples, of truths in full and in part, so weary of earth and so eager————O what's the use to continue. Your escape mechanism is beautiful—and a wonderful release for you from the emotional pressure within—and is truth—half-truth—and pure fancy—and comes from the partial full knowing—partial understanding—and recurrence of vague sights and scenes and conversations reconstructed from the ragged edge of partially remembered things long, long agone that rise to the surface of the conscious from the very depths of the subconscious. You have always had them in one way or another—and you will always have them—until progress from this dimension relieves you. However, they are not harmful; they are really a beautiful relief—and partial satisfaction—though very far from full satisfaction.

Andrew, who could both read and write, born in Bethsaida, was an Apostle of John, called "the Baptist," a brother of Simon Peter. Andrew was the third disciple called by Jesus and who became an Apostle of our Lord. Andrew who introduced his brother, Simon Peter, to the Master. Andrew who was martyred by flogging and crucifixion on a date corresponding to November 30th, in the year 67 A.D., by the Roman proconsul because he converted the wife of the proconsul, Maximilla, to the sect of the Nazarenes. Andrew who was crucified on a cross in the form of the letter X, and ever since this day this symbol has been known as "St. Andrew's Cross."[5] A close friend of ABNER, who became one of the 76 disciples who were sent out to carry the word to the Jew and the Gentile, and who built the church of the Nazarene, so called, in Philadelphia, in Perea, across the Sea of Galilee.

Love from Ma and I to you all,

[5] Loose seems to have derived this information from the apocryphal "Acts of His Passion" and other apocrypha.

15

A Special Message from 1933

DIARY *December 6, 1942*

FORUM—Paper 13: "THE SACRED SPHERES OF PARADISE"

As we passed into the Forum room today we were greeted by Christy and then by Dr. Sadler who stood in the inner doorway. Martha nodded as she passed him, and he half extended his right hand to Harold, who shook it with his left as he continued to his seat. There is still an air of reserve. Mr. Steinbeck gave us a snapshot of the dinner party we attended at Mrs. Palmer's. Harold asked Elsie Karle (a couple of rows ahead) about Dent, who reported he had finally flown by Army plane on up to Alaska from Seattle. She said she had talked to him by phone on Friday. Mrs. Trent, who had not been present for several weeks, seated herself beside Harold and told him how very much she had gotten from his book *Your Key to Happiness.* She said her husband's eye operation had relieved his continuous headache and that she was eager for us to meet him and help him get his mind off himself. From her statements we inferred that he regards anyone interested as she is in these spiritual revelations as "slightly balmy." Harold deferred acceptance of her invitation to visit their home.

Bill's reading of today's paper on the twenty-one worlds surrounding Havona [*sic*] and Isle of Paradise proved of extraordinary interest. The paper dealt specifically with the seven spirit worlds of God the Father which were the concurrent result of the Father-Son relationship. They are by name: Divinington, Sonarington, Spiritington, Vicegerington, Solarington [*sic*], Seraphington, and Ascendington.

Divinington is the secret world which has to do with personal beings of high order created by act of the Father, alone, and is the residence of the mystery beings, the Father fragments, which indwell the ascending mortals of time and space. Preserved on this world forever is the secret of the origin and creation of these beings. No other beings who did not originate on Divinington are ever permitted to reach its shores.

Sonarington is the place of origin of beings created by the Eternal Son, and one seventh of this sphere contains forever the secret of the incarnation of Creator Sons in the bodies of mortal men throughout the countless worlds of time and space in all the seven superuniverses. It also contains the secrets of all manner of incarnation of beings of different orders assigned to special services on the worlds of time and space.

Spiritington is the domain of the beings of Infinite Spirit on which is contained the secret of the power of reflectivity—that miraculous faculty of ascertaining at all times, in any part of the vast grand universe, a specific knowledge of what is taking place there either individually or collectively. There are actual beings who by some unknown union of their own bodies form a "reflectivating intelligence circuit" enabling high orders of beings to see and perceive events transpiring anywhere in the furthermost regions of time and space.

Vicegerington is the world on which reside the beings of Trinity origin and the Trinitized Sons of God. One-seventh of this world preserves the secret knowledge of the manifestation of the Father-Son creative relationship which produces these beings.

Solarington [*sic*] contains many mystery beings unknown to humans but is the headquarters during this two-billion-year universe cycle of the Universe Power Directors. The Perfector of Wisdom (author of this paper) said that could he be taken to this world it would seem to him to be a place totally devoid of personalities and utterly barren because of his incapacity to perceive the type of beings resident there.

Seraphington is the abiding place of the various orders of seraphic hosts engaged in the countless services being constantly performed for the ascending mortals of time and space. This world contains the secret of the ability of these seraphic beings to wrap their own substance about other non-material beings, thus forming a transport which can convey them at incredible speeds throughout the boundless reaches of time and space.

Ascendington is the world reserved as the receiving station for all ascending mortals from the worlds of time and space on their way inward to Havona and the ultimate attainment of the status of Finaliters in the Reserve Corps of Destiny. Ascendington is forever to be known as our permanent cosmic address and, in the inconceivable time to come, we are to go out from it and return to it as we engage upon missions of service to the still-to-be-created beings in the universes now being formed in the outermost space levels beyond the periphery of our present Grand Universe. Once having passed from the superuniverse, and qualifying for the transcendent experience on the billion heaven worlds of Havona, all Ascendington is open to us at all times, including the secret of our fusion with the mystery being, the God fragment known as the Thought Adjuster, which secret will forever be preserved by us from all beings of different origin.

The most perplexing mystery of all creation to beings of other origin, however high, is the evolution of the soul in mortal man and its co-joining with this pre-personal fragment of the Father to form, at last, an eternal identity and to partake in an unimagined and unparalleled service in the majestic destiny of worlds and beings and things yet to come. We, as ascending mortals, eventually, knowingly, realize the fusing of our human entities with this segmented personality of God the Father in such a manner that we never lose this human side of us, regardless of the elevation of our spirit status. It is on Ascendington that we will spend many of our vacations between highly-to-be-enjoyed assignments. It is here also that unspeakably thrilling unions will take place with other fellow ascenders with whom we have associated in the unfolded past on the various worlds of our temporary sojourn in time and space.

It was brought out in today's paper that many spirit beings of which we have no conscious awareness respond to our deep soul aspirations and render service to us but are governed entirely by our free-will choice, and are powerless to aid when and if we lose these spiritual aspirations. It was stated, too, that there are many orders of beings active on this earth who are invisible to us and which are not mentioned or discussed in the Book of Urantia.

Harold told the Burtons he was leaving for a few days, and they said cordially, "Hurry back." Mrs. Steinbeck announced a collection to be taken up in payment of flowers for Mr. Gusler's funeral. Comment among Forum members indicated that few had known him, although many recalled Mrs. Gusler and the fine paper she had read on her plans for presenting the Urantia truths before the Forum body. Harold made our contribution toward the flowers to Mr. Kellogg at the reception desk downstairs. Bill Hales stopped Harold on the way out to ask how he was getting along on the Jane Addams story. Harold surprised him by saying he had finished it but had not disposed of it yet, and likened it to the development of his Twain material, which had subsequently been sold to Warner Bros. with the picture due to be released early next year. Bill said, "We're looking forward to seeing it." No doubt there was wonderment among Forum members as to how long we would be staying on here, and there will be more wonderment now that Harold has told Bill he has finished the Jane Addams work.

Mrs. Githens was present but did not speak, as were Clyde Bedell and his wife, who looked at Harold with no sign of recognition.

December 9, 1942

While out shopping this a.m., Martha met Leone who greeted her with exceptional cordiality. Leone explained she had been Christmas shopping, with Jimmie [*Ed. note:* probably Charlie], for a doll for Patty which had to be dressed, and she didn't know how she was going to find time to do it, etc.

Immediately afterwards Martha met Mrs. Steinbeck, who reported that the Sunday meetings had gone quite as usual last Sunday except that, while Alvin Kulieke was reading a fine paper associating the Book of Urantia with music, Bill, who was sitting in the front row, had suddenly had a "horrible" hysterical laughing spell. She said if it had been anyone else she didn't know what would have happened. As it was, Alvin had made a rather sharp comment and then went on with his paper. Mrs. Steinbeck said she and Mr. Steinbeck and also Miss Baumgartner were invited to one o'clock tea at Dr. Sadler's on Sunday next.

December 13, 1942

FORUM—Paper 14: "THE CENTRAL AND DIVINE UNIVERSE"

As we crossed the street, a car drew up in front of the Sadlers' residence containing the Bedells and Bill Hales. We nodded a greeting and then met Elsie Karle, who was on foot, having come via train and two changes of streetcar. She said Dent was really on his way now, and showed us a good picture of him taken at Seattle with some army officer.

Inside we met Mr. Hill, who greeted us cordially. Martha stepped into Mr. Kellogg's room to tell him Mary would be late, and she fancied a warmer feeling on Mr. Kellogg's part though he did not smile. Leaving Kellogg's office to go upstairs, Harold ran face to face with Clyde Bedell coming in, who said, "Hello, Harold," but with a distinctly unfriendly expression. His attitude since this "development" has been as strange as any, particularly since he was the one who drew up the petition.

Upstairs, Mr. Hales shook hands with Harold. Mr. Hill followed us in and sat beside Harold. He chatted amiably about non-Forum matters. The Steinbecks and Mrs. Palmer came in, the latter playfully pulling Harold's hair and telling him she had gotten Martha's permission to do so. This little informality indicated, at least, the feeling of cordiality existent.

Bill's reading of the paper seemed especially tiresome to us today, interspersed as it was with his own attempted profound statements and witticisms which only served to confuse and annoy rather than to help, as far as we were concerned. Mr. Hales Sr. and Clyde Bedell are usually the ones who ask questions from the floor, and Bill gives his answers in a tone of final and complete authority. Occasionally he throws a crumb to his audience by saying, "If any of you can think of a better answer, I'd like to hear it," but he immediately goes on reading as though he expected no reply. We were glad when the paper was over, but not from the standpoint of its contents. It is increasingly evident to us that the interjection of a human personality between the truth as contained in the papers and the individual desirous of receiving this truth, greatly detracts from clear and unadulterated understanding.

Elsie Baumgartner spoke to Harold a few minutes at intermission, saying she had not yet reported by mail to Harry Loose, as she was too bewildered and was hoping that time would straighten out many things in her mind. Harold said that he would like to say to her that none of the accusations made against us were true, including the most outrageous of all, that Ruth Kellogg had said we had tried to plot with her parents to seize the papers. Miss Baumgartner said this accusation had been made in her hearing, in the presence of the group she went with when seeing the Doctor. She said she could not comprehend what possessed the Doctor to make such a charge if unfounded, and that she had a hard time believing it from the first. Then, too, she said that the treatment of us did not seem at all in the spirit of the papers or even humanly considerate. She said that the Doctor had talked in such a manner that no one could tell which of his statements represented spiritual instructions and which his own human viewpoint and attitude. She said, "I think now that he purposely wanted to so confuse us. I, personally, am greatly disappointed in the human side of some of the personalities in charge and it has upset me so that I've had all I can do to make myself attend since. If I had not felt it to be my duty, and if I did not have faith that higher powers would clear up this state of things in due time, I wouldn't know what to do."

Harold said that his asking for a hearing before the Forum at the 9/13/42 meeting was made necessary by the charges the Doctor had preferred without giving him an opportunity to answer them, and she probably had noticed that the Doctor was afraid to air these charges before the Forum body as a whole in Harold's presence. Elsie said, "Yes. And I very much disliked his statement that we were 'only guests in his home.' It has made me feel ever since that I was not really welcome here, not only at the Sunday meetings, but the Wednesday night meetings as well. I think he did this deliberately to intimidate everybody, and while I think he has lived up to his devotion insofar as the guarding of the papers is concerned, he has fallen down very much on the human side."

She then said she would like to give us a ring and have a good chat with us some night. She indicated that many people were terribly confused and uncertain, and that they were wondering why, if we had done anything so bad, our case had not been disposed of. Harold said we had asked that we might face the contact commissioners in the presence of the entire Forum body, but this had been refused. Harold said he felt certain the Doctor was afraid to face him in public on such charges.

Christy, for the first time since we can remember, was not in evidence today. On the wall just outside the Forum room was an invitation to an "open house" for all Forum members at Dr. Sadler's, New Year's afternoon. While Harold was talking to Miss Baumgartner, Martha had a talk with Mrs. Burton about Sholem Asch's *Nazarene*[1] and his concept of Joshua ben Joseph and Lazarus in contrast with the papers. Mr. Burton was warm and friendly as always.

We met Alvin Kulieke, Mr. Kulieke Sr. and Lucile [Olson], and Martha asked Alvin about the fine paper we heard he had read at the Seventy. He said he had likened the papers to a great symphony, and Harold said he thought this a fine concept and that we would like to see his paper sometime. The Kuliekes seemed genuinely cordial, Mr. Kulieke particularly.

Mrs. Githens came in about the middle of the paper but avoided looking in our direction at any time.

HARRY LOOSE to MARTHA SHERMAN

Monterey Park, December 18, 1942

Dear Martha:-

I want to acknowledge receipt of your letter with the enclosure of Harold's beautiful "Through Death." I imagine that Harold will do more of these, and I know that the Forum folks in general would much appreciate them if they could get them. Something may work out.

Am much interested in how the talks came out in Marion, December the 9th. Have been so very hopeful that a sponsor would be located for a radio program through John Matter or some contact that he would make. . . .

Things here go along just about the same for the time of year that it is. The meat allotment here has run short because at the time the allotment was made they didn't take into consideration the fact that before the year was over there would be an addition in the population here of over 300,000; workers in the war industries around here. There has been no beef available in any of the butcher shops for over two weeks and very little of anything else. Eggs are a nickel apiece. There is no butter to be had. Today I went to the butcher shop to order a small turkey for Christmas and they told me that they couldn't take any orders, for there weren't sufficient turkeys in the market as the

[1] Sholem Asch, *The Nazarene* (New York: G. P. Putnam's Sons, 1939).

Government has taken 6,000,000 pounds of turkeys for the boys in the armed forces. I may be able to get a chicken later but the prospects are not good. . . .

Do not neglect a single Forum meeting. Mr. Gusler has been released. He is far better off to be rid of the flesh. The grief that we feel over the release of a dear one from the flesh is purely because "WE" have lost something and so we grieve—we do not grieve because the one who has gone on has been promoted surely. There is very little friendliness—charity—love—or any other godly emotion expressed in the Forum—at any time. There has been much of other emotions—hate—fear—and other opposites. I don't believe that you would be strong enough to know the whole setup and the details. It would sure sicken you.

I have forgotten to remark the receipt of the magazines—and to express thanks—I'll get a lot of reading out of them a little later on. . . .

Yes, Harold, Swedenborg WAS a highly developed Soul—and he reached some heights. He presented a very interesting study in his lifetime—and even more interesting since his death. He arrived at the conclusion that "all life is and was God." In his way, he was right. Right—in the fact that all Life has within it some PART of God or it could not exist. All too long to argue—or to explain—here. And his real name was not Swedenborg. That name was a "taken name," such as was a very prevalent thing to do in those times—and still exists in no small measure right up to now. His correct name was, or should have been, the same as his father—which was Ohlson. He lived next to "the House of the Olive Men" from the time of his birth until his 12th year. The "House of the Olive Men" was so called because of the Italian merchants and traders who owned and occupied this well-known place. It is quite an interesting story—his birth and development—his clairvoyant powers, so called—O there is a lot there—the name of the woman who delivered him, what we today call a midwife, also had the same last name as his father but spelled with an "e" instead of an "o".[2] Read his philosophy. It will be interesting and entertaining—not that it will ever convert you to the philosophy.

Well, Martha—and Harold—I will have to close for now—so with love to you ALL, I will stop for this time. With every good wish for a very happy time at Christmas—and the same for New Year.

As always,

[2] What Loose says here about eighteenth-century Swedish scientist and mystic Emanuel Swedenborg contradicts all known information about him.

HAROLD SHERMAN to HARRY LOOSE

Chicago, December 20, 1942

Dear Harry:

I have been jammed up with work—or, at least, trying to get work in Chicago—and have lacked the time to write. My Marion trip was a heartwarming occasion, and my two talks, before the Kiwanis Club and the Foreman's Club, were exceedingly well received. I also gave a short talk to Mother's Women's Club, which seemed to please her. The 12-13 Club, a unique little organization of 13 men, who used to meet at 13 minutes after 12 noon, every Friday, held a reunion for me, after 20 years . . . this used to be the publicity committee of the Chamber of Commerce, and we put over some of the biggest civic events ever accomplished in Marion. The affection shown for me was touching, and indicated again the priceless value of true friendship. Several men embraced me and unashamedly kissed me, with tears in their eyes . . . and the whole evening was one never to be forgotten. It made me feel again, how much I must constantly strive to be worthy of such regard . . . and how important it is to give personal attention to even "the least of these." Different Marion people would stop me and remind me of something I had done or said which had meant so much to them . . . and which I had long since forgotten . . . or what even one little word of encouragement or faith may mean, exercised at the right time.

The situation across the street remains the same . . . and apparently the Doctor is playing a waiting game, figuring he will tire us out or we will leave the city . . . which makes us even more determined to solve our economic problems and remain here. We sent Christmas cards to those who have befriended us and to the Kelloggs, but NOT to the Doctor or Christy or Bill. And when we go over to the Forum today, I suppose these last three will know, by this time, that others have been remembered and they have not. The Doctor has announced open house on New Year's afternoon, which we are NOT attending. He has not shown us the Christian spirit, let alone the Christmas spirit . . . The papers are absolutely wonderful and direly needed by this sick and sorry world. I only hope and pray the higher powers take a hand at the proper time to clear the atmosphere over there. . . .

There is a chance of my radio program being sold to a Chicago sponsor . . . and I have made many connections which I feel, in time, are going to be profitable. Just now the going is temporarily tough . . . and I have been notified that the Twain case is up for a hearing in New York on January 5th. I am trying to get another postponement until I am financially able to make the trip . . . and I have hoped this matter would be cleared up so that I would not have to go to all this trouble, anyway.

Harry, wherever money is involved, trouble usually arises. Isn't this world's standard of values all cockeyed . . . that we have to depend so upon money . . . and have to strive so hard to get it? I hope in worlds to come that this won't be so.

John Matter, this Chicago friend, who knows so many prominent people here and is introducing me around, feels I should let him canvass the members of the Hull House board and see if consideration of my play cannot be reopened. But my feeling is that I should wait until the Twain picture is out . . . or at least until I have a private showing here . . . and then invite Mrs. Bowen, Mr. Schwartz, Miss Carr and others to see the picture . . . and GO BACK to them after that, and see if I can win them over . . . rather than playing politics and trying to influence board members to overrule Mrs. Bowen, etc. . . . Don't you think this is the best procedure? . . .

Our thoughts go out to you this Yuletide and we wish we could be together in the flesh . . . but we will certainly be in spirit . . . with our hearts full of gratitude for all you people have done for all of us. Mary, Marcia, Martha and I send LOVE and the prayer that health and good things will be with you through 1943.

Sincerely,

DIARY *December 20, 1942*

FORUM—Paper 15: "THE SEVEN SUPERUNIVERSES"

As we entered the Forum room with Martha in the lead, Dr. Sadler limply extended his hand which we both shook in passing. Christy of course had greeted us but distantly as she always does when Doctor is present. There were even fewer on hand at the start, many being late arriving; gas rationing and snow had made their inroads.

Bill read Chapter 15—the longest paper of all—which called for an intermission in itself and lasted until almost 4:30. The paper had to do with the layout of the grand universe, and while heavy reading was magnificent in content.

At the finish, Mrs. Steinbeck told us she had just learned that the meeting of the Seventy was being dispensed with and Dr. Sadler was going to read some special message of some kind so it would be okay for us to stay. We declined, however, as we had planned to attend open house at Hull House where Mary was aiding in the reception and serving. Due to the overlong meeting, we were already late in leaving.

Mrs. Burton, Miss [Ruth] Carothers, Mrs. Palmer, Mrs. [Julia] Early and the Steinbecks all spoke to us. Russell Bucklin, who spoke especially to several other members seated at different points, only nodded to us. His continued aloofness is perhaps as difficult to understand as that of any. We sent Christmas cards to all who had befriended us particularly. These were the Burtons, Steinbecks, Mrs. Palmer, Mrs. Gusler and Elsie Karle. On deliberation we decided to show our friendliness toward the Bucklins and the Kelloggs, but we did not send cards to the Sadlers or to Christy. The Haleses had already sent us a Christmas greeting and we mailed them one of ours in return.

Mrs. Early spoke of her sons having read quite a number of Harold's books and being thrilled at having sat beside him some Sundays before.

December 21, 1942

In order that we might have a report as to what happened following our departure Sunday, Harold phoned Mrs. Steinbeck tonight. She said Dr. Sadler canceled the Seventy meeting without notice or announcement and took that hour to read and to comment on some shorthand notes made during a session with the instrument in 1933 when they tuned in on some doings which they were not supposed to hear. This was a conference of spirit entities having to do with pre-war conditions and conditions which were to exist after the war. According to the Doctor we are heading toward a socialistic state and some of the changes, revealed through what was recorded that night, have already come to pass. The Doctor explained that he was not supposed to make known any of this material, but that since some of these changes had now come about he was taking the authority to speak of them for they had nothing to do with the papers as such.

Mrs. Steinbeck said Dr. Sadler interspersed so many remarks on Stuart Chase's work, a series of books on war and peace containing predictions on the world we are destined to live in, that she could not tell half the time which of the information the Doctor was giving out pertained to his own records and which had to do with Mr. Chase's writings.

Harold commented that he distinctly remembered the Doctor's declaring on the occasion of the Sept. 13th meeting that he had never permitted, nor would he ever permit, any subject to be brought up during the regular Forum meetings which was not directly connected with the papers.

Mrs. Steinbeck said, "Yes, I recall that too, but the Doctor said lots of things have happened to change his mind and methods of procedure, so none of us can tell any more what he is going to do next. He just seems to suit himself."

Harold said, "It must have been confusing and it certainly was inconsiderate for the Doctor to cancel the Seventy meeting without any notice."

Mrs. Steinbeck said, "Yes, but I guess you've got to expect that when you're dealing with him."

Harold said he had heard nice comments about different little speeches on the papers given at the Seventy meetings, particularly Alvin Kulieke's. Harold further remarked about Bill Jr.'s strange outburst of laughter in the midst of Mr. Kulieke's address. Mrs. Steinbeck said, "Yes, Bill did blurt right out and laugh, but Mr. Kulieke answered him back when he made fun of the paper and went right on. Nobody else laughed, and we didn't see anything for Bill to laugh at, but apparently he did. It was very strange."

Mrs. Steinbeck said she had made notes on Dr. Sadler's talk and was going to compare them with notes made by several others, including Charles Rawson, and then write them up so we could see them. She said she had the Seventy program all lined up now through the month of January if the Doctor would let her hold the meetings. This indicated how little say anyone actually has in association with developments under the Sadler roof, and how little consideration is shown when the Doctor wants to go off on some excursion of his own.

[*Addendum 12-21-42:*] Mrs. Steinbeck told Harold that Mr. Bucklin and Miss Baumgartner were the only ones present at the last intended meeting of those interested in studying the charters and other plans for Urantia Book publication and organizations. These meetings have never been encouraged by Dr. Sadler and have deliberately been let go by default. Mr. Bucklin went to Dr. Sadler this particular evening and asked him what should be done about them, whereupon Dr. Sadler said, "Just forget about them. There isn't any interest in these matters anyway." So the meetings have now been abandoned.

December 27, 1942

All Forum meetings called off for today (as of last Sunday).

HAROLD SHERMAN to HARRY LOOSE

Chicago, December 28, 1942

Dear Harry:

There has been a big blow-up at Hull House and Charlotte Carr is out! Mrs. Bowen felt she was entering too much into partisan politics, as did other members of the Board. A Miss Wing, who was going to give Hull House a bequest of $20,000, also walked out with Miss Carr, and Hull House is temporarily in a tight economic spot, due to this crisis. I have been *impressed* to lay low during this period and not try to press things . . . and I can see WHY now, because I think conditions are much better for me to step in and complete my deal—since Hull House needs money . . . and should be happy to sell Jane Addams' life story as a means of aiding the settlement. . . .

Ruth Kellogg, before I forget it, has been out on the coast during the holidays . . . visiting a soldier friend whom she intends to marry . . . and she may have married him on this trip. I was in hopes she would look you up, but I doubt if she has. We have had a nodding acquaintance with the Kelloggs since this difficulty . . . sent them a Christmas card with no acknowledgment . . . they must be scared to death. I wish, when you can, you would fill in the rest of the story about ACROSS THE STREET. I do not believe I could be more nauseated than I am at present, over some of the attitudes and atmosphere.

Harry, I had a most unusual dream or vision last night, and I am writing you in confidence about it as the ONLY ONE I can confide in. I seemed to be told . . . or taken ahead in time, and shown that [popular radio host] Walter Winchell meets a sudden death. I was instructed to prepare a radio program, based upon the Urantia material, for the fifteen-minute spot now held by Winchell . . . to file several sealed letters with different friends, containing a note addressed to the Jergens company, in which I predict the sudden passing of Winchell and then enclose this program submitted to TAKE THE

PLACE of Winchell's presentation. The friends are not to open the sealed letters, protected by government postmark, until so advised by me—and ONLY THEN in the presence of officials from the Jergens company. When this time occurs, I am to go to Dr. S. regardless of his present attitude, show him the evidence, and tell him that I have been impressed that the time has now come to introduce the Urantia material, through this RADIO OUTLET.

It was intimated to me, in this dream or vision, that AT THIS TIME a message would be received by Dr. S. through the instrument, CONFIRMING my action and INSTRUCTING the Doctor to co-operate with me. Then the Jergens officials, impressed by this FOREKNOWLEDGE of Winchell's death and the preparation of the material in advance anticipation of this event, are to be SHOWN the EVIDENCE . . . the Urantia Book in preparation . . . so that reference can be made to the source . . . and the BROADCASTS BEGIN . . . before the book is published or ready for publication . . . so that the public appetite is enormously whetted . . . and a *LITTLE* KNOWLEDGE given to mankind each week. Winchell controls the biggest audience of any program in America, and is short-waved to all other countries . . . his audience in the U.S. is said to reach a total of 30,000,000. Here would be a ready-made audience, which would be electrified by such a development.

This may sound fantastic . . . this dream or vision came to me last night. I could proceed quietly, in preparation, if you think it wise to follow through. I wish I could get some verifiable confirmation of these impressions . . . I dare not breathe this to a soul beyond Martha, whom I awakened to tell at five this morning. But if I had consciously tried to figure out a method of presenting this TRUTH, I doubt if I could have hit upon a more simple but powerful medium, made to order, for this SUDDEN and DRAMATIC switchover. You see, Jergens Lotion has that MOST VALUABLE fifteen-minute spot on SUNDAY NIGHT . . . and they would be paralyzed if something suddenly happened to Winchell, with no plans made to fill in for him. If I suddenly appeared on the scene with the evidence that I had known for some months of his sudden demise (protected by affidavits) it is bound to have quite an influence. Can you ascertain anything from higher sources, to throw any more light on this unusual "suggestion"?

We spent a quiet Christmas and sent our thoughts out to you and yours. Mother is here from Marion, Indiana, to stay until after

New Year's. There is no Forum meeting this coming Sunday . . . but an open house at Dr. S.'s on New Year's Day afternoon, to which we are *not* going.

Please save the postmarked envelope to this letter as well as the letter, in some safe place, unless you do not think it advisable.

I am auditioning for the possible sale of my radio program on personal philosophy next week—and hope to sell it and thus settle my financial problem. . . .

LOVE TO ALL.

DIARY *December 28, 1942*

This a.m. Harold passed the Doctor on the street returning home from the corner drugstore. He looked old and somewhat woebegone, with a soft hat turned down and collar of overcoat up, plodding along. Harold said, "Good morning, Doctor" and the Doctor looked up, startled, to reply "Oh! Howdy," with a little gesture of the hand toward his hat.

This a.m. we received a wedding announcement from the Kelloggs of Ruth's marriage which took place on the West Coast. We knew she had left to visit her soldier sweetheart and surmised the wedding would take place. We've received no Christmas card from the Kelloggs and feel they thought it only proper to formally let us know of Ruth's marriage.

HARRY LOOSE to HAROLD and MARTHA SHERMAN

Monterey Park, December 29, 1942

Dear Harold and Martha, "small Martha of the biscuits,"

Thank you and small and necessary Martha for your unique Christmas card. It is very different, and has been admired by some interesting intelligences.

I have not seen Ruth Kellogg. I do not expect to see her and I do not want to see her. I am very hopeful that you will not have to go to N.Y.C. on the Twain thing. Rec'd a printed Christmas greeting from the Matterns—quite out of the ordinary—from their N.Y. address. . . .

Your vision is very interesting. I have made inquiry and found Winchell is alive—to the date of this letter, anyway.[3] Do not let this in any way discourage your reception of these impressions, however, for this is a favorite way of the introduction of a subject which, through

[3] Winchell died in 1972.

fear of the above-normal, could not be as well received otherwise. The Bible is filled with such illustrations. However, you may be sure that your work here has hardly begun. Have patience; you will be knowingly active. Such vision as you had, when legitimate, will be repeated and will receive other and further confirmatory identification of a positive nature. You will be SURE when the time comes—there will be no hesitancy.

Do not neglect attendance at the Forum as long as it is available. Do not think that your polite attendance is without result. Do not allow yourself to slump in interest—or appear to slump—or allow thoughts of "O what is the use—I am making no progress" enter your mind. (Attention Martha to assist.)

I am writing under pressure—hurried and condensed. There continues much activity regarding ALL that you are interested in.

Glad that your Mother came up from Marion for Xmas and do hope that you were able to give her considerable information.

Please do not forget Ronayne etc. in the present stress.

I have oft told you that evil continues into the next dimension. It has some power there. It has more power and some representatives here. I hope that this tells you something. . . .

I advise you to make every effort to get the O.K. from Mrs. Bowen to the sale of Jane Addams and then to market it as soon as possible for the best market available—by which I mean the best price. I also very much hope that you will find a sale on the radio for a program on your own philosophy. Push this and the Addams matter just as hard and as fast as you can. . . .

I miss you both a great deal and wish that I could shed the responsibility of this receiving station and power house and spend a little time with you. I did so wish to get to Chattanooga but it didn't work out. From what I can put together of mixed messages that pass, there is activity for much good in the present great war need. I wish that I knew more myself.

Will stop for now. As always, our "much love to you ALL,"

Harry

APPENDICES

Appendix A

[An undated and unaddressed letter written in 1942 in which Harry Loose instructs Harold to form a group of seven.]

At once start to assemble about you seven very carefully chosen intelligences. No more than this—no less than this number. Of this grouping there must be a balance in favor of male intelligences. Be satisfied with one to begin with. Be slow, careful and cautious. Add to this one very carefully and only after a most positive surety of their loyalty, intelligence, interest and ability to retain this matter in secrecy until such time as is arrived when they will be further advised as to their service.

Accept only intelligences of middle age—not old—not young—with physical and mental health. Choose intelligences that give a positive impression of eventual ability to teach and to talk from a platform. Do not begin to teach until you have fully assembled the seven whom you are sure answer the requirements. To assemble this grouping, before you start to teach, they may be given only such very minor information as will arouse their immediate and positive interest. This whole must be handled very diplomatically and with extreme care. No mistake must be made with the choice of the seven as there is no remedy if a mistake in judgment is discovered later. This is very personal to you as what is to follow will be your own individual responsibility.

Those of the seven, being married, may transfer nothing to their husbands, or wives, unless with your permission, after their own request and recommendation. None of these wives or husbands may join the original seven. Their only information is to come through their husbands or wives. None being present in the circle of seven. Be doubly careful of and searching of these thus added individuals desirability after such request and recommendation. A refusal is far better for you than an error discovered later.

In the eventual, these, your students, will be in the beginnings of the makings for furtherance of a great work coming later. These chosen intelligences are only to know YOU. They are not to know anything of or about other intelligences interested in this matter and are to know nothing of other locations where such information is being revealed. They are surely to know that *there are* many other chosen intelligences and that there are other locations in distant places where this work is being similarly done. You, however, are their only contact—for this time and period. You are their only supply and their only direct knowledge of entity. They are only to know that you are in contact with other intelligences and other locations interested in the same matter.

Be sure and positive in the very beginning to very much stress the great need for patience. You will find each eager for more haste. This cannot be. Explain that you are limited, and directed, in the amount that you give. This will be correct. Bind them, on honor, that there will be no written matter—no memoranda—no notes taken. This is positive. Loss of place in the circle—and other things—may happen in such instances.

I may tell you that in the accomplishing of the above, satisfactorily and well, you are starting along the way that will eventuate, in the not far future, a year maybe, or in even a shorter time, in the reception of a higher intelligence in the presence of the seven. You may, of course, speak of the Book. Its course of preparation and the time elapsed. Not of its present location. You may speak of the time of its possible release when it will be available to them. You may speak of your original contact—how it was accomplished—naming no names—or locations. You may, and must, speak with positiveness and authority. You may have the backing in such of Martha in such positiveness and authority. Martha and the children must be abjured to silence as to the identity or location of your local contacts with intelligences existing here. [*Handwriting:* All, however, may [illegible]]

Appendix B

CLYDE BEDELL to WILFRED KELLOGG

Mr. Wilfred Kellogg
Diversey Parkway
Chicago

Chicago, October 30, 1933

Dear Mr. Kellogg:

Will you kindly throw this letter into the hopper with whatever other suggestions you may be receiving—for consideration by Dr. Sadler and the rest of you?

I am doing this typing on a borrowed typewriter, I am not a stenographer, and my time is short. I ask pardon in advance for miscues.

Please don't impute to me a desire to see a loose-knit or nondescript board for the U Society. I perceive that precautions must be taken. I too wish to see stable direction of this revelation's distribution. But I feel there must be a middle course which will appear to be fair and defensible. Fair to the book itself, fair to the directors whoever they may be, and fair to the people for whom after all we incorporate—the part of the public we can interest.

The following points are self-explanatory. First though, I wish to say that unless it would handicap him professionally, I believe there are inescapable reasons why Dr. William should be on the board—if indeed he is not its chairman.

WHY SHOULD A SELF-SUPPORTING BOARD HOLD OFFICE FOR LIFE?

1. I believe we cannot warrantedly expect any religious or secular enterprise on earth to be better governed by old men in their dotage than by a board deliberately designed to avoid that possibility.

2. A board for "life" smacks of the papacy—but has the worse aspect of never being swayed by counsel when one man is won, but only when four or more are won.

3. The incorporators are placed in the position of saying, "We are the only persons on earth qualified to do this job, and the only seven in our lifetimes who COULD do it—but, let the unwashed and misguided public provide the money to do our bidding."

4. The incorporators may be made to appear to place their interest in the society before the society's welfare, inasmuch as they presume no persons so well qualified as themselves will become members of the organization as it grows and develops.

5. Why should ANY seven of those fortunate to be in on this revelation to date, say that, out of the thousands of splendid people we hope to have join us, none can ever qualify so long as the seven may live, to participate finally, actively, and directly in the society's direction?

6. Jesus took no such water-tight precautions in connection with the dissemination of the new conception of religion. Should we be so circumscribing and narrow in connection with this book?

7. If genuinely aged men can do the job well, why not seek some such to participate now?

8. To me, closing the board, as proposed, is entirely out of harmony with the spirit and the breadth of the revelations we wish to see promulgated.

9. It seems inconsistent to me to say in one breath, "This is too vital and important to risk letting the mob have a voice," and in the next, "It will be of so little importance in a few years that the direction of old men will be good enough."

10. WHAT GOOD REASON is there for doing it? If it is to keep good and trusted men in, they can re-elect themselves every year or five or ten, as may be arranged—so long as their consciences would permit. If it is to form an inviolate autocracy to keep other good men out, it discredits the incorporators.

11. A conscientious young man would, I believe, refuse to accept life membership on such a board. I would never want inviolate right of tenure to keep me on a body which should occasionally draft onto itself enthusiastic and fresher blood.

12. Your proposals contemplate "kicking off" unworthy members. That is an admission of human fallibility. A simple provision for

"terms of so many years" would obviate all necessity for so deplorable a possibility as you contemplate.

13. Failure to reelect a man would appear more desirable to me than trial and recrimination and bitterness.

14. The great disseminators of religion have generally been young men. There was some militancy even in Jesus. Venerable men may be splendid for sitting and counselling, but they have never been generally famed for active direction and aggressive enterprise. There should be a little of that always on the board, should there not?

15. If the "permission is given," we owe it to this revelation to permit it every possibility for wider and more adequate promulgation as the years go by. I cannot prescribe to the guess in the dark that the society's work will possibly be done in twenty or thirty years and that an aged board at that time will be no handicap. We owe it to the revelation to presume work of its dissemination may be even more important to be directed by strong and sure hands then than now.

16. We deliberately deny some hardihood and sincere heartfelt devotion to the revelation for a future date—when we deny its board the opportunity to grow and keep alive and active, which the revelation itself has in itself. That's poorly said. I mean, the revelation is a great potential all in itself. It is young and new and vital and alive. Its growth and acceptance may be dependent on the vitality and aliveness, the great devotion and sincerity and stamina, of the men who direct its distribution. Should we deny the book a board kept always partially vital and refreshed?

17. If we believe the work will be completed (I don't) before the first board becomes impaired and befogged by too much living, why incorporate? If we incorporate to provide a continuing entity to the Society, why not provide that the entity be a vigorous one as well as illustrious, sincere, dignified—and whatever, or whatever the case may be?

18. The Supreme Court was not incorporated—or elected—or sponsored—by itself.

19. The Supreme Court is a receiving and digesting body. It has never advertised or tried to sell or distribute a decision. Our society's board should be a disseminating and radiating body. Please don't believe I want to see it a cheaply commercialized thing. But the preaching of John the Baptist—and of Saul to nearly all the Greeks—was warm, alive, vigorous, aggressive.

I am afraid I weary you. Let me more briefly come to the other point.

WHY DENY A VOICE—TO SOME EXTENT AT LEAST—TO THE PEOPLE WHO PAY? TO THE PEOPLE WHO MUST CARRY THE WORD ON? TO THE PEOPLE FOR WHOM WHEN ALL IS SAID AND DONE—THE REVELATION IS MADE—THE PUBLIC WE CAN INTEREST?

1. It seems hardly fair to ascribe religious perception to those who would join us and then to call them a mob unfit to participate even indirectly in the choice of men who will direct further efforts to get more men like them to perceive.

2. It seems hardly fair to say, "Give us your money, but not your opinion. You can practise this religion in your own sphere, but we don't think you have enough of it to help elect a minority of our directors."

3. It rather appears to me that to refuse supporting members some voice in naming directors directly or indirectly is subversive of a lot the world has learned politically, economically, and spiritually.

4. After all, too—we are seeking live thinking dynamic people to embrace this book—not sheep.

5. Disseminators of a new revelation might be warranted in leaning over backwards in taking precautions to avoid appearances of an unwarranted "divine preceptorship."

6. I feel it is a little specious—or something of the kind—to extend a "Jesus book" while saying, "We must protect ourselves against pollution by associates of your choosing."

7. Do we wish to say, "You are spiritual enough to see that this book should be disseminated, but you are not spiritual enough to see that one man can do a better job than another of disseminating it."

8. It hardly seems fair to me to impugn today, the motives of the people whom we will have won to this book five or ten years from today.

9. After this inviolate board begins to die off, will we not have to turn to people such as we propose barring for a long period of years? If we say, "The job will be done then," it might be remarked that Jesus started a dissemination 2000 years ago which isn't done yet. Nor did he appoint a closed regimen to carry it along. Although a certain group of believers did.

I am sorry I am so verbose.

Let me start to stop.

Without jeopardizing the interests of the society, or lessening the protection you wish it afforded, terms could be made for stated periods, with power of re-election in the hands of the board. Thus you would cause each director to face squarely at the termination of a term the question as to his fitness, and the possibility of some new adherent who might serve better. You would secure the security you wish. You would eliminate a good share of the possibilities for regret.

Next, why have the entire board from any one source? Or elected in any one way? Dr. Sadler's thought that the council might name a few directors would solve most of the objections which occur to me in connection with denying the membership a voice.

* * *

Is the following worth thinking about?

Three incorporating directors to serve until the book is about to be published, or is published?

Then, upon publication, let them start terms of six years. Then, at the start of those terms, let them name three more directors to serve for two years each.

And let the council concurrently, and upon its election, name three directors to begin terms of fours years each, one of whom would be chairman of the council.

Then, as terms expired, the directors would name a new directors' directors, and the council, the council's directors, always for 6-year terms.

* * *

Perhaps a few things might be said in favor of having each group of three named above, including a 2-year and a 6-year director. And as each term expired, the new term would be for 6 years. Thus, instead of a group of three from the council expiring together, one would expire each two years, et cetera.

* * *

Had I not made so sudden a departure for New York, I would have sent this to you sooner. All best wishes, and be sure I have confidence that your final decisions—be they one way or another—will work out. Somehow, they always do.

Yours,

Clyde Bedell

Appendix C

LYCEUM LECTURE TUESDAY.

Dr. Wm. Sadler, Noted Chicago Surgeon, at Senior High School, 8:15 Tomorrow Night.

The Teachers' Lyceum Course is presenting a variety in the way of programs, and a great many people will find very interesting and profitable the lecture arranged for Tuesday evening at 8:15 o'clock, at the Senior High School, when Dr. William S. Sadler, surgeon, author and lecturer, appears.

Dr. Sadler is a practicing physician and surgeon of Chicago, a professor of the Post Graduate Medical school, and medical director of the Chicago Therapeutic Institute, one of the most unique establishments of its kind in the country.

His medical books are so popular that they have been numbered among the six best sellers. He is a member of the leading medical association and is the exponent of some of the most modern views. One of his lectures is entitled, "Faith and Fear, or How the Mind Influences the Body;" another is "Americanitis, or the High Pressure Life."

He has lectured successfully for twenty years on the Chautauqua platform, and he has been much sought after as an after dinner speaker. The ticket price is very reasonable.

DR. SADLER HERE MONDAY

Will Address Parent-Teacher Association in Afternoon

Dr. W. S. Sadler, who is to appear on the lyceum course next Monday evening, has very kindly consented to address the meeting of the Parent-Teacher Association next Monday afternoon. He is one of the strongest speakers who has ever appeared in Junction City, and the association is very fortunate in having a chance to hear him. The public is very cordially invited to be present and hear him on Monday afternoon.

Two notices of Sadler's appearances in Kansas in January 1923. The Sadlers began the Forum shortly after he returned to Chicago. LEFT: from Fort Scott Daily Tribune *and* Fort Scott Daily Monitor, *Mon. Jan. 15. RIGHT: from* Junction City Daily Union, *Fri. Jan. 19.*

Appendix D

"HOW I WOULD PRESENT THE URANTIA BOOK," by Mrs. Carl [Rachel] Gusler (1942)

In the endeavor to formulate an acceptable way to present the Urantia Book just published, I have chosen the following plan addressed to a general group of listeners. By that, I mean a group of various religions or faiths or unbeliefs. In so doing, that universal appeal which the book has will keep its universal appeal and will engage the interest of each sufficiently to wonder what there might be in it for him.

The group may be our sons and their wives some Friday evening. It may be two couples to whom I wish to lend a copy each, or it may be a group such as you. I believe the *presentation* should be the purpose of every arranged gathering, large or small. There will be plenty of accidental opportunities, where there can be more or less personal and specific approaches and discussions.

Not knowing what license, if any, we would have as Forum members, it seemed best to me to proceed as one of those who had read the Urantia Book just published. My purpose is to so interest this group that they or a reasonable percent will waste no time to make its contents their own.

If you can imagine yourselves to be the group, and I can so interest *you* as you place yourselves in pre-Forum days, perhaps that will be the test of my effort.

This is in general one presentation I'm sure I shall some day make:

I have read the Urantia Book.

It claims to be the first revelation for all races and peoples that has been given to the world since Jesus' life on earth.

It claims to have been sent by authorities in the Great Beyond to give us a fuller understanding of the heavenly Father and his Son, Christ Michael, and of the Infinite Spirit; a fuller understanding of the plan of the Heavenly Father for his human children in all the far-flung worlds; a knowledge of the origin and cosmology of the Universe; the analysis, co-ordination, and unification of the physical, mental and spiritual spheres of life and thought and being; and very much of consuming interest concerning the personnel—to us unseen—of this planet and of the wondrous spirit worlds which will some day be part of our experience.

The Urantia Book evidently is for the whole world, for men of all races and creeds—and will be published in every major language.

According to this remarkable book, our planet's name is Urantia and we are known as Urantians. We belong to the Universe of Nebadon of which Christ Michael, our Jesus of Nazareth, is the sovereign son ruling his worlds in infinite love and mercy.

I believe the Urantia Book is the revelation it claims to be. I see no reason for insisting that the world should not expect direct interracial or planetary revelation, and even if I *did*, to read it would be amply convincing to me that it is of supernatural origin. It has given to me a complete satisfaction and abiding faith, a deepened desire for the realization in my own life of those qualities which are of survival value, a consuming interest in the life in the Great Beyond and yet an ever-intensified and widening interest in this planet where we Urantians find ourselves living. It has also given me an awakened, alive interest in many phases of knowledge which my school days did not seem to generate. Some are beyond my ability to comprehend except in part and yet the interest is there.

In fact, the book, besides being a spiritual guide—an enlarged way of responsible life along undreamed-of, intriguing pathways—is a liberal education for one who aspires to Universe citizenship. It imparts the outward look and the drive to know, to understand, and above all to share this first revelation given to the races of our world since the life of the Master.

We are a mixed group. Some of us dipped only from the surface of the unfathomable riches of the Master's teachings; some searched hither and yon, never able to come to a knowledge of the truth; others relegated to the realm of un-understandable things—those perplexing, controversial or irreconcilable facts—and pressed forward in unbounded faith to those things which are ahead. These last have our deep admiration and regard. Such men and women do we have by the thousands upon thousands in our churches and cults today. If there claims to be a fuller revelation of this Jesus and his universal message, is it not reasonable that we should search? And if the truth it be, enjoy that fuller knowledge?

In place of seeing through a glass darkly, we might come into a more abundant life here; look forward with joy—and I mean joyful anticipation—to the life in the Great Beyond; and somehow have deep within a sense of universe citizenship, with its manifold responsibilities and privileges.

For myself, I found the same heavenly Father, the same Jesus, both more fully revealed; the account of the origin and cosmology of the universes, grand beyond finite comprehension; and the far-reaching plan of the heavenly Father for all his children in the inhabited worlds, a wondrous journey worth all the effort it will involve.

There have come changed conceptions, some quite revolutionary but withal a fulfillment rather than a curtailment of human aspirations and longings.

Everything is not made simple to mankind, I found. How can man hope to grasp the infinite? But the different manifestations of creation on its different levels are coordinated and synthesized into a magnificent whole; and there is opportunity to catch a glimpse of a truly integrated, unified personality. The conception through eons of ages is growth and progress and fulfillment of purpose. It seems to me its drawing power for men of every belief is inexhaustible. It searches out men's hearts, helps them to reconcile cumbersome prejudices and then to discard them. Each can find a point of contact, disentangle himself in the pursuit of truth, beauty and goodness. I venture to say that, whatever a man's belief, earnest study will bring him that experience.

Have you delved into Theosophy? You will find much along your line of thinking, you who search for an answer to the riddle of the universe.

Are you a Christian Scientist? You will be able to shift into gear with much of the teachings, really more easily than I.

Have you been interested in reading Swedenborg? Read the Urantia Book and you will see why it has been sent direct.

Besides being a way of life in the spiritual sense, it touches every sphere and plane of knowledge. Parts deal with the scientist's world; parts with philosophy; parts deal with economics and government; parts with the evolution of this planet, material and physical. You will be intrigued by the story of life on a neighboring planet and a world settled in life and light.

It is a book for the scientist, philosopher, statesman, economist, the practical man, the idealist, for all those interested in the origin of the universe, in the cosmology and character of the universe, and in the evolution of its inhabitants through worlds hitherto unrevealed to us.

To me it is the revelation it claims to be. I cannot but pass it on in its entirety of truth, beauty and goodness. To me, it is the fuller revelation of the fatherhood of God and the brotherhood of man, and the Father's plan for the children of men through all the ages to come.

It is as if God had given to his children a sort of blueprint of whence we came, our relation to the universe and the joyous, intriguing pathway we may tread as his children on earth and through all eternity.

It is a book which lends itself most advantageously to group discussions; and after you have read at least parts of the book, I'm sure I should like to join with you to form just such a discussion group.

If you feel, as I did, the need for a religious experience you had somehow failed to realize, I believe you will find peace and satisfaction through the study of the Urantia Book.

If you are one of those who is, with unbounded faith, carrying on, on a high spiritual plane, devoting your life in the service of the Master by serving his human family, you have awaiting you a joy and vision, far surpassing your ability to conceive, for the enrichment of life on all its levels.

As to books, the one I have is one of a rather expensive edition. But I understand it is available in an edition so priced that every family may own one.

Appendix E

HAROLD SHERMAN'S 1942 POEMS

ETERNAL GLORY

They die beyond our world of sense
But live in fuller measure.
Our senses limit what we know
And, blind to spirit treasure,
We struggle here encased in flesh—
Our souls the body may enmesh,
The animal in us is rife
From origin of bestial strife.
But, as we climb our Godward way,
We loose our hold on house of clay
And death is given as the key
To realms which, now, we cannot see,
But which were destined from the first
To quench man's growing spirit thirst.
Tho' low our being in His sight,
Our climb from darkness into light
Will one day find us by His side—
Earth sons in whom He has great pride.
Mere chapter of a greater story
That leads us to eternal glory!

—November 20, 1942

WHEN GOD SPEAKS

The end for which beginning was
Is coming unto man.

He now must face what sinning does
As best the human can.
His free will choice of sense desires
Has warped his growing soul
And cut him off from spirit fires
Which light man's inner goal.
Long ages past man's stumbling feet
Have bruised his sensual way.
Life's pages are a balance sheet
Demanding that man pay.
No longer can the human wait
His passions to appease;
The tempo of his spirit fate
Will bring him to his knees
And cause the God in him to speak,
As crushed he is and low,
Reduced, at last, in spirit meek,
The truth he now must know.
For man the animal must leave—
This time the way divides—
The human part, itself, may grieve.
The soul, with spirit guides,
Will rise to heights before undreamed,
As mankind sees the way,
And naught will be as it has seemed
When God's Word rules the day.
—November 22, 1942

YOUR SPIRIT VOICE

If strive you would to seek the good
That's buried deep within you,
You'll need to reach the spirit guide
Beyond your nerve and sinew.
The animal in which you live
Is powerless to aid you
And you must sense the greater truth,
It's really God who made you!
A kingdom lives within your mind
In which your spirit dwells

But you, in blindness, fast are tied
And live a thousand hells.
A voice within you fain would speak
To point unerring way,
But you, with ears of spirit dulled,
Hear not what God may say.
When soul, from body reaches up
To realms where it belongs
And catches, now and then, the tone
Of truthful spirit songs.
For harmony abounds on high
And with man must reside
Before the animal in him
Will yield and step aside.
Your spirit voice determines choice
Of steps you yet must take
And he who listens guides his feet
His destiny to make.

—November 22, 1942

A UNIVERSE IS BORN

About a billion years ago,
Before this world was made,
God's architects surveyed this space
In which their plans were laid.
They martialed all the lines of force
And energies that flowed
From out the central universe
Of God's supreme abode.
And all was motion in this sphere,
Dark islands swirling round,
As force directors gave commands
That matter might abound
In all the myriad forms designed
For evolution here,
Before the breath of life from God
Was destined to appear.
Long eons passed and vast the task
Of beings from on high

As step by step this mighty work
Brought light to this dark sky.
A sun blazed forth, it's brilliant rays
Seen gleaming from afar
By creatures watching breathlessly
Upon a distant star.
And joy there was in all the realms
Of life-pervaded space
When birth of this new universe
By God's decree took place.
The neighboring suns,
In greeting joined
Their warm and friendly hands
To grip this new sun's fiery form
In strong, magnetic bands.
And hold, in gravity embrace,
These planets newly born
Which Sons of God, in earthly form
Would one day soon adorn.
Oh wondrous is the pattern schemed
For lowly creature man
Which his evolving soul must weave,
Each strand as best it can!
Oh merciful is God on high,
In love and wisdom just,
As he awaits man's climb to Him
Through human faith and trust!
Oh glorious is the goal ahead—
Unspeakably sublime—
When man's evolving soul survives
The worlds of space and time!
—November 24, 1942

SONS OF GOD

Before all time and space God was;
His presence, Paradise,
A stationary central Isle
Unbounded, without size.
Dimension, yes, in consciousness,
Beyond our grasping here,

Abiding place of Father-Son
A timeless, spaceless sphere.
But Son in Father could not be,
And time and space were born
That God might take eternity
His being to be shorn
Of countless other Sons of Him—
Descendants of this One—
On whom God smiled
And found no fault,
His own Eternal Son.
So greatly pleased was God in Him,
His very first creation,
He spoke the word that freed this Son
To share God's great elation
In moving out from Paradise,
With tools of time and space,
To fashion worlds of finite power
And found the human race.
A creature man, quite animal,
In early stature made,
With Son of God a Creator Son
To keep him unafraid—
A Father watching over him—
The selfsame loving care
That God, through His Eternal Son
With all alike does share
As universes new spring forth,
In stately grand procession;
With always for the beings there
A spirit intercession
That God, through all ascending Sons,
His own may glorify
As they evolve through time and space
To mansion worlds on high.
Eternal Son is our birthright—
Sonship with God above—
Our goal beyond all time and space
Sustained alone by Love.

—November 25, 1942

THE VOICE WITHIN

Though time and space their fetters place
Upon the mind of man,
Through Faith, each soul may reach beyond
And sense God's mighty plan.
No story can be told complete
To struggling humans here
For many cannot face the Truth
While lives are ruled by Fear.
And many more are quite content
To go their stumbling way
Indifferent to the Voice within
And what it tries to say.
"Oh Man, the road ahead is long
And far away your goal.
Look up, not down, give spirit wings
And free your earth bound Soul.
Each step you take can be toward God
With vision rightly centered.
You may walk with Him and talk with Him
The moment He has entered
Your sacred realms of mind and heart.,
Upon your invitation.
And great will be the changes wrought;
It's true of all creation
For soon as man the door unlocks,
And lets the God force in,
He starts to climb upon a path
That leads away from sin.
The flesh itself is always weak
So destined from the first
For man was not intended here
To quench his spirit thirst.
But, even so, the plan of God
Man's free will choice allowed
That he might climb to worldly heights
Of which he might be proud.
Thus far, man's willful, lustful sway
Has pushed God quite aside

And in the depths of untold souls
Their faith has all but died.
To gain again the vision lost
Through hateful, Godless living,
A cataclysmic time must come,
And man must be forgiving
Of all the evil done to him
As he has done to others;
And come to know and love all men
As equals and as brothers
For God indwells the lowest soul
As He indwells the highest.
To those who seek to do His will
His presence comes the nighest.
And Faith in Him, unfalteringly,
Throughout all grief and strife
Will lead your soul unerringly
Into Eternal Life.

—November 27, 1942

THROUGH DEATH

The fear of death has panicked Man
From time he came to earth—
And yet, through death, the soul of him
Is given its free birth.
Imprisoned deep in fleshly house,
The Godward side of man
Has sought to leave the animal
Since human state began.
For spirit joined with flesh that day,
When freewill choice took place,
And God, from that great moment on,
Indwelt this lowly race.
His architects, who planned this world
And all its forms of life,
Had witnessed through the years untold
Its upward, struggling strife.
That Man, of all the creatures here,
Should have evolved so high,

Brought joy to hosts administering
As God, Himself, drew nigh.
For all creation seeks to find
From what source it has sprung
Since all life-forms are but the beads
Upon which life is strung.
But freewill choice may be attained
By every worldly creature.
This faculty, when once achieved,
Becomes its spirit teacher,
Preparing it for realms beyond,
Through trial and error here.
The choice of good or bad by man,
His vision none too clear,
Keeps lifting him, slow step by step,
Upon the rungs of time
And builds for him a soul within
Which starts its homeward climb.
For God, Creator of all things,
In Heaven-world resides
And draws all seeking souls to Him;
Unerringly he guides.
For man to die, is then to gain
A blessed sweet release
From all that plagued him here on earth
And kept his soul from peace.
The animal, in which he lived,
Returns its form to dust
But, rising out of it is man,
In God's Love placing trust.
And standing by his quivering soul,
As death his body takes,
A part of God, in spirit form,
The bonds of soul now breaks.
A seraphim, an angel shape,
Appears on mission graced
And into her safe custody
Man's sleeping soul is placed.
A transport waits with passengers

Bound for the mansion worlds
With heavenly insignia
Upon its side unfurled.
Majestic is the trip through space
Unconscious though the soul!
Conditioned is man's spirit now
For waking at its goal.
God's messenger who dwelt with him
Has made report on High—
A record of the earthly life
And of man's soulful try
To rise above the animal,
Its fear and lust and hate,
And claim his promise destiny
Before it was too late.
But now God speaks and what He says
Sends spirit guide a-winging
"This is my Son in whom I'm pleased,"
All angel voices singing.
And then the soul of man bestirs,
Sweet music fills his ears
And, in the twinkling of an eye,
His new-born form appears.
God's spirit guide is by his side
To take him by the hand
And lead him onward on his path
With all the joyous band
Of those who have survived this life
Upon the World of Cross,
And know, at last, that in God's Love
There never can be loss.

—December 2, 1942

THIS WORLD OF CROSS

Three days Christ Michael lay in death,
The same as creature man.
He rose in spirit just to prove
That what He did we can.
The path He trod we are to tread;

No darkness can enshroud
His Spirit is a light to us
A guide through storm and cloud
As fleshly mists rise up, at last,
And earthly' shadows fall,
While man's soul struggles to be free
And leave the worldly pall
Of low vibrating forces here
(a part of this dark planet)
Which strive to bind the soul of man
And finally to ban it
From going on to realms beyond,
As God, Himself decreed
Before this earth. through Lucifer,
Its evil ways did breed.
O struggling man, you lost the path
In ages now far gone!
Your free will choice was led astray
By leaders who did wrong.
And fellow creatures, in that day,
Who followed those they trusted
Became the servants, not of God,
Their souls with sin encrusted,
Until conditions here on earth
The Angel Beings sickened.
And man, in anguish, cried for help
That spirit might be quickened
Else he might lose all he had gained
On stumbling, upward path;
Nor find escape from Satan's sway
And God's eternal wrath,
The destiny of man was set
From day he made first choice
To build for self a better world
And listen to God's voice.
But, through default of those on High,
Assigned to guide man's way,
Strange things were brought to pass on earth
A long and evil day,

Which only a Creator Son,
Whose children were in danger,
Could save by being born on earth.
And so, it was a manger
That first embraced this Son of God—
In last bestowal life—
Who chose to visit this dark world
With sin and lust most rife.
A world where Adam, yes, and Eve,
Had also failed in mission
By fusing with the races here
And weakening through emission,
Life's plasmic forces given them
For raising high the stock
That man might gain new spirit power
And set ahead the clock
Of his evolving earthly state,
So much in need of aid,
With man beset, within, without,
His very soul afraid.
How sorrowfully Creator Son
Looked down on what He saw!
And He knew then that only He
Could now restore God's law.
To do this, He must needs come down
From His accustomed place
To be then born as other men,
A human form to grace.
A baby born as other babes,
And yet, as not another
E'en though of actual flesh and blood
And earthly father mother;
A babe into a growing man
With angel hosts attending,
Creator Son on earth as man,
And not the least pretending
But living just as man has lived
And evermore must live,
Nor calling on His higher powers

Surcease from trials to give;
    Experiencing the ills of flesh
And, tempted as we are,
    By evil loosed upon this earth
Which God will not yet bar
    Since, in His mercy infinite,
All creatures gone astray
    Are given every soulful chance
To find again their way.
    Christ Michael then, in coming here,
Existing as a creature,
    Sought by living as He did
To be man's spirit teacher;
    To show to man the truths of God,
The universe on high,
    The kingdom of another world
To which man's soul could fly
    Escaping from the house of flesh
So battered, weak and weary
    And leaving, far behind, this earth
With pain and grief so dreary.
    But man, in anguished ignorance,
The Master could not see
    Nor recognize in human form
Just who He chanced to be;
    That He who walked this earth in flesh
Was really his Creator,
    A drama ne'er before so great
In any world theater.
    And O! the tragic climax when,
A cross with nails was plied
    To fasten bleeding hands and feet
A lance wound in His side,
    The broken form of this, our King,
Beloved Son of God,
    Was crucified by us that day
And beat with stone and rod
    And spat upon and deep reviled
By children of His own

Whom He had come to earth to save.
And they, His Truth disowned!
And yet, in giving up His life
As man, himself, must give it,
He bore the cross that we must bear.
We're not to die, but live it!
For how we live and what we think,
If choose we do God's will
Is all that really counts on earth
And gives our soul its fill
Unto the day when comes the call
And we through death must pass,
With spirit freed, our soul now joins
A graduating class
Of beings destined to partake
Of joys prepared on high;
Reward for all we've suffered here
From One who, too, did die
That we again might live with Him
In worlds of finer hue
And know the love He holds for us
Eternally is true.

—December 5, 1942

Index

This index is limited to persons, events and issues related to the Shermans' Urantia experience. Harold Sherman, Martha Sherman, Harry Loose, William S. Sadler, Sr. and William S. Sadler, Jr. occur too frequently in this and later volumes to be listed, except in connection with particular issues.

CONTACT COMMISSIONERS, THEIR RELATIVES, AND EMPLOYEES OF 533

Penn (married name Boike), Mary Esther (proofreader), 333
Pickard, Jerry (fiancé of Ruth Kellogg), 43, 429, 431
Sadler, Charles (son of Bill and Leone, "Charlie"), 6, 179, 314, 358-359, 361, 396, 420
Sadler, Lena Kellogg (1875-1939), 31, 88, 97, 106, 116, 118-119, 127, 145, 147-149, 159, 199, 259, 270, 278, 295, 322-323, 328, 373, 375
Sadler, Leone Gill, 6, 33, 86, 157, 159, 179, 244, 283, 311, 314, 359, 361, 396, 399, 420
Sadler, Patricia (daughter of Bill and Leone, "Patty" or "Patsy"), 6, 179, 283, 358-359, 361, 396, 420
Sadler, III, William S. (son of Bill and Leone, "Billy"), 6, 179, 283, 358-359, 361, 396
Thurman, Helen Gill (sister of Leone Sadler), 244
Wilson, Herschel (cousin of Dr. Sadler), 31

THE LOOSES, AND FRIENDS AND FAMILY OF THE SHERMANS WHO BECAME FORUMITES

Hesse, Sophie Dorothy (sister-in-law of Harry Loose, "Auntie," joined Forum in 1932), 65, 107, 328, 336
Loose, Emily Hesse ("Mother Loose," "Ma," joined Forum in 1931), 18, 23-24, 45, 61, 65, 272, 302, 324, 328, 336
Loose Burkhart, Josephine (daughter of Harry and Emily, "Jo" or "Josie," joined Forum in 1931), 65, 107, 336, 402-403, 406
Matter, John (friend of the Shermans, future candidate for Forum), 382-383, 403, 415, 423, 426
Mattern, H.C., 140, 144, 151, 156, 159-161, 163, 165-167, 178, 183-184, 190, 201, 211, 218-219, 221-222, 228-229, 234, 236, 238, 240, 243, 246-248, 256, 267, 272, 280, 317, 333, 335, 407, 414, 431
Mattern, Mary, 140, 144, 151, 156, 159-160, 163, 165, 167, 178, 183-184, 211, 218, 222, 229, 234, 236, 238, 243-244, 246-247, 272, 280, 317, 333, 335, 407, 414, 431
Sherman, Mary, 3-4, 8-9, 13-14, 16, 21, 45, 63, 95, 107, 112, 197, 214, 263, 314-315, 324, 359, 393-394, 403, 408, 421, 426-427
Wilkins, Sir (George) Hubert, 3, 7-10, 14, 17, 21-23, 30-32, 35, 38-39, 41-42, 44, 51, 57-58, 61, 86, 140, 152-153, 180-181, 183, 207, 220, 224-227, 256-258, 264, 281-283, 287, 295-297, 311, 323, 358, 366, 374, 378. 382-388, 396, 402
Wilkins, Suzanne, 10, 39, 41

GENERAL FORUMITES

Allen, Jennie, 309, 332, 336
Baumgartner, Elsie, 16, 21, 207-208, 210-213, 223, 229, 241, 243, 260, 273, 283-285, 288, 306-307, 321, 348, 367-372, 406, 411, 420-423, 428
Beattie, Harry, 134
Bedell, Clyde, 95, 104, 110-112, 134-135, 142-143, 145, 153-154, 157-158, 163-164, 166, 175-177, 180-181, 183, 210,

MEETINGS AT 533, FORUM COMMITTEES, AND ANNUAL PICNIC AT HALES HOUSE

ISSUES AND INTRIGUES

COMMUNICATIONS FROM HIGHER BEINGS

PLANNED URANTIA ORGANIZATIONS

DEVELOPING URANTIA MANUSCRIPT

PRE-FORUM HISTORY AND APOCRYPHA

THE URANTIA DIARIES
of Harold and Martha Sherman

VOLUME 1: 1898-1942

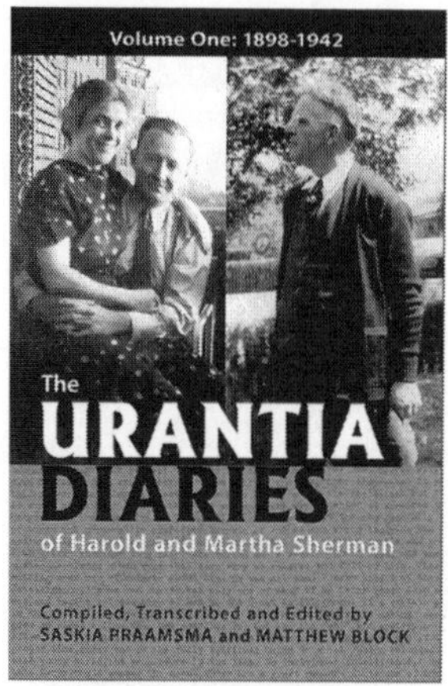

ISBN: 978-0-9967165-9-8
eISBN: 978-0-9982556-0-6

VOLUME 2: 1942

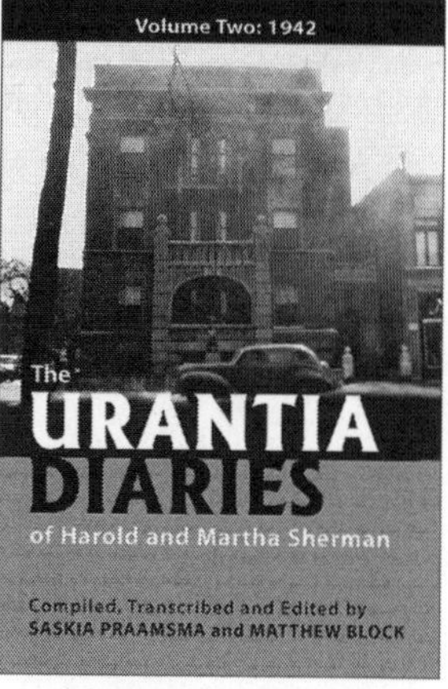

ISBN: 978-1-7321796-1-5
eISBN: 978-1-7321796-2-2

VOLUME 3: 1943

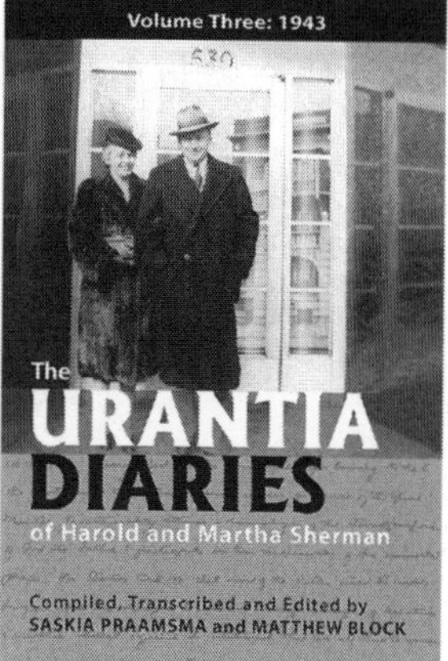

ISBN: 978-1-7321796-3-9
eISBN: 978-1-7321796-4-6

VOLUME 4: 1944-1945

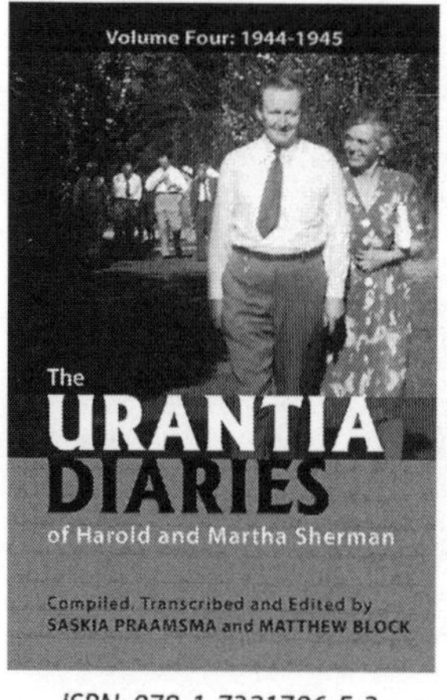

ISBN: 978-1-7321796-5-3
eISBN: 978-1-7321796-6-0

VOLUME 5: 1946-1955

ISBN: 978-1-7321796-7-7
eISBN: 978-1-7321796-8-4

VOLUME 6: 1955-1998

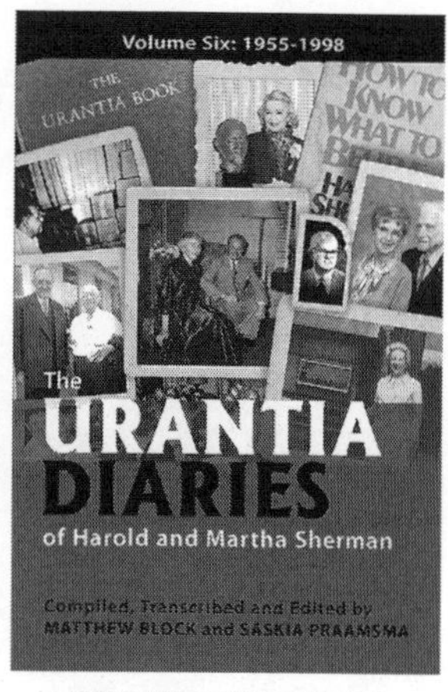

ISBN: 978-1-7344621-3-5
eISBN: 978-1-7344621-2-8

Made in the USA
Middletown, DE
30 September 2021

49400865R00288